ECONOMICS   Made Simple

The Made Simple series
has been created
primarily for self-education
but can equally well
be used as
an aid to group study.
However complex the subject,
the reader is taken
step by step,
clearly and methodically,
through the course. Each volume
has been prepared by
experts,
using throughout the
Made Simple technique of teaching.
Consequently the gaining
of knowledge now becomes
an experience to be enjoyed.

In the same series

Accounting
Acting and Stagecraft
Additional Mathematics
Advertising
Anthropology
Applied Economics
Applied Mathematics
Applied Mechanics
Art Appreciation
Art of Speaking
Art of Writing
Biology
Book-keeping
British Constitution
Business and Administrative
   Organisation
Calculus
Chemistry
Childcare
Commerce
Company Administration
Company Law
Computer Programming
Cookery
Cost and Management
   Accounting
Data Processing
Dressmaking
Economic History
Economic and Social
   Geography
Economics
Electricity
Electronic Computers
Electronics
English
English Literature

Export
Financial Management
French
Geology
German
Human Anatomy
Italian
Journalism
Latin
Law
Management
Marketing
Mathematics
Modern Electronics
Modern European History
New Mathematics
Office Practice
Organic Chemistry
Philosophy
Photography
Physical Geography
Physics
Pottery
Psychology
Rapid Reading
Retailing
Russian
Salesmanship
Secretarial Practice
Social Services
Soft Furnishing
Spanish
Statistics
Transport and Distribution
Typing
Woodwork

ECONOMICS Made Simple

Geoffrey Whitehead, B.Sc. (Econ.)

Made Simple Books
W. H. ALLEN   London
A Howard & Wyndham Company

© W. H. Allen & Co. Ltd, 1970

Made and printed in Great Britain
by Richard Clay (The Chaucer Press), Ltd., Bungay, Suffolk
for the publishers W. H. Allen & Co Ltd.
44 Hill Street, London W1X 8LB

First edition, October 1970
Ninth edition, January 1979

ISBN 0 491 01751 0 paperbound

Foreword

This book covers all the basic aspects of the economic organization of free-enterprise societies, with special reference to Great Britain's position in the European Community and the Commonwealth. It explains clearly and simply the production, distribution and exchange of goods and services, both within a country and internationally. The activities of plants, firms and industries are examined, so are the influences upon them of great institutions: banks, insurance companies, trade unions and local and central government bodies. The part played by governments in controlling abuses, promoting social progress and managing prosperity is fully described, and likely trends— such as the control of population—considered. The historical development of Economics is incidentally recounted.

Although principally designed for self-study, the book is of equal value to schools, colleges and universities. Teachers and lecturers will find that it adequately covers the syllabuses of various examining bodies for G.C.E. 'A' Level Economics, the new BEC National Diploma and Certificate courses and the Higher National Certificate Conversion course. It also covers relevant material for the professional examinations for Accounting, Company Secretaryship, Cost Accounting, etc., the Intermediate Examination for the Chartered Institute of Transport and the first year Degree Courses at University level. It is particularly suitable for students reading Economics as a liberal study accompanying main courses in other disciplines. It is a sound background reference book for more elementary studies at O level and C.S.E. level.

In preparing this book I have received much helpful assistance from a number of public bodies, firms and individuals. I wish to express my thanks to the following: the Controller of H.M. Stationery Office for permission to reproduce and adapt sundry tables from official publications, particularly the National Income Accounts, the Balance of Payments Accounts and the Progress Reports of the Departments of Employment and Trade; the Clyde Port Authority for permission to reproduce its map on the Maritime Industrial Development Area; the Bank of England for permission to reproduce statistics from its Quarterly Magazine; *Barclays Bank Review* for permission to reproduce a chart on the advances made by bankers; the Cooperative Union, Ltd., for help with recent statistical data and permission to reproduce its photograph of the original Toad Lane, Rochdale, Co-operative shop; and Mr. R. C. Meadows of the Eastern Electricity Board for advice about the structure of the industry.

I should particularly like to acknowledge the help of two colleagues; Mr. Derek Lobley, for his criticism and helpful suggestions in the preparation of the manuscript, and Mr. Leslie Basford, whose meticulous work in editing and improving the text was invaluable.

GEOFFREY WHITEHEAD

Table of Contents

CHAPTER ONE

SOME BASIC IDEAS

(1) What is Economics?

Economics was defined by the late Alfred Marshall, one of the great Victorian economists, as 'the study of mankind in the everyday business of life'. There are other definitions which are discussed later in this book, but Marshall's definition draws attention to that unique feature of human society: that unlike other animals, man provides for his everyday needs by means of a complex pattern of production, distribution, and exchange. This everyday business of providing the means of livelihood is called by the general term 'economy'. Economics is the study of economies, and in particular of modern economies such as those of Western Europe and the United States of America. In passing we take note of primitive economies, but it is the advanced economies that interest us most. How do we produce all the things that we need? How do we distribute the products among the various groups in the society? What institutions have we developed to promote economic activity, and how does each institution play its part in the intricate relationships of everyday life?

(2) 'Wants' and 'Utilities'

The study of economics begins with understanding human 'wants'. By 'want' the economist means the endless succession of material 'wants' which are displayed by all living things. Everyone needs air, food, and water to support life. If we live in some climates we need clothing and shelter from the weather. Everyone needs a home to call his own; some territory which is his, by right.

Even when we have these basic 'wants', other more advanced 'wants' present themselves. We want comfortable homes, entertainment, education, and transport. As the things we need increase in variety and become more and more sophisticated, the economy becomes more intricate too, until thousands of men are co-operating in different countries to produce the raw materials, designs, and specialized machinery which are necessary for a single thing we 'want'—such as an aeroplane or a motor vehicle.

The student of economics has to learn many new words in the course of his studies. There is nothing complicated about these new words; but once they have been learnt and understood they make conversation between economists easier, because everyone then knows exactly what the other man is talking about. Outsiders often dismiss this specialized vocabulary as jargon, but this is a mistake. The words 'table' and 'chair' describe particular household objects: they are the jargon of the dining-room.

The first piece of economic jargon we need to learn is the word **utility**. In ordinary language this means something that has usefulness, and to some extent this is still its meaning in economics; but the particular form that this usefulness takes is to satisfy our 'wants'. Thirst is a 'want', and water has 'utility' because it satisfies this want. A glass of water does not always have the same utility, its satisfying power depends upon the extent of our want. Consider a thirsty child in a school playground: for her a glass of water has utility. To the airman whose plane has crashed in the desert, the same glass of water would have greater utility, for his need is greater. To an Indian peasant in a monsoon flood, water has no utility at all.

When we reduce economics to its basic elements it is the study of how mankind produces utilities to satisfy wants. In satisfying the wants we consume the utilities, so that they cease to exist and we must start producing them again. A large part of the everyday business of life involves the repetitive production of well-tried utilities to satisfy well-known wants. Inventors and designers, however, constantly produce new forms of satisfaction—a blue rose, or a 'whiter' detergent, or a new motive power—so that man progresses to higher levels of satisfaction.

(3) The Production of Utilities

Satisfaction can be achieved in two ways: by the enjoyment of goods or the enjoyment of services. **Goods** are tangible items which either satisfy the basic requirements of human life or make that life fuller and richer. Common examples are foods, clothing, housing, furniture, books, television sets, and motor cars. The actual point of satisfaction occurs when we consume the food, or beverage, wear the clothing, make use of the furniture, and so on, so that the name **consumer goods** is usually applied to these tangible utilities. There is another class of goods, dealt with more fully on page 23, called **producer goods**. These are goods which do not yield personal satisfaction to consumers but are part of the capital assets of production. A drilling machine, or an assembly line in a factory, are examples of producer goods.

Services are intangible 'utilities', which satisfy our needs by personal attention. The dentist who extracts a painful tooth; the surgeon who sets a broken leg; the television personality who brightens an otherwise dull evening; or the hairdresser who prepares us for a social occasion are examples of people offering **personal service**. As with goods, there is a class of services which is not directly personal in this way, but forms part of the productive organization. Such services are **commercial services**; trade, banking, transport, insurance, and communications are the chief examples.

The whole purpose of production, which makes use of producer goods and commercial services in the course of its activities, is to create utilities by providing an endless flow of consumer goods and personal services. In order to achieve this production of utilities the resources available to mankind must be mobilized. These resources are called the **factors of production.**

(4) The Factors of Production

There are three factors of production which together enable advanced economies to create the goods and services needed by mankind. These three sets of resources are given the names land, labour, and capital.

Land is a term used by the early economists to describe resources provided by the bounty of nature. It includes not only agricultural land but also the mineral resources of the earth, the gases of the atmosphere, the products of the fields, forests and oceans, and even the extra-terrestrial resources which man may one day begin to haul in from space.

Labour includes all the human resources of the earth, the physical and mental abilities of the peoples of the world. It embraces a wide variety of skills in specialized trades and occupations, and abilities of organization and management that are crucial in the productive processes. We shall see later that a dispute exists between economists as to whether this last type of skill is so different from occupational skills as to deserve being classed as a separate factor. For the moment we will not try to separate off organizational skills in this way.

Capital resources are the 'producer goods' to which we have already referred. They are a store of physical assets owned by businessmen and others which enable the production of consumer goods and services to be carried on more effectively. Capital assets of this sort have to be constructed from natural resources by human skill and energy, so that whatever stock of these assets is available must have been accumulated in an earlier period.

(5) The Organization of Production

If the factors of production are to be combined to create utilities which will satisfy man's wants, someone must take the initiative. Even in the most primitive tribes there is some leader who displays above-average ability in hunting, fishing, or food-gathering. In more civilized groups other skills become important. Master craftsmen discover, develop, and hand down the secrets of spinning, weaving, pottery-making, and the smith's arts. Enterprising merchants travel the mountain and forest trails, or cross trackless deserts and seas to bring the precious products of the world to market. In more advanced nations the complexity of production calls forth classes of men who are skilled in making the necessary arrangements. They may possess special technical ability, like the great engineers of the Industrial Revolution. They may possess, or know how to collect, financial resources which will enable production to be organized. They may even be unscrupulous, quick to take advantage of the weaknesses or indecision of others. Whatever their particular ability, the economic effect is the same. Production is achieved by the enterprising activity of such individuals who combine the factors of production in the best possible way to achieve outputs of goods and services. These organizers of production are called **entrepreneurs.**

(6) Consumption and Production

When production has been achieved, the goods and services produced are used to satisfy the wants of mankind. In consuming the utilities created we destroy the fruits of our earlier labours. The fuel mined is burnt; the cloth woven is worn; the crops harvested are eaten, and the shelter built is enjoyed. Consumption destroys production, and we return to our former condition. We must begin again an endless cycle of production and consumption.

(7) Scarcity and Choice

No matter how much we produce, we shall never be able to satisfy men's wants, for these develop and extend with every advance of technology. Appetite grows with feeding, and every growth of output which raises man to a new level serves but to reveal a more extensive horizon. In his book, *Nature and Significance of Economic Science*, Lord Robbins defined economics as: 'The science which studies human behaviour as a relationship between "ends" and scarce "means" which have alternative uses.' Man's insatiable 'wants' are Robbins's 'ends' which exist to be satisfied. The resources of the earth are the scarce 'means' which are available to satisfy these ends. Economics becomes a study of how men behave when there are insufficient 'means' to satisfy the 'ends' they have in mind.

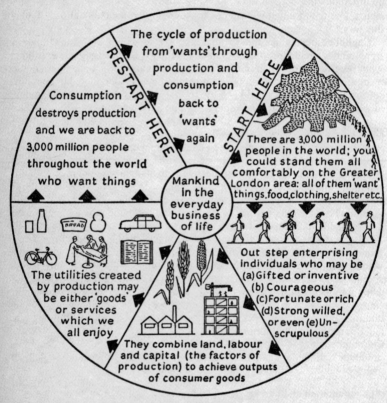

Fig. 1. The cycle of production

If the utilities that can be created are limited compared with the insatiable appetites of men, then we must exercise some sort of choice as to what shall be produced and in what quantities. Just how we exercise this kind of choice depends upon the type of society in which we live. In the so-called 'free-enterprise' societies choice is exercised by a wide range of individuals and groups. Millions of housewives exercise choice when they do their shopping. Motorists buy, or do not buy, from countless garages which they pass on the way to work. Councils and other elected bodies choose equipment and buildings according to their sense of priorities. This apparent freedom of choice is marred a little by influences which are at work to persuade us to exercise choices in a way different from our own natural inclinations. Informative, or persuasive, advertising may influence our demand for goods. In the free-enterprise countries the choices of millions of people take effect through the **market**. The existence of markets is a characteristic feature of such economies, and the major commodity markets and financial markets lie at the root of the prosperity of such nations.

(8) Cost and Opportunity Cost

Everyone who is familiar with a money system understands the ordinary meaning of 'cost', as the amount of money that has to be given up in order to obtain a particular commodity or service. In economics we have a term 'opportunity cost', or 'alternative cost', which expresses the cost of a commodity not in money but in terms of the alternative forgone. If we exercise choice we must have alternatives from which to choose. The housewife who decides to give a party on an anniversary or birthday will tend to reduce expenditure on ordinary meals so that she can accumulate reserves for the party. The true cost of the party is the reduced enjoyment at other meals. The student who chooses to cut a lecture in order to escort a young lady to the theatre is sacrificing one opportunity for another. The true cost of the theatre visit is the lecture he has missed.

When we take one opportunity, or follow a particular policy, we shall never know what would have happened if we had taken the other alternative opportunity, or policy. The student who cut the lecture might have had his interests in the subject triggered off into a lifetime pursuit. On the other hand, the theatre visit might end in a more permanent attachment to the young lady, so that he marries and lives happily ever after. Similarly, a decision by a local authority to have only comprehensive schools in its area will divert resources of building accommodation and teaching staff towards this type of education. We shall never know whether these resources would have given greater satisfaction if used in other ways.

(9) 'Free' Economies, 'Controlled' Economies and 'Mixed' Economies

Economic activity is pursued in a climate which to some extent reflects the political framework of society. In all nations it developed originally in a framework of free enterprise where little interference was made in the activities of those engaging in economic activity. This framework of free enterprise was described by men like Adam Smith (see page 9), and perhaps today is best represented by the American economy. Outright free enterprise does lead, regrettably, to some abuses. In particular it leads to gross inequalities of incomes, and to various types of monopoly practices. Political solutions to the injustices of outright 'free' enterprise have given us Communist (controlled) economies like the Soviet and Chinese economies. Military solutions have given us situations like the Ugandan controlled economy; as yet insufficiently developed for its success to be appraised. In many other countries, but notably in the United Kingdom, a 'mixed' economy, featuring certain centrally controlled industries and a rich pattern of other 'free enterprise' industries, has been evolved.

In fact all countries must be, to some extent, mixed economies. It is impossible for bureaucratic supervision of every aspect of production to be achieved even by the most authoritarian governments, while the monopolistic exploitation of the mass of any people in a truly 'free-enterprise' system is totally unacceptable in the increasingly egalitarian atmosphere of the modern world.

This book is largely concerned with the free-enterprise economies and mixed economies of the western world, but readers should relate their readings to the broader world scene.

(10) Summary of Chapter One

1. Economics is the study of the ways in which man provides for his everyday needs of food, clothing, shelter, etc.

2. 'Utilities' are goods and services that have the power to satisfy the 'wants' of mankind.

3. Production of utilities is achieved by making use of the factors of production, land, labour, and capital.

4. The initiative in production is taken by businessmen called 'entrepreneurs', who combine land, labour, and capital to create goods and services.

5. Consumption destroys production; 'wants' devour 'utilities'.

6. Since the resources available to mankind are limited, we must exercise choice. In choosing, the true cost of one opportunity chosen is the 'next-best' alternative opportunity we did not choose.

(11) Suggested Further Reading

Hanson, J. L.: *A Textbook of Economics* (Chapter 1). Macdonald & Evans: London, 1970.

Marshall, A.: *Principles of Economics* (Book 1, Chapters 1–3). Macmillan: London, 1961.

Whitehead, G.: *Commerce Made Simple* (Chapter 1). W. H. Allen: London, most recent edition.

Exercises Set 1

1. Draw up a list of 'wants' likely to be experienced by: (*a*) a shipwrecked mariner on a desert island; (*b*) a citizen of an advanced nation.

2. Distinguish between 'consumer goods' and 'producer goods'.

3. What are 'utilities'?

4. What is an entrepreneur?

5. Explain 'the endless cycle of production and consumption'.

6. What do you understand by 'opportunity cost'? Suggest true costs for the following: (*a*) a high level of armament production; (*b*) a bottle of wine at a dinner party; (*c*) a refill of notepaper in a student's ring binder; (*d*) a field of wheat.

8. Aristotle said, 'Man is an economic animal'. What do you think he meant?

9. Why is a market of significant importance in free-enterprise societies? In your answer suggest the important features of a free market.

10. 'In primitive societies man is preoccupied with satisfying his basic wants; in advanced societies he is still preoccupied with production, but now services are his main interest.' Discuss.

SECTION TWO: PRODUCTION

CHAPTER TWO

BASIC IDEAS ON PRODUCTION

(1) What Does an Economist Understand by 'Production'?

We have already seen that production is the creation of 'utilities' to satisfy 'wants'. It follows that the creation of both goods and services is 'production' to an economist. Economists do not draw any distinction between the farmer, the factory worker, the lorry driver, the doctor, or the actor as far as production is concerned. All these workers are specializing in the creation of some commodity or service which is required by their fellow men. The farmer is not more productive than the doctor; he is only providing a different sort of utility. Physical labour is not more worthy of reward than mental labour, for all producers are engaged in a common endeavour to satisfy man's wants. If we make the mistake of belittling the 'service' trades because they are unproductive, and divert their workers into other occupations, we shall decrease satisfaction. In fact, it is precisely these occupations which are insusceptible to mechanization which are expanding fastest in the advanced nations. Whereas fewer and fewer agricultural workers can grow more and more food by a thoughtful use of machinery and fertilizers, it is much more difficult to mechanize personal services. We are unlikely ever to see mass production in the dentist's chair or the operating theatre. Higher levels of satisfaction in health services must therefore be achieved by training more dentists and doctors. In rather a different way the services devoted to distribution and exchange, such as transport, wholesaling, and retailing, must expand as specialization in large factories or farms produces greater and greater surpluses to be shared out among the population. An increased number of people engaged in the provision of services is therefore inevitable and advantageous.

It follows that workers in service trades are equally entitled to a reward for their activities, for they are just as much part of production as the factory worker or the farm labourer. A manufactured commodity has not been fully 'produced' in the economic sense until it reaches the consumer. It is therefore quite wrong to claim that the actual grower or producer is entitled to the full fruits of his labour, and mean by that the entire price paid by the consumer for the commodity. The middleman who brought it to market and the retailer who handled it are also entitled to a reward. Unless they receive a reward for their efforts they will not handle the goods, and the grower will be unable to realize any reward for his work, while the factory worker will soon be laid off because stocks are rising.

Production to an economist, therefore, is the creation of utilities to satisfy wants; whether that means the creation of a 'good' itself in agriculture or industry; its transport from the point of production to the point of consumption (geographical distribution); its transport through time from the moment of pro-

duction to the moment of consumption, in stock-piles, cold stores, warehouses, or granaries (distribution through time); or the provision of 'personal services' directly enjoyed by individuals or groups, such as health, education, and entertainment services.

For convenience production is divided into three categories.

(2) The Three Classes of Production

We all specialize in some sort of work, producing some useful commodity or service, but to study production we must try to sort out the different classes of producers. The three main types of production are known as **Primary Production**, **Secondary Production**, and **Tertiary Production**. Table 1 names some of the specialists who work in the three types of production.

Table 1. Types of production

(a) THE PRODUCTION OF GOODS		(b) THE PRODUCTION OF SERVICES	
1. *Primary Production*	2. *Secondary Production*	3. *Tertiary Production*	
(The production of goods made available by Nature. Man's inheritance of natural wealth)	(The production of sophisticated products which are derived from the natural primary products)	(The production of services)	
		Commercial Services	*Personal Services*
Coal miner	Engineer	Wholesaler	Doctor
Gold miner	Electronic Engineer	Retailer	Dentist
Tin miner	Builder	Banker	Nurse
Lead miner	Decorator	Insurance agent	Teacher
Oil driller	Cabinet maker	Stockbroker	Lecturer
Lumberjack	Carpenter	Importer	Policeman
Farmer	Plastics engineer	Exporter	Detective
Fisherman	Refinery technologist	Transport driver	Entertainer
Whaler	Stillman	Merchant-Navy	Vocalist
Pearl diver	Potter	Captain	TV Personality
Herdsman	Tailor	Ship's crew	Clergyman
Fur trapper	Steelworker	Communications	Undertaker
etc.	Shipbuilder	engineer	Editor
	Aeronautical engineer		Author
			Psychologist

The reader should consolidate his grasp of these three types by attempting to think of ten more occupations in each of the four groups shown.

(3) Direct Production and Indirect Production

(a) *Direct Production*. If a person works directly to satisfy his own wants he is said to engage in **direct production**. Thus a castaway on a desert island would be forced to find his own food, build his own shelter, and make such garments as he could from the leaves of trees or the skins of animals. He must be a jack-of-all-trades: a hunter, farmer, builder, tailor, and so on. He would never have the time to do half the things he would like to do, and he would never develop the skill that comes from repetition. Similarly, tribes of primitive peoples, even though they co-operate together in a primitive communal existence, rarely satisfy all their wants, and are easily exterminated by natural disasters. The Bushmen of the Kalahari go naked except for a leather strap hanging from the shoulders and tied around the waist. They build only the most primitive shelters, for they are constantly on the move following game. Those who are too feeble to keep up are left, in a protective thorn shelter with all the water that can be spared, until thirst or the hyenas or leopards put an end to them. Clearly direct production is an inefficient type of organization.

(b) *Indirect Production* is production by specialization. People choose an occupation that appeals to them, usually because they have a natural talent or interest in it. They either have already, or hope to achieve, an advantage over their fellow men in that particular field of activity. The advanced nations offer an incredible variety of employment to their citizens. Not only are there many specialist trades, but within each trade there are many separate occupations. A popular television programme, in which a panel of personalities had to guess the occupations of viewers who challenged the panel, ran for ten years before it was retired at last—without having run out of trades.

If production is **indirect** it means that the producer is not attempting to satisfy his own wants directly, except to a very limited extent. A tailor no doubt makes himself a suit occasionally, and an oil-refinery engineer probably buys cheap petrol from the company pump. The bulk of the products of both trades will go to other people—to the general public. In return, the tailor and the refinery engineer will obtain a balanced share of the world's goods through the exchanges arranged by wholesalers and retailers, using money as a medium of exchange.

(4) Specialization and the Division of Labour

Indirect production takes place when entrepreneurs combine the factors available to them to secure the required goods and services. People are employed in their specialist occupations, to take the fullest advantage of their natural talents or acquired abilities. Adam Smith, the first great economist, drew attention to this specialization as the chief source of the Wealth of Nations. The reader should know more of this great economist. Let us make a small diversion to consider his contribution to economics.

Adam Smith—the Optimist who started the 'Dismal Science'

Adam Smith was born in 1723, the son of the Comptroller of Customs at Kirkcaldy in Fife. He went to Oxford, but was dissatisfied with his course because it had nothing much to do with the things that interested him. His great treatise on *The Nature and Causes of the Wealth of Nations* was publ shed in 1776. It was the result of 20 years study of the industrial developments taking place around him in Britain, which was just passing through the stage known to history as the Industrial Revolution.

Adam Smith started the central economic tradition, which holds that economics attempts to understand and explain the world in which we live, but not unduly to change it. His emphasis on the natural competitive forces in the market as the thing that regulated the economy led to the idea that there were inevitable forces at work which human beings were unable to control, and should leave strictly alone.

His central doctrine was that a system of natural liberty, where free men were able to follow their inclinations, would lead to the best results for both the individual and society itself. Man's natural inclination is to increase his well-being by producing wealth. If each man is thrown on his own resources he will labour for his own enrichment, and will incidentally enrich all society. Adam Smith's book, appearing at the same time as the American colonies declared their independence, prophesied that their system of free enterprise would make them the greatest nation in the world.

The weaknesses of Smith's doctrine lay in its disregard of the distribution of wealth. He was talking about total wealth, or **aggregate wealth.** He had little hope that the distribution of wealth between manufacturers, merchants, and landlords, on the one hand, and the mass of working people, on the other, would ever be such as to benefit the ordinary people. He said, 'We have many Acts of Parliament aimed against combining to raise wages; but none against combining to lower them.' This led Smith and other economists to conclude that although wages could not fall below the point where they would keep the workers alive, they were unlikely to rise much above that point. For this reason economics was referred to as 'The Dismal Science'. It was for later economists such as John Stuart Mill to point to the distribution of wealth as a matter of fundamental importance in society.

Smith died in 1790, a man of international reputation whose central doctrine has passed into history as the doctrine of *laisser faire*: leave men to please themselves, and they will do the best for themselves, and everyone else too. It remains a doctrine which has much to recommend it, but has been largely abandoned today for policies directed at the management of prosperity and at increasing individual welfare.

Specialization—the Key to the Wealth of Nations

In the first chapter of his book Smith described the specialization of labour used in a local pin factory with which he was familiar. He wrote:

'A man not educated to this business could scarcely perhaps with his utmost industry make one pin a day, and certainly could not make twenty. . . . But in the way this trade is carried on it is divided into a number of branches, of which the greater part are likewise peculiar trades. One man draws out the wire, another straights it, a third cuts it, a fourth points it, a fifth grinds it at the top (for receiving of the head). To make the head requires two or three distinct operations. To put it on is a peculiar business, to whiten the pins is another. It is even a trade by itself to put them into the paper, and the important business of making a pin is divided in this way into eighteen different processes, which in some manufactories are all performed by distinct hands.

'I have seen a small manufactory of this kind where ten men only were employed, and where some of them consequently performed two or three distinct operations. But although they were very poor, and therefore but indifferently accommodated with the necessary machinery they could, when they exerted themselves, make among them twelve pounds of pins a day. There are in a pound upwards of 4,000 pins of a middling size. Each person, therefore, could make one-tenth of 48,000 pins in a day. But if they had wrought separately, without having been educated to this peculiar business, they certainly could not have each made twenty, and possibly not even one.'

The Advantages of Specialization

Adam Smith went on to examine the advantages of specialization. He found the main advantages to be as follows:

(a) *People are free to choose the work they like.* When a person is free to choose his employment he generally chooses a trade which interests him and in which he has some natural talent. He therefore works more effectively and more willingly, so that output rises and the nation becomes more prosperous.

(b) *The specialist uses the same set of tools all day.* A 'Robinson Crusoe', alone on his desert island, has many tasks to perform every day. He may dig his field for a short while, and then put his spade away while he makes fish hooks for an hour or two before going down to the beach. This is both wasteful of time and an inefficient use of equipment. The specialist uses the same set of tools all day. They are constantly at work, so that they contribute more intensively to production, and there is no waste of time clearing away between different activities. The intensive use of capital equipment is very desirable, because it is then worn out before it is made obsolete by new techniques of production.

(c) *Constant use of the same tools and materials leads to a close study of both, resulting in improved equipment and better methods of work.* A man who specializes in a particular trade soon discovers methods of production that are an improvement on previous methods. These 'tricks of the trade' are often jealously guarded secrets. Even in mass-production systems, where layout and procedure have been carefully planned, improvements are still possible. Many firms offer cash prizes to employees who suggest improvements which save time or materials.

(d) *Specialized production is associated with mechanization, and machines can be speeded up.* Wherever specialization enables work to be subdivided into processes, it becomes possible to mechanize the activity. This enables the power of the machine to replace the muscle power of the worker. The activity may be carried on at high speed; machines do not tire like workers, nor do they grow bored with the repetition of actions for which they have been designed or programmed.

(e) *Repetition brings increased skill.* Of course this is over a more limited field. Readers who have marvelled at the intricate windings of an electric motor or the complex circuits of a television set are strongly recommended to visit a factory where such things are made. They are usually assembled by female workers who have become so accustomed to the work that they can talk quite freely to their neighbours about everyday affairs and still produce faultless assemblies. Admittedly they are only putting in one or two components each, but over this narrow field they have acquired enormous skill.

The Nature of Specialization

The increased output achieved by specialization is the result of the **division of labour**. The process has proceeded historically along the following lines:

(a) *Specialization within the Family or Tribal Group.* We have seen that direct production generally results in poverty. Man quickly finds that working together gives better results. The best hunters go hunting, the best anglers fish, the best potter makes pots for the entire village, and so on. The fruits of their labours are then shared among the whole family or tribe.

(*b*) *Specialization into Trades*. Here the natural divisions of production are performed by specialists: bakers, butchers, engineers, doctors, and so on. The medieval guilds were combinations of such skilled tradesmen, designed to keep trade secrets within the guild, admission to which could be achieved only by properly trained apprentices. The persistence of trades into modern advanced societies has produced the great craft unions like the printers, engineers, and electricians. The organization of doctors, dentists, accountants, and similar groups is an extension of specialization into higher levels of professional and administrative life. Originally organizations were small and centred in towns all over the country; now they have grown to national importance.

(*c*) *Specialization into Sub-trades*. The further division of work into particular aspects of a particular trade increased skill by concentrating the attention of tradesmen on those jobs that for some reason (usually profit) interested them most. In the early days of the cotton industry a division soon sprang up between spinning and weaving, between dyeing and fabric-printing, etc. Skill increased, but for each entrepreneur it was over a more limited field. This spreading of specialized activities throughout a region led to the localization of production, which is dealt with more fully on page 60.

(*d*) *Specialization into Processes*. Here the division of labour reaches its greatest concentration. The manufacturing process is broken down into a series of separate activities, each of which is performed by a separate operative. This operative becomes highly skilled over a very limited field, and mass production results.

The term **mass production** is used to describe any system which aims at producing, with the fewest workers, the greatest output of goods. In nearly every industry today techniques have been developed which allow manufacturing processes to be carried on continuously, often day and night. The work flows through the factory in an endless stream, and workers at various stages perform individual operations with specially designed machinery.

Henry Ford in America developed the motor-car industry from a system whereby one man built a car completely to a system where hundreds of men, each performing one operation repeatedly, produce a continuous flow of cars. At one time a car was rolling off the production lines every ten seconds. Henry Ford's definition of mass production reads: 'It is the focusing upon a manufacturing project of the principles of power, accuracy, economy, system, continuity, speed, and repetition.'

Two other factors have been found to affect greatly the volume of production. They are **simplification** and **standardization**. Together with **specialization** they are the source of wealth in our affluent society. These three methods, simplification, standardization, and specialization, are sometimes called **the three Ss**.

Simplification is the process of making a manufactured article as simple and functional as possible. Many modern plastic household articles, such as bowls and buckets, display this quality of simplicity. There are no decorative embellishments of any sort. The design is such that once the plastic has been pressed into shape the article will fall out of the press instantly. The surface of the mould is polished to a mirror finish by the toolmaker, and this perfect finish is reproduced on the plastic article, which is consequently shiny and attractive to the customer.

Standardization is the process of making things in standard parts, which can be used in many similar articles. For instance, a transistor in one type of radio set is very like a transistor in another. Where standard parts can be used in many appliances the factory making these parts has very long production runs indeed. These long runs mean that the unit cost per component is reduced, because the expensive design costs are shared out among millions of units of output.

Automation and Computerization in Industry. These modern developments carry specialization to its highest levels. When a design has been reduced to its simplest, most standardized form automation becomes possible. The whole process is not only mechanized but also automated so that human operatives are not required. Computerization adds a further refinement, enabling, for example, decisions to be made about dynamic changes in the operation of plant. These developments open up very great possibilities for the future satisfaction of wants, and it is these prospects that have led economists such as Prof. Galbraith to assert that man is approaching a final solution to the problems of the production of wealth.

(*e*) *International Specialization of Labour.* Modern technology has developed specialization so fully that a further geographical change becomes possible. Instead of regional specialization, national specialization becomes a distinct possibility. Italian styles of shoes are sold all over the world, American machine tools are universally recognized, Japanese cameras, Scotch whisky, and Swiss watches are demanded everywhere.

We therefore see that technically the division of labour has moved through the following stages:

  (i) The use of individual skills and talents.
 (ii) The development of specialized trades.
(iii) The subdivision of these trades into specialized aspects.
(iv) The further subdivision of these aspects into processes.
 (v) The mechanization and automation of processes.
(vi) The computerized control of automatic processes.

These changes have resulted in a growth of large-scale industries which have developed territorially in the following way:

  (i) From the family to the village or tribal unit.
 (ii) From the countryside to the medieval borough or town.
(iii) From the town to the geographical region.
(iv) From the regional to the national level, with particular nations supplying a major part of the world's requirements.

The advantages offered by a fuller development of specialization are not achieved without some adverse effects. We must now consider the disadvantages of specialization.

(5) The Disadvantages of Specialization

Despite the obvious advantages of simplification, standardization, and specialization, there are certain disadvantages to offset the gains achieved.

The net effect is still a higher level of satisfaction of human 'wants', but it is not as high as at first seemed possible. The chief disadvantages are:

(*a*) The growth of tertiary production.
(*b*) The monotonous nature of many highly specialized employments.
(*c*) The decline of craftsmanship.
(*d*) Structural unemployment and regional unemployment.
(*e*) Industrial unrest and social discontent.

(*a*) *The Growth of Tertiary Production.* Specialization concentrates production in large factories, most of whose output is surplus to the requirements of the employees in each factory. This means that the commercial activities of distribution and marketing are greatly increased. Wholesalers specialize in warehousing stocks at appropriate points until they are required by consumers. This clears the production lines, which would otherwise be choked by the volume of goods produced. Retailers buy from wholesalers and display goods where consumers can inspect and purchase them. Clearly some of the gains achieved by mass production must be dissipated in these activities.

(*b*) *The Monotonous Nature of Many Highly Specialized Employments.* The work involved in a particular process can soon become an automatic activity which the operator performs without difficulty. Some people prefer this type of employment, which carries little responsibility and finishes as soon as the factory siren blows. Others find it irksome in the extreme. Often such employees feel trapped in a manufacturing system from which there is no escape. This is particularly true in areas where one or two large enterprises dominate the local employment scene and few alternative occupations exist for those who dislike work as operatives.

(*c*) *The Decline of Craftsmanship.* Mass production greatly reduces the skills required of ordinary workers. They become highly skilled at particular processes but know little of the entire range of activities in their craft. Of course, a few super-craftsmen on the design staff still play an influential part in the whole enterprise, but the mass of employees are unable to take part in any truly creative activity. This leads them to regard work as of little importance, for their true personalities can be developed only in leisure hours. Thus production suffers and the total effectiveness of enterprises is reduced.

(*d*) *Structural Unemployment and Regional Unemployment.* Structural unemployment is unemployment caused by changes in the world demand for a particular product. The whole structure of an industry changes as world demand falls. Even if world demand grows, but is supplied from a different source, serious unemployment can occur in the formerly prosperous supplier's industry. In 1870–1900 the United Kingdom ship-building industry built ships for the whole world, and her merchant navy carried about 80 per cent of world trade. Today she builds ships for only a few nations and carries only 11 per cent of world trade. The consequent structural changes in the British ship-building industry are a cause for concern to men, management and governments. The risk of being laid off is understandably unsettling to a labour force, and causes unrest and hardship.

Regional unemployment arises when an area of a country has too high a proportion of its work force tied to a particular industry. Technology is not static, but dynamic. Advances in technology make previously prosperous industries obsolete: victims of declining world demand. For instance, synthetic fibres such as nylon and Acrilan have made serious inroads into the markets for natural fibres such as silk, cotton, and wool, and earlier synthetic fibres such as rayon. In rather a different way a region may suffer setbacks because its previously advantageous position is eroded away for some reason. Perhaps it is the exhaustion of natural supplies of raw material, or economic changes may reduce the demand for its products. For example, the change to oil, gas and electric central heating has affected coal mining. Where a region is over-specialized, a serious depression in one major industry leads to a general decline in associated industries in the area; migration of skilled workers and a general decline in prosperity follows.

(*e*) *Industrial Unrest and Social Discontent.* If high degrees of specialization are introduced, mechanization and automation must replace existing labour forces. It is generally recognized that such trends are inevitable and benefit the whole community by raising the volume of production. The displaced workers must be retrained to new employment, and these new jobs will inevitably be in tertiary production rather than in primary or secondary production. Even with the fullest co-operation between management and unions, it is often difficult to resolve these problems—particularly as, by its very nature, specialist production is easy to disrupt. If work flows continuously through a factory any operative who downs tools interrupts the production line. 'One out—all out' is the cry, and it is easily achieved.

Industrial unrest tends to be local, but social unrest can be country-wide. If advanced societies are to prosper everyone must share in the prosperity, for disruption is easily arranged. Some reasonable distribution of wealth has to be achieved which, without disrupting incentives to hard work, keeps society stable.

(6) Limitations to the Division of Labour

Although the division of labour will usually result in lower costs per unit of output, there are limitations to its effective use. These limitations are:

(*a*) *The Extent of the Market.* There is little point in mass production of goods which are not in mass demand. Therefore refined division-of-labour techniques are inappropriate in industries serving a small market only. Artificial limbs are unlikely to be mass produced, for the number of disabled persons is fortunately small. Similarly, a shop in a country district, sparsely inhabited, is unlikely to employ specialist bacon cutters, ham slicers, etc. The sole assistant will perform such activities to the best of his ability at times when customers are not present waiting to be served.

(*b*) *Technical Impossibility.* Sometimes it is impossible to subdivide a technical process beyond a certain point. When each process has been reduced to a minimum activity further division of labour is impossible, and increased output will have to be achieved by duplication of the existing processes. Parallel units of production in an industry indicate that no further economies could be achieved by the subdivision of labour.

(*c*) *An Inadequate Monetary System.* If the money system is inadequate in some way, perhaps because of general distrust of the currency or fear of depreciation, the production of large outputs becomes more risky. Entrepreneurs will play safe and content themselves with lower levels of production than in more favourable circumstances.

(7) Production and Welfare

Many economists have defined economics in terms of welfare. In Britain, the Welfare State was established in the years following the Second World War, and although it has its critics, it also has many staunch supporters. If the aim of an economy is to create utilities to satisfy wants, and if social unrest develops in societies where manifest inequalities exist, then it seems inevitable that some attempt at a Welfare State must be made in most societies. The alternative appears to be repression of some sort.

At this point economics merges with politics. It is inappropriate in *Economics Made Simple* to go further than this. Applied economics, usually regarded as a field of study that can be approached only when basic principles have been examined, inevitably merges into politics, and instead of merely observing man in the everyday business of life attempts to suggest acceptable policies which will maximize human welfare.

(8) The Pattern of Production in an Advanced Economy

Great Britain holds a Census of Production at regular intervals. Such a census is difficult to take. It involves problems of definition—how shall we classify the production of each type of factory, for example; of collection—how shall we deal with manufacturers who refuse to send in their figures; and of statistical presentation.

The latest data available after full statistical analysis are the 1974 figures. Compared with the figures for 1963, they show the pattern of production in Britain today. They also reveal how inflation has affected the money value of production. At 1963 valuations the total 1974 production of £102,387 m was really only £50,984 m.

Table 2. Production in Great Britain, 1963–74

Industry	1963 Output of Goods or Services in £ millions	Changes by 1974
Food, Drink, and Tobacco	4,477	14,598
Chemicals and Allied Industries	2,692	13,447
Metal Manufacturing	2,479	7,177
Engineering and Allied Industries	9,013	27,827
Textiles, Leather and Cloth	3,081	7,200
Other Manufacturing Industries	3,771	13,530
Mining and Quarrying	1,031	1,196
Construction Industry	3,930	12,531
Gas, Electricity, and Water	1,593	4,881
Estimated Total Production All Census Industries	32,067	102,387

(Source: Annual Abstract of Statistics, 1976)

Table 2 demonstrates the overriding influence of manufacturing industry, particularly engineering and allied industries. It is also clear that *secondary* production is the major contributor to the national output of Great Britain.

(9) Summary of Chapter Two

1. To an economist all workers are producers, whether they are engaged in producing goods or services.

2. Production can be divided into primary production (natural resources), secondary production (manufactures), and tertiary production (commercial services and personal services).

3. Direct production is the production of goods for one's own immediate personal use.

4. Indirect production is production by specialists, who perform either in particular trades or in processes arranged along mass-production lines.

5. The division of labour secures high levels of productivity and achieves a high national income. This national income must be shared fairly if industrial and social unrest is to be avoided.

(10) Suggested Further Reading

Allen, G. C.: *The Structure of Industry in Britain*, 3rd Ed., 1970. Longmans.

Marshall, A.: *Principles of Economics* (Book II, Chapters 1–3). Macmillan: London, 1961.

Smith, Adam: *Wealth of Nations* (Book I, Chapters 1–3). Dent, Everyman Series: London, 1960.

Tugendhat, C.: *Oil: The Biggest Business*. Eyre & Spottiswoode: London, 1968.

Turner, G.: *The Car Makers*. Eyre & Spottiswoode: London, 1968.

Exercises Set 2

1. Discuss whether (*a*) the conductor of a symphony orchestra, and (*b*) a dental mechanic, are productive workers.

2. How might the following be made to increase their productivity: (*a*) a garage foreman in the repair section, (*b*) a bus conductor; (*c*) a tailor; (*d*) a schoolteacher; (*e*) a politician?

3. What similarities, and what differences, as far as production is concerned are there between: (*a*) a peasant fishing from a balsa raft in the Peruvian Current; (*b*) an owner-operator fishing from a modern trawler outside the Icelandic limit?

4. Consider the advantages and disadvantages of specialization in the motor-vehicle-servicing industry from the points of view of: (*a*) a large motor-vehicle manufacturer considering to whom he should give his sole agency for servicing in Transitshire; (*b*) a householder about to go on holiday who wants his car to be serviced cheaply and reliably; (*c*) Ivor Waywivem, a motor-vehicle mechanic.

5. 'To an economist all occupations are productive.' Explain.

6. 'We factory workers made the goods—we are entitled to the full rewards from them.' Explain why they can't have the full rewards from the sale of these goods.

7. Eskimos practised polyandry (one wife having many husbands) because of the killing-off in infancy of girl children. Why do you think the Eskimos killed off children in this way?

8. What do you understand by the division of labour?

9. List the advantages of specialization and illustrate them by considering some industry you know about.

10. 'Mass production is the focusing upon a manufacturing project of the principles of power, accuracy, economy, system, continuity, speed, and repetition' (H. Ford). Explain these principles as applied to the motor-vehicle industry.

CHAPTER THREE

THE FACTORS OF PRODUCTION

(1) Introduction

We have already seen that enterprising individuals organize production by employing what are called **factors** (land, labour, and capital) in such proportions as seem the most appropriate to them. In making business decisions the aim is generally to achieve the greatest output of utilities from the minimum input of factors. This will usually result in the greatest profit to the enterprise, but if not some conflict may develop between the greatest output of utilities and the greatest profit to the owners. The true aim in this case is probably profit maximization. Generally speaking, economists expect entrepreneurs who are behaving rationally to maximize profits; but some entrepreneurs may have reasons for deliberately not doing so. For instance, the prospect of labour unrest may lead them to use more labour and less capital (e.g. machinery) so that, instead of maximizing profits, they maximize satisfactions. There are some satisfactions which are not monetary, and the employment of our fellow men in useful and rewarding labour may be one of them.

(2) The Factors of Production—Land

By 'land' the economist means those resources made available by the bounty of Nature. At present these resources are found only on earth, because although man has reached the moon he has not yet started to exploit extra-terrestrial sources of minerals. Land therefore consists of the following:

(a) The agricultural areas of the earth's surface.
(b) The natural grasslands, woodlands, and jungles.
(c) The deserts and ice deserts.
(d) The oceans and seas.
(e) The chemicals of the earth's crust and of the atmosphere.

The last are of three types: the elements formed before the earth was born in the atomic furnace of some great Sun; the compounds resulting from the interaction of elements, for example, sodium chloride and carbon dioxide; and other compounds which are the accumulation of animal and vegetable material resulting from life on earth. Sometimes these compounds are very complex, or are mixtures of many chemicals—for example, crude oil. Sometimes they are simple, like the chalk which forms the white cliffs of Dover.

Land as a Free Gift of Nature. Since land has either existed in its present form from time immemorial or is provided annually by the bounty of Nature, it is often regarded as a free gift which all citizens should be entitled to share. In some countries, even today, reasonable quantities of land may be taken by anyone. In Tanzania, for example, nationals may build a house anywhere they like without permission, provided the holding taken is a reasonable one for a family. In the United States in the nineteenth century land was similarly available to settlers, so that the workman of today became the independent landed proprietor of tomorrow. In Australia the word 'squatter' came to mean 'independent landowner': he acquired his rights to a farm or ranch by occupying and working the land. In that great Australian song 'Waltzing Matilda' it is the squatter who is the property owner and is harassing the swagman, or tramp, for stealing his sheep. In Britain the ownership of natural resources has developed from an original seizure of the land during the Norman invasion of A.D. 1066 through the granting of leases and freeholds to a situation where many people own land, but all land is owned. There are no free gifts of Nature except atmospheric ones. For instance, anyone who gets planning permission could set up a factory to obtain oxygen by liquefying air, but even he would need some land on which to build his plant.

Land as a Geographical Site. Like the entrepreneur referred to above, every enterprise requires a geographical location. The location of industry is an interesting topic and is dealt with on page 55. Geographical location is also of importance to individuals, who must have some territory they can call their own. Where peoples are dispossessed of their land they become refugees seeking a geographical location by the kind permission of other nations.

Land—Mobile Factor or Immobile Factor. The mobility of factors is important, since it is often necessary to move them if they are to be combined with other factors. Alaskan oil is of little use in Alaska, and Burmese teak is not appreciated as greatly there as in the fashionable homes of Western Europe. But some resources are immobile. We cannot move Niagara Falls to a more desirable location, but must utilize its electrical potential *in situ*. We cannot move a building site we wish to dispose of to a more desirable location, where it will fetch a higher price. An important aspect of mobility of land is the short period taken by crops to grow. This increases the mobility of land, in that it can be turned over to other uses very quickly. For instance, once a field is sown with wheat it is 'immobilized' until harvest time; but after the wheat has been harvested the land can be used for growing a different crop or for rearing cattle or sheep. If it is converted to industrial or domestic uses by being built on its mobility declines considerably, for it cannot now be turned over to different uses until the buildings have served their useful purpose, which may not be for 100 years.

Land—Limited in Supply or Inexhaustible. The early economists were much impressed by the limited supply of land, and our inability to increase it. This may have been because they were British, and in Britain, unlike some other countries, land has been wholly owned since 1066. Today some economists are preoccupied with the possibility that we may soon exhaust the resources of the earth's crust. It is commonly believed that oil resources are only sufficient to last about fifteen years at the present rate of consumption. World supplies of tin are scarce, and deposits in Cornwall formerly regarded as uneconomic are now worth working again because of the prices reigning in world markets. It appears that while most natural resources are still in abundant supply, we may soon exhaust supplies of one or two products. We are also in danger of over-hunting such creatures as the whale (now so scarce that most nations have ceased to send out whaling fleets), and population pressures are seriously reducing wild life in Africa.

Even though the actual territory of the earth is limited, it can be used much more intensively than at present, as those who live in Hong Kong or Singapore have proved. Reclamation of land also takes place on quite an extensive scale, as in Holland, and irrigation can restore deserts to fertility. A particularly great advance will be made in the next year or two in Libya, where a search for water in desert areas has revealed enough underground water to fill the River Nile for 200 years. This should enable huge areas of desert to be irrigated, so perhaps the early economists were pessimistic in their statement that the supply of land could not be increased.

Land—Subject to the Law of Diminishing Returns. The early economists held that land was a factor which suffered particularly from the Law of Diminishing Returns. This early doctrine held that, given a certain quantity' of the factor land, with which the entrepreneur combined increasing quantities of labour or capital, sooner or later the addition of further quantities of these other factors would result in diminishing returns, that is less output per unit of other factors applied.

Table 3. Diminishing returns from land

Area of land (in acres)	Weight of fertilizer used (in cwts)	Output of potatoes (in tons)	Increase in output over untreated land	Marginal output (i.e. output achieved by each extra cwt. used)
1	—	5	—	—
1	1	6	1	1
1	2	8	3	2
1	3	10·5	5·5	2·5
1	4	11·5	6·5	1
1	5	9	4	−2·5

An example of this is given in Table 3. Successive increments of capital (in the form of artificial fertilizer) are being added to an acre of land by a smallholder growing potatoes. Untreated, the land yields 5 tons per acre. When successive increments of fertilizer are added output rises. The first sack yields an increase of 1 ton per acre, the second sack yields an extra 2 tons per acre, and the third sack an extra 2½ tons per acre. The fourth sack only yields an increase of 1 ton, so that diminishing returns have already set in, while the fifth sack produces no better results at all, tonnage actually decreasing. At this point the fertilizer has become too concentrated. Maximum output is achieved at four sacks of fertilizer, but by this time both the marginal output (i.e. the extra output achieved from each sack) and the average extra output have begun to decline.

Diminishing returns must inevitably follow the addition of successive increments of capital to land.

The early economists were wrong in thinking that the Law of Diminishing Returns applied particularly to land. Industry appeared to them to be able always to achieve increasing returns, because in general industry in their day was on a fairly small scale. Today we know that diminishing returns can set in when firms become too large. Difficulties over communication between the board of directors and the ordinary work-people may result in production losses which are greater than the gains achieved by a more perfect division of labour.

The Law of Diminishing Returns can be seen in operation in real life almost everywhere. The following examples will illustrate this point, but the reader is urged to find local examples drawn from his own experience.

Example 1. A firm moves into a new town to set up a clothing factory. At first it employs only fully qualified machinists. As it expands production, the supply of suitably trained machinists is exhausted and it has to recruit inexperienced female staff and train them. Expense incurred in the training scheme reduces overall profitability. Later still, when it has trained the suitable female labour, it has to accept for training less and less satisfactory labour. Training periods have to be lengthened and larger wastage (due to spoilt work) accepted as inevitable. Finally, it may have to adopt a home-sewing scheme for out-workers, because the pool of workers available to travel daily to the factory is exhausted. This will involve extra expense in delivery and collection of the product.

Example 2. A country attempts to increase agricultural output. At first it utilizes all the best land; but as the programme develops, more and more unsatisfactory land has to be cultivated. Diminishing returns at each successive stage of expansion are inevitable.

(3) The Factors of Production—Labour

'Labour' to an economist is the supply of human resources, both physical and mental, which is available to engage in the production of goods and services. The supply of labour depends on two things: (*a*) the total labour force available, i.e. the population less any sections of the population who do not work; and (*b*) the number of hours per week the population is prepared to work.

The Working Population

Population is dealt with more fully on page 360. The 'groups who do not work', referred to above, consist of:

(i) *Young People*. The number of young people available for work varies with the education available. If education is largely a matter of parental instruction and the handing down of techniques from father to son, as in many peasant communities, children will participate in production from an early age. If education is a matter of specialist tuition by professional educators the labour supply will be correspondingly reduced as pupils and students are withheld from the labour force during their schooling.

(ii) *Married Women*. Where it is traditional for married women to cease work when they have young children to care for, the labour force is correspondingly reduced. In Britain since the end of the Second World War the employment of married women has been the the greatest single change in the labour force. Despite recent legislation calling for equal opportunities for women it remains true that for many married women the family is more important than the career. Decisions to take up career opportunities are deferred while the children's welfare requires it. Instead employment is deliberately taken in fields where good incomes can be earned without irksome responsibilities. It is impossible to generalize, of course, and many gifted women carry both home and family responsibilities with an equanimity which inspires the admiration of all who know them.

(iii) *Retired Persons.* The age of retirement affects the supply of labour. If, for example, retirement at the age of 65 is normal, so that perfectly healthy and energetic men and women retire compulsorily at that age, the supply of labour is reduced. Many people of retirement age today are quite capable of continuing in productive employment.

The Hours Worked per Year. If the working week is reduced the supply of labour falls, unless the resultant improvement in health enables more efficient labour to take place in the shorter working week. For instance, in early industrial Britain men, women, and children commonly worked a 12–14-hour day. It is probable that the Ten Hour Act, introduced in 1847 to reduce the working day, improved the effectiveness of the work done in the ten hours to offset the shorter day. This is probably not true of present-day conditions, where, for example, reducing the 40-hour week to 35 hours almost certainly lowers the supply of labour. Productivity may still rise if the reduction of hours is secured by the workers in return for an agreement to use new machinery, etc., but the factor capital has produced the increase. Holiday periods operate in a similar way to reduce the supply of labour. An extreme example is the case of the Californian shipyard which is currently giving its workers 91 days holiday a year. In the United States generally a 30-hour week is quite common. Some workers prefer extra income to shorter working hours, so that 'moonlighting' (doing one job by day and another in the evening) is quite common. 'Moonlighting' therefore increases the supply of labour available to entrepreneurs.

The Quality of Labour. More important perhaps than the actual supply of labour is the quality of the labour. Is it skilled, semi-skilled, or unskilled? Is it willing? Is it adaptable? Skilled labour is labour which has either mastered a particular craft, like toolmaking or printing, or has been professionally trained, like doctors, dentists, lawyers, and accountants. Semi-skilled labour is in some ways a misnomer, since the operatives who are described as semi-skilled have in fact reached very high degrees of skill over a very limited range of activities. A spot-welder in a motor-vehicle assembly plant and a stator winder in a vacuum-cleaner factory are examples. Such labour can be very quickly trained, in from four to six weeks at the most. Similarly, one manu-facturer of accounting machines considers an operator can be fully trained in two days. Unskilled labour, as its name implies, requires little specialized training. What training there is can be acquired on the job itself. Even so this labour becomes more efficient as it grows used to the work. When the canals were dug in Britain, and later when the railways were laid, the entrepreneurs found it took a full year to turn a strong, healthy ploughboy into a navvy. Not only did he need to learn the economy of effort which would enable him to work long hours without tiring but his whole physique had to change. To build the muscles that were necessary for the work, and to acquire the strength of character to withstand the rough life was not the work of a single day.

Generally speaking, skilled labour tends to be more *specific* than semi-skilled or unskilled labour. The idea of 'specificity' is an important one in economics. If a factor of production is specific it can be used in only one particular task: for instance, a dentist must be employed in dentistry if his true talents are to be used. If we take a dentist and turn him into the fields to cut sugar cane we shall be wasting his talents. Of course it may do the dentist a world of good to find out what a hard life the cane-worker leads, but this is no substitute for the efficient use of his services in caring for his patients' teeth. A spot-welder in a motor-car factory is a less specific form of labour. He will probably be equally useful servicing cars in a garage, or drilling assemblies in an electronics factory.

Factors affecting the efficiency of labour include:

(*a*) The general education and background knowledge of the labour force. If it has been born into the television era of an advanced society it will be knowledgeable, adaptable, and sophisticated. If it has only recently left a peasant community it will be unsophisticated, superstitious, nervous, and slow to adapt itself.

(*b*) The general health of the labour force. This may be improved by diet, and by adequate welfare services of all sorts. A developing nation's progress may be slow because a fully effective labour force depends on raising the standard of living. This is a slow process and depends on an efficient labour force. We therefore have a vicious circle, which spirals slowly upwards, but at an increasing pace as the years go by.

(*c*) The incentives offered to labour. Where there are few incentives labour will be less efficient. Where the incentives are great labour will apply itself more assiduously.

(*d*) The availability of other factors of high quality. This is the commonest method of increasing the efficiency of labour. If it is backed by good quality land, labour itself will be more efficient. If it is backed by well chosen tools and adequate power supplies, even a poor labour force will be highly productive. One explanation of the great wealth of the United States, despite the short working week and long holidays of its citizens, is that during his working hours every worker is supported by an array of power tools appropriate to his activities.

(4) The Factors of Production—Capital

The word 'capital' is used in many different ways today, but all its meanings refer to some stock of physical assets which have been created in the past and are available for present use. Thus **social capital**, such as schools, roads, and municipal swimming baths, has been created over the years by contributions in the form of rates and taxes. As a factor of production, capital means the stock of **producer goods** which are available to entrepreneurs for use in production.

Producer goods are defined as goods which are not made to satisfy wants directly but are made to increase the eventual output of consumption goods by raising productivity in the fields, forests, and factories of the earth. Thus a motor-driven saw raises the volume of timber cut by workers in the forestry and timber trades, resulting in an increased flow of timber products at cheaper prices into our homes. A refinery fractionating column turns the experimental work of the research chemist into a productive reality, yielding up a flow of hydrocarbon products into the petrol tanks and oil sumps of our cars and the service bays of garages.

Types of Producer Goods. The commonest types of factor capital are:

(*a*) Constructional works of every sort: factories, offices, mines, power stations, dams, piers, docks and harbour improvements, aerodromes, roads, railways, canals, hospitals, schools, etc.

(*b*) Plant, machinery, tools, and equipment of every sort.

(*c*) Stocks of raw materials and partly finished goods. Some economists hold that stocks of finished consumer goods which are being transported (either geographically or in time) are 'capital' too. This idea ties in with our definition of 'production' as a process that continues until the final consumer actually receives the goods; but for practical purposes it is probably better to leave this class of finished goods out of our calculations of the factor capital.

Specific Capital. Capital assets tend to be more specific than either land or labour. Many types of plant are purpose-built, and are of little use if the demand for the product they make changes. Many tools are designed to do particular jobs: a hammer is less specific than a press tool for making plastic tea-plates. The extent to which his capital assets are specific may vitally affect the decisions made by an entrepreneur. For example, a tailor faced with a reduced demand for suits may use his sewing machines to make overalls or skirts—for sewing machines are non-specific. A cement manufacturer faced with reduced demand must either stock-pile or shut down, for a cement works can only make cement.

Capital, Income, and Wealth. These words are clearly connected, for a wealthy man usually has a regular income and also a house, car, often investments, and so on. The exact relationship is simple. Income is a flow of wealth accruing over a period of time. Thus a man receiving a salary of 400.00 per month is receiving an income with which he can select a basket of goods and services, i.e. a flow of wealth spread over the month. Capital is a stock of goods existing at any particular moment of time.

The Accumulation of Capital. In order to create capital assets of the types listed above it is necessary for work to be performed without any immediate gain or reward in the form of consumer goods. In primitive societies the workers making stone axes must be kept alive by the other members of the tribe who hunt or collect food. These hunters and food gatherers must eat less today so that capital assets can be produced which will increase productivity in the future. In other words, we must postpone current consumption to provide future improvements in living standards. Economists put it in the form of an equation:

$$\begin{array}{ccc} Consumption \\ postponed \end{array} = Savings = \begin{array}{c} Capital\ available \\ for\ investment \end{array}$$

The early stages in any country's accumulation of capital are very bitter years. Promises of jam tomorrow do not compensate the poor eating dry bread today. Were the early capitalists of Great Britain, whom Dickens called 'The Iron Gentlemen', justified in paying such low wages to accumulate the capital for their industries? At least they practised self-denial themselves too. Similarly, Henry Ford, the American industrialist, asked by his son for some money, reputedly gave the boy a penny. The boy indignantly flung it into a bush in the garden. Ford insisted on finding it, and read the boy a lecture on the value, and unique properties, of copper. Was Stalin right to let five million Russians die of starvation while he built up heavy industry? Economists do not attempt to answer such questions, which cannot be settled by reference to facts. As a result of Stalin's policies, Russia did succeed in accumulating capital, but this might have been achieved equally well in other ways.

Skills as Capital. Hidden behind the actual producer goods themselves there is another kind of capital, the accumulated skill and knowledge of the people. This can be established only over lengthy periods of time, although the process is speeded up by modern education. Great Britain took a great many years to discover the basic industrial processes which brought her to greatness. From about 1700 until 1850 these skills and processes were slowly mastered. Other nations, like France, Germany, and the United States, made more rapid progress because they benefitted from lessons already learned in Britain. They sprang to industrial power in fifty years (1860–1910). The Japanese made even more rapid strides. In each case there is the further point that when you come in later you start from a better base. Germany rose to power in the electrical age rather than the steam age, and Japan has made its progress in the electronic era. Leap-frogging in this way, the late developers not only challenge but surpass others who, having invested capital in earlier technologies, are slow to destroy what they have so painfully accumulated. The process of accumulating capital is perhaps less bitter for those who begin today than in the early days of industrialism.

Once a nation has advanced through the initial period of the accumulation of capital it is much easier for it to accumulate capital, because it already has a skilled and sophisticated labour force. The best example of this was the rapid recovery of Germany after the Second World War. Despite the appalling devastation of the country's resources and the punitive reparations demand, Western Germany rose like a phoenix from the ashes. This was not entirely due to her own efforts. Enlightened behaviour by the Allies contributed a great deal, but the hard work and skill of the West Germans themselves was chiefly responsible for restoring a shattered economy to a leading position in Europe in the space of a dozen years. It has been calculated that the total capital assets of even an advanced nation represent less than two years of national income. The rebuilding of Germany in such a short time appears to support this calculation.

Net Capital Formation and Savings

The following ideas about capital formation are important.

(a) *Capital formation is possible only if consumption is postponed somewhere in society*. This postponement of consumption may be voluntary, involuntary, or State-induced. Voluntary self-denial occurs when we postpone present consumption quite deliberately, perhaps to save resources for bad times ahead, or to pursue some long-term policy aimed at capital formation. Involuntary savings occur when someone else prevents us from enjoying our full consumption. This may happen when there is overcharging by entrepreneurs in favourable positions. Gambling dens, which are usually considered as anti-social, might be justified on the grounds that they remove funds from the pockets of those who clearly do not know what to do with their money and put it into the pockets of others who will invest it in solid enterprises. State-induced savings are effected by taxation. If, as a matter of Government policy, income is taxed away to reduce personal consumption these funds will be available for capital formation. Taxes may be imposed on the rich to help the poor. Such taxation will not help capital formation at all, for it encourages consumption.

(*b*) *Savings release resources to support workers engaged in the creation of capital assets.* It is the postponement of current consumption (savings) which enables unproductive workers to be supported. The word 'unproductive' is used here to mean 'unproductive of consumer goods', because the end product of these workers will be a capital asset. This capital asset will make available a bigger flow of consumer goods eventually.

(*c*) *The savings made must not merely be hoarded, but must be 'invested'*, i.e. used to support the workers engaged in producing the capital assets required. As there is always some risk involved in this type of activity, the savings which have been invested may, or may not, yield a future increased flow of consumer goods. The process of investment is carried out directly by the entrepreneur who sets up in business using his own savings as capital to support himself while he creates the capital assets he requires. It is carried out indirectly when a person who wishes to save invests his money with an institutional investor (such as a bank, building society, or unit trust) which records the loan made to it and then makes the savings available to an entrepreneur in search of funds. The claims of the individual who saves the money against current consumption are handed on to the entrepreneur who intends to build a factory, or dig a mine, or create some other producer good. Self-denial on the part of the saver makes possible capital formation by the borrower.

(*d*) *Not all the new assets created represent an increase in capital.* The capital formation of any country in a given year does not all represent an advance in national wealth. Some of the new capital assets created will merely be replacing old assets which have become obsolete or have depreciated to the point where they must be scrapped. The term **net capital formation** is used to signify that portion of created capital assets which is in excess of depreciation in the period under review. If Britain builds 300,000 houses per year but pulls down 200,000 older properties in slum-clearance schemes the net capital formation is 100,000 houses.

Capital Consumption

Where the net capital formation is a negative quantity, because less new assets are created than old assets are retired from production, we may say the nation is *living on its capital* or *consuming its capital*. This often happens in war-time, when heavy destruction of capital assets may occur at a time when replacement is particularly difficult because able-bodied men are away fighting. The slow recovery of Britain after the Second World War was partly due to heavy consumption of capital during that period. Not only was serious destruction of capital assets experienced but also heavy debts were incurred with overseas countries. The repayment of these debts reduced net capital formation in the years 1945–55.

Every nation must take care to maintain its capital and attempt to increase it. As populations rise, larger supplies of capital are needed to maintain existing living standards. Since most people expect their standard of living to improve year by year, it is essential that a positive net capital formation be achieved.

(5) Is the Entrepreneur a Factor of Production?

At one time the activities of entrepreneurs were considered to be so different from those of other humans that entrepreneurs were regarded as a separate factor of production. They provided 'enterprise', which was essential to the productive process. The development of the limited-liability company as the chief type of business unit has led to a careful examination of the activities of entrepreneurs, for in this form of organization different persons perform different activities, which were formerly performed by the sole proprietor, or partners.

The activities undertaken by an entrepreneur are as follows:

(a) *Ownership*. The early entrepreneur was the source of the capital of the enterprise, which he had accumulated by postponing consumption. In placing that claim against the goods and services available at the disposal of the business, he ran the risk that the business would prove to be a failure. The function of ownership is to carry risk: to bear the uncertainties of business life.

(b) *Management*. Early entrepreneurs, and sole traders or partners today who control their own businesses, work in the business. They make the major business decisions: what to produce, in what quantities, whom to employ, when and where to market the output, whether to expand or contract the activities of the firm, etc. In the limited-liability company such activities are performed by the board of directors, who are not the owners of the company (except that they must hold some shares).

Today we regard the two activities in the typical firm (the limited-liability company) as having been largely separated from one another. The difference is between 'the entrepreneurs' and 'the entrepreneurial function'.

The **entrepreneurs** are the *owners* of the business who contribute the capital and *bear the risks of uncertainties in business life*. They may be sole traders, partners, limited partners, or shareholders.

The **entrepreneurial function** is the *control and management of an enterprise*. It adjusts the enterprise to the dynamic situation in which it is being conducted, co-ordinating factors to achieve the maximum return on capital invested by the owners. It is a special type of human labour, increasingly performed not by sole traders and partners with personal interest in the affairs of the firm but by professional managers who may also own a few shares. The increasingly complex industrial structure of advanced societies throws up a whole career structure of management and junior management, taking an active share in the entrepreneurial function but quite divorced from true ownership of the business.

Enterprise is therefore no longer generally regarded by economists as a fourth factor of production, even though countless old-style entrepreneurs may be observed running their sole-trader or partnership business and wielding powerful influence in many private limited companies. The public limited company is of such overwhelming importance that it justifies regarding the entrepreneurial function as one performed by ordinary labour, not a special type of labour.

(6) Combining the Factors of Production

The entrepreneurial function of management is to maximize the return on capital invested. In order to do this, management combines the factors of land, labour, and capital in what it considers to be the best possible way. It then observes the achievements of the resources used, and makes adjustments if necessary. Some possibility exists of **substitution between factors,** replacing an expensive factor by a cheaper one, for example, but complete substitution of one factor by another is usually impossible. Suppose that land prices are high. The management may increase the proportion of capital to land, so that capital-intensive use of the land is achieved. In rural areas it may mean the use of battery systems for producing poultry and eggs; in London it means building tower blocks of flats instead of bungalows.

In employing resources the management will measure the factors in terms of cost, to achieve the most economical input of factors. Factor costs are dealt with in detail later, but the names given to the rewards paid to factors are

Factor	*Reward paid to the factor* (*Factor Cost*)
Land	Commercial rent
Labour	Wages (salaries has the same meaning)
Capital	Interest (paid to the owner for surrendering his claims to current consumption) Profit (paid to compensate the owner for the risk he runs)

(7) Summary of Chapter Three

1. Production is achieved by the combination of land, labour, and capital in the creation of goods and services.

2. Land as a factor means the resources made available by Nature. To some extent these are free gifts by Nature to mankind. Every enterprise must have a geographical location. The early economists noticed that land was subject to the Law of Diminishing Returns, but this law is today held to apply to all factors, not exclusively to land.

3. Labour is the human factor, and depends upon the working population available, its quality and suitability for the types of activity proposed.

4. Capital is a claim against the resources of goods and services available to mankind. It has to be accumulated by a reduction in current consumption, and makes possible the creation of producer goods and social assets of all sorts. These assets then enable even greater production of consumer goods and services in the succeeding period.

5. The entrepreneur is today regarded as the owner of a firm. The entrepreneurial functions of management control and co-ordination of business activities are regarded as being performed by labour today. The typical modern business unit, the limited-liability company, displays this separation between ownership and management.

6. In combining the factors of production, substitution between factors is possible to some extent. Management aims at the best possible combination of factors.

(8) Suggested Further Reading

Benham, F.: *Economics* (Chapters 6–8). Pitman: London, 1967.

Cairncross, A.: *Introduction to Economics* (Chapter 4). Butterworth: London, 1966.

Harvey, J.: *Intermediate Economics* (Chapter 4). Macmillan: London, 1971.

Hicks, J. R.: *The Social Framework* (Chapters 6 and 7). Oxford U.P.: London, 1960.

Exercises Set 3

1. What factors would be controlled and manipulated by a retired sea captain using his life savings to run an inn in freehold premises near a major port?

2. Suggest how the following might save labour by using capital: (*a*) a cotton plantation manager; (*b*) a sugar refiner; (*c*) a garage proprietor; (*d*) the board of governors of a college; (*e*) the chief accountant of a multiple-shop organization.

3. Which types of 'land' are used by the following entrepreneurs: (*a*) a grain farmer; (*b*) a cattle rancher; (*c*) a chemical engineer in an oil refinery; (*d*) a frozen-fish-finger manufacturer; (*e*) a manufacturer of neon tubes?

4. List the likely 'capital goods' employed by: (*a*) a gold-mining company; (*b*) an electric-shaver assembly firm; (*c*) a trawler operator; (*d*) a bespoke tailor; (*e*) a hire-purchase finance company.

5. Discuss the Law of Diminishing Returns as it applies to the following factors in the given situations: (*a*) land—used for market gardening; (*b*) labour—one man employed to repair watches; (*c*) capital—a machine for filling milk bottles.

6. What do we understand by an 'entrepreneur' today? Who performs this function in the following cases: (*a*) a sole trader; (*b*) a partnership; (*c*) a public limited company?

7. To some extent all factors are interchangeable. Explain, giving examples drawn from primary, secondary, and tertiary production.

8. Distinguish between specific and non-specific assets. The liquidator of a company is appointed to sell off the assets to pay the creditors. What will be the effect on his activities of a high degree of specificity in the assets?

9. An American company has a choice between setting up a factory in Belgium or Turkey. Discuss the likely labour situations facing them in these two countries, and the probable advantages and disadvantages of each.

10. 'The sole purpose of capital is to exploit working people'—European Trade Unionist. 'We would welcome capital investments from any country on terms fair to both parties'—African politician. Discuss the accumulation of capital, referring in your answer to the different attitudes displayed by these two spokesmen.

CHAPTER FOUR

THE TYPES OF BUSINESS UNIT

(1) Introduction

Firms are units of business organization carrying on some productive activity resulting in the creation of goods or services to satisfy wants. These types of business unit show a progression from small-scale businesses, often run by sole traders or partnerships, to large-scale enterprises of national and even international importance. Since the accumulation of capital is a difficult process, at first the scale of operations must be small. As the profits made are re-invested in the enterprise it grows, and growth accelerates as the years go by. Finally, its manifest success makes investment in the firm attractive to outsiders as well.

The size of the business therefore reflects the amount of capital invested. Differences between the various units reflect: (*a*) the ownership of the capital concerned; (*b*) the control of the conduct of the enterprise; (*c*) the accountability of the controllers to the investors, in so far as they are different people; (*d*) the division of the profits.

(2) Types of Business Unit

Business units in Britain may be divided into three main groups: *Private enterprises*, *non-profitmaking units*, and *public enterprises*. A full list includes:

Private Enterprises
   Sole Traders
   Partnerships
   Limited Partnerships
   Private Limited Companies
   Public Limited Companies
   Holding Companies (a more advanced type of Public Company)

Non-Profitmaking Units
   Clubs of many sorts
   Co-operative Societies

Public Enterprises
   Municipal undertakings
   Nationalized undertakings

Readers in other countries may find the British pattern of enterprises slightly different from their own.

Ownership is the key to the difference between these three types of undertaking. Private enterprises are owned and operated by certain clearly identified people, who are also entitled to the rewards of the enterprise. Non-profitmaking groups exist in order to confer benefits on the members which are outside the commercial activities of the unit. Profit is a mere incidental, but any surplus is shared among the membership. With public-enterprise units, the enterprise is socially owned and operated, possibly on a commercial basis, but with the intention of supplying goods and services at reasonable prices for the benefit of the whole community.

(3) Sole-trader Enterprises

A sole trader is a person who enters business on his own account, contributing the capital to start the enterprise, labouring in it with or without the assistance of employees, and receiving as his reward the proceeds of the venture. The advantages are as follows:

(*a*) No formal procedures are required to set up in business. A licence must be obtained for certain classes of business, and the name of the business must be registered under the Registration of Business Names Act, 1916, if it is anything other than the true name of the proprietor.

(*b*) Independence is a chief feature of these businesses. Having no one to consult, the sole trader can put his plans into effect quickly.

(*c*) Personal supervision ensures effective operation at all times. Customers are known to the proprietor, who can cater for their tastes and avoid bad debts by a personal assessment of credit-worthiness; employees are under personal supervision; waste is avoided.

(*d*) Expansion need be pressed only to the point where the market is adequately supplied. In isolated areas this makes the sole trader the effective business unit.

(*e*) He is accountable only to himself and (apart from taxation authorities) need reveal the state of his business to no one.

The disadvantages include:

(*a*) Long working hours and little time off for vacations.

(*b*) Sickness can lead to business difficulties.

(*c*) The proprietor has 'unlimited liability', which means that he is personally liable to the full extent of his private wealth for the debts of the business. Insolvency may mean the sale of his house and home to pay the creditors.

(*d*) Expansion is usually possible only by ploughing back the profits of a business as further capital. The sole trader may be able to borrow from a bank, or privately, but he is not allowed to borrow from the public. He may take a partner, but this means a loss of independence. He can keep this independence if he takes a 'limited partner', but these are not easy to find in present conditions of high taxation.

(*e*) The business is part of the estate of the proprietor at his death, and it may be necessary to sell the business in order to pay Capital Transfer Tax.

(*f*) Like most small-scale enterprises, it will be a high-cost enterprise, because the degree of specialization is usually small.

Vulnerability of the Sole Trader

In recent years there has been a decline in the number of sole-trader enterprises, as the advantages of large-scale enterprise have become more noticeable. Every improvement in transport and communications exposes the local shop and the local factory to a blast of competition from larger and more efficient enterprises. The general raising of social standards (hygiene, sanitation, working conditions, and safety) has made it more and more difficult for the small man to compete. One small factory owner complained that when trade is booming he cannot find the raw materials at a price that pays him to manufacture, and when trade is bad he cannot find a customer for his product. Sole traders are therefore of less importance today than formerly, but in one respect they are still of considerable value. Despite the high proportion of new ideas and new products which are discovered by the research departments of large-scale organizations, a significant contribution is still made by the small-scale entrepreneur. Inspired individuals still come up with completely new ideas. One has only to think of Frank Whittle's jet engine, Christopher Cockerell's hovercraft, the Williamson Diamond Mines, or Butlin's Holiday Camps to realize that the age of the individual entrepreneur is not yet past entirely. Economists call such enterprises **nodal points** in the economy. A 'nodal point' is a biological term meaning a 'growth' point. Some of the most significant growth points in recent years have developed in small enterprises.

(4) Partnerships

In seeking to achieve larger scale, a sole trader may consider entering into partnership.

Why take a Partner?

There are several reasons why sole traders combine together to form partnerships. The chief advantages are:

(a) Increased capital, permitting the business to expand more rapidly than is possible by the 'ploughing back' of profits earned.

(b) The responsibility of control no longer rests with one person. This makes possible holidays and free week-ends, and reduces the worry the sole trader experiences in times of ill health.

(c) Wider experience is brought to the firm, and some degree of specialization is possible; this is particularly true of professional partnerships. A physician and a surgeon may form a partnership; or lawyers with experience in different fields—divorce, criminal law, commercial law—may combine to offer a more comprehensive service to the public.

(d) Very often a young man teams up with an older man. The young man has his health and strength; his partner has the capital and the experience. Together they make a satisfactory team.

(e) The affairs of the business are still private.

Disadvantages of a Partnership

(a) The partners still have unlimited liability for the debts of the business.

(b) Each partner must consult the other and consider his views every time a decision has to be made.

(c) The partnership is adversely affected by the death of a partner, whose share may be withdrawn to pay the beneficiaries. It is therefore desirable for each partner to take out life assurance to provide a lump-sum benefit in the event of the other partner's death.

The partnership is particularly suitable for professional people, such as doctors, lawyers, and accountants. It is also suitable for small-scale enterprises of all sorts, in retail trade, manufacturing, agriculture and horticulture, road haulage, and local wholesaling.

(5) Limited Partnerships

The law affecting partnerships was modified in 1907 by the Limited Partnership Act. This Act permits a partnership to be formed between an active partner or partners and one or more 'sleeping' partners who are accorded the privilege of **limited liability.**

The Privilege of Limited Liability

Where a person has funds available for the promotion of business activity, but does not wish himself to take any part in the conduct of the business or the management of the firm, it seems unfair to require him to carry the burden of unlimited liability which attaches to sole traders or partners. The principle of limited liability holds that such a person should be liable to the extent of the capital he has contributed, but no further than this. The limitation of liability in this way unlocks savings which would otherwise merely be hoarded by their owners, and releases them to play a productive part in the industrial and commercial fields.

In the early days of the Industrial Revolution people who contributed capital to industrial firms were held to be full partners, and many lost their homes when speculative projects collapsed and the partners were required to contribute to pay the debts of the firms concerned. Only in 1855, when the increasing demands for capital met resistance from savers who had already seen others suffer hardship through no fault of their own, did Parliament sanction limited liability for shareholders.

The 1907 Act sanctioned limited liability for partners with capital to contribute, provided that there was at least one partner, the **general partner,** who did assume unlimited liability for the affairs of the business, and provided that the limited partner took no part in the management of the firm. The reader should notice that the division between 'ownership' and the entrepreneurial functions of management control begins to appear at this point.

Some of the risks of the enterprise are now being borne by partners who are statutorily forbidden to take any part in the conduct of its affairs.

(6) The Private Limited Company and the Public Limited Company

These two types of business unit are very closely connected, and both are controlled by the Companies Acts of 1948–1976. Since 1967 they have been brought even closer together by the removal of the exemption clauses which had previously made the exempt private company so attractive a form of business organization. Before considering these points let us look at the formation of such a company.

Floating a Company

The promoter of a company must find either one more (in the case of a private company) or six more (in the case of a public company) persons prepared to join with him as **members** in signing a **Memorandum of Association.** This document governs the relationship of the company with the external world. Its seven main clauses are as follows:

(*a*) The name of the company, with 'Limited' as the last word. This word tells anyone who does business with the company that the shareholders have limited liability. It is a warning to them not to deal with the company unless they are quite sure they can afford the risk. Many people think a company is more reliable to deal with than a sole trader or partnership, but this is not necessarily so.

(*b*) The address of its registered office.

(*c*) The objects of the company. This states what the company will do when it is established, and forms the legal basis for its activities. It will have to keep its activities within the fields specified, or the courts may rule them *ultra vires* (outside the powers). This is a protection to the shareholders. Suppose I invested £500 in a company that was to develop a revolutionary type of aero engine, which I believed had a great future. I suddenly discover that the directors are using my money to buy sugar which happens to be rising on world markets. I would naturally feel that this was not the purpose for which I had subscribed my capital, and would be able to obtain an injunction restraining the directors from using my money in an *ultra vires* way.

(*d*) A statement that the liability of the members is limited.

(*e*) The amount of share capital to be issued, and the types of share.

(*f*) An undertaking by the signatories that they desire to be formed into a company registered under the Acts, and to undertake to purchase the number of shares against their names.

(*g*) By the 1976 Act a seventh rule requires that the names, addresses, etc., of the first director (or directors) and the first company secretary shall be stated in a prescribed form. This statement must be signed by the other members and contain the consents of the director(s) and secretary.

Having drawn up and signed the Memorandum of Association, the directors usually then draw up detailed **Articles of Association,** which control the internal affairs of the company. Such matters as the procedure to be followed at meetings, the duties of the managing director, the borrowing powers that may be exercised, and so on are considered and agreed. A set of model articles, called Table A, is printed in the Acts. These articles will be effective and binding on all companies issuing shares, unless the company's own articles specifically invalidate them on some point.

Registration of the Company

The promoters of the company may now proceed to register the company under the Acts. They present to the **Registrar of Companies** the Memorandum of Association; the Articles of Association; a statement of the nominal capital, on which a tax of 0·50 per cent is payable; a list of directors and their written consents and promises to take up shares; and a statutory declaration that the Company Acts have been complied with.

If all is in order, the Registrar will issue a **Certificate of Incorporation,** which bestows upon the company a separate legal personality. The company may now do all the legal things that an ordinary person can do: for example, it may own land and property, employ people, sue and be sued in the courts, etc. Before it may begin trading, however, it must secure the capital it needs. With a private company this will largely be contributed by the founders, anyway. With a public company it must be obtained from the public, either directly or indirectly through the institutional investors.

Classes of Shares

People with savings to spare have to be tempted to invest in an enterprise; hence the wide variety of shares and bonds offered to them. Some people want a high return on their capital, and to obtain it are prepared to run some risk. Others want security for their savings, even though the rate of interest is lower. Security is particularly difficult to ensure in inflationary times. For instance, savings in Government Securities are absolutely secure; if you leave them in for fifty years you will receive £1 back for every £1 invested, but if that £1 will only buy goods worth 20 new pence, because of **inflation** over the years, you have really lost money on the investment. We say that the **nominal value** (nominal means 'in name only') has remained the same, but the **real value** (in terms of what it will purchase) has declined.

A full explanation of the types of share is given in *Commerce Made Simple*, but for readers unfamiliar with the main points a comparative Table is shown on page 36.

A further comparative Table on pages 38–9 deals with the main aspects of private-enterprise units.

Certificate of Trading

Before a limited company can begin to trade it must secure a **Certificate of Trading.** This is issued by the Registrar of Companies when registration is finally completed by lodging with him the following documents:

(a) A statement that the minimum capital has been subscribed.

(b) A statement that the directors have paid for their shares.

(c) A statutory declaration that the Companies Acts have been complied with.

The minimum capital is that amount of capital stated in the prospectus as being the minimum which, in the directors' opinion, is necessary for the success of the enterprise. If this minimum is not reached all the capital collected must be returned to the shareholders. Directors can ensure a successful commencement of trading if they have the issue underwritten by financiers prepared to buy the shares should the public not do so.

How a Company is Formed and Financed

Fig. 2 shows how most public companies are formed. Starting in a small way, often as a family business and operating as a private company, they expand to the point where they can fulfil the strict requirements of the Stock Exchange Council.

When permission to deal in a company's shares is accorded by the Stock Exchange Council the public will be invited to subscribe for shares. The new capital thus made available enables the firm to expand its activities and achieve the advantages of large-scale production.

Invitations to the public to subscribe for shares are made in a **prospectus,** which is a full and frank account of the history of the company to date, its profit record, and every detail likely to be of interest to an investor trying to assess his risks in making an application for shares.

This prospectus must be registered with the Registrar of Companies before the public are invited to subscribe.

Table 4. Comparison of different types of share

Type of Investment	Reward earned	Degree of risk	Who buys them	Who issues them
Ordinary Shares	Equal share of profits, hence nickname 'Equity Shares'	Carry the main risk	(a) Well-to-do investors who want big returns. (b) Institutional investors, for a balanced portfolio. (c) People interested in capital gains, rather than revenue profits	Private and Public Companies
Deferred Ordinary Shares. (Founder's Shares)	Share of profits after Ordinary shares have had some (say 10%) profit	Same as Ordinary Shares	They are taken by the vendor of a business when he sells it to a company, as an earnest of goodwill	Public Companies chiefly, but also Private Companies
Preference Shares	Definite rate of Dividend (say 7%), but only if profits are made	Less than Ordinary Shares as they *usually* have a prior right to repayment	Investors seeking security rather than large dividends	Public and Private Companies
Cumulative Preference Shares	As above, but if profits are not earned in one year the dividend accumulates and is not lost	As above	As above	As above
Participating Preference Shares	After taking the fixed rate (say 7%) these shares earn extra dividend if the Ordinary shares get more than 7%	As above	As above	As above
Debentures (Loans to companies: Debentures are not really shares)	Fixed Rate of interest (say 6%), payable whether profits are made or not	Very small	Timid people wanting a secure investment	Public and Private Companies, if permitted by their Articles

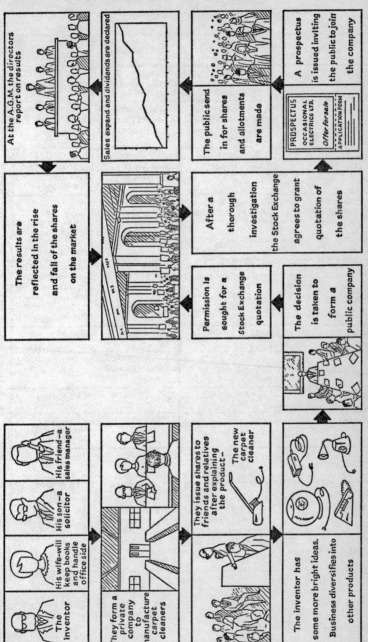

Fig. 2. The formation of a company

Table 5. Comparison of private-enterprise units

	Aspect	Sole Trader	Partnership	Limited Partnership
1	Name of firm	Any name provided it is either the proprietor's true name or their names, or has been registered under the Registration of Business Names Act, 1916		
2	How formed	By commencing business without formality except (1) above	By agreement, which may be oral or written; limited partnerships must be registered	
3	Control of the firm	Proprietor has full control	Every partner is entitled to manage	Only the general partner(s) can manage the business
4	Liability for debts	Liable to the limits of personal wealth	Jointly and severally liable for debts to limits of personal wealth	General partners fully liable; limited partners not liable beyond the capital contributed
5	Relationship between owner and business	The business is the owner, or owners, and has no seperate legal existence		The business is the same as the general partners; the limited partner is not the business
6	Membership of firm	One	Two or more	Two or more
7	General powers	At will	At will, subject to agreement; if no agreement, Partnership Act 1890 applies	
8	Transfer of ownership	By sale of 'goodwill'	Only with unanimous consent	
9	Controlling Acts	None	Partnership Act, 1890	Limited Partnership Act, 1907
10	Disbanding of firm	At will or by bankruptcy	Firm may go bankrupt or be dissolved by notice or mutual consent	
11	Advantages	Independence. Personal control of staff and granting of credit. Decisions acted upon at once	Increased capital. Days off and holidays possible. Wider experience of partners. Privacy of affairs	Limited liability for some partners. Larger capital
12	Disadvantages	Long hours no holidays. Illness affects conduct of business. Unlimited liability. Small capital.	Unlimited liability. Death or retirement ends firm. Profits must be shared	Unlimited liability for the general partners. Also as for partnerships

	Limited Companies	
	Private	Public
1	The registered name, registered under the Companies Acts, 1948 – 1976 ending in the word 'Limited', as a warning to future creditors	
2	By registration under the Companies Acts, with due legal formality	
3	Directors control the company. Members have no control at all, but may elect a new board at the Annual General Meeting if they wish to do so	
4	Limited liability for all members – only liable to the limit of capital contributed	
5	The business is a separate legal personality from the members	
6	Minimum two, maximum fifty (excluding employees)	Minimum seven, no maximum limit
7	As laid down in Memorandum of Association and Articles of Association	
8	Shares may only be transferred with consent of fellow shareholders	Shares are freely transferable
9	Companies Acts, 1948 – 1976	
10	Company may go into voluntary or compulsory liquidation	
11	Limited liability Death of shareholders does not affect the firm. Capital can be found from fifty members. Privacy to some extent on affairs	Limited liability Death of shareholders does not affect the firm. Very large capital can be collected.
12	Publication now required, but since February 1972 turnover need not be revealed unless it exceeds £250,000. Only fifty members.	Full public knowledge of affairs

(7) Non-Profitmaking Units

A certain number of business units are non-profitmaking clubs and societies. They are formed to confer on their members certain benefits in the way of club facilities, discount trading, or value for money. Such clubs and societies often make profits on the year's trading, but these are not profits in the normal commercial meaning of the word. They really represent over-payments by the members for the services they have received, and are usually called 'surpluses'. Examples of such business units are the Working Men's Clubs of the north of England and the Co-operative Societies.

Co-operative Retail Societies

The first successful 'Co-op' store was founded in 1844 in Toad Lane, Rochdale, by twenty-eight weavers nowadays remembered as the 'Rochdale Pioneers'. The idea was to buy foodstuffs at wholesale prices and sell them (to members only) at market price. Profits were divided among members in proportion to the value of their purchases. The share-out (dividend) took place twice a year. By 1845 there were seventy-four members, the turnover was £710, the profit £22.

The Co-operative movement spread rapidly. Societies were set up in towns all over the United Kingdom. In 1862 the members voted to set up a wholesale organization, the Co-operative Wholesale Society. This society not only supplied the retail societies like any ordinary wholesaler but also ran factories, farms, transport services, and even tea gardens to provide everything the retail societies needed. The retail societies joined the wholesale society in exactly the same way as the ordinary members joined the retail society. All the profits of the Co-operative Wholesale Society are shared among the member retail societies, and all the profits of the retail societies are shared among the members. Thus in the end all the profits return to the members of the retail societies, whose purchasing power actually keeps the Co-operative movement going. In 1975 there were about 11 million members in 253 retail societies Sales totalled £2,132 million, three quarters of which was groceries.

Fig. 3. The Rochdale Pioneers' historic store as it was in 1844

Agricultural Co-operatives

These are very common in many countries and enable the small-scale farmer to achieve some of the economies of large-scale organization. They may be **marketing co-operatives,** which grade, pack, and distribute farmers' produce; or **purchasing co-operatives,** which buy seed, fertilizer, and equipment at discount prices, supplying or hiring these items to farmers.

(8) The Public-enterprise Sector of the Economy

In Britain about half of the economy and about two thirds of the commerce is conducted by the private enterprise firms already described. The remainder of the activities of the economy are conducted by socially owned enterprises. Some, like the Army, Navy, and Air Force, are clearly the sort of institutions that the State itself should control. Others have tended to be performed by the State because they are non-profitmaking, and as such are unlikely to be attractive to businessmen. Such activities as education, medical care, and sanitation are best operated as socially provided amenities for the benefit of all citizens.

In the industrial and commercial fields certain goods and services are by their nature monopolies. Among these **natural monopolies** are gas, electricity, and water supply. The capital costs of such enterprises are too great for competition to be possible. We do not install three sets of gas pipes into our houses in order to be able to enjoy Jones's, Smith's, or Robinson's gas according to which is the 'best buy' this morning.

Transport is another natural monopoly. It would be uneconomic to run two railway lines from London to Reading, or two different sets of half-empty buses along a country road. These natural monopolies have, for economic, political, or social reasons, come to be run in the United Kingdom by the State or by municipal authorities, who provide the services required at reasonable prices.

The Case for Public Enterprises

(*a*) They provide socially necessary facilities like education and sanitation which, being unprofitable, are unlikely to be provided by private enterprise.

(*b*) They are the best way to provide services which are a natural monopoly, like railways, electricity, and gas supply.

(*c*) Capital can be provided by taxation and rate assessment, as well as by borrowing, with Government guarantees about interest and repayments. This is useful where profits are unlikely for some time, as with airlines.

(*d*) The provision of services without a principal emphasis on profitmaking renders the goods or service cheaper than otherwise they would be. This amounts to a social subsidy enjoyed by domestic and business consumers.

(*e*) The large-scale operations performed enable great use to be made of the economies of scale. Local undertakings cannot do this. The best example is electricity supply.

(*f*) Sometimes competition is wasteful, and leads to reduced safety standards and 'cut-throat' price cutting. Despite legislation and licensing, this was a feature of the road-haulage industry, where unscrupulous hauliers operated vehicles with insufficient maintenance and ignored rules about drivers' hours.

(*g*) Where Government policy requires clear lines of control in financial affairs, the existence of a National Bank is desirable.

(*h*) Where labour relations are utterly embittered, as in coal-mining in Britain, nothing but a complete clean sweep will revitalize the industry.

Disadvantages of Public Enterprises

(*a*) There is a conflict between economy of operation and adequacy of service which it is difficult to reconcile. For example, the public will demand as perfect a service as possible, but will complain loudly if they have to pay too much for it. Some people claim that the recent modernization of British Railways to provide an efficient service, especially on particular routes, was money misspent because it occurred at a time when traffic of all sorts was deserting the railways for the roads. Comparable expenditure on roads would have promoted the efficiency of the economy far more.

(*b*) Dis-economies of scale occur, particularly if the enterprise is very large or closely controlled by local or central government. This involves an excessive degree of caution on the part of managers fearful of being blamed for innovations they otherwise would introduce. This disadvantage may be simply the result of choosing the wrong sort of business structure for the industry.

(*c*) Politicians and councillors may know little of business, and may influence the enterprises along unbusinesslike paths.

(*d*) Waste is sometimes not discouraged, since losses are borne by the ratepayers or taxpayers.

(*e*) If political repercussions are likely, or if the enterprise is subject to political or parochial pressures, it may not develop in the best way for the industry.

(*f*) State-operated services often have the opportunity to discriminate against privately owned firms in the same line of business. For instance between 1946 and 1960 B.O.A.C. and B.E.A. were able to prevent competitive civil airlines from operating services that were later proved to be desirable and beneficial to the nation as a whole.

Whatever one feels about the desirability or otherwise of State-run enterprises, some degree of State ownership seems to be inevitable. Over a wide range of activities, nationalized industry appears to operate certainly as well as, and possibly better than, the private-enterprise industry it has replaced.

Municipal Undertakings

Commercial enterprises run by Borough and County Councils include such units as municipal swimming baths, bus services, piers and seaside entertainments, theatres and community centres. The capital costs are usually borne by borrowing against the general security of the rates; the idea is to price the facilities to the public at such a figure as to recover both the operating costs and the interest and capital repayments during the lifetime of the asset.

Nationalized Industries

The major nationalized industries in the United Kingdom are coal, gas, electricity, atomic energy, steel, and rail transport. Many other undertakings, while not actually nationalized, are run as public corporations which carry out most of the activities in their particular fields. For instance, while there are many civil airlines, British Airways handles the vast majority of the business. A nationalized industry in Great Britain is formed by the expropriation of the assets of the major firms in the industry in return for adequate compensation, and the setting up of a Board to run the industry under an Act of Parliament bestowing the necessary authority. The industry is expected to run as a business venture, making enough profit to pay the interest on the Government stock issued to finance the compensation. The adequacy of compensation is very difficult to fix. In some cases it has been less than fair, in others more than generous. Usually appeal on compensation is possible to an independent tribunal. In 1976 the British National Oil Corporation was formed, followed in 1977 by British Shipbuilders and British Aerospace.

Organization and Control of Public Enterprises

No hard-and-fast rules about the organization and control of these enterprises has been laid down, since every enterprise is controlled by its Act of Parliament, which aims at devising the organization most suited to the particular industry. The most general features are as follows:

(*a*) The industry has been set up to operate as a commercial business without day-to-day Parliamentary control of its activities. Any type of Civil Service organization is deemed to be too slow-moving for the conduct of what is essentially an industrial undertaking.

(*b*) Taking one year with another, the business is expected to be economically self-sufficient. The phrase 'taking one year with another' means that rates and charges to the public shall be such as to achieve an overall cover of expenses, but a loss in a particular year is not important if subsequent years will recoup the loss. This has not always been the case, especially where very heavy initial debts were taken on to pay compensation to former owners. In these cases Parliament has simply been forced to free the industry from debt by writing off the losses to the Exchequer. Recently it has been decided that a five-year period is the best for judging these enterprises.

(*c*) Parliamentary control of the industry is achieved by:

(i) The annual publication of accounts, which are scrutinized by the Public Accounts Committee.

(ii) An annual debate. One day of Parliamentary business in each session is given up to a debate on the industry's affairs. In fact, these days are not always used for their true purpose, for by tradition the Opposition has the right to choose some other topic of business if it is felt that there is little cause for criticism of the industry.

(iii) The appointment of a Minister to assume general control of policy; he has no right to query day-to-day administrative matters.

(*d*) Parliament usually sets up a Consumers' Council of interested parties to represent the consumer and raise questions about the services and its charges. There are no shareholders able to vote the Board out of control, though the Minister may remove the senior officials. Security of office promotes a proper career structure within the industry and ensures a regular supply of qualified and experienced personnel for senior posts.

(9) Nationalization in Britain

British Overseas Airways Corporation (B.O.A.C.), set up in 1940, was the first public corporation of the type which came to be known as the 'Nationalized Industries'. After the Second World War the Labour Government was elected on a programme which included large measures of nationalization, and the following industries and services were nationalized:

(*a*) The Bank of England (1946).

(*b*) The coal industry—under the National Coal Board (1947).

(*c*) Civil airways—under British European Airways Corporation (1946).

(*d*) The electricity industry—under the Electricity Council. Below the Council a Central Electricity Generating Board generates electricity, and sells it to twelve Area Boards for distribution and supply, e.g., the Eastern Electricity Board (1948).

(*e*) The gas industry—under the National Gas Council and with twelve Area Boards, e.g. the North Thames Gas Board (1949).

(*f*) Transport—under the British Transport Commission (1947). This proved to be such an enormous undertaking, with 900,000 employees (more than any other employer in the country), that it was eventually partially denationalized and considerably decentralized in later Acts.

(*g*) The iron and steel industry—under the Iron and Steel Corporation (1951). This was later denationalized, but renationalized in 1967 under the British Steel Corporation.

(*h*) The National Health Service, which is rather a different form of organization, was set up in 1948.

(*i*) In 1976 the British National Oil Corporation took control of the nationalized part of the North Sea oil and gas industries.

(*j*) British Aerospace and British Shipbuilders were nationalized in 1977. The impact of these later Acts of Nationalization cannot yet be assessed.

A discussion of the part played by these industries in the economy is to be found on pages 334–64.

(10) Summary of Chapter Four

1. Business units may be small-scale, medium-scale, or large-scale undertakings.

2. Differences between the forms of business organization reflect differences between: (*a*) the capital contributed; (*b*) the ownership of that capital; (*c*) the control of the enterprise, and (*d*) the accountability of the controllers to the owners.

3. Sole-trader enterprises are very numerous, but are vulnerable to competition from low-cost large-scale firms. Some of them represent valuable growth points in the industrial structure of the nation.

4. Partnerships offer advantages to small-scale entrepreneurs, but still suffer from the defects of unlimited liability.

5. Limited partnerships permit investors or retired partners to provide capital for firms without the added risk of unlimited liability, but there must be at least one general partner who is liable to the limit of his personal wealth.

6. Private and public limited companies permit the collection of large sums of capital from shareholders who are protected by having limited liability.

7. Non-profitmaking organizations play some part in business life, particularly the Co-operative Movement in retail trade, and in agriculture.

8. The nationalized undertaking or public corporation has an increasingly important part to play in most countries as some attempt is made to control natural monopolies, or provide goods and services which for some reason cannot be provided by private enterprise.

(11) Suggested Further Reading

Allen, G. C.: *The Structure of Industry in Britain.* Longmans: London, 1970.
George, K. D.: *Industrial Organisation: Competition, Growth and Structural Change in Britain.* Allen & Unwin: London, 1971.
Turner, G.: *Business in Britain.* Eyre & Spottiswoode: London, 1969.

Exercises Set 4

1. Alan Grant is a sole trader operating a roadside garage. His main areas of trade are: (*a*) petrol and oil sales; (*b*) spare parts and accessories; (*c*) routine servicing and testing of vehicles; (*d*) major repairs to damaged vehicles. Suggest the ways in which he could change the form of his business so as to provide: (i) more capital; (ii) less worry; (iii) more leisure.

2. Discuss the possible reasons why most countries have a nationalized railway system but road haulage is often run by private enterprise.

3. There are 15,000 public limited companies in Great Britain but 450,000 private limited companies. What are the reasons for this great disparity?

4. Discuss why there is such a wide variety of shares and debentures available. Which types are likely to prove attractive to: (*a*) a widow, aged 55, wishing to invest a £10,000 Life Insurance payment received on the death of her husband; (*b*) a millionaire, looking for a big yield; (*c*) a trade union investing sickness contributions from members?

5. Discuss the advantages to independent bus operators of a co-operative organization. Consider particularly the fields of activity where it would be most beneficial.

6. Consider (*a*) the advantages and (*b*) the disadvantages of limited liability. Your viewpoints should include those of: (*a*) entrepreneurs; (*b*) investors; (*c*) creditors; and (*d*) society as a whole.

7. What are the main forms of business units in private enterprise? Which form would most likely be found operating a chain of grocery shops? Give your reasons.

8. Describe the powers and responsibilities of a public corporation. How does Parliament control such corporations?

9. Explain the difference between debentures and shares. In your answer bring out the attractions of these two types of investment to those who buy them.

10. In Great Britain nationalization has occurred in different industries in different ways. For instance, the railways were nationalized after many years of private operation. The airlines were nationalized after only a few years of private operation. The Atomic Energy Authority was set up as a nationalized body immediately atomic power became a practical proposition. Suggest reasons for the very different treatment accorded these industries.

11. What are the chief differences between a private limited company and a public limited company?

12. 'Penniless inventors search in vain for someone to finance development of their inventions, while prosperous companies are deluged with funds whenever they invite the public to subscribe.' Explain why this is so.

13. What are the disadvantages of a one-man business? Why do so many continue to exist?

CHAPTER FIVE

THE SCALE OF PRODUCTION

(1) The Plant, the Firm, and the Industry

One of the obvious features of the modern production scene is the existence of large-scale firms. The word 'scale' means size. There are usually advantages to be gained by increasing the size of the business; such advantages are called **economies of scale**. In discussing scale in this context we must distinguish between production units or plants, firms and industries.

Plants are production units devoted to the creation of a particular utility, or group of utilities. Such a unit will have a distinct geographical site and a distinct output, or range of outputs, in the form of goods or services.

Firms are business units exerting ownership over one or more plants. They may be sole traders, partnerships, limited partnerships, private limited companies, public limited companies, or public corporations. The production units they own may be in one particular industry, or they may have diversified so that they are engaged in a number of different industries.

An **industry** consists of a group of firms producing similar goods or services for a particular market. They will generally be in competition with one another, but occasionally are found to be co-operating. The complex pattern of industry today defies precise definition. Official definitions embrace groups of industrial and commercial firms which appear to have a mutual bond of interest. These bonds justify the name 'industry'. The major branches of industry in Britain, for example, are set out in the census of production Table given on page 16.

(2) Size of Production Units

Each production unit, or plant, will have an ideal size which is decided either by the technical processes of production or by the market. Technical factors make their impact on the supply side, since they usually involve some increase or reduction in costs which affects the profitability of the plant. Market factors are effective on the demand side, dictating the size of the plant by restricting its growth to the point where the supply satisfies the demand for the goods or service concerned. Among the technical factors are:

(*a*) *The Nature of the Processes Involved in Production.* The technology to be used in the plant often decides the scale of the production unit. For example, chemical processes often require large indivisible units of capital which are economic only if operated at certain levels of output. In other industries the capital unit is quite small, and the size of a production unit can therefore also be small. Examples of these two contrasting scales of production are the modern oil refinery, which consists of a complex of interdependent capital units of great size, and the clothing factory, whose capital units consist of relatively small items like sewing machines and pressers.

(*b*) *Increased Scope for the Division of Labour.* The more specialized the production system, the greater the scale of the enterprise and the number of machines or men required.

In the motor-vehicle industry, besides large-scale units which stamp out whole parts of vehicles in a single process, the multifarious activities of many individuals are joined into a continuous process by the 'belt' system of production. Such activities become possible only if the scale of production is large, since they depend upon the fullest use of the division of labour.

(c) *The 'Lowest Common Multiple' Principle.* Where there are components entering into a product, the major components often dictate the scale of production. If component *A* is made on a machine which can produce 10 units per hour, while the other major component *B* is produced at a rate of 6 units per hour, the lowest common multiple is 30 units per hour. If the management provides three machines for component *A* and five machines for component *B*, then all machines will be kept busy at an output of 30 units per hour. Where there are many components, it is not possible to arrange that every machine is kept busy all the time; the components which are produced very quickly will have to be stored until required. Nevertheless, the entrepreneur will try to achieve the best possible rate of utilization for all machines bought.

Market Factors

Where the market is limited, the size of the production unit will be small. The specialist firm, using small-scale methods of production, can supply the demand for many items which are not in popular use. Where goods are in wide demand or are essentials for everyday life, large-scale methods of production will have been devised to satisfy the market. The situation is not static in this respect, and items of specialist interest today may be in widespread demand tomorrow.

(3) Economies of Scale

The economies of scale may be divided into **internal economies** and **external economies**. Internal economies arise within the firm itself. External economies arise in the locality around, where ancillary firms and services contribute to the efficient conduct of its operations.

(a) Internal Economies of Scale.

The chief internal economies of scale come under six headings: technical, administrative, financial, marketing, research, and welfare economies.

Technical Economies arise from the increased use of specialization and from mechanization, automation, and computerization. Of particular interest is the more economic combination of factors that large-scale operation makes possible. A 32-ton truck with a driver and mate is a more economic combination of labour and capital than a 5-ton truck and driver. A hedging machine will serve a 500-acre farm as easily as a 50-acre farm. Capital tied up in stocks of both raw materials and finished goods need not be increased in proportion as firms grow. This is particularly true of slow-moving items in warehousing, where a minimum stock will serve a large firm supplying many retailers quite as easily as a small firm.

Administrative Economies. There are many administrative economies to be achieved in large-scale firms. Doubled output in the factory does not necessitate two factory managers. It need not mean twice the paper-work; invoices may simply deal with larger quantities. When firms grow larger the specialist skills of particular managers are used to greater effect, and more sophisticated decision-making techniques may be introduced. Probably the administrative field is one of the last areas left where major economies of scale can now be achieved, since firms have brought manufacture and distribution to a fine art.

Financial Economies. Many large-scale firms find it easy to borrow money at favourable rates of interest. They can usually offer collateral security, such as title deeds to property and mortgages on fixed assets or stocks. They can often afford fire appliances and security guards, so that they obtain favourable insurance rates, or they may even act as their own insurers, setting aside funds for contingencies. Their 'public company' status attracts investors, who willingly subscribe capital, often paying a premium on shares or debentures for the privilege of becoming members or creditors.

Marketing Economies. In recent years competition between firms has led to very efficient use of manufacturing and financial resources. Competition has not been pressed so heavily in the marketing field. Considerable economies are now being achieved in distribution by the optimum siting of depots and warehouses, the elimination of small orders, the cash-and-carry principle, careful calculation of re-order points, etc. Where large-scale firms operate marketing agencies handling an assortment of products, they achieve economies because marketing costs are increased less than proportionately for each new product carried.

Research Economies. The competitive position of many firms depends on their ability to keep ahead of rivals in the range and quality of their products. Research not only reveals new products, new methods of work, and new markets: it results in more efficient use of present resources, waste products, etc. Large-scale firms can usually afford research departments, since the cost can be spread more thinly over the larger volume of production.

Welfare Economies. Welfare concerns the health, living conditions, and recreation of staff. Large firms which can offer attractive conditions, recreational facilities, and pension schemes attract good-quality labour and foster a spirit of loyalty which keeps the organization in good heart.

(b) External Economies of Scale

Surrounding any firm is a locality which soon reacts to the firm's arrival in the area. Sometimes the siting of the firm will depend on favourable arrangements made with local authorities to provide suitable facilities, housing, water supplies, sanitation and health facilities, training courses at local colleges, etc. Entrepreneurs in related fields or in service industries likely to be needed will make approaches offering goods and services. Labour will seek employment, and may undertake special training when it hears of vacancies. The six types of economies already discussed may equally be achieved externally.

External Technical Economies are particularly important. They involve the sub-contracting to local firms of ancillary activities or particular aspects of the firm's work. This may result in a more perfect division of labour. Technical components in the motor-vehicle industry are often produced by this type of sub-contractor

An entrepreneur, about to set up in a particular industry, would be ill advised to site his factory in an area remote from similar firms. To do so would be to reject deliberately any opportunity of achieving external technical economies. This is one reason why Government policies aimed at directing industries to areas where unemployment is high often meet opposition from entrepreneurs fearful of being out of touch with the rest of the industry.

External Administrative, Financial, and Marketing Economies. The growth of local tertiary services is of enormous importance to large-scale firms. Specialist mailing agencies, advertising agencies, and employment bureaux; local banking, security, and insurance services; haulage, warehousing, shipping and forwarding firms; Chambers of Trade and even organized markets spring into existence.

Welfare, Training, and Research Economies. The locality is where the firm's employees will live. The provision of housing, educational, and recreational services makes for a contented, trained, and stable labour force. Financial contributions to local facilities are less expensive than the private provision of these for employees' use only, and co-operation with other firms can promote research facilities at lower cost.

(4) Diseconomies of Scale

While there are many economies of scale, large size is also a disadvantage in some respects. As the output increases, the tertiary problems of distribution and marketing increase. Advertising expenses may rise, discounts may need to be larger if customers are to be found, and export trade involves extra costs. Relations between management and employees become increasingly impersonal, with a long chain of command which discourages enthusiasm. It becomes increasingly difficult to achieve a consensus of opinion, so decision-making is deferred; and when decisions are made they lose effectiveness in the more remote parts of the organization.

Even the external economies of scale can prove disadvantageous if large firms experience setbacks due to changes in world taste or fashion. The associated secondary and tertiary firms in the locality are dependent on the prosperity of their chief customers. A whole locality may quickly become a depressed area. Some structural unemployment (see page 58) is inevitable, anyway, in industries affected by changes of taste or fashion.

(5) The Optimum Firm

Where a firm is operating at a scale which gives it the lowest unit cost possible it is said to be operating at the optimum. It is almost impossible to know when the optimum level has been achieved, and in practice, entrepreneurs work on subjective hunches of where the optimum is. In an increasingly involved technological world few products are the result of one process, but are an assembly of components. The optimum level of production of one component is unlikely to be the same as that for another. Sometimes this difficulty can be overcome by batch production of parts, a single department producing two or three components in rotation, where each batch is sufficient to carry the factory through a period of future output. The question of costs is dealt with more fully in Chapter Eight.

In a particular industry there may be two or three optima. For instance, some relatively low-level division of labour may be open to small-scale firms who, using this technology, can achieve a certain optimum position. By changing to a more highly capitalized form of production they may be able to reach new levels of efficiency. Firms of this type will be found clustering around a second optimum size. There may even be one or two very large firms at a third higher level. The continued existence of the less efficient firms must reflect some separation of the markets which enables them to survive.

Even when the enterprise is operating at or near the optimum, various influences are at work to erode its position. For instance, depreciation of equipment gradually turns a low-cost firm into a high-cost firm. Changes of technology bring the same effect about more rapidly as obsolescence ensues. Changes in the availability and price of factors render present combinations less efficient and change the optimum arrangement in favour of newer firms entering the industry.

(6) Small-scale Business Units

Despite the dominance of very large-scale firms in most industries, a very large number of small-scale firms continue to exist. There are a number of reasons for this, including the **small size of the market.** This has already been referred to on page 47. Where demand is not great, the division of labour to intensify output is pointless. When Henry Ford was about to set up in business he seriously considered watch production. From his early youth he had been fascinated by chains of gear wheels and had repaired clocks and watches for friends and neighbours. Concluding that the demand would be insufficient for a full system of mass production, he turned his attention instead to motor cars. Of course, today mass production of watches does take place, but only because a general increase in the standard of living has raised the demand for watches since that time. In an isolated community we often find a general shop selling everything: groceries, drapery, footwear, ironmongery, etc. The market for each of these groups of commodities is insufficient to support a specialist retail outlet.

Personal Service. Where the enterprise offers personal service, large-scale operation simply cannot be achieved. The hairdresser who employs assistants to perform certain activities like washing hair, preparing customers for styling, etc., is still limited as far as the scale of his business is concerned by the number of customers to whom he can give his personal attention. Too fleeting a visit from the maestro will send customers elsewhere.

'Exclusive' Products. In some businesses, like the fashion trades and interior decorating, exclusive creations which are the work of particular artists or designers are the basis of the enterprise. Standardization or mass production is quite impossible in such businesses.

Psychological Factors. Independence of the proprietor is an important reason why some businesses remain small. Where growth can be achieved only by the sacrifice of independence, taking partners, or borrowing from banks or finance houses, the owner may well feel that peace of mind is worth more than extra profits. Sometimes the same results can be achieved by co-operation with other independent operators, pooling resources, and sharing marketing facilities.

(7) The Advantages and Disadvantages of Small-scale Production

The advantages may be listed as follows:

(*a*) *Effectiveness of Decisions.* Having all matters under his personal supervision, the entrepreneur can put decisions into effect at once. Time-consuming procedures such as are used in large-scale enterprises, where authority has to be obtained before effective action can be taken, are eliminated. Personal supervision ensures that the work proceeds with maximum speed.

(*b*) *Personal Control Promotes Goodwill and Reduces Risks.* Where the proprietor has the affairs of his business under continual supervision he is able to ensure that the service he gives is of a high standard. Frequently, by living on the premises, he is conveniently placed to control situations such as the late arrival of supplies after normal business hours, or special requests by valued customers. Because the proprietor personally sanctions credit, bad debts are reduced.

(*c*) *Employer–Employee Relations.* The proprietor's relations with his employees are personal, so the employees are encouraged to be efficient and are not tempted to take advantage of an absentee owner. His understanding of their personal problems encourages staff loyalty, mutual consideration, and respect.

The disadvantages are:

(*a*) *The division of labour will be small.* Resources will therefore be uneconomically used. The most efficient factor combinations, particularly of labour and capital, can be achieved only in large enterprises. It follows that only certain types of business or businesses catering for small localities will not face competition from more efficient units.

(*b*) *The personal abilities of the entrepreneur decide the scale of the business.* These abilities may be affected by ill health or absences caused by domestic problems.

(*c*) *The proprietor will be personally responsible for the debts of the business* to the full extent of his personal assets, unless, of course, he chooses to convert the enterprise into a private limited company.

(8) Combination of Business Units

Under this heading we are concerned with the present trend of large units absorbing small businesses. In the past, all businesses began in a small way because of the necessity to accumulate capital. Nowadays, in a wealthy nation, firms can actually start off as large-scale enterprises, provided that enough interested people (shareholders) can be found to furnish the capital. Many of these shareholders are insurance companies, banks, and investment companies. Such firms are called **institutional investors.** They collect savings from the general public, investing them wisely for the mutual benefit of all parties.

Today there is a growing tendency to increase the size of businesses in nearly all trades, manufacturing, building, wholesale, and retail. Because the advantages of large-scale projects are so great, there is a tendency for small businesses to grow into bigger businesses, and for them to be **absorbed** by the bigger firms. There is also a tendency for firms to **amalgamate** to form a bigger firm, and there is a tendency for similar firms to co-operate with one another for good reasons (greater economies) or bad reasons (price fixing). Such associations are called 'cartels' (a German word), or 'trusts' (an American word). On the whole, the domination of an entire industry by one firm is probably undesirable, because it leads to monopoly profits. In many countries such huge firms are banned altogether, but in Britain they are controlled fairly effectively by legal methods. The difficulty is to prevent the huge firm abusing its power while at the same time encouraging efficiency by allowing firms to reach the optimum size.

If we try to increase size we may do so either horizontally or vertically.

Vertical Integration tries to control all the stages of a particular product. Examples are found in many industries. In the shoe industry some firms make the shoes, distribute them, and sell them in their own retail shops. Some tea firms own tea estates, process tea in their own factories, import it, blend it, package it, and deliver it to the shopkeeper. Some oil companies own oil-fields, tankers, refineries, delivery vehicles, and garages where the refined products are sold. Further good examples of vertical integration are to be found in the brewing and motor-vehicle industries. Frequently a major brewery will jealously guard its water supply against pollution; it will buy its barley and hops, if not from its own farms, at least from accredited suppliers; it will manufacture, wholesale, and transport its branded products, and retail them in 'tied' houses. In the automobile industry there are many specialist manufacturers producing components, but the major elements of the assembly process—the body-building, upholstering, power-unit assembly, and vehicle assembly plants—are controlled by the parent company, which also licenses sole agencies in the retail trade.

Horizontal Integration is where firms try to control all aspects at one level. For example, wholesalers try to gain control of wider and wider areas; multiple shops take over small businesses all over the country; and chain stores set up branches in every town.

Limited companies may achieve either horizontal or vertical integration by 'holding' other companies.

Lateral Integration is the amalgamation of firms using similar techniques to produce similar products. A maker of pressure gauges may absorb a thermometer manufacturer and make both products in future.

Holding Companies

Where a company has acquired control of another company by the purchase of 51 per cent of its voting shares, it is said to be a **holding company.** This is one way of building up a large-scale business, and it takes advantage of specialization within an industry. For example, where in years gone by a motor-vehicle manufacturer may have found it convenient to allow a specialist firm to supply him with particular components, a growth in the size of his own business may make it desirable to bring the subsidiary firm within his own direct control. By purchasing 51 per cent of the voting shares, control can be secured and the subsidiary company brought within the direct influence of the parent company.

The integration may permit the smaller company to preserve its goodwill while sharing in the large-scale benefits: research, technical, marketing, and welfare economies achieved by the parent firm. The parent firm can gather under its wing subsidiaries in the raw-material, transport, component-supply, marketing, advertising, and research fields; this will ensure that it is never starved of raw materials, components, or markets. Here we have an example of *vertical integration*: integration from top to bottom of an industry. The same process enables a holding company to diversify into other areas outside its major field, and thus avoid disaster if its major industry should experience a recession. This is called **diversification.**

(9) Returns to Scale

We have already seen that the adjustment of factors in combination with one another results in increasing or decreasing returns. The Law of Diminishing Returns refers to the effect on output in the short-run of adjustments of a variable factor when it is in combination with a fixed factor.

'Returns to scale' refers to the returns achieved when an existing combination of factors is increased so as to change the scale of the enterprise. In these circumstances the proportions of all the factors of production can be altered, and the output may increase in the same proportions as the scale, showing that constant returns to scale have been achieved. Alternatively, output may increase more, or less, than proportionately: in these two cases we have increasing returns to scale or decreasing returns to scale. Decreasing returns to scale is a fairly rare occurrence; constant returns to scale occurs more frequently in real life, and increasing returns is the most usual of the three.

(10) Summary of Chapter Five

1. Plants are units for production; firms are business units which own plants; industries are groups of firms with a common interest in the provision of a particular class of goods or services.

2. The size of business units depends on technical factors connected with production or on the market for the product.

3. The economies of scale may be internal or external to the firm. Internal economies include technical, administrative, financial, marketing, research, and welfare economies. External economies accrue to a firm because of its connections with the other firms and institutions in the locality.

4. Diseconomies of scale arise from excessive size and decreased personal interest in the enterprise by management and staff.

5. The optimum firm is that firm which is able to achieve minimum average cost per unit of output.

6. Small-scale production continues to exist for technical, marketing, or psychological reasons.

7. Large-scale production is likely to achieve economies. This leads to amalgamations, or to absorption of small firms by outright purchase or as subsidiaries of a holding company. Integration may be vertical or horizontal.

8. When an increase in the size of a production unit results in a more than proportional increase in output we have increasing returns to scale.

(11) Suggested Further Reading

Lipsey, R. G., and Stilwell, J. A.: *An Introduction to Positive Economics.* Weidenfeld & Nicolson: London, 3rd. Ed., 1971.

Stacey, N. A. H.: *Mergers in Modern Business*. Hutchinson: London, 2nd. Ed., 1970.

Townsend, H.: *Scale, Innovation, Mergers and Monopoly*. Pergamon: Oxford, 1968.

Exercises Set 5

1. What is meant by 'the economies of scale'? Illustrate your answer by reference to a local industry with which you are familiar.

2. What financial economies are likely to be achieved by a large-scale firm which a small firm would be unable to enjoy?

3. Discuss the most suitable size of business unit for the following enterprises, giving reasons for your choice in each case: (*a*) cement manufacture; (*b*) coastal fishing; (*c*) a bakery; (*d*) electricity generation; (*e*) aircraft manufacture; (*f*) legal advice on bankruptcy procedures; (*g*) hosiery manufacture.

4. Discuss, from the point of view of a customer who requires an electric point to be installed in her home, the advantages and disadvantages in each case of asking (*a*) a local electrician, (*b*) a nationalized electricity board, to do the job.

5. Discuss the technical economies likely to be achieved in: (*a*) large-scale agriculture (refer to wheat or other staple crop grown locally); (*b*) light engineering (refer to the manufacture of domestic consumer durables such as electric hair-dryers, shavers, toasters, or radio and television receivers).

6. Considering your own locality, decide what external economies might be enjoyed by a manufacturer moving into the area. What further inducements might a forward-looking local authority offer to an industrialist to encourage him to set up a plant in the area?

7. 'You say I am in business to make money; I know I am in business to make shoes' (a footwear manufacturer). What might be the effect of this attitude on the scale of his enterprise?

8. Discuss the merits and demerits of small-scale business from the point of view of the employee.

9. What is meant by 'the optimum firm'? How can an entrepreneur bring his firm to the optimum position, and what influences are at work to erode the position when it has been achieved?

10. Is it ever likely that the small-scale business will completely disappear? Justify your answer.

11. Is it true to say that the typical firm in advanced economies is large, even though there are a great many small firms? Explain fully.

12. Distinguish between internal and external economies of scale, with particular reference to manufacturing firms.

CHAPTER SIX

THE LOCATION OF PRODUCTION

(1) The Theory of Location

A firm will locate its production units on sites which are convenient and economical. Since the aim of an entrepreneur who is acting rationally is to maximize profits, he will pick that site which enables him to produce at the lowest average unit cost. If there are two such sites the final decision may rest on some other factor, which may be psychological or may maximize non-economic advantages, like staff access to entertainments, housing, or schools.

(2) Causes of Location

Industry tends to be located:

(*a*) Near a source of raw material.

(*b*) Near a source of power.

(*c*) Near a means of transport, e.g. a port, river, railway, road, canal, or airport.

(*d*) Near an educated working class or other source of labour.

(*e*) Near a market.

(*f*) Near a centre of commerce, particularly financial institutions.

(*g*) Near a centre of Government.

(*h*) In a suitable climate.

(*i*) In a stable political atmosphere.

The following examples of each type of location should give a general guide to location, but the reader is asked to consider his own home area and country and decide why the business units near at hand have been sited in their present position.

(*a*) *Closeness to a Source of Raw Material.* Generally speaking, raw materials are heavy and expensive to move. The manufacture of bricks in the clay fields north of London is a typical example of location close to a source of raw material. Another is the world's largest hardboard factory near Sao Paulo in Brazil, which is situated near a forest of 16 million eucalyptus trees. Its consumption of timber is equal to the annual growth rate of the forest, so that the source of supply is never exhausted.

Sheffield, the British steel centre, was founded because it was conveniently placed for an iron industry, with local supplies of the three basic raw materials: coal, iron ore, and limestone.

(*b*) *Closeness to a Source of Power.* An early example of this cause of location is the migration of the English cotton and woollen industries to towns in the Pennine valleys of Lancashire and Yorkshire. Here the damming of the rivers running off the Pennine hills drove water-mills to provide power for the machinery. Later the invention of the stationary steam engine, which was more powerful, caused the cotton industry to move again to areas where coal was in plentiful supply. Manchester, situated on a coalfield, therefore became the chief centre of the cotton industry.

Another excellent example of location of an industry near a source of power is Kitimat in British Columbia. Here there is a lake high in the Rocky Mountains which, because of its geographical situation, could be one of the world's largest hydroelectric-power sources. Unfortunately it is so remote that heat losses in the cables transmitting power to any civilized area would have made it uneconomic. The problem of utilizing this source of electricity was solved by erecting an aluminium smelter and subsidiary industries at Kitimat itself. Aluminium smelting requires vast quantities of electrical power. The lake, which was on the wrong side of the mountains, was reached by tunnelling through, and the power station was built into the rock. The natural outlets from the overflow of the lake were dammed up so that the sole exit for water lies through the power station in its cavern far below.

(*c*) *Closeness to a Method of Transport.* There are innumerable examples of location of an industry at a suitable point for easy transport. Historical examples are the growth of industrial areas along the banks of the British canals as these were dug during the Industrial Revolution, from 1760 to 1820. The growth of the Potteries is a particularly important example. Later the development of towns on railway lines opened up new areas of the country, and in more modern times we have the development of industrial areas around great motorways. The development of port areas is particularly striking. In recent years the M.I.D.A.S. proposals aim at locating huge Maritime Industrial Development Areas at appropriate points on the coastline. Here ocean transport of large size, up to 1,000,000 tons eventually, will deliver bulk cargoes of ores, wheat, crude oil, and other products direct to the steel mills, flour mills, and refineries where they are required. This will enable really economic use to be made of bulk carriers.

Rotterdam, in Holland, is a typical example of this type of development. The visitor to modern Rotterdam finds the whole port area covered with a complex of industrial projects. Already sited in an excellent position for serving the industrial might of Western Germany through its river and canal links with the Rhine, these new terminals for grain, oil, iron ore, sulphur, and many other commodities make Rotterdam the finest example in the world of location near methods of transport.

(*d*) *Closeness to an Educated Working Force.* Labour is one of the factors of production. Entrepreneurs are therefore likely to site their production units near a source of labour. It is often helpful if the available labour is sophisticated and trained, since this will reduce the amount of in-plant training required. When siting his first plant in Great Britain, Henry Ford was influenced by the new housing areas being set up at Dagenham in Essex. This area represented a supply of educated labour of good quality. There was cheap land available in the marshes near by, and a large market was available in the London area. The River Thames gave good access for raw materials and made export of finished vehicles easy. Such a combination of advantages led to the erection of the Dagenham plant of the Ford Motor Company.

Human beings become attached to the areas where they are born and brought up, so that many are reluctant to move. One economist has called labour 'the immobile factor'. It is a paradox that the only factor that can move by itself should display an almost characteristic immobility. Often this

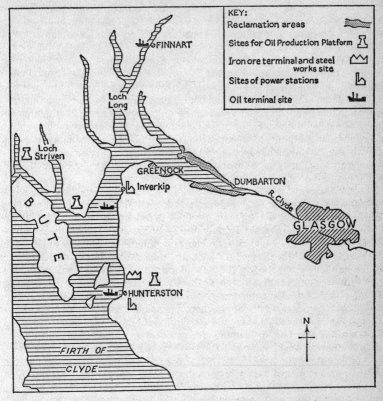

Fig. 4. The Maritime Industrial Development Area at Clydeport

Notes:
1. Requirements for a M.I.D.A. are:
   (*a*) At least 5,000 acres of flat land;
   (*b*) Adjacent water to a depth of 50 feet at high tide.
2. Clydeport offers 6,000 acres and depths of 50–60 feet at L.W.O.S.T. (low water of a spring tide).
3. Channels in the main estuary are 240 feet deep in places and right up to Finnart in L. Long 110 feet is available; Finnart is currently used by tankers of over 300,000 tons and 82 feet draft.
4. Oil terminals have been built at Finnart and Hunterston.
5. A nuclear power station, an ore terminal and a construction site for oil production platforms have been built at Hunterston. A site for steelworks has been earmarked.
6. The container port is situated at Greenock.
7. Freightliner and motorway links to the area are already in existence.
8. The reclamation areas would provide extensive berthing facilities and industrial sites for primary industrial users, and associated secondary industries and tertiary services.
9. A power station at Inverkip is now operational.

immobility presents problems when **structural unemployment** occurs. Structural unemployment is unemployment caused by a permanent change in demand for a product. For example, Lancashire cotton goods have been in much less demand since the development of synthetic fibres like nylon and Terylene, and also since the growth of cotton mills in overseas territories such as Hong Kong. The resultant decline in the Lancashire cotton industry produced a good deal of unemployment in the area. Other areas have been hit by declines in the demand for British ships and coal. These areas have been given special attention by Governments to encourage industries to move to the area in need of redevelopment. Firms find that these development areas offer a pool of good-quality labour, educated in industrial processes and techniques. Such labour is a very valuable asset, and this is one reason why location in a development area may give firms a useful economic advantage over similar firms in more prosperous, and therefore higher-cost, areas.

(*e*) *Closeness to a Market*. Although raw materials are heavy and awkward to transport, they rarely suffer damage when moved. Today the end product often decides location. If the end product is fragile, or highly polished, or liable to be stolen it may be preferable to produce it near to the eventual market, or close to its biggest markets. This reduces the journey to be made by the majority of the finished product, and thus lessens the risk of damage or pilferage. This explains why household furniture is usually manufactured close to large cities rather than near forests. It also explains the attraction of London as a site for consumer-goods industries. Areas like the Ruhr in Germany, the Benelux area of Northern Europe, the Paris area, and the continuous sweep of industry from Liverpool through the Midlands down to London and the Home Counties are excellent examples of the growth of industrial areas near large populations which will consume their products.

Another consideration in the decision to locate near the market is the relative importance of transport costs to the value of the product. If transport costs are high compared with the unit's value—as, for example, with car bodies—such units will be made near the assembly plant. If transport costs are tiny compared with the value of a unit of output—as with transistor radios —transport half across the world will not be too expensive. Japan's excellent transistor radios are an example.

(*f*) *Closeness to the Financial Institutions*. In Britain the changes in taxation policy since the Second World War have had a profound effect on the financing of industry, which has in turn affected location of industry. The redistribution of income associated with the Welfare State has reduced the personal fortunes of the well-to-do, and raised the levels of income of the mass of the people. This has resulted in an increasing influence of the financial institutions like banks, insurance companies, and finance houses. No longer can industry be financed by private individuals. Wealth is shared more evenly, and savings have to be collected in small sums from a mass of people. This makes the institutions which are skilled in collecting such sums (particularly insurance companies, banks, building societies, and trade unions) of great importance to anyone seeking capital. The entrepreneur may therefore prefer to locate his business with reasonable access to such institutions. In Britain this has played some part in the development of the South-east, with the City of London at its centre.

(*g*) *Closeness to the Centre of Government*. Heavy taxation levels increase the proportion of the National Income which is being spent by the Government. If the public sector of the economy grows, firms find it advantageous to site their offices and factories near to the Centre of Government. This again partly explains the heavy concentration of industry in the South-east of England, near Westminster. The best example, however, of this type of location is the growth of industry in and around the Eastern Seaboard areas of the United States of America, under the influence of lucrative contracts from Washington for the Space Programme, the Poverty Programme, and similar Government policies.

(*h*) *In a Suitable Climate.* Sometimes climate has an important part to play. Clearly we cannot grow vines or sugar cane in regions where the sun rarely shines. Humidity is sometimes important: for instance, because threads snap more easily in a dry atmosphere, cotton is manufactured best in damp climates.

(*i*) *In a Stable Political Atmosphere.* Capital is scarce and capital assets are expensive. They may take years to construct and decades to return the capital invested. Stable political life, absence of revolutions, and freedom from fear of expropriation are prerequisites to heavy capital investment. For this reason industry tends to locate itself in spots where volatile behaviour of political groups is at a minimum. The construction of refineries near oilfields used to be a feature of the oil industry, and large processing plants were built in the Middle East, in Indonesia, and elsewhere. Today there is a much greater tendency to build them in more stable areas, and to transport the crude oil in mammoth tankers to the refinery.

(3) Industrial Inertia

Inertia is the tendency of a natural body to go on doing what it is already doing. It is difficult to overcome the inertia of a stationary boulder, and once we get it on the move it is equally difficult to stop it. The same thing is true of industries; they display 'industrial inertia'. This industrial inertia keeps an industry in a particular area long after the original reasons for its location there have ceased to be important. Many external economies of scale would be lost if the industry moved away from an area where specialist subsidiary firms and local government facilities have been created over the years. More important, the technical knowledge and skill of the local work-force is crucial to the success of the industry.

Sheffield, which is still a world centre for steel production many years after the local supplies of iron ore have been exhausted, is a good example of industrial inertia. It has proved cheaper to import iron ore from Sweden and Spain than to disband the complex of experience, know-how, and research which Sheffield offers the British steel industry.

Hollywood is another example of the inertia of an industry. Long after the original reasons (concerning reliable climatic conditions) for location there have ceased to have importance the motion-picture industry persists, despite enormous changes in its techniques and in the requirements of the public. Television, a completely new industry, turns to the old industry in the old place.

A further aspect of inertia is the tendency of huge firms with very large capital assets to persist and develop even when the management is not very dynamic. It becomes difficult for younger and more energetic firms to obtain capital in the face of the great industrial capacity of their well-established rivals.

(4) The Drift to the South-east in Great Britain

During the present century a significant change in the location of industry in Great Britain has occurred under the twin influences of electrification and road transport. This change in location has moved many industries into the Midlands and South-east, and away from the older industrial areas of the North, Scotland, and Wales, which as a consequence have become victims of structural unemployment. The inertia which has kept industries like steel centred in the old industrial areas cannot be effective on new industries like aviation, motor-vehicle manufacture, electronics, and petrochemicals. Such industries have, until very recently, been free to locate themselves in the optimum positions, and the optimum position has often been near London.

Electricity makes power available to industries throughout the length and breadth of the country at the flick of a switch. This has set industry free from the coalfields, and new industries have not needed to look for power to the old sources of coal and steam.

Road transport has permitted door-to-door delivery of raw materials and finished goods. The increasingly sophisticated products of modern factories are easily damaged or pilfered. Closeness to the market becomes, as we have seen, more important than closeness to raw materials.

Besides these factors the changes in the distribution of income have made both closeness to the institutional investors and closeness to the Government of great importance. All these factors have tended to pull industry to the South-east, where the resulting traffic concentrations, housing problems, and inflation of prices have presented serious diseconomies of scale. A fuller account of Government intervention to redistribute industry more evenly is given later (see page 358). Here it is sufficient to note that the location of industry in the Midlands and South-east has produced an almost continuous conurbation from Liverpool to Brighton. Some reversal of this tendency seems inevitable if a large part of the British population is not to be deprived entirely of country air and quiet.

(5) Localization of Production

One defect that is not apparent in South-east England is an excessive 'localization of industry'. This phrase refers to an excessive concentration in one locality of industries which are interconnected, so that a setback in the main industry causes a general depression in the locality. In South-east England industry is very diverse, and it is rare for diverse industries to experience a depression at the same time. If the furniture industry is quiet the clothing industry or the motor-vehicles industry may be booming.

Excessive localization occurs because of the advantages of the external economies of scale. Subsidiary industries grow up around the main industry, and service trades grow up around the housing estates associated with all the firms in the area. If a change in world taste or fashion, or the development of new materials, or increased competition from abroad reduces activity in the main industry subsidiary industries decline too. Unemployment causes a decline in the services required by householders, and the whole area experiences hard times. Like the farmer's wife with all her eggs in one basket, one piece of bad luck can ruin all.

Reference has already been made to the structural unemployment that results. Government solutions to these problems are discussed on page 359.

(6) Summary of Chapter Six

1. Industries are located in places where they can produce at the least possible cost.

2. Important causes of location in earlier times were closeness to a source of raw material and closeness to a coalfield (as a source of steam power). Closeness to a means of transport was also important.

3. Today location is influenced chiefly by closeness to the market; to the institutional investors; to the centre of Government, and to transport. Closeness to Europe may influence location in the future.

4. Industrial inertia often keeps an industry sited in a particular locality long after the original reasons for its location there have ceased to be important.

5. Localization of industry is the excessive concentration of related firms in one area, so that a depression in a major firm spreads to all the other firms around. This causes hardship as structural unemployment sets in.

(7) Suggested Further Reading

Deverell, C. S.: *The Location of Industry*. Editype: London, 1968.
Wright, M.: *Industrial Location and Regional Policy*. Longman, 1970.

Almost all major textbooks of geography include a useful section on this topic.

Exercises Set 6

1. Consider the capital city of your own country. Draw up a list of reasons why: (a) it was originally established where it is; (b) what caused industry and commerce to develop it to its present size; (c) if it is still growing, what factors continue to make it attractive as a location; and (d) if it is declining, why it is no longer attractive as a location.

2. In your own country select two examples of location near each of the following: (a) a source of raw material; (b) a river; (c) the seashore (if available); (d) a railway; (e) a main road; (f) a source of power; (g) a centre of Government.

3. Rotterdam is now the biggest port in Europe. Consult a map of Europe and suggest why.

4. Discuss the geographical position and the location of industry at any two of the following sites: (a) Chicago; (b) Southampton; (c) Lagos; (d) Johannesburg; (e) Sydney; (f) Liverpool; (g) Singapore; (h) Hong Kong; (i) Cape Town; (j) Canberra; (k) Auckland; (l) Hawaii.

5. Discuss whether industrial inertia has played any part in the continued prosperity of: (a) London; (b) Bristol; (c) the capital of your own country; (d) your own local town.

6. The location of industry near power sources is less important today than in former times. Do you agree, or disagree,? Give your reasons and examples to support them.

7. To what extent does closeness to the market affect the location of business establishments?

8. How may location affect the costs of a firm?

9. What is industrial inertia? Give examples.

10. Once oil refineries were located near oilfields. Today they are more frequently located near centres of industrial population. Discuss the reasons for this change in policy.

11. It is better to bring the timber to the factory than to take the factory to the timber. Explain the economic arguments behind this statement.

SECTION THREE: THE THEORY OF PRICE DETERMINATION

CHAPTER SEVEN

BASIC IDEAS OF DEMAND

(1) Definition of Demand

If production is undertaken in order to supply the 'wants' of mankind demand must be the most basic idea in economics. Every individual demands goods and services. When all the individual demands are put together the resulting composite demand is what the industry must supply if people are to achieve satisfaction.

In defining 'demand', however, economists cannot equate 'demand' with 'want', because an industry cannot be expected to supply goods and services without payment. In attempting to discover the demand for a particular commodity we only consider demand that is backed by purchasing power. Man's wants are unlimited, but his demand for a particular item is very often limited if the price he must pay is too high.

The demand for goods or services is therefore that quantity of the goods or services which purchasers will be prepared to buy at a given price, in a given period of time.

Note particularly that price is crucial to any discussion about demand. It is meaningless to discuss the demand for motor vehicles unless we know what price range is being considered. The demand for family cars at £1500·00 each will be very different from the demand for limousines at £10,000·00 each.

(2) The Conditions of Demand

Demand is not fixed, but varies with changing conditions. The demand for silk stockings has been completely altered by the invention of nylon fibre, and the demand for bicycles in advanced nations has been greatly reduced by the development of motor vehicles.

The chief factors affecting demand may be divided into those factors affecting the individual consumer or family of consumers and those factors affecting the total demand of the whole market.

Factors Affecting the Demand of Households

(*a*) *The Tastes of the Household.* Every family is different, and even members of the same family have different tastes and preferences. In most countries populations are not these days homogeneous, but have been formed from mixed racial groups. This is not always obvious if the country has had a long period of settled history, and intermarriage between different racial groups has occurred. All that is left perhaps of originally quite different peoples is a variety of tastes and preferences which have very ancient origins. Superimposed on these ancient patterns of taste are other more modern patterns: religious, social, and economic pressures which influence choice in food, clothing, living conditions, entertainment, and recreation. These tastes and preferences play some part in deciding the total demand for a commodity or service.

We may therefore demand goods because they satisfy innate wants which we cannot explain but still feel are necessary; or because they are fashionable; or because we have been convinced by advertising that they are desirable. The demand for all such goods will rise, and the demand for goods which are not to our personal taste or which are less fashionable or less well promoted will decline.

(*b*) *The Income of the Household.* Family income is often decisive as to whether a commodity is demanded or not. Few ordinary households demand light aircraft as a means of personal transport, but a millionaire may keep one available. Many families run a car, some run two cars, and many are resigned to the fact that they will never be in the car-buying income range. Most housewives know what their families can afford, and buy within quite narrow price bands. Even so-called impulse buying, where consumers buy a thing because they happen to see it, tends to occur within the price range each housewife knows to be appropriate for her family.

(*c*) *The Necessity of the Commodity, and its Alternatives if Any.* Some goods are demanded by everyone because they are necessities. We all require food, clothing, shelter, etc. Some goods become necessities because they are habit-forming, like tobacco and alcohol. Where a commodity has alternatives it is not a necessity, but the alternative must be in the same price range. Rolls-Royce cars are not substitutes for small family saloons, and Savile Row suits are not substitutes for ready-made garments as far as the majority of consumers are concerned.

(*d*) *The Price of Other Goods.* If the price of a commodity is high compared with the price of other goods the demand for it will be relatively weak. If the goods are close substitutes for one another, as for example, motor cycles and motor scooters, the price of one will be seriously affected by a lower price of its competitor. Even if the goods are not close substitutes for one another, there is usually some competition between them, because the money to be spent represents all the possible alternatives of satisfactions available to the consumer. The young lady who decides against a bottle of perfume and in favour of a pair of new shoes has been influenced by the price of the perfume into thinking that the shoes will yield her greater satisfaction. They are not close substitutes for one another, but they are still in competition.

Factors Affecting the Total Market Demand

(*a*) *The Size and Structure of the Population.* If there are many people to be fed, clothed, and housed demand will tend to be strong, especially if the population is able to back its 'wants' with purchasing power. The structure of the population will influence demand for particular items. A bulge in the birth-rate for any reason will alter demand as the children born develop through to maturity. In the early years the demand for children's clothes, toys, etc., will be increased. Gradually the increased demand will change to school books and games equipment, later to cosmetics and motor cars. Later still the growing numbers of mature young people of marriageable age may lead to a new bulge in the birth-rate. Finally, an increased demand for wheel-chairs and hearing aids may result.

(b) *The Distribution of Income among the Population.* Some societies are so organized that classes of rich and poor persons appear. Others are organized to achieve greater equality of wealth. A progressive system of taxation, which taxes the rich to help the poor, is often used to achieve greater equality. Market demand will be stronger in egalitarian societies than in those where obvious inequalities exist, for the mass of the people in egalitarian societies can back their 'wants' with purchasing power. The strong level of demand in Great Britain over the last quarter of a century reflects the more even distribution of wealth that has been achieved since the introduction of the Welfare State.

The Consumer's Scale of Preferences

The result of these conditions, often called the determinants of demand, is a **scale of preferences** for each consumer. High on each consumer's scale of preferences come the things he needs most or likes best. Lower on the scale come things he will buy if his income permits, once all the more satisfying items have been purchased. The scale of preferences changes with the pressure of daily events. We all know of things we have been meaning to buy for years, but somehow their purchase eludes us because more pressing requirements prevent them reaching the top of our scale of preferences.

Table 6. Mrs. Brown's weekly demand for lamb cutlets

Price per unit	Cutlets demanded
0·11	—
0·10	2
0·09	2
0·08	3
0·07	3
0·06	4
0·05	4

(3) A Personal Demand Schedule

A schedule is a list, and the list of demands for any individual is called an **individual demand schedule.** Table 6 shows the demand schedule of such an individual for an everyday requirement like lamb cutlets. This schedule takes for granted that the only thing that has changed to alter the demand is the price of the commodity. All other conditions of demand, like family income, or personal taste, or fashion, have not changed. The phrase *ceteris paribus* ('other things being equal') is often used in economics to describe a situation where only one aspect of a situation is deemed to be changing.

Note that Mrs. Brown has a relatively small demand for lamb cutlets. There are only two people in the Brown family. When cutlets are expensive they have one each. When cutlets are cheaper Mrs. Brown buys Mr. Brown an extra cutlet. When they are very cheap she has two herself as well. When

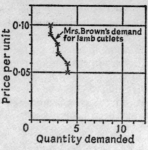

Fig. 5. An individual demand curve

displayed graphically, as in Fig. 5, the line joining the points plotted on the graph is a rather jerky line moving out from the vertical axis of the graph and sloping down towards the right.

Table 7 shows three more demand schedules.

Table 7. Three more weekly demand schedules

Price per unit	Mrs. Green Cutlets demanded	Mrs. Gray Cutlets demanded	Mrs. White Cutlets demanded
0·12	4	—	—
0·11	5	—	—
0·10	6	—	—
0·09	6	—	—
0·08	7	—	—
0·07	7	—	—
0·06	8	1	—
0·05	8	2	—

What can you guess about the size of Mrs. Green's family?

What can you guess about the income of Mrs. Gray's family?

What can you guess about Mrs. White's family's fondness for lamb cutlets?

Quite apart from the size of Mrs. Green's family, would you gather from this schedule that her family are poor or relatively well to do?

Fig. 6 displays the individual demand schedules for the two families who are requiring some of this product. Once again we notice that the curve slopes downwards towards the right, though once again the motion is rather jerky in the case of Mrs. Green's demand curve.

(4) A Composite Demand Schedule

If we now imagine the demand schedules for all these individuals added together, and if we add in the housewives who are demanding legs of lamb, shoulders of lamb, etc. (it would be unrealistic to imagine that only cutlets were being demanded and the rest of the carcases being wasted) we arrive

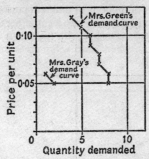

Fig. 6. Two more individual demand curves

at a **composite demand schedule** or **market demand schedule** for lamb. This demand schedule is given in Table 8.

The important point about the composite demand schedule is that, generally speaking, *the quantity demanded of any commodity will increase as the price falls.* This well-known everyday fact is shown quite clearly by the schedule. At a price of 3·00 the consumer requires only 200,000 lambs to be brought to the dinner-table. At a price of 2·00 the article is much better value for money, and as many as 2,000,000 lambs are demanded. Whether any farmers are prepared to supply at that low price is quite another matter, which is discussed on page 81.

When graphically presented this information now looks as in Fig. 7.

Table 8. A composite demand schedule

Weekly demand schedule for lamb carcases	
Price (in currency units)	Quantity demanded
3·00	200,000
2·90	250,000
2·80	300,000
2·70	500,000
2·60	750,000
2·50	1,000,000
2·40	1,200,000
2·30	1,400,000
2·20	1,600,000
2·10	1,800,000
2·00	2,000,000

Note: As explained in the text, the prices here refer to whole carcases, not the price for cutlets only as in Tables 6 and 7. It would be unrealistic to imagine that the rest of each animal is wasted.

Notice that the inclusion of millions of different customers has smoothed out the jerky demands of each individual into a smoother curve. This curve slopes downwards towards the right, in line with the rule noticed above that as the price decreases the quantity demanded will increase.

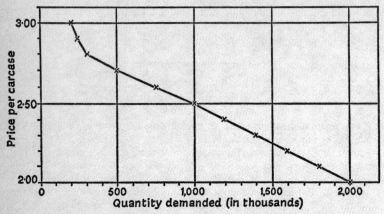

Fig. 7. A market demand curve for lamb; quantity demanded in thousands of carcases

(5) The General Demand Curve

For the sake of convenience economists disregard the details of particular demand schedules, although a great deal of research has been carried out on such schedules. In ordinary discussion about the likely effects of changes in demand, etc., it is sufficient to use a general diagram which can be varied to envisage different possibilities. The conventional arrangement is to call the vertical axis OY and the horizontal axis OX. The prices and quantities are not marked in with mathematical precision, but are simply assumed to be evenly graduated along the axes from the origin O. The *general demand curve* shown in Fig. 8 is labelled DD, and its general shape conforms to the first 'law' of demand and supply.

The first 'law' of demand and supply states that *the more the price of a commodity is decreased, the greater the quantity that will be demanded.*

Note: It is convenient to use the word 'law' to describe these general observations which appear to be true in many real-life situations. The student of economics should remember that they are not 'laws' in the scientific sense. Economics is an inexact science at best.

(6) Extensions and Contractions of Demand

From a demand curve of the sort shown in Fig. 7 it is possible to read off an infinite number of demands at various prices, which makes it possible to discuss demand quite fully. For instance, in Fig. 9 we can read off for prices P_1, P_2, P_3, and P_4 the quantities demanded, which are Q_1, Q_2, Q_3, and Q_4. Clearly at each of these prices a different quantity has been demanded, so we could say that the demand has changed. However, in economics the phrase 'a change of demand' has a quite different meaning. This phrase is used to

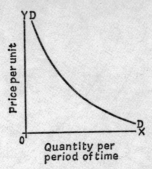

Fig. 8. The general demand curve

describe a change to a new demand curve, so that at every price a different quantity will be demanded.

We therefore refer to changes in demand along an existing demand curve as extensions or contractions of demand. Although economists do talk loosely about demand 'changing', readers are urged to use the better terms 'extending'

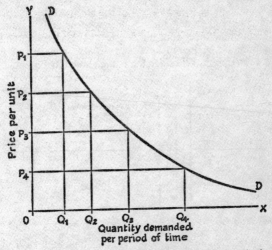

Fig. 9. Extensions and contractions of demand with changes in price

or 'contracting', unless they mean the sort of change illustrated in Fig. 10. Here we really *do* have a change of demand at every price. This type of change is not responding to price alterations on the market, but is responding to some more fundamental change, such as a change in taste or fashion or a change in income. In the last twenty years in Great Britain an enormous change in the demand for motor cars has occurred, due largely to a change in income. More people can afford cars today.

(7) Regressive Demand Curves

Some demand curves behave in an unusual fashion. They do not obey the first law of demand given on page 68. Instead of continuing progressively along

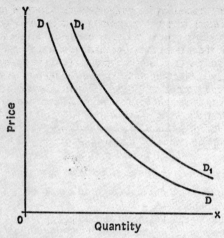

Fig. 10. A change in demand, to a new demand curve

the general demand path, they suddenly turn and become regressive. A regressive demand curve is a demand curve that turns and starts to go backwards. This exceptional behaviour may occur at either end of the curve.

Regression at the Upper End of the Curve—Goods of ostentation and goods expected to become scarce. Consider the curve shown in Fig. 11.

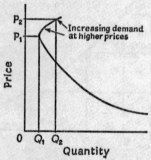

Fig. 11. Regressive demand curve I: (*a*) goods of ostentation; (*b*) expectations of higher prices to come

At a price of P_1 the quantity demanded is Q_1, a very small quantity. At a higher price P_2 we would expect demand to be even less, but demand for this product is exceptional and it increases when the price is raised. Such goods are called **goods of ostentation**; they are purchased not because of their intrinsic worth but because they are required to emphasize status. There are many levels of status. Retailers often find that cheap costume jewellery on sale at very low prices sells poorly. The same jewellery offered at ten times the price sells quite well. Nobody wants to buy his girl friend a brooch that costs 10 pence: he would lose face if she discovered the price. Yet the same brooch at 1·00 makes a 'worthwhile' gift.

A quite different reason for regressive demand curves of exactly the same shape as above occurs with the **expectation of future price increases**. This is commonly met on the major commodity markets. Dealers fear even higher prices may follow the present increases because world shortages are developing, and press in to buy up whatever supplies are available, even though they are more expensive. Speculative fevers on foreign-exchange markets are particularly common examples of this kind of regressive demand, prices soaring upwards in a frantic attempt to choke off demand, but demand becoming ever stronger as the prices soar.

Regression at the Lower End of the Curve—inferior goods and goods expected to become even cheaper. Consider the curve shown in Fig. 12.

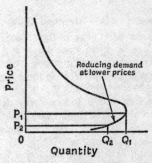

Fig. 12. Regressive demand curve II: (*a*) inferior goods or 'Giffen' goods; (*b*) expectations of even lower prices to come

Here we have a demand curve showing regression at its lower end. This time, despite the reduction in price from P_1 to P_2, the quantity does not increase. The curve turns and goes backwards, indicating a reduced demand despite lower prices. This effect occurs with a class of goods called inferior or 'Giffen' goods.

Inferior goods are goods that are very cheap, and inferior to some other readily available goods. The best example is rye bread, which is a cheap and inferior substitute for white bread made from milled wheat. When such a commodity forms a large proportion of the purchases of a consumer, say a poor peasant, a fall in its price may mean that less of it will be purchased. It is now so cheap that the peasant is enjoying a higher income in real terms, and can vary the pattern of his purchases to buy some of the superior white bread. Cheaper inferior goods may therefore result in less of them being demanded. When the price of such inferior goods rises, the need to pay more for this item may lead to insufficient income being available to buy alternative goods. The first economist to describe this behaviour was Sir Robert Giffen, who noticed that during a time when wheat was very expensive and bread consequently rose in price, the consumption of bread actually increased among the poorest classes in Victorian England. As prices rose from P_2 to P_1 quantity demanded rose as consumers were forced to reduce their diets to a bare subsistence on bread. Hence inferior goods are often called **'Giffen goods'**.

An interesting example of regressive demand is the experience of the Co-operative Movement, which has always historically been most prosperous when times were hard and prices and wages low. At such times Co-operative goods, which have always been good-quality products at fair prices, appeal strongly to consumers, and their stores are filled with busy shoppers. In prosperous times, when wages are high and retail trade is booming, the Co-operative Movement tends to do less well. Value for money is less important to affluent people, who buy with less discrimination.

On highly organized commodity markets and stock exchanges it is possible for demand to be regressive when prices are falling, if speculators hold off in expectations of further falls. When the market is 'bearish' speculators not only refuse to buy but actually sell in expectations of buying back later at even lower prices. So, far from strengthening demand, the lower prices have the opposite effect and weaken it still further.

(8) Choosing a 'Basket of Goods'—Marginal Utility as the Basis of Demand

We now have to consider what governs the choice of the consumer in satisfying his wants. Why does he reject some goods and decide on others? Why do some people find satisfaction in filling their baskets with fruit and bread, while others choose meat and eggs? Why do some pay for piano lessons while others buy motor cycles?

There are several factors that influence every decision, but all are subordinate to the desire to obtain maximum satisfaction. The ability of a good to give satisfaction is called its 'utility'. In thinking about utility we have to distinguish between *total utility* and *marginal utility*.

Total utility is the total satisfaction we derive from the possession of a commodity. Usually total utility will continue to rise as we acquire more and more of the same goods. This would certainly be true, for example, of a collector's acquisition of antiques. It might not be quite so true of a smoker's purchases of cigarettes. There might come a point with many commodities where total utility had reached a maximum and a further supply would be a positive nuisance.

The Margin in Economics

One of the commonest ideas in economic analysis is the concept of the margin. The word 'margin' means 'edge'; poets talk about 'the margin of the lake', and teachers instruct pupils to draw margins in their exercise books. In economics there are many margins, and they are always very important points because it is at the margin that business decisions are made. For instance, marginal cost is the cost of a unit of production that is just on the edge of current output. If we cut some output it will be that unit which is cut. Similarly, the marginal firm is the firm just about to leave a contracting industry, or the firm that has just entered an expanding industry. Marginal utility is another of these margins.

Marginal utility is the satisfaction we receive from possessing one extra unit of a commodity, or the satisfaction we lose by giving up one unit. Shall I buy another shirt? The satisfaction I shall derive from it is its marginal utility to me. I am weighing the marginal satisfaction of the shirt against the satisfaction of having the money for the shirt instead—the money representing everything else that I could have instead. This is an example of choice, and as we have already said, choice is fundamental to economic life. If I decide on the shirt it is because the marginal utility to me of a shirt is high. If I decide on some other alternative, perhaps a textbook or a visit to the theatre, it is because the marginal utility of the shirt to me is low. Business decisions are always marginal decisions. A million housewives every day weigh up the marginal utilities to them of another tin of soup, or packet of tea or pound of sugar. At other levels entrepreneurs are pondering whether to make another 10,000 chairs, or switch production over to some other line of furniture.

Marginal Utility Diminishes as Total Utility Rises. If marginal utility is the extra satisfaction to be derived from a further unit of a commodity it is clear it will not be the same for every unit obtained. Smokers are on record as saying that the first cigarette of the day is the most satisfying. Subsequent cigarettes have a smaller marginal utility, and even the veteran chain-smoker finds himself indifferent to the eighty-first cigarette of the day. The housewife buying bread certainly needs a loaf or two. She is less enthusiastic about the third loaf, and positively embarrassed by the twentieth, for she cannot either carry it home or use it before it goes stale. Clearly the marginal utility of the twentieth loaf may even be negative.

If we imagine some unit in which we can measure utility, say 'units of satisfaction', we can illustrate marginal utility and total utility diagrammatically as shown in Fig. 13.

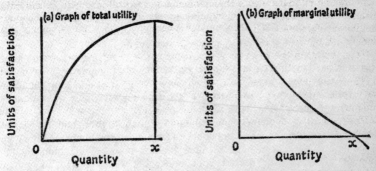

Fig. 13. Total utility and marginal utility measured in units of satisfaction

Notes:

1. Total utility continues to rise, but reaches a maximum where the commodity is such that there is an absolute limit beyond which marginal utility is negative.
2. Marginal utility begins to fall away at once, as soon as we have the first unit. From then on each successive unit gives less and less satisfaction. At point *X* the marginal satisfaction to be gained is zero, and total utility is at a maximum. Any further purchases of this commodity would now be irrational, for there is no sense in buying goods when the further supply will only be a nuisance, and leave us more dissatisfied.

'Free Goods' and 'Marginal Utility'

Some goods are completely free of cost, and some goods are so cheap that they are almost free of cost. For example, air is free, and it is unlikely that anyone will ever be able to monopolize the air and insist on us paying for a breath of it. In many countries water is in sufficient supply for it to be provided at very nominal charges. In such circumstances consumers become very careless about the quantity of water they use, for once the small bill has been paid they can use as much as they like. This attitude is completely changed when the water is metered and the charge is based upon the quantity used.

The marginal-utility curve for such a free commodity is shown in Fig. 14.

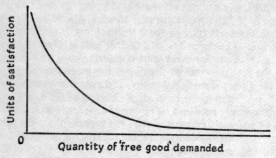

Fig. 14. The marginal-utility curve of free goods

Note: The marginal-utility curve does not cut the X axis because the marginal utility of the goods never becomes negative. However, the marginal utility does become very low indeed, so that the commodity is almost wasted. The housewife who leaves the garden hose running throughout a long summer afternoon so that the children can cool themselves under the sprinkler is getting very little utility from a great quantity of water.

Conclusions about the Selection of a 'Basket of Goods'

Consumers who are basing their choice of a basket of goods on the utility (i.e. satisfaction) they can obtain, will try to achieve the maximum satisfaction possible. This leads to two conclusions.

(*a*) They will push their consumption of free goods to the maximum possible position, continuing to demand supplies even when the marginal utility has become very low indeed. A good example of this occurred in Britain when no charge was made for prescriptions under the National Health Service. Families had large supplies of drugs like penicillin and other antibiotics which had been given to the family during illness. On a recurrence of the illness further supplies were demanded, even though some of the old supplies were still available. It was free, so demand continued strong even though the utility of the extra supply was very low. Eventually a prescription charge had to be imposed to reduce the nation's drug bill.

(*b*) They will balance the marginal utilities of the goods they are thinking of buying against their prices. Eventually, when maximum satisfaction has been achieved the ratios of the marginal utilities of all the goods to their prices will be equal. This is illustrated in Fig. 15.

In this situation the consumer cannot increase his satisfaction. Suppose he decides to give up one unit of Commodity 3. It will realize 9·00 for other purchases, but satisfaction of 18 units will be lost. If the 9·00 is spent on Commodity 2 it will buy $(9{\cdot}00/7{\cdot}50) = 1{\cdot}20$ units. At 15 units of satisfaction per unit he will get 18 units of satisfaction from the extra supply of Commodity 2. However, because marginal utility declines as quantity increases, the next unit of Commodity 2 will not yield 15 units of satisfaction but a little less. He will therefore achieve less than 18 units of satisfaction. He has there-

fore not improved his satisfaction by the change. The same result arises from
the purchase of 9·00 worth of Commodity 1.

A more modern approach to the problem of choosing a basket of goods is
called the 'Revealed Preference Theory'. This is discussed on page 142.

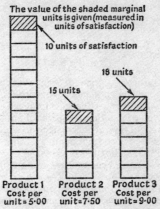

The value of the shaded marginal units is given (measured in units of satisfaction)

10 units of satisfaction

18 units

15 units

Product 1
Cost per
unit = 5·00

Product 2
Cost per
unit = 7·50

Product 3
Cost per
unit = 9·00

Fig. 15. Three goods selected for the basket of the consumer such that the marginal
utilities relative to price are equal

Note: The following equations apply:

$$\frac{\text{Marginal utility of commodity 1}}{\text{Price of commodity 1}} = \frac{\text{Marginal utility of commodity 2}}{\text{Price of commodity 2}} = \frac{\text{Marginal utility of commodity 3}}{\text{Price of commodity 3}}$$

i.e.

$$\frac{10}{5 \cdot 00} = \frac{15}{7 \cdot 50} = \frac{18}{9 \cdot 00}$$

(9) Summary of Chapter Seven

1. The demand for a commodity or service is that quantity of it which
consumers are prepared to buy at a given price in a given period of time.

2. Every consumer subconsciously has a personal demand schedule for each
class of goods, which reflects his individual attitudes and inclinations.

3. These individual demand schedules can be collected together into a composite demand schedule.

4. From such aggregate demand schedules we can draw a demand curve
for the product.

5. This demand curve slopes down towards the right because it displays the
general tendency of consumers to demand more when the price is low.

6. In certain situations and for certain products, demand curves can be
regressive, i.e. they turn back on themselves.

7. In choosing a selection of goods and services the consumer is motivated
by his desire to achieve maximum satisfaction.

8. In achieving maximum satisfaction he will balance the marginal utilities
of goods against their prices, one with another. Marginal utility is the satisfaction derived from a further unit of a commodity by a consumer who
already has some of that commodity.

(10) Suggested Further Reading

Boulding, K. E.: *Economic Analysis* (Chapter 4). Harper & Row: London, 1966.

Hanson, J. L.: *A Textbook of Economics*. Macdonald & Evans: 3rd. Ed., 1970.

Lipsey, R. G., and Stilwell, J. A.: *An Introduction to Positive Economics*. Weidenfeld & Nicolson: London, 3rd. Ed., 1971.

Livesey, F.: *Economics* (Chapter 3). Polytech Publishers: Stockport, 1972.

Exercises Set 7

1. Define 'demand'. Distinguish 'demand' from 'want', and illustrate by reference to demand in India and the United States of America.

2. Suggest reasons why Mrs. Brown's demand for bread may be very different from Mrs. Smith's. (In this type of question a superficial answer is usually insufficient. Students are urged to think of several factors likely to affect demand.)

3. What is the first 'law' of demand and supply? Illustrate it graphically, indicating different levels of demand along the curve drawn.

4. What is a regressive demand curve? How can a regressive demand curve for 'Giffen' goods be explained?

5. 'Copper is cheap, I will buy some immediately' (speculator). 'Copper is cheap, I will sell copper at once' (same speculator on another occasion). Discuss the difference in attitudes displayed.

6. 'In ordinary everyday decisions marginal utility is more important than total utility.' Explain, using the demand for breakfast cereals as an example.

7. 'Total utility usually rises, marginal utility always falls.' Is this statement true, or largely true? Explain.

8. Explain how a housewife decides on a selection of goods for the family.

9. What are 'free' goods? Why is the marginal utility of most free goods small in everyday life? Do we, then, cease to demand them? Explain.

10. When a housewife's selection of goods is complete the marginal utilities of the goods selected relative to their prices will all be equal. Explain.

CHAPTER EIGHT

BASIC IDEAS OF SUPPLY

(1) Definition of Supply

The responses that entrepreneurs make to the demands of consumers bring on to the market a wide variety of goods and services. In deciding what quantity to supply, each entrepreneur will be influenced by a number of factors, discussed in (2) below. The total quantity of a good, or service, made available to the general public as a result of the business decisions of the entrepreneurs in the industry is called the **supply** of that good, or service. We may therefore define supply as follows: *the supply of a commodity or service is that quantity of it which entrepreneurs are prepared to make available at a given price, in a given period of time.*

As with demand, we must notice that the price is crucial to any discussion of supply. There is no such thing as the supply of family cars *per se*. It is the supply at £1,500·00 each or £10,000·00 each which can be estimated and discussed.

(2) Factors Affecting Supply

The chief factors affecting supply are: (*a*) the price of the commodity, and (*b*) the conditions of supply. Under (*b*) we may particularly note: (i) the costs of production; (ii) the state of technological development; (iii) natural influences, and abnormal political influences.

The Price of the Commodity. The price of the commodity affects the prospects of profitability of an enterprise. Every entrepreneur is assumed in economics to be engaged in production in order to achieve maximum profit. He must certainly achieve a normal return on capital invested, or there is no incentive at all to stay in the industry. He will hope to do rather better than this in actual fact, and will attempt to operate at the best level possible. Good prospects of profitability will encourage him to come in and produce the supplies required. He will expand the production of his enterprise until output reaches such a level that profit is at a maximum.

The Conditions of Supply: (i) costs of production. The costs of production are of such importance that a whole profession is engaged in calculating and controlling them. The cost accountant distinguishes between two major sets of costs, **fixed costs** and **variable costs,** but the specialized vocabulary used in a full discussion of costs is very extensive. A simple chart of costs is given in Table 9 overleaf.

The Conditions of Supply: (ii) the state of technological development. Not only does an advanced technology reduce unit costs by achieving the economies of scale but without it the production of even a single unit may be impossible. When the early pioneers of the motor car built their first models it was necessary to cut each component for the gear-box by hand. They started with rods of steel and brass, and sheets of wrought iron, and built the whole vehicle. The elementary level of motor-vehicle technology prevented any appreciable supply from coming on to the market. The more advanced the technology, the greater the flood of supplies that pours on to the market.

The Conditions of Supply: (iii) natural influences and abnormal political influences. Supply is particularly subject to external influences, which may disrupt either the actual output itself or the distribution system moving the supplies to the point of consumption. Hurricanes, tornadoes, hail, frost, snow, and drought disrupt output. Similarly, war, fire, strikes, and civil unrest prevent the normal activities of production. All these things interrupt transport by rail, road, sea, and air.

Table 9. A simple chart of costs

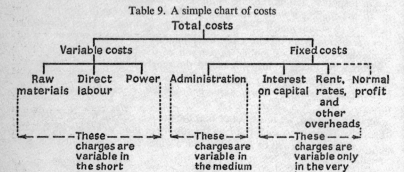

Notes:

1. *Variable costs* are costs that vary with the volume of output; if we double the output of furniture, for example, we must use twice as much wood, more labour, etc.
2. *Fixed costs* do not vary with output; for example, rent is the same whatever the output produced.
3. *Normal profit.* To an accountant profit is the difference between costs and selling price, but economists include *normal profit* as an element of cost. This is very helpful, because it draws attention to the entrepreneur's desire for profit. If he cannot achieve a reasonable return on capital invested he will leave the industry— in other words, the costs he *must* cover include normal profit.
4. *Variability in the short run, the medium run, and the long run.* This is important in understanding the decisions made by entrepreneurs, but cannot be fully discussed at this point. *Variable costs* can be reduced at once by cutting back production and dismissing workers. Such harsh treatment of workers is becoming less easy in advanced societies where trade unions are strong. *Administrative costs* can be reduced in a rather longer time by dismissing employees on monthly contracts, or by giving 'golden handshakes' to those with longer contracts of service. Other *fixed costs* cannot be reduced so easily, and may involve finding a buyer for factory premises or paying lump sums for the privilege of surrendering a lease.

A further type of political activity is Government interference with the market. For instance, taxation may cause demand to change and thus make output unprofitable, or it may simply reduce the profitability of some enterprises below normal. Normal profit is that profit which is just sufficient to retain a firm in the industry but is not sufficient to attract a firm outside the industry to enter. When taxation is imposed the high-cost firms in an industry may find that profit falls below this normal return on capital invested. Such firms will leave the industry and supply will be reduced.

For any given firm the prospects of profitability and the conditions of supply dictate production policy. What the entrepreneur decides to produce in the prevailing conditions leads to an individual supply schedule.

(3) Individual Supply Schedules

There are millions of consumers demanding products, but the number of suppliers is much smaller. Sometimes there is only one supplier, called in economics a **monopolist.** Sometimes there are two or three main suppliers only, as in the British detergent industry, where two great combines dominate the scene. This situation is called **oligopoly** (from the Greek *oligoi* meaning 'few'). The commonest situation is where there are many suppliers competing with one another. Sometimes we talk about **perfect competition.** A full discussion of what economists mean by perfect competition is given on page 86. As a rule some imperfections exist in the market, usually because goods have been 'branded' to make them artificially different from similar goods. This situation is called **imperfect competition** or **monopolistic competition.**

In considering demand we discussed the demand schedules of certain housewives for lamb cutlets, and eventually of the whole body of consumers for lamb carcasses. We must now consider the **individual supply schedules** of some suppliers of lambs, i.e. some farmers who raise sheep for wool and mutton.

Just as consumers vary in their preferences for goods, suppliers vary in their ability to supply. Some, because they are better situated, or more skilful, are low-cost producers, while others are high-cost producers.

Examples of high-cost and low-cost producers are illustrated in Table 10. When these schedules are drawn as individual supply curves the result is as shown in Fig. 16 overleaf.

(4) A Composite Supply Schedule

If we now imagine that the supply schedules of all the suppliers in the industry have been added together we find that the supply schedule of the industry looks like Table 11 (see page 81).

Table 11 illustrates a very important aspect of supply, which is known as the second 'law' of demand and supply.

The second 'law' of demand and supply states that *the higher the price, the greater the quantity that is supplied.*

The reader is advised to consider every such Table in this book carefully. Can you visualize the industry clearly? At a price of 2·00 only the most efficient farmers are bringing their animals to market. They are such low-cost producers that even at a price of 2·00 they can make a profit. As the price rises more and more inefficient producers are able to make a profit, and bring their flocks in to be culled. The higher the world prices for mutton, the more producers will join the industry. The lower the price, the more producers will leave the industry and either give up farming altogether or change over to some aspect of it more lucrative than sheep-raising.

Graphically presented this information appears as shown in Fig. 17.

Notice that this supply curve slopes upwards towards the right. This is because the quantity supplied rises as the price rises—exactly the opposite of what happens with the demand curves shown in Figs. 7 and 8.

Table 10. Two individual supply schedules

Price per unit	Number of animals supplied weekly	
	A. Smallholder	A. Bigboy Ltd.
3·00	500	10,000
2·90	450	9,000
2·80	250	8,000
2·70	100	7,000
2·60	—	6,000
2·50	—	5,000
2·40	—	4,000
2·30	—	3,500
2·20	—	3,000
2·10	—	—
2·00	—	—

Notes:

1. Mr. Smallholder is a high-cost producer. He cannot supply any animals at a price below 2·70.
2. The limited company is a low-cost producer; perhaps because it achieves economies of scale, or is more favourably situated.
3. Unlike a demand schedule, where consumers demand more when the price is low, suppliers offer to supply *less* when the price is low. The higher the price, the greater the quantity that is brought to market.
4. Neither of these producers can suddenly increase supplies of lambs. It takes time for flocks to be bred. What they can do is to send existing animals to market if the price is right, or retain them on the farm until prices improve.

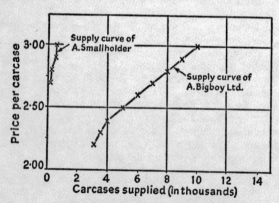

Fig. 16. Two individual supply curves

Table 11. A composite supply schedule

Price per unit	Animals supplied weekly by whole industry
3·00	2,000,000
2·90	1,800,000
2·80	1,600,000
2·70	1,400,000
2·60	1,200,000
2·50	1,000,000
2·40	800,000
2·30	700,000
2·20	600,000
2·10	500,000
2·00	400,000

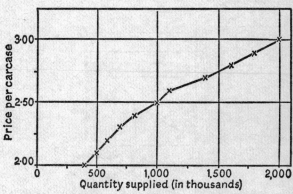

Fig. 17. The supply curve for lamb

(5) A General Supply Curve

Once again we do not bother in theoretical discussions with the actual shape of supply curves for particular industries. Instead, as with demand, we use the **general supply curve** as a basis for discussion. Its characteristics are that uniform graduations are assumed along both axes, and the curve obeys the second 'law' of demand and supply, in other words, it indicates increased supplies coming on to the market as prices rise. This curve is shown in Fig. 18.

(6) Extensions, Contractions, and Changes in Supply

Once again we must distinguish between extensions and contractions of supply, on the one hand, and changes in supply, on the other. The term

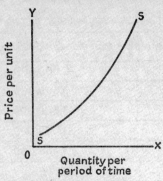

Fig. 18. The general supply curve

'extension of supply' refers to an increased supply coming on to the market due to the attraction of higher prices being offered there. When the farmer decides to market his lambs, because prices have risen and will now yield him a profit, there is no 'change' in supply as far as economists are concerned. Similarly, when supply contracts under the influence of falling prices there is only a movement along the same supply curve. These extensions and contractions of supply are illustrated in Fig. 19.

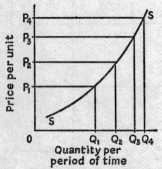

Fig. 19. Extensions and contractions (but *not* changes) of supply

To an economist a change in supply means a change causing a new curve altogether. Such a change must be due to a change in the conditions of supply: perhaps a change in the techniques of production, or some natural or political event which interferes with the supply of the commodity. All such changes result in either a larger or a smaller supply coming on to the market at every price. This produces a new supply curve, as shown by S_2S_2 in Fig. 20.

(7) Regressive Supply Curves

The regressive type of curve shown in certain cases of demand is not very common with supply. However, a good example is afforded by the supply curve for labour. This is often regressive when very high wages are being paid, since workers can then earn sufficient to provide for their families in shorter work-

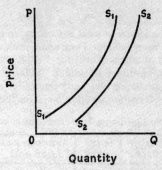

Fig. 20. A change in supply, brought about by a change in the techniques of production

ing periods. Consequently absenteeism grows, especially if the work is hard and unpleasant. In Great Britain absenteeism in the coal mines became a serious problem a few years ago when higher wages for workers at the coal face meant that men could take greater leisure periods without reducing their standards of living. As income rises, the marginal utility of income falls and the marginal utility of leisure rises; especially where work is dangerous and unpleasant. Fig. 21 illustrates the supply of such labour.

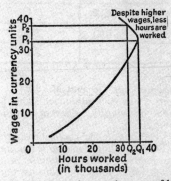

Fig. 21. The regressive supply curve of labour

Note: At P_1 the wages paid are sufficient to call forth 35,000 hours of work per week at a particular coalfield. At P_2 the extra wages result not in an increased supply of labour but a decreased supply as absenteeism reduces the total hours worked.

(8) Deciding to Supply—Marginal Cost and Marginal Revenue as the Basis of the Firm's Output

Just as consumers make decisions to demand goods or services, entrepreneurs make decisions to supply them. The decision to demand is based on the marginal utility of the good to the consumer, as already explained on page 74. The decision to supply is based on the relationship between the marginal cost and the marginal revenue. We must now define these terms, and note a number of interesting points about each.

Marginal Cost

    Marginal cost is the addition to total costs incurred in producing one extra unit of production—the marginal unit. Once again decisions are being made at the margin. It is not a question of whether I shall produce 100,000 cars or none but whether I shall produce 100,000 or 95,000; or will perhaps 105,000 be best. Table 12 suggests some imaginary figures for a business whose fixed costs are 100·00. Variable costs start off at 50·00 for the first unit, but are less

Table 12. Marginal cost and average cost

Output	Fixed costs	Variable costs	Total costs	Average cost per unit	Marginal cost of the extra unit
0	100	—	100	—	—
1	100	50	150	150	50
2	100	90	190	95	40
3	100	128	228	76	38
4	100	176	276	69	48
5	100	240	340	68	64
6	100	320	420	70	80
7	100	418	518	74	98
8	100	540	640	80	122
9	100	674	774	86	134

Notes:
1. Fixed costs, as their name implies, are constant.
2. Variable costs, the costs of raw materials, direct labour, power, etc., increase as output rises, but not in a constant way, because of increasing returns to scale and then decreasing returns to scale.
3. The alterations to variable costs are the marginal costs of successive extra units. Notice that they decrease from 50 to 38 under the influence of the economies of scale, but then begin to rise as diminishing returns set in.
4. Average costs per unit fall from 150 to 68, but then begin to rise. The reader should note that marginal cost starts to rise before average cost, which continues to fall as long as marginal cost is below average cost.

for the second unit and even less for the third. This is because economies of scale are being achieved. After the third item the variable costs begin to rise more and more rapidly. This means that the *marginal* cost of each unit is going up fast—diseconomies of scale are beginning to creep in. Consider the notes below the Table, and the relationship between marginal cost and average cost.

The Relationship between Marginal Cost and Average Cost

    It is important to understand the relationship between marginal cost and average cost. The marginal cost is the cost of the last unit to be produced. It is therefore the vital thing that controls the average cost. If the marginal cost is lower than the average cost the average cost will fall. If the marginal cost is greater than the average cost, then the new average cost—now that one extra unit has been included—will rise. A simple illustration of this is the effect on the average age of any group of the arrival of one more member. Suppose a class of night-school students has an average age of 19 years. If they are joined by one new class member (the marginal student) aged 17 years, his age, being lower than average, will reduce the average age of the class. If the new arrival is a mature student aged 42 his higher-than-average age will increase the average age of the class.

Returning to the effect on average cost of changes in marginal cost, we can see the result in Table 12. As long as marginal cost is less than average cost, the average cost falls with every new unit. As soon as marginal cost becomes higher than average cost, i.e. at 80·00 for the sixth unit of production, the average cost starts to rise. It must do, because the high cost of that extra unit drags up the whole average. This is shown graphically in Fig. 22.

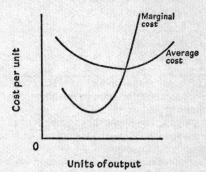

Fig. 22. Average- and marginal-cost curves

Notes:
1. As long as marginal cost is lower than average cost, average cost is falling.
2. As soon as marginal cost rises above average cost it drags the average cost up with it.
3. Therefore the marginal-cost curve always cuts the average-cost curve at its lowest point.

Marginal Revenue

We are still not quite ready to understand at what point the entrepreneur decides to stop supplying his goods or service. This is because we do not yet know what **marginal revenue** is. Even when we have defined marginal revenue, we have to look at the different types of market situation before we can fully understand it.

Marginal revenue is defined as *the increase in total revenue to be achieved by supplying one further unit of a commodity.*

One might think that this would be the same as the price for which the unit is sold, but in fact this is often not the case. To explain why, we must consider the market situation in which suppliers and consumers meet.

Markets in Economics

A market is a place where buyers and sellers are in contact with one another to fix prices. There are many types of market. The highly organized commodity markets and financial markets of the City of London are as near as one can get in real life to the perfect markets which economists like to imagine and discuss. By contrast, a thief who is trying to dispose of a stolen ring does so on a very imperfect market. He cannot offer it openly in the market-place in case someone informs the police. Any potential buyer becomes a threat if the thief refuses to sell the ring at the price offered. The illegality of his transaction is what makes his market imperfect, but there are many legal market situations which are imperfect. What is a **perfect market**?

A perfect market is one which displays the following characteristics:

(*a*) a large number of buyers and sellers, none of whom dominate the market;

(*b*) a homogeneous commodity, so that buyers are indifferent from whom they buy;

(*c*) an absence of friction in the market;

(*d*) perfect knowledge in the market;

(*e*) no one receiving preferential treatment.

(*a*) *There must be a large number of buyers and sellers, none of whom dominate the market.* If there are a large number of buyers and sellers competition on the market will be strong. In perfect market conditions no producer is so large that he can raise the price by withholding his supplies, and no consumer is so important that he can lower the price by refusing to buy. As examples of markets with large numbers of buyers and sellers, we may quote the London Stock Exchange and Lloyd's. The former has hundreds of brokers and jobbers buying and selling shares; Lloyd's has 6,000 underwriters and over 200 firms of brokers selling and buying insurance.

(*b*) *The commodity dealt in must be homogeneous.* In other words each unit of the product must be exactly like every other unit. This is sometimes easy to achieve, and sometimes quite impossible. With silver, for example, on the Silver Bullion Market in London contracts are made for silver which is 0·999 fine, i.e. 999 parts per thousand fine. On the London Wool Exchange in Mark Lane such perfection is impossible, for sheep are temperamental creatures, and the quality of the fleece varies with the animal. Bales are sold after inspection by the buyers, who form personal estimates of the value of each bale. Wool is not a homogeneous commodity; silver is, or can be refined until it is.

This homogeneity of the product makes both buyers and sellers indifferent with whom they conclude a contract. No one's 0·999 fine silver is different from anyone else's 0·999 fine silver. A share in Imperial Chemical Industries from one jobber is as good as the same share from any other jobber. Price becomes the only reason for changing jobbers.

(*c*) *There must be an absence of friction in the market.* Friction, in science, is a force that reduces the efficiency of a machine. Friction in a market similarly reduces the efficient fixing of prices. Fig. 23 shows friction in the market for potatoes in two market towns, *A* and *B*.

Any such friction reduces the perfection of the market. Transport costs are a typical example of friction in the market. Tariffs are another, while trade-union restrictive practices reduce perfection in the market for labour.

(*d*) *Perfect knowledge must exist in the market.* In certain of the London Commodity Markets dealing is by 'open outcry'. Everyone dealing on the market knows the prices being asked, for he can hear them. Such perfect knowledge is rare. The housewife, shopping in her local supermarket, has not the time to tour round comparing prices for groceries. By contrast, when she buys furniture or something expensive and long lasting she may 'shop around' for several weeks before she finally decides what to buy. This improves her knowledge of the prices being charged by different firms.

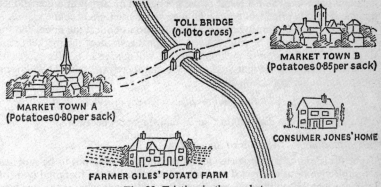

Fig. 23. Friction in the market

Notes:

1. The toll bridge charges 0.10 for each sack of potatoes crossing. It is the 'friction' in this market.
2. Farmer Giles, if there was an absence of friction in the market, would take his potatoes to town *B* and sell them at 0·85 per sack. Because he will have to cross the bridge and pay 0·10 per sack, his earnings from the market in town *B* would be cut to 0·75 per sack. He will instead sell them in town *A* for only 0·80 per sack.
3. Consumer Jones would like to buy his potatoes in town *A* at 0·80 per sack. To cross the bridge will cost him 0·10 per sack, making 0·90 altogether. He is therefore forced to pay 0·85 at town *B*.

(*e*) *There must be no preferential treatment for any particular class of buyers or sellers*. Discrimination against one buyer in favour of another reduces the perfection of a market. In times of shortage shopkeepers who keep goods in short supply 'under the counter' for special customers are displaying discrimination. Discrimination is not always unjustified—businessmen are entitled to look after their best customers—but if it does exist it results in prices being different in the imperfect market from what they would be in more perfectly competitive circumstances.

The perfect market has only one price. If a market is perfect there can be only one price for each good. If there were two prices buyers would rush to buy at the lower price, forcing the price up; sellers would rush to sell at the higher price, thus lowering it. Before we can look fully at these market operations we must finally clarify the supply position. This section is about the decision to supply. The crucial point in that decision is the marginal revenue to be received.

Imperfect markets. A full discussion of these is given on page 132. At present we must return to our supplier, and the marginal revenue which he will earn by the output decision he makes.

Marginal Revenue in Perfect Competition

In a perfect market there are many buyers and sellers, none of whom is such a large dealer that he can influence price. This means that for any given producer the price is fixed at market price. We are not quite ready to see how market price is decided; this is discussed on page 93, but if we accept the idea of a price fixed as the result of the interaction of supply and demand we can see that this price will prevail all over the market, because the market is perfect. Nothing any producer can personally do will affect the price, and for every unit that he sells he will receive a **marginal revenue** of the market price. If the price of a family motor car is £1,600 he will receive £1,600 for every one he makes, including the marginal unit. We can therefore make the following statement: in perfect competition

price = marginal revenue = average revenue.

Now consider the diagram in Fig. 24 and the notes below it.

Conclusions about Decisions to Supply

The decisions of entrepreneurs about the quantity of goods to be supplied are subjective decisions based on personal estimates of the marginal costs of their products. Even the best accountant can only guess what is the cost of a particular unit, but he does his best to supply the board of his company with as accurate a view as possible of the current situation.

In perfect competition the entrepreneur produces until the marginal-cost curve cuts the marginal-revenue line. In other types of market, where some element of monopoly enters, the entrepreneur will still produce to the point where marginal cost equals marginal revenue, but the marginal revenue will not be the same as the price. This is explained more fully on page 133.

The total quantity supplied to the market helps decide the market price, and it is this determination of price which is examined in the next chapter.

(9) Summary of Chapter Eight

1. The supply of a commodity or service is that quantity which entrepreneurs are prepared to make available at a certain price, in a given period of time.

2. Supply is affected by the costs of production, by the general level of technological development, and by the prospects of profitability.

3. Generally speaking, the higher the price, the greater the quantity of goods that is supplied.

4. Regressive supply curves are not common, but the supply curve of the factor labour is often regressive when high wages are being paid, because then the marginal utility of leisure rises.

5. Marginal cost is the addition to total costs incurred by producing one further unit of output.

6. Marginal revenue is the additional revenue achieved by the sale of one further unit of output. In perfect competition it is the same as the sale price of the article.

7. A supplier stops production when marginal cost rises to equal marginal revenue. Beyond that point he loses money on every extra unit.

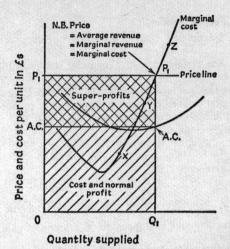

Fig. 24. Deciding what quantity to supply in perfect competition

Notes:

1. We are considering *one* supplier only in this diagram.
2. For this supplier, price is fixed at market price.
3. This supplier is a low-cost firm, because his average costs are well below market price. He is therefore going to make some very useful temporary profits.
4. Consider the point X on his marginal-cost curve. At this point the marginal cost is £X, but he will receive £P_1 for the sale of this unit. This will be a profitable unit.
5. At point Y the marginal unit is costing him £Y, but he will receive £P_1 for its sale, so that this will again be profitable, but not as profitable as the unit costing £X.
6. At point Z the marginal unit costs £Z, but he receives only £P_1. He will therefore lose money on it.
7. It follows that an entrepreneur will stop production when his marginal cost becomes equal to marginal revenue. The next unit will cause him to lose money.
8. We can therefore say that for every producer in perfect competition at the point where he ought to cease production

$$Price = Average\ revenue = Marginal\ revenue = Marginal\ cost.$$

9. This producer is receiving $OQ_1P_1P_1$ of income. His average costs at this output are found where the quantity line cuts the average-cost curve, i.e. at $A.C.$
10. The area shaded in single hatching, $OQ_1A.C.$, $A.C.$ is the income received to cover costs + normal profit, so that this income includes a reasonable return on his invested capital.
11. The area shaded in double hatching, i.e. $A.C.$, P_1, P_1, $A.C.$, is the income he receives over and above normal costs and profits; we will call this 'super-profit' for the moment. We can thus see that this entrepreneur is doing very nicely.
12. However, the entrepreneur cannot hope to enjoy these super-profits for long. Freedom of entry will mean that competitors will join the industry, supplying goods which will lead to price reductions, and his super-profits will be competed away from him as price is lowered to $A.C.$ and even lower. This situation is explained more fully on page 97.

(10) Suggested Further Reading

Boulding, K. E.: *Economic Analysis* (Chapter 5). Harper & Row: London, 1966.

Cairncross, A. K.: *Introduction to Economics* (Chapter 16). Butterworth: London, 1966.

Hanson, J. L.: *A Textbook of Economics*. Macdonald & Evans: London, 1970.

Lipsey, R. G., and Stilwell, J. A.: *An Introduction to Positive Economics*. Weidenfeld & Nicolson: London, 3rd. Edn. 1971.

Exercises Set 8

1. Define 'supply'. What motivates an entrepreneur to supply a commodity or service?

2. Distinguish between fixed costs and variable costs, illustrating your answer by reference to any manufacturing industry with which you are familiar.

3. What is 'normal profit'? What justification is there for regarding normal profit as a cost of production?

4. 'Mass production lowers average costs by dividing fixed costs between large numbers of units of output.' Discuss this statement, saying whether you agree with it or not.

5. 'Millions of people demand goods. Only a few thousand supply them. That is why demand schedules and supply schedules look so different.' Illustrate the differences by drawing up an imaginary demand schedule and supply schedule for tea, or cheese.

6. What is a regressive supply curve? Under what circumstances is supply likely to be regressive?

7. Copy this diagram (Fig. 25) and then label it fully.

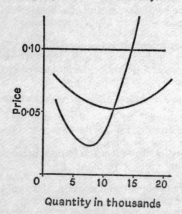

Fig. 25

Now answer these questions:

(*a*) Is this a diagram of a high-cost producer or a low-cost producer?

(*b*) Estimate the output of this supplier.

(*c*) Will this supplier make normal profits, or more than normal profits, or less than normal profits?

(*d*) Is this industry likely to increase in size, decrease in size, or stay at its present size?

8. Write short notes about each of the following: (*a*) an extension of supply; (*b*) a change in supply; (*c*) the shape of a supply curve; (*d*) regressive supply.

9. How does an entrepreneur in perfectly competitive situations decide what output to produce? Illustrate your answer with a diagram.

10. What is marginal cost? What is average cost? What is the relationship between them?

11. What is marginal revenue? What is average revenue? When are they the same?

12. What is a perfect market? Do they exist in real life? Give examples of: (*a*) near-perfect markets; (*b*) imperfect markets.

13. 'Perfect knowledge is impossible in markets unless they are highly organized.' What is 'perfect knowledge' and how can an organized market ensure that knowledge is perfect?

14. Discuss the likely frictions in the market for wool.

CHAPTER NINE

HOW PRICE IS DECIDED IN PERFECT MARKETS

(1) Equilibrium in the Markets

In perfect or perfectly competitive markets prices are fixed in an atmosphere of **pure competition**. This is a theoretical concept in the minds of economists rather than a real-life situation, but some public markets are very nearly perfectly competitive. In such markets the price adjusts upwards or downwards to achieve a balance, or **equilibrium**, between the goods coming in for sale and those being requested by purchasers. Demand and supply react on one another until a position of stable equilibrium is reached where the quantities of goods demanded exactly equal the quantities supplied. The price at which goods are changing hands varies with supply and demand. If the supply exceeds demand at the start of the day prices will fall. This may discourage some of the suppliers, who will withdraw from the market, and at the same time it will encourage consumers, who will increase their demands. A twin force is therefore at work to achieve equilibrium, and establish a **market price** which equates demand and supply.

We can best see how this occurs by comparing the demand and supply schedules already used in Table 8 and Table 11.

(2) Demand and Supply Schedules in Equilibrium

These schedules are given together in Table 13.

As already noted, when price is high the quantity demanded is small, but

Table 13. Demand and supply in equilibrium

Price in currency units	Weekly demand by consumers	Weekly supply by producers
3·00	200,000	2,000,000
2·90	250,000	1,800,000
2·80	300,000	1,600,000
2·70	500,000	1,400,000
2·60	750,000	1,200,000
2·50	1,000,000	1,000,000
2·40	1,200,000	800,000
2·30	1,400,000	700,000
2·20	1,600,000	600,000
2·10	1,800,000	500,000
2·00	2,000,000	400,000

the quantity offered by suppliers is great. As price falls the quantity demanded increases, but the quantity offered by suppliers is reduced, since the least efficient suppliers cannot offer the goods at the lower prices. Equilibrium is reached in this example at a price of 2·50 per carcass, when one million animals are demanded by consumers and supplied by producers. This illustrates the third 'law' of demand and supply, which states that '*Price adjusts to that level which equates demand and supply.*'

(3) Diagrammatic Presentation of Equilibrium Price

A general diagram illustrating the determination of price at the point where demand and supply are equal is given in Fig. 26.

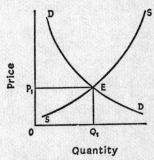

Fig. 26. The determination of equilibrium price

Notes:

1. Demand is small when the price is high, and great when the price is low.
2. Supply is great when the price is high, and small when the price is low.
3. At E (equilibrium) the demand curve and supply curve intersect.
4. At this point E, demand and supply are in equilibrium: as much is being brought into the market as is being taken away by consumers.
5. The price P_1 is called *equilibrium price* or *market price*. It is that price which equates supply and demand.

(4) Changes in Price under the Influence of Changes in Demand and Supply

Changes in the conditions of demand result in a completely different demand curve for a product. Changes in the conditions of supply similarly result in a completely new supply curve. Such changes result in more, or less, goods being demanded, or supplied, at every price. When such changes occur they result in a change in market price, for the equilibrium position described in Fig. 26 is disturbed. There are four possible disturbances:

    (*a*) an increase in demand;
    (*b*) a decrease in demand;
    (*c*) an increase in supply;
    (*d*) a decrease in supply.

A close study of the four cases illustrates equilibrium price very clearly. The reader should follow through the development in each case so he is quite clear how the market regulates price to achieve equilibrium. Before doing so there is one further point to note: the responsiveness of demand and supply to changes in price are different.

The Responsiveness of Supply and Demand to Changes in Price

Demand is very responsive to price changes because consumers are able to adjust their demands quickly. A momentary calculation of the utilities involved, a quick decision, and the housewife presses in to buy the most desirable commodity available. Supply cannot possibly react in this way. At the very least, the entrepreneur has to replan his activities and switch to a new product. In many cases he has to erect a new factory, or plant fields or dig mines before he can produce any output. This means that there is always a time-lag when demand changes before supply can adjust itself. When supply changes, the reactions of customers demanding the product are almost immediate.

The reader is now urged to consider Figs. 27–30 and the notes below them, bearing in mind that in each case the changes result from a change in the *conditions of demand* or the *conditions of supply*. They show respectively:

(*a*) The effect on price of an increase in demand (Fig. 27).
(*b*) The effect on price of a decrease in demand (Fig. 28).
(*c*) The effect on price of an increase in supply (Fig. 29).
(*d*) The effect on price of a decrease in supply (Fig. 30).

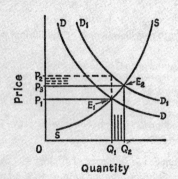

Fig. 27. Effect on price of an increase in demand

Notes:

1. Due to some change in the conditions of demand, perhaps a change of taste or fashion, or a change of income, demand has altered from DD to D_1D_1.
2. Supply cannot react at once because entrepreneurs have to modify plans. There is therefore a shortage and price rises steeply to P_2, the point where a supply of Q_1 cuts the new demand curve. Entrepreneurs supplying the goods are now making excellent profits.
3. Under the influence of these profits, firms expand output and supply begins to creep up from Q_1 to Q_2.
4. As supply increases the price falls from P_2 to P_3.
5. The new equilibrium price of P_3 is established at E_2, where the old supply (which has *extended* to E_2) cuts the new demand curve, which has *changed* to D_1D_1.
6. *Conclusion:* an increase in demand raises price and increases the quantity supplied by the industry.

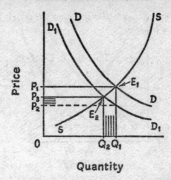

Fig. 28. Effect on price of a decrease in demand

Notes:

1. Due to some change, perhaps of taste or fashion, demand has decreased from DD to D_1D_1.
2. Entrepreneurs supplying the commodity cannot immediately cease production of it, and as a result there is too great a supply for the demand. Price falls drastically to P_2. Some entrepreneurs at this price are making losses.
3. Under the influence of these losses, entrepreneurs reduce production, and supply falls from Q_1 to Q_2.
4. As the supply decreases price begins to recover and creeps up from P_2 to P_3.
5. The new equilibrium price P_3 is decided where the old supply curve (supply having *contracted*) cuts the new demand curve D_1D_1.
6. *Conclusion:* a decrease in demand lowers the price and leads to a decreased supply from the industry.

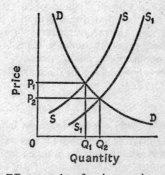

Fig. 29. Effect on price of an increase in supply

Notes:

1. For some reason, perhaps a change in the techniques of production, supply has changed from SS to S_1S_1.
2. The increased supply causes a surplus on the market, and price falls.
3. Due to the swift reactions of consumers, demand extends to take up the new supply at the price P_2.
4. *Conclusion:* an increased supply causes a fall in price and an increase in the quantity demanded.

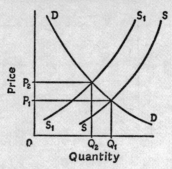

Fig. 30. Effect on price of a decrease in supply

Notes:
1. For some reason decreased supplies are available: perhaps a war has interfered with the output in a country which has previously been a major supplier.
2. The decreased supply causes a shortage, and price rises.
3. Consumers react quickly and the demand contracts to Q_2, achieving equilibrium at the new price P_2.
4. *Conclusion:* a decreased supply causes an increased price and a decrease in the quantity demanded.

(5) The Effect of Price on Firms in Competitive Industries

On page 89 we looked closely at a firm producing for a perfect market, and said that this firm would produce that output which maximized its profit. In order to do so it would stop production when marginal cost equalled marginal revenue. We also saw that, for a firm in a perfectly competitive market, the marginal revenue and the average revenue are equal to price. No firm can do anything about price—there are so many buyers and sellers that any given firm wields no influence at all on price.

Now consider five firms all producing for the same market. Their situation is illustrated in Fig. 31 (*opposite*).

(6) When Will a Firm with Specific Assets Leave the Industry?

In the notes to Fig. 31 on page 97 opposite it was stated that where a firm has 'specific assets', that is assets which are of little use in any other industry, it is difficult for that firm to leave the industry. There are many examples of firms with this type of asset. A catalytic cracking tower is not of much use outside the oil industry. Much of the point of a methane carrier built to carry compressed gas at very low temperatures will be lost if we use it to carry wheat at ordinary temperatures.

Similarly, a coffee bush cannot be converted to yield tea if there is a slump in world demand for coffee. At what point will such a producer cease production and leave the industry? The answer is that *a producer with specific assets leaves the industry when the price will not even cover average variable costs.* Fig. 32 on page 98 explains why.

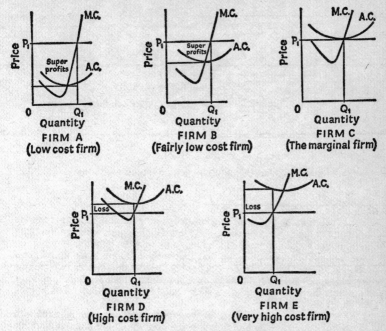

Fig. 31. Five firms in the same industry

Notes:

1. These five firms are all supplying in the same market. They range from a very low-cost firm (Firm *A*) to a very high-cost firm (Firm *E*).

2. Firm *A* is like the firm already discussed on page 89, Fig. 24, making super-profits because it is a low-cost firm with modern, highly productive plant.

3. Firm *B* is not as efficient as Firm *A*, but it is still making more than normal profit. It is operating closer to optimum production. Optimum production is production where average cost is at a minimum. (See Firm *C*.)

4. Firm *C* would be the marginal firm in an ordinary competitive industry, but, as will be seen below, this industry is unusual because it has 'specific assets' which are of no use in other industries. Firm *C* is making normal profit and is operating at the optimum, i.e. minimum average cost.

5. Firm *D* is a firm that is looking for a way out of the industry. It looks as if it is making losses, but this might not actually be true—it might just be making less than normal profits. In other words, its capital could be better used elsewhere. Why doesn't it get out? It would like to leave, but it can't, because its assets are no use in any other industry.

6. Firm *E* is really making losses, and it would go if it possibly could. It looks as if this industry must have *very* specific assets. This is explained in Fig. 32.

7. In the short run even a competitive industry can have high-cost firms and low-cost firms. In the imaginary case of *perfect competition*, especially in the long run, all firms like *D* and *E* will leave the industry. Firms like *A* and *B* will have their super-profits competed away from them. All firms will be like Firm *C*, the marginal firm. For the marginal firm in perfect competition, we can say that

Price = Average Revenue = Marginal Revenue = Marginal Cost = Average Cost.
The firm will be working at the optimum level with average cost at the minimum.

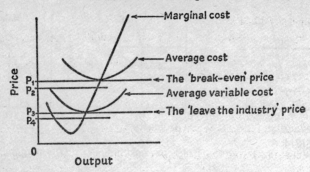

Fig. 32. Leaving the industry—let the specific assets rust

Notes:

1. At P_1 the firm is making normal profits: it is the marginal firm.
2. At prices below P_1 the firm is making less than normal profits. Suppose it receives a price of P_2 when it is paying costs of P_1. It is definitely now earning a less-than-normal return on capital invested, and ought to leave the industry.
3. If we examine the costs of P_1 we find that these costs are made up of *Fixed Costs + Variable Costs + Profit*. The fixed costs have already been suffered (the entrepreneur has already built the factory, installed the plant, etc.); indeed, some accountants describe these costs as **sunk costs** because they have already been sunk into the business.

   The variable costs are payments for wages, raw materials, etc., incurred with each unit of output. These are shown in the diagram by the Average Variable Cost curve.

   As long as price is above average variable costs, it will pay the entrepreneur to keep production going. At the price P_2 for each unit of production sold he receives: (*a*) everything he spends on variable costs, plus (*b*) *something* towards his 'sunk' costs or 'fixed' costs. It is still worthwhile producing.
4. At price P_3 he is receiving back his variable costs, but nothing more.
5. Suppose price drops below P_3, say to P_4. The entrepreneur will now be paying for wages and raw materials a price of P_3, but will receive back less than P_3 for the goods produced. Clearly this is ridiculous: it would be throwing good money after bad. The only thing to do here is to put the plant into mothballs and shut down. P_3 is therefore the 'leave-the-industry' price, even for an entrepreneur with very specific assets. He must then wait for better times to return.

(7) Summary of the 'Laws' of Demand and Supply

1. Generally speaking, demand increases as price falls.
2. Generally speaking, supply increases as price rises.
3. Equilibrium price is that price which equates demand and supply.
4. An increased demand raises price, and also calls forth an extension of supply.
5. A decreased demand lowers price, and also brings about a contraction of supply.
6. An increased supply lowers market price, and causes an extension of demand.
7. A decreased supply raises market price, and causes a contraction of demand.

(8) Summary of Chapter Nine

1. Price is decided under perfect competition by the interaction of demand and supply.

2. Market price is that price which equates demand and supply, so that the quantity of goods supplied by producers exactly equals the quantity demanded by consumers.

3. Other things being equal, an increase in demand or a decrease in supply leads to a rise in price.

4. Similarly, a decrease in demand or an increase in supply leads to a fall in price.

5. In competitive conditions, in the long run, all firms tend to be marginal firms making normal profits and producing at the optimum (minimum average cost) level.

6. Where a firm has specific assets, it cannot leave the industry if price levels fall to the point where it is making less-than-normal returns on capital invested. Such a firm continues in production until price falls below average variable cost, when it shuts plant down and waits for better times

(9) Suggested Further Reading

Harvey, J.: *Intermediate Economics*. Macmillan: London, 2nd. Edn. 1971.
Lipsey, R. G., and Stilwell, J. A.: *An Introduction to Positive Economics*. Weidenfeld & Nicolson: London, 3rd. Edn. 1971.
Samuelson, P. A.: *Economics: An introductory analysis*. 8th. Edn. 1971.

Exercises Set 9

1. Fill in the missing words in the sentences below:

(a) The price of a commodity rises when —— is supplied.
(b) The price of a commodity rises when —— is demanded.
(c) The price of a commodity falls either because —— is supplied or because —— is demanded, or both.
(d) In a competitive market, price is established where demand and supply are in ——.
(e) A change in supply is caused by a change in the —— of supply.
(f) An extension of supply results from an —— in ——.
(g) A change in demand is caused by a change in the —— of demand.
(h) A contraction of demand results from an —— in price.

2. Write about half a dozen lines on each of the following: (a) a demand schedule; (b) a supply schedule; (c) a graph showing a demand curve and a supply curve; (d) equilibrium price.

3. What are the 'laws' of supply and demand? Why do we write the word 'laws' in inverted commas?

4. What is equilibrium price? Consider in your answer the example of tomatoes on sale at Covent Garden Market in London: (a) in August; (b) in December. Account for any difference in the prices observed.

5. Why does the price of lettuces fluctuate more than the price of tinned soup?

6. Discuss the likely effect of: (a) a good harvest on the price of wheat; (b) a sudden frost on the price of autumn flowers; (c) a change to automation in the electronics industry on the price of television sets; (d) rising family income on the price of cars.

Illustrate your answers with diagrams.

7. 'In this industry once you have set up in production you cannot turn back. All you can do is keep production going and hope prices will be large enough to make it all worth while.'

What sort of industry do you think this speaker was describing? Outline the problems of such an industry as far as price is concerned.

8. 'United States' stockpiling for strategic reserves has virtually ceased. This has eased the markets for most primary products.'

Discuss the likely effects on: (*a*) the price of copper; (*b*) the supply of magnesium; (*c*) the demand from Zambia for British manufactured goods (Zambia is a large copper producer).

9. 'For the marginal firm in perfect competition average cost, marginal cost, and price are all equal.' Explain, with the help of diagrams.

10. The prices of shares fluctuate daily. The prices of motor-vehicle accessories hardly ever change. Explain why.

CHAPTER TEN

ELASTICITY OF DEMAND AND SUPPLY

(1) Definition of Elasticity

The 'elastic' used in clothes extends and contracts under the influence of forces applied to it. Demand and supply similarly extend and contract under the influence of such forces as changes in price. It is often useful to know the degree of extension or contraction that will follow a given price change. For instance, a Finance Minister who is about to impose a tax of 10 per cent on some commodity with a view to raising revenue would like to know in advance the probable contraction in demand that his new tax will inevitably cause. The extension and contraction of demand and supply with changes in price has been termed the 'price elasticity of demand and supply'.

Price elasticity of demand is the responsiveness of demand to changes in price.
Price elasticity of supply is the responsiveness of supply to changes in price.

Since responsiveness changes at different points along most demand curves, price elasticity always refers to particular points along the curve—which is the same as saying it refers to a particular price. Thus the elasticity of demand for a commodity at 1·00 per unit might be different from its elasticity of demand at 0·50 per unit.

The most useful measure of elasticity is a relative measure. Measuring change in absolute terms is not very helpful. As an example, if we lower the price of petrol by 1 per cent and as a result sell 40,000 gallons more per week, this absolute figure sounds impressive. If we then compare it with weekly sales of 40 million gallons we see that sales actually only rose by 0·1 per cent. The percentage figure gives us a much better idea of what really happened—an insignificant increase in business as a result of the price cut.

The usual formula for discovering price elasticities is

$$\text{Price Elasticity} = \frac{\text{Percentage change in quantity}}{\text{Percentage change in price}}$$

Besides price elasticity of demand it is possible to have **income elasticity of demand,** i.e. the responsiveness of demand to changes in income; and **population elasticity of demand,** i.e. the responsiveness of demand to changes in population. We also have **cross elasticities,** where a change in the *price* of one commodity produces changes in the *demand* for another

Besides price elasticity of supply it is possible to have *factor cost* elasticity of supply, the responsiveness of supply to changes in factor prices.

(2) The Price Elasticity of Demand

The price elasticity of demand is the responsiveness of demand to a change in price. If demand responds more than proportionately to a change in price the demand is said to be **elastic**; if it responds less than proportionately to a change in price it is said to be **inelastic**. Consider the following examples:

(*a*) Housewives demand potatoes every day, and regard them as a staple diet for the family. Suppose potato prices rise by 10 per cent. Will this cut back demand by 10 per cent? It is unlikely, it might even increase demand, for potatoes are inferior goods.

$$\frac{Percentage\ change\ in\ demand}{Percentage\ change\ in\ price} = \frac{say\ 1\%}{10\%} = \frac{1}{10}$$

Hence the demand for potatoes is inelastic, i.e. less than proportional response.

(*b*) The price of beef rises by 10 per cent. Will housewives cut back on their purchases of beef? Probably they will, for there are several good substitutes, such as lamb and pork. Suppose the demand drops by 25 per cent:

$$Elasticity = \frac{25\%}{10\%} = 2\tfrac{1}{2}$$

The demand for beef is therefore elastic, i.e. a more than proportional response.

(*c*) The price of lettuces rises by 10 per cent and demand falls by 10 per cent.

$$Elasticity = \frac{10\%}{10\%} = 1$$

The demand for lettuces is said to show **unitary elasticity**, i.e. the response is exactly proportional to the change in price.

The price elasticity of demand is nearly always negative, i.e. quantity reduces as price rises, so that in example (*a*) above the real changes are:

$$\frac{-1\%}{10\%} = -\frac{1}{10}$$

By convention we disregard the minus sign.

(3) Five Typical Cases of Price Elasticity of Demand

It is difficult to be precise about elasticity without using mathematical terms which are beyond the scope of *Economics Made Simple*. Of the multitude of possible elasticities, the five most common cases are:

    (*a*) infinite elasticity of demand with respect to price;
    (*b*) zero elasticity of demand with respect to price;
    (*c*) unitary elasticity of demand with respect to price;
    (*d*) fairly elastic demand with respect to price;
    (*e*) fairly inelastic demand with respect to price.

Let us first look at the limits of elasticity. These limits (infinite elasticity and zero elasticity) are illustrated and described in Fig. 33 (*opposite*).

Unitary Elasticity

Midway between these two limits lies the case of unitary elasticity, where the responsiveness of demand is exactly proportional to a change in price. Fig. 34 shows such a curve *(see page 104)*.

Fairly Elastic and Fairly Inelastic Demand

Consider the demand curves shown in Fig. 35 *(see page 105)* which intersect at the price P_1. These demand curves are not related in any way, but both goods can be bought at price P_1. What is the elasticity of such curves? The notes below Fig. 35 explain their elasticity.

Demand Curves with Constant Elasticity

We cannot as a general rule talk about the elasticity of demand curves, for there are only three curves that have constant elasticity. They are:

(*a*) The perfectly elastic curve, Fig. 33(i), whose elasticity is infinite.
(*b*) The perfectly inelastic curve, Fig. 33(ii), whose elasticity is zero.
(*c*) The curve with unitary elasticity (Fig. 34), whose elasticity is 1.

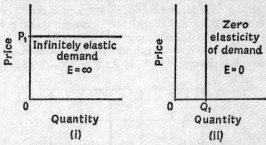

Fig. 33. (i) Infinite elasticity of demand, i.e. $E = \infty$; (ii) Zero elasticity of demand, i.e. $E = 0$

Notes:

1. At prices above P_1, in diagram (i), no quantity at all is demanded.
2. As the price falls to P_1, quantity increases to infinite demand.
3. This seems to be a highly theoretical situation, and it is chiefly to be regarded as a mathematical limit: elasticity can go no farther than infinity. It is, however, highly realistic if we think of the demand in perfectly competitive markets for the supplies of a single producer. If the market price is P_1 for 'Hoover' shares and I offer them for a little less than P_1 I shall immediately dispose of my entire supply.
4. By contrast, in diagram (ii) the quantity demanded does not change at all: there is absolutely zero response to any change in price, however great. The demand curve is a vertical straight line.
5. Again this is a highly theoretical situation, for it is difficult to imagine such a commodity. The demand for some things, for example, habit-forming drugs, is very inelastic. Addicts have been known to beg, borrow, steal, and even murder for the price of a shot of heroin. Demand does not change, however high the price.
6. You should now read about Fig. 34 (page 104).

Other curves have different elasticities at each point along the curve, even though the absolute changes might appear to be regular. This is illustrated by the demand schedule and graph of Fig. 36 and the calculations below it.

The typical straight-line demand curve is shown in Fig 37. It can be established mathematically that the elasticity along this curve varies from infinity at the price axis to zero at the quantity axis (*see page 106*).

(4) Total Revenue and the Elasticity of Demand

To an entrepreneur the amount spent by consumers on his product is the total revenue that will accrue to him by his activities. It can be found by multiplying price by the quantity sold, so that at any point on a demand curve the total revenue earned is represented by the rectangle price × quantity, which is the area OQ_1DP_1 in Fig. 38 (*see page 107*).

Entrepreneurs are interested in the total revenue, and the effect upon total revenue of changes in price. If an entrepreneur cuts price, will it lower his total revenue? This depends on the elasticity of demand at this point. If demand is elastic, so that quantity sold increases more than proportionately, total revenue will rise. If demand is inelastic it will not pay him to cut price, for a cut in price will reduce the amount spent by the public on his product.

In Fig. 39 a straight-line curve (whose elasticity varies from infinity at the price axis to zero at the quantity axis, as explained earlier) is used to demonstrate the change in total income caused by a change in price (*see page 108*).

Wherever the point of unitary elasticity lies, a change at that point will not alter total revenue, for the shaded area of revenue lost by the decreasing price equals the shaded area of revenue gained from the increased quantity sold. This can be seen in a change from P_3 to P_4. (See Fig. 39, Page 108.)

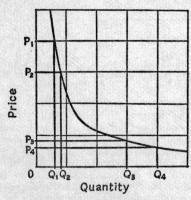

Fig. 34. Unitary elasticity, $E = 1$

Notes:
1. Here we must remember that it is the relative changes that are important. As we move down the price axis, equal absolute changes become relatively more and more significant. As we move along the quantity axis, equal relative changes have to be bigger and bigger in absolute terms. From P_1 to P_2 is a $33\frac{1}{3}$ per cent change in price; from Q_1 to Q_2 is a $33\frac{1}{3}$ per cent change in quantity. From P_3 to P_4 is also a $33\frac{1}{3}$ per cent change in price, while at this point a $33\frac{1}{3}$ per cent change in quantity requires demand to shift from Q_3 to Q_4.
2. It is often said that the slope of a demand curve gives an indication of the elasticity. But in this diagram elasticity is unitary everywhere (i.e. demand is changing proportionately to price all the way along the curve), even though the gradient of the graph varies from almost vertical to almost horizontal.

(5) What Determines the Elasticity of Demand?

The elasticity of demand depends chiefly on the availability of substitutes for the goods concerned. If there are no close substitutes for a commodity, demand for it will be inelastic, since customers will be forced to buy it if they want that particular class of satisfaction. Thus while the demand for cabbage is elastic, since there are many other vegetables, the demand for tobacco is relatively inelastic, since there are no close substitutes for tobacco. A shortage of close substitutes is a particular feature of goods that are habit-forming, like tobacco and alcohol, the demand for which tends therefore to be inelastic.

The other main factor affecting the elasticity of demand is the relative importance of the price of the goods to our total income. Where a commodity represents a very tiny fraction of total income, demand for it will be inelastic. The satisfaction to be derived from a box of matches or a newspaper is great relative to its cost, so that demand will be unresponsive to price changes.

Although it is sometimes said that the demand for *luxuries* is elastic and the demand for *necessities* is inelastic, this statement is not necessarily valid. Thus luxuries having no near substitutes, like diamond engagement rings, are usually in inelastic demand, while necessities like brown bread are in elastic demand, for there are dozens of similar products available on the shelves of supermarkets as substitutes.

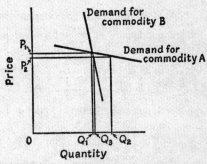

Fig. 35. Demand curves with different elasticities at a given price

Notes:

1. At a price of P_1 the quantity demanded of both goods is Q_1. This coincidence is purely fortuitous, for the demands for these goods are quite unrelated: they might be, for example, the demand for beef (Commodity A) and cigarettes (Commodity B).
2. Imagine a small change in price, say a reduction of 5 per cent, to P_2.
3. In the case of Commodity A the quantity demanded would change more than proportionately to Q_2 (it looks about a 25 per cent change). Therefore

$$Elasticity = \frac{25\%}{5\%} = 5$$

4. In the case of Commodity B the change, to Q_3, is less than proportional (say $2\frac{1}{2}$ per cent). Therefore

$$Elasticity = \frac{2\frac{1}{2}\%}{5\%} = \frac{1}{2}$$

5. It follows that where two demand curves pass through the same point the more gradually sloping curve is the more elastic of the two.
6. The numerical values of elasticity for points where demand is elastic must lie between 1 and infinity. In note (3) above the value is 5, which *is* a number between 1 and infinity.
7. The numerical values of elasticity for points where demand is inelastic must lie between 1 and zero. In note (4) above the value is $\frac{1}{2}$, which *is* a number between 1 and zero.

Price	Quantity
0·60	1,000
0·50	2,000
0·40	3,000
0·30	4,000
0·20	5,000
0·10	6,000

Fig. 36. A demand schedule and its demand curve

Notes: What is the elasticity of demand at price of 0·40? If we are envisaging a decrease in price we have

$$Elasticity = \frac{\%\ change\ in\ demand}{\%\ change\ in\ price} = \frac{\frac{1,000}{3,000} \times 100}{\frac{0·10}{0·40} \times 100} = \frac{33\frac{1}{3}\%}{25\%} = 1·3$$

which represents a fairly elastic demand, whereas at a price of 0·20 the figures are

$$Elasticity = \frac{\frac{1,000}{5,000} \times 100}{\frac{0·10}{0·20} \times 100} = \frac{20\%}{50\%} = 0·4$$

which represents a fairly inelastic demand.

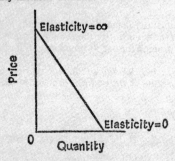

Fig. 37. A straight-line demand curve

(6) The Importance of Elasticity of Demand

There are a number of business decisions which are affected by the elasticity of demand. It is not easy to predict what the elasticity of demand is at any particular price, for the evidence available is usually slight. For example, a businessman may know what current sales are at current prices, and he may know that there are few close substitutes for his product. This may lead him to think that if he raises price, demand will prove to be inelastic, so that the change in sales will be less than proportional. But there is no guarantee that his decision is the right one. Since elasticity is different at every price, he may discover to his chagrin that the price increase was the last straw as far as his customers were concerned and that as a result sales fell more than proportionately.

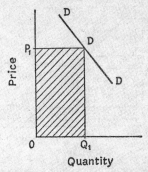

Fig. 38. Total revenue of an entrepreneur or an industry

Important decisions affected by elasticities include the following:

Price-fixing by a Monopolist

The monopolist wishes to set such prices as will yield him the maximum profit. If we refer to Fig. 39 again we see that when the demand is inelastic it will pay the monopolist to raise prices. Suppose he can make comfortable profits at a price of P_5. He will make even more profits if he raises the price towards P_4. When he raises the price past P_3, however, demand will become elastic, and from that point on he will find increased prices less profitable. The monopolist will therefore always find it profitable to restrict output and force price up until the demand for the good becomes elastic.

Taxation Policy of a Chancellor

Taxes are imposed for a variety of reasons. The raising of revenue is one common aim, but the discouragement of undesirable industrial development is another.

If a Chancellor wishes to raise revenue he must tax goods which are in inelastic demand. Since there are no close substitutes for these goods, consumers will be unable to avoid the tax by reducing purchases of the goods. Taxes on tobacco, wines and spirits, and on tea have always been good revenue raisers in the United Kingdom. There are no close substitutes for any of these products, though the non-smoking teetotal citizen will avoid tax on the first two. Petrol tax has also been a very prolific source of revenue.

If a Chancellor wishes to influence what he deems to be undesirable developments he may do so by imposing taxation. The extent to which the policy succeeds will depend on the elasticity of demand. An interesting example occurred in the Autumn Budget of the United Kingdom in 1974. The VAT rate on petrol was raised from 8 % to 25 % to discourage the use of private vehicles in view of the high oil prices. This effectively added 8½ pence to the price of a gallon of petrol. It seems clear that this increase did not have the desired effect. The demand for petrol is notoriously inelastic. The increased tax only produced increased revenue for the Chancellor.

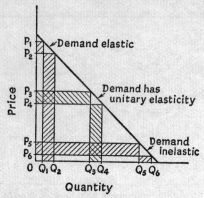

Fig. 39. Changes of total revenue with price changes

Notes:

1. A change from P_1 to P_2, where demand is elastic, results in a greater total income. The shaded area of extra income is greater than the shaded area of lost income, as quantity changes from Q_1 to Q_2.
2. A change from P_5 to P_6, where demand is inelastic, results in a decreased total income. The shaded area of income lost is greater than the shaded area of income gained as demand extends from Q_5 to Q_6.
3. Clearly somewhere between an infinitely elastic demand and a demand which has zero elasticity there lies a point where elasticity is unity. With a straight-line curve this point lies half-way along the curve.

Devaluation or Depreciation of the Currency

These are explained more fully on page 282. Briefly, to devalue or depreciate the currency is to lower it in value against all other currencies. This enables foreigners to buy our exports more easily, for they become cheaper, while at the same time foreign goods become more expensive to our own citizens. This should improve the Balance of Payments position, by increasing exports and reducing imports. The elasticity of demand for exports and imports may affect the success of this policy. If the demand for exports is elastic, so that even though each unit of exports sold brings in less foreign currency the extra demand more than offsets this, foreign earnings will increase. If the demand for exports is inelastic with respect to price the policy will be worse than useless, for the volume of exports will not increase, and those sold will bring in less earnings than before. There are similar effects on imports.

(7) Income Elasticity of Demand

Income elasticity of demand is the responsiveness of demand to changes in income, and is found by the formula

$$\text{Income elasticity of demand} = \frac{\text{Percentage change in the quantity demanded}}{\text{Percentage change in income}}$$

Income elasticity of demand is very important in planning both industrial and social requirements. In Great Britain, for example, people seem to expect that their incomes will double every twenty-five years. In order to achieve such an increase in incomes the national income must grow, at a compound rate, by $2\frac{1}{2}$ per cent per year. In other countries much more rapid rates of growth are being achieved, though the actual volume of goods being produced is not so large. Readers will remember that the volume of real goods needed to secure a 10 per cent increase in a country with a low standard of living is smaller than the volume needed to produce a $2\frac{1}{2}$ per cent increase in a wealthy country like Great Britain. It all depends on the size of the base from which you start.

When incomes rise people do not merely increase their demands for the goods they consumed formerly, but change to new products. They may enrich their lives by more varied diets, or more sophisticated consumer goods. Entrepreneurs and Governments must predict these requirements, and form opinions as to the likely elasticities of demand for various goods and services as incomes rise.

Consider a rise in incomes of 10 per cent, which leads to the following changes in demand for the five commodities shown in Table 14.

Table 14. Income elasticity of demand

Effect on demand of a 10% increase in income	Commodity				
	A	B	C	D	E
Change in demand	Fall of 10%	No change	Rise of 1%	Rise of 10%	Rise of 50%
% Change in quantity / % Change in income	$\frac{-10}{10}$	$\frac{0}{10}$	$\frac{1}{10}$	$\frac{10}{10}$	$\frac{50}{10}$
Value of elasticity	-1	0	0·1	1	5
Income elasticity of demand	Negative income elasticity	Zero income elasticity	Inelastic demand with respect to income	Unitary income elasticity	Elastic demand with respect to income

Generally speaking, the demand for inferior goods has negative elasticity as incomes rise, while the demand for consumer durables and tertiary services rises more than proportionately with rising incomes.

(8) Cross Elasticity of Demand

Sometimes it is helpful to know the change in demand for a commodity that is likely to follow a change in the price of some other commodity. This is particularly true where the goods are substitutes for one another, or are complementary goods. For example, a change in the price of butter might cause a large change in the demand for margarine, while a change in the price of petrol might influence the demand for new motor vehicles.

The responsiveness of demand for one commodity to changes in the price of another commodity is called the cross elasticity of demand. The formula is

$$\text{Cross elasticity of demand} = \frac{\text{Percentage change in quantity demanded of commodity } X}{\text{Percentage change in the price of commodity } Y}$$

(9) The Price Elasticity of Supply

This is the responsiveness of supply to changes in price. Once again it is found by the formula

$$\text{Price elasticity of supply} = \frac{\text{Percentage change in quantity supplied}}{\text{Percentage change in price}}$$

Supply Curves with Constant Elasticity

Once again perfectly elastic supply is a straight line, parallel to the X axis, while zero elasticity (supply completely unresponsive to price) is a straight line parallel to the price axis.

Perfectly elastic supply is rather improbable in real life, it indicates that at prices below P_1 suppliers are not prepared to supply at all, but at the price of P_1 they are prepared to supply any quantity required.

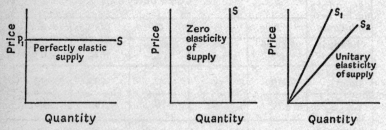

Fig. 40. Supply curves with constant elasticity

A supplier motivated by non-economic motives might behave this way, for example, if as a matter of principle he would not supply below the 'fair' price, nor charge more than the item was 'worth' even when demand was strong.

Supply with zero elasticity is quite common in real life; the paintings of Rembrandt have zero elasticity of supply and sell on the market for whatever price they will fetch.

Unitary elasticity of supply is a special case. Every straight-line supply curve passing through the origin must have unitary elasticity. Quantity supplied must change proportionately to price if the 'curve' is to be both straight and through the origin.

When Will Supply Be Elastic (i.e. Responsive to Changes in Price)?

Supply will be elastic (elasticity greater than 1) in the following cases:

(*a*) Where an entrepreneur produces for several different markets and can divert supplies to the market offering the best rewards.

(*b*) Where an entrepreneur produces a variety of products and can turn production over easily from unprofitable lines to more profitable ones.

(*c*) Where the costs of entering the industry, or the losses suffered by leaving it, are small. A stallholder whose overhead costs consist of a £2 rental charge is unlikely to hesitate about leaving his field of activity if the produce he sells proves unremunerative. A manufacturer with specific capital assets is less mobile (see page 98).

In each of these cases an increase in price will quickly attract supplies into the market, while a decrease in price will drive supplies away, or discourage the supplier so that he reduces output.

Time and the Elasticity of Supply

Time has a great effect on the elasticity of supply. In the short run the supply of many items is inelastic. For instance, milk production cannot be raised until cows are brought into calf. Apple trees take several years to grow and tea gardens even longer. To build a new factory is not the work of a week or so, but may take years to design and equip. The effect of this time-lag on prices is illustrated in the next section.

(10) Price Fluctuations and the Elasticity of Supply and Demand

Fluctuations in price are a source of much inconvenience both to producers and to consumers. In the market economies (as distinct from the planned economies) of the world the development of highly organized markets is an attempt to smooth out fluctuations in price. Chapter Eleven is devoted to a full discussion of these matters.

Generally speaking, the prices of primary products fluctuate more than prices of secondary products. Not only are the agricultural products susceptible to interruptions of supply due to bad weather, crop diseases, etc., but all primary products tend to be carried long distances to the market, so that they are peculiarly susceptible to delays due to strikes, wars, or rumours of wars. Diversion of shipping, for example, due to the closure of the Suez Canal changed the pattern of supply for many products and led to a dramatic growth in the size of oil-tankers and other bulk carriers.

Fluctuations in price are difficult to illustrate because of the ease with which wrong ideas about elasticity can be conveyed. Readers are apt to forget that elasticity refers only to a particular price: it is *not* constant all the way along a demand curve, except in the special cases of infinite elasticity, zero elasticity, and unitary elasticity.

To avoid confusion, Fig. 41 has been drawn showing two demand curves and two supply curves meeting at a point. The diagram has then been split into four parts, to illustrate the effect of four possible cases which will cause prices to fluctuate. These cases are:

(*a*) a change in demand, supply being elastic;
(*b*) a change in demand, supply being inelastic;
(*c*) a change in supply, demand being elastic;
(*d*) a change in supply, demand being inelastic.

Fig. 42 shows the effect of a change of demand, when supply is elastic or inelastic, on the price of the commodity being demanded.

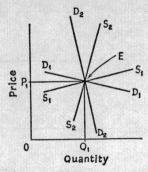

Fig. 41. Demand and supply curves with different elasticities

Note: At the price P_1 the demand curve D_1 is more elastic than the demand curve D_2, and the supply curve S_1 is more elastic than the supply curve S_2.

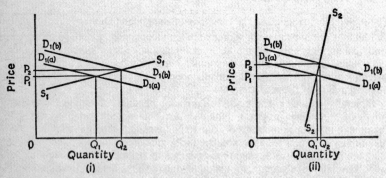

Fig. 42. Elasticity of supply and change of demand: (i) supply elastic; (ii) supply inelastic

Notes:

1. Demand is elastic like D_1 in Fig. 41.
2. The result of an increase in demand in Fig. 42 (i) is that supply adjusts easily to the changed demand, turning out the increased quantity required with only a small increase in price.
3. The result of an increase in demand in Fig. 42 (ii) is that supply adjusts with difficulty to the changed demand. To call the extra supplies on to the market at all, very large increases in price are needed, because supply is inelastic.
4. The reader should work out for himself on a piece of scrap paper what would have happened in each case if: (*a*) demand had decreased, instead of increased; (*b*) demand, instead of being like D_1 in Fig. 41, had been like D_2 in Fig. 41, i.e. less elastic.

   Fig. 43 opposite shows the effect of a change in supply when demand is elastic, or inelastic, on the price of the commodity being demanded.

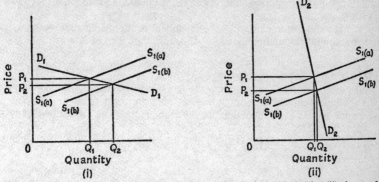

Fig. 43. Elasticity of demand and change in supply: (i) demand elastic; (ii) demand inelastic

Notes:

1. Supply is elastic, like S_1 in Fig. 41.
2. The result of an increased willingness to supply is that demand, in Fig. 43 (i), extends rapidly to consume the increased supply offered. Price falls only slightly, and the increase in goods supplied is large.
3. The result of an increased willingness to supply in Fig. 43 (ii) is that demand extends only slightly, price falls a good deal, and the extra quantity supplied is small.
4. The reader should again work out for himself the effects of: (*a*) a decrease in supplies offered by producers; (*b*) the changes that would have resulted had the supply curve, instead of being elastic as in S_1, been inelastic like S_2 in Fig. 41.

(11) Summary of Chapter Ten

1. Price elasticity of demand is defined as the responsiveness of demand to changes in price.
2. It is found by the formula:

$$\frac{\textit{Percentage change in quantity demanded}}{\textit{Percentage change in price}}$$

3. There are three demand curves with constant elasticity: the infinitely elastic curve, the unitarily elastic curve, and the curve with zero elasticity.
4. All other demand curves have elasticities which change along the curve. For such curves elasticity refers to a particular point on the curve, i.e. to a particular price.
5. Total revenue to the producer (i.e. total expenditure by the consumer) varies with price. Since fluctuations in price depend on the elasticity of demand, total revenue varies with elasticity.
6. Elasticity of demand chiefly depends on the availability of close substitutes.
7. Elasticity of supply is defined as the responsiveness of supply to changes in price. Its formula is similar to that given in note (2) above.
8. Prices fluctuate widely if supply or demand are inelastic.
9. Prices are stable if supply or demand are elastic.

10. Primary producers suffer more from fluctuating prices than secondary producers.

11. Besides price elasticity of demand and supply, income elasticity of demand, and population elasticity of demand are also of interest.

(12) Suggested Further Reading

Lipsey, R. G., and Stilwell, J. A.: *An Introduction to Positive Economics.* Weidenfeld & Nicolson: London, 3rd. Edn., 1971.

Samuelson, P. A.: *Economics: An introductory analysis.* McGraw-Hill: 8th. Edn., 1971.

Stonier, A., and Hague, D.: *A Textbook of Economic Theory.* Longmans: London, 1964.

Exercises Set 10

1. Define elasticity of demand. A refrigerator priced at 100·00 currency units is selling 1,000 models per week. When the price is cut to 95·00 the sales increase to 1,750 models per week. What was the elasticity of demand at a price of 100·00?

2. A motor car retailing at 500·00 currency units is bringing in a total revenue of 5,000,000·00 per month. When the price is lowered to 475·00 the total revenue increases to 5,500,000·00. What is the elasticity of demand at 500·00?

3. Why are percentage changes more useful than absolute changes when measuring elasticities? Illustrate your answer by reference to the elasticity of demand for two products, A and B, whose prices are cut by 10 per cent. Each improves its sales by 5 units per week. A had previous average weekly sales of 10 units, B had previously been selling 100 units per week on average.

4. In a perfect market the demand for the output of a single producer is infinitely elastic. Explain.

5. What is the relationship between the elasticity of demand and the total expenditure on a commodity by the consuming public?

6. Explain the term 'price elasticity of demand' and discuss its relevance to the taxation policy of a Finance Minister.

7. 'It is no good cutting the price of our rail tickets,' said the accountant, 'the elasticities are against us in these affluent times.' What elasticities was he referring to? How were they operating against the railway company?

8. Draw and label fully: (*a*) an infinitely elastic demand curve; (*b*) a supply curve of zero elasticity; (*c*) a curve of unitarily elastic demand.

9. What factors affect the elasticity of demand? What is the likely elasticity of demand for the following goods (assume reasonable market prices): (*a*) oranges; (*b*) iron ore; (*c*) penicillin; (*d*) a 'Spinitdry' washing machine; (*e*) petrol (gasoline); (*f*) a box of matches.

10. 'Natural rubber is in inelastic supply.' Do you agree with this statement? Justify your answer. What effect will a war affecting a major rubber-growing area have on the incomes of rubber planters in areas unaffected by the hostilities?

CHAPTER ELEVEN

COMPETITIVE MARKETS—THE INSTITUTIONS WHERE PRICE IS DECIDED

(1) Definition

A market is defined as a place where buyers and sellers are in contact with one another to fix prices.

This contact may be established directly, e.g. where retailers buy supplies at the wholesale produce markets, such as Covent Garden or Billingsgate; or indirectly through specialists, such as the brokers and jobbers on the London Stock Exchange. Physical presence in the market is not necessary; indeed, the Foreign Exchange Market is largely conducted by telephone.

Generally speaking, the major markets are such specialized affairs, and dealings are conducted in such large quantities, that the general public is ill equipped to deal upon them. For instance, the minimum contract for wheat on the Liverpool Wheat Exchange is 125 tonnes, and the minimum contract for sugar is 50 tonnes on the London Sugar Futures Market. Such markets are called **highly organized markets**, and only experts may deal on them.

While absolute perfection in the market is difficult to achieve, some of these institutions come very close to the perfect competition imagined in theoretical economics, and equilibrium price is established in conditions where perfect knowledge of the market and complete absence of friction exist. A full list of these institutions as far as the United Kingdom is concerned is given below. Overseas readers are urged to consider the institutions of their own countries, and to decide how comparable they are with British institutions.

(2) Competitive Markets in Great Britain

A full list of these markets includes:

Commodity Markets

(a) *The London Metal Exchange*, in Whittington Avenue, where copper, tin, lead, and zinc are bought and sold.

(b) *The London Tea Auctions*, in Sir John Lyon House.

(c) *The London Commodity Exchange Group*, in Cereal House. This is a group of commodity markets, some of which have been established for a very long time. Others are very recent, like the London Fishmeal Terminal Market and the London Vegetable Oil Terminal Market, both of which were set up in 1967. An interesting case which illustrates the dynamic nature of market institutions is the London Shellac Trade Association, which ceased to trade in 1966. This market, which formerly handled enormous transactions, has been affected partly by technological change (gramophone records are no longer made from shellac), but more seriously by price control in India. This has resulted in merchants obtaining the commodity at a fixed price, whatever orders they place, so that there is little point in laying in stocks when the commodity is cheap. For this reason speculation ceased to be possible and the market in 'futures' has ended.

The other products dealt in on the London Commodity Exchange group markets are:

  (i) Cocoa.

  (ii) Coffee.

  (iii) Copra, the dried 'meat' of the coconut, rich in vegetable oils, used in the manufacture of margarine and soap.

  (iv) Fishmeal (made chiefly from anchovies caught in millions off the coast of Peru). This is very rich in protein and has become vital to the broiler industry, one of the fastest-growing sections of Britain's intensive agriculture.

  (v) General Produce. This very old market was the original centre for many commodities which now have a separate market to themselves, such as rubber, coffee, tea, and cocoa. Its members still handle over 100 commodities, of which pepper and spices, aromatic oils, bristles, hair, gum, waxes, mica, and ivory are examples.

  (vi) Jute (a stong fibre from Bengal used in making sacking and carpets).

  (vii) Rubber.

  (viii) Sugar.

  (ix) Vegetable Oils. This market deals in soya-bean oil, and it is hoped to extend the market to deal in other vegetables oils in due course.

  (d) *The London Wool Terminal Market* at Mark Lane, where Australian greasy wool for future delivery is brought and sold.

  (e) *The Fur Market* in Beaver House, Garlick Hill.

  (f) *The London Grain Futures Market* at the Baltic Exchange.

  (g) *The Uncut Diamond Market* run by the Central Selling Organisation in Holborn Circus, and the *Hatton Garden Market* associated with it.

  (h) *The English Grains Market*, in the Corn Exchange, Mark Lane.

  (i) *The Gold Bullion Market*, in St. Swithin's Lane.

  (j) *The Silver Bullion Market*, Great Winchester Street.

  (k) *The Manchester Royal Exchange*, where cotton and rayon yarn, and cloth are dealt with.

  (l) *The Bradford Wool Exchange*, where 'tops' and 'noils' are bought and sold.

  (m) *The Liverpool Cotton Exchange*, traditionally the market for raw cotton.

  (n) *The Liverpool Wheat Exchange*.

Financial Markets

  (a) *The Stock Exchange*, in Throgmorton Street.

  (b) *The Discount Market*, centred around Lombard Street and Cornhill.

  (c) *The Foreign Exchange Market*, in which a few authorized dealers exchange sterling for foreign currencies.

Other Markets

  The Insurance Market, centred around Lloyd's.

  The Baltic Exchange, in St. Mary Axe, where shipping and air freight space can be chartered.

  Wholesale Produce Markets. These are very widespread, but the London ones are famous and attract produce from a wide area. They are:

(i) Covent Garden, the fruit and vegetable market, recently moved out of central London.

(ii) Spitalfields, the East End fruit and vegetable market.

(iii) Smithfield, the meat market.

(iv) Billingsgate, the fish market.

The situation of the London Markets can be seen on the map of the City of London in Fig. 44.

(3) Methods of Dealing

The methods of dealing in the commodity markets vary greatly because they are the result of a century or more of trading in the particular commodities concerned. To some extent the method is affected by the commodity itself.

Where a product has, or can be given, a uniform standard quality, dealings are made much easier, because the dealers know with certainty what they are buying and selling. For example, on the London Metal Exchange the commodities dealt in are called Standard Copper, Standard Tin, etc. The quality of these products can be scientifically tested and established.

Tea, on the other hand, is insusceptible to standardization. The quality varies not only from growing area to growing area but also seasonal differences in rainfall, etc., make the product different from year to year in the same area. Even on a given bush the leaves vary from poor to top quality. Similarly, no two sheep give wool that is alike: some sheep are contented and docile, with a good fleece, while others are temperamental and grow a poor-quality fleece. Products such as tea and wool must therefore be sampled by the buyers before they can decide on a fair price.

In particular, if a commodity can be standardized so that dealers know with certainty what they are buying and selling it makes possible a 'futures' market. Futures markets are particularly useful in reducing the risks of business life (see page 124).

The chief types of dealing are:

(a) auction sales;
(b) ring trading;
(c) challenging;
(d) private treaty;
(e) a special case—diamonds.

Auction sales occur where the product is not susceptible to standardization. It must be sampled beforehand if the buyers are to decide a fair price for the goods. At the London Tea Auctions in Sir John Lyon House the buying brokers sit round in tiered seats while the brokers representing the tea growers in India and Ceylon mount the rostrum to auction their lots. The buying brokers know which particular lots they require and have decided the limits of prices to which they will go. The highest bid wins, but sellers may specify a reserve price below which they will not sell.

The London Wool Terminal Market now operates at a much reduced level because of competition from synthetic fibres, and an increase in trading on the market at Sydney, Australia. From a peak of over 280 million *lb.* in 1959 trading has declined to less than 5 million kilograms today. This decline in trading has led to London adopting the Sydney contract, which is for 1,500 kg of Australian CWC Type 78 good merino fleece.

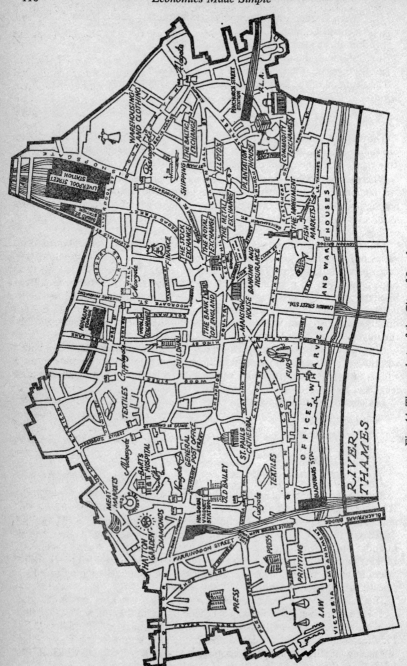

Fig. 44. The markets of the City of London

Ring trading is a method of dealing used at the Metal Exchange and the Sugar Exchange in Mark Lane. The name originates from the use of a chalk ring on the floor in years gone by to separate the buyers from the sellers.

In the Metal Exchange the ring now consists of a circle of curved benches, and there are forty members who take their seats at twelve noon for the first of the three daily sessions. Dealings are allowed for five minutes only in each metal, and are started by the Secretary of the Exchange with the hanging up of a notice bearing the name of the metal to be dealt in and the appropriate words; for example 'Tin, gentlemen, tin'. Members with tin to sell shout their offers, and those wishing to buy approach the seated sellers. Clerks standing behind make a note of the deals concluded. After five minutes the notice is changed, and the cry 'Copper, gentlemen, copper' is heard.

Besides these open-market periods when trading takes place in a very public way, private contracts are concluded outside market hours between dealers who wish to get their books straight or to complete unfilled orders. This may be done in the centre of the Metal Exchange floor, or in private offices, or by telephone.

At the Sugar Exchange a white circle is marked on the floor and buyers and sellers meet inside the circle to make binding deals. Sugar prices fluctuate very widely, because sugar is a vital food, and changes in the international situation may cause demand to rise suddenly. Also a large proportion of cane sugar is grown in the West Indies, where hurricanes can destroy a whole island's crop in a few hours. This raises prices throughout the world. The Sugar Market at Mark Lane is one of the most modern in the world, with soundproof telephone boxes and closed-circuit television to help the dealers.

In the Coffee Market at Mark Lane a similar method is used. It is called 'open outcry' on the floor of the market, and calls are made four times a day at 10.45 a.m., 12.30 p.m., 2.45 p.m., and 4.50 p.m. The wide range of qualities and varieties on offer in world coffee markets makes 'trading in actuals' a complex operation, and dependent entirely on the sellers and buyers honouring their contracts. For instance, if the grade, size, roast, or 'cup' of a consignment of coffee proves to be different from the original sample disputes can and do arise. There is no arbitration body to decide such disputes, probably because no one has more knowledge of the product than the dealers themselves.

Challenging. The London gold and silver bullion markets are less boisterous, because the number of dealers authorized to deal in these metals is limited. The half-dozen brokers sit around a small table and challenge one another until a firm price is agreed. This is said to be the price at which gold has been 'fixed' for the day, and the room where the brokers sit is therefore called the 'Gold Fixing Room'.

Whether a perfect market can be said to exist when the number of buyers and sellers is limited to half a dozen is debatable. To the extent that they are speaking on behalf of most of the users of these metals, it is probably fairly perfect.

Private treaty is the method used by the dealers on the Stock Exchange, the Baltic Exchange, the Foreign Exchange Market, the Corn Exchange, and the Insurance Markets. In the Copra Market the business is done mainly in the offices of the firms themselves. In the General Produce Market private treaty now fixes the price of most of the bargains. In the Rubber Market the floor of the house is used to conduct business, but it is by private treaty and not open outcry. Private 'treaty' means private discussion of the price to be paid. Despite the fact that the bargains they strike are private contracts between the parties, fierce competition exists in these markets.

Diamond market Some 85% of all newly mined rough gem and industrial diamonds are sold through the London based Central Selling Organisation (CSO), whose companies sort, value and sell rough diamonds to the world's major diamond cutting centres and industries. Companies within the CSO enter into agreements with the various diamond producers to purchase their entire output. In times when certain categories (there are over 2,000 of them) are in excess of demand, the CSO will hold them in reserve and offer them for sale only at a rate at which world markets can absorb them. This has created price stability for diamonds, confidence in the diamond industry and ensured that the producers do not have to worry about fluctuation in demand.

When the diamonds reach the CSO in London they are sorted and valued according to size, colour, shape and quality before they can be sold. Industrial diamonds are sold through Industrial Distributors (Sales) on a day-to-day basis to meet the demands of modern industry. Gem diamonds are sold at the ten annual sights held by The Diamond Trading Company. The Company's customers are advised of the sights and send in their requirements which are equated against present stocks. They will then come to London to inspect their diamonds, although they cannot argue about the price of the diamonds except in the case of a large stone. The customer can refuse to take the entire parcel but cannot merely take any particular part of it; however, should an error in valuation occur this would be rectified.

In Hatton Garden, close to the CSO offices, there are many traders in diamonds both rough and polished. There, diamonds are available in much smaller quantities than those supplied by the CSO.

Table 15 shows some interesting details of the major markets.

(4) Specialists who Promote Perfection in the Markets

The specialists who operate on highly organized markets fulfil a variety of functions. Their range of activities is wide, and no general description can hope to give a clear picture of a particular market or a particular transaction.

Merchant Functions. Where a dealer buys and sells on his own account, as a principal to the transaction and not as an agent, he is performing the merchanting function. The commodity belongs to him, to be resold at a profit at some future time. Whether or not he actually takes possession before reselling depends on the trading period in the market. In some situations, like the fruit and vegetable markets, physical possession of the goods is commonplace; in other markets the vast majority of the items dealt in are not handled physically by the dealers.

Agent functions. Some dealers act only as intermediaries between the producer and the retailer, selling the goods on a commission basis. Such men are called **agents**. Strictly speaking, an agent is anyone who does something on behalf of another. In commerce we call them 'mercantile agents'. A mercantile agent is defined in the Factors Act of 1889 as a person 'having in the customary course of his business as an agent the authority either to sell goods, or to consign goods for the purpose of sale, or to buy goods, or to raise money on the security of goods'.

The two most important types of mercantile agent are **brokers** and **factors.** The difference between them is a difference in the extent to which they handle goods.

Table 15. British Terminal Markets

Market	Basic commodity for 'future' contracts	Price quoted in	Minimum contract
London Rubber Terminal Market	Ribbed smoked sheet rubber Grade 1	pence per kg	5 tonnes
London Cocoa Terminal Market	Good fermented Ghana	£ per tonne	10 tonnes
Coffee Terminal Market of London	Robusta	£ per tonne	5 tonnes
	Arabica	$ per 50 kg	5,865 kg
United Terminal Sugar Market	Raw cane (or beet) sugar	£ per tonne	50 tonnes
London Wool Terminal Market	Australian CWC Type 78	pence per kg	1,500 kg
London Metal Exchange	Standard Copper	£ per tonne	25 tonnes
	Standard Tin	£ per tonne	5 tonnes
	Standard Zinc	£ per tonne	25 tonnes
	Standard Lead	£ per tonne	25 tonnes
	Silver 0·999 fine	pence per troy ounce	10,000 oz. (10 bars)
Baltic Exchange (GAFTA) (Grain and Feed Trade Association)	E.E.C. barley	£ per tonne	100 tonnes
	E.E.C. wheat	£ per tonne	100 tonnes
Silver Bullion	0·999 fine	pence per troy ounce	2,000 oz. (2 bars)
Liverpool Wheat Exchange	Varieties	£ per tonne	100 tonnes
Liverpool Cotton Exchange	Varieties	pence per kg	At will

(a) Brokers' Functions

Brokers merely sell the goods for their principals: delivery of the goods sold is left to be arranged later, for the broker does not have them in his possession. A broker knows the field of activities and the correct procedures to follow. He knows who is short of a particular commodity and who has (or will have) supplies available. His function is to bring buyer and seller together at an economical price for both. Mutual benefit is the essence of contracts, and brokers are agents who arrange contracts for the benefit of their principals. Thus stockbrokers buy and sell shares at the best market price available. Lloyd's brokers buy insurance for their clients from underwriters at the lowest premiums possible, while shipbrokers negotiate on the Baltic Exchange to sell space on ships and aircraft to cargo owners trying to move their goods.

(b) Factors' Functions

The factor (unlike the broker) is in possession of the goods. He sells the goods for his principal, delivers them up to the buyer for payment, and renders an account (less his commission) for the sums due.

Speculators' Functions. A chief feature of highly organized markets is the development of speculative functions. Practically all dealers on the market engage in speculation at some time or another, and some dealers specialize in these activities. The historical development of this function is interesting.

In any productive process there are a number of activities to be undertaken. Formerly these were all done by one firm. For instance, in the early days of the cotton trade, merchants went to America, bought cotton, arranged export procedures, shipped the cotton to Lancashire, running the risks of its physical loss or damage and the economic risks of changes in its price, paid import duties, and finally manufactured it.

Gradually these functions were split away from one another. The shipowner, for example, appeared as a specialist functionary, and the insurance underwriters assumed the risks of physical loss of the cargo. With the development of the highly organized markets the speculator appeared. His function is to carry risks through time so that the manufacturers can make contracts involving the future manufactures of finished goods in the face of fluctuating raw-material prices. If raw-material prices fluctuate, and on page 111 we have seen that they do fluctuate because of the inelastic nature of both supply and demand, then a manufacturer's contracts and tenders could be seriously upset. By assuming these risks, the speculator performs a useful function (see Fig. 45).

(5) How Speculation Works

The purely speculative activity depends on the prediction of future prices based on informed opinion. It cannot arise in situations where price control over a commodity is established, as already explained on page 115 with reference to shellac.

Suppose the speculator expects a future rise in prices. His activities are outlined in Table 16. In Table 16 the references to specific assets might be illustrated as follows:

Primary Producers. Weak demand for primary products may result in the eventual destruction of coffee plantations, return of rubber plantations to the jungle, abandonment of uneconomic mines, etc. The speculators' activities mean such actions are no longer necessary, and the very reverse may occur: new plantations may be laid out with the most modern methods being used.

Secondary Producers. Faced with high prices for raw materials, the factory owners may reduce activity to less than optimum levels, or may even close down plant. The release of speculative stocks lowers price and enables plant to continue in use, or even be expanded and improved.

(6) 'Spot' Markets and 'Futures' Markets

Markets which deal in goods for prompt delivery are called **'spot' markets** because the goods are there on the spot and can be delivered as soon as payment is made. This is true of tea, raw wool, gold, and diamonds.

'Futures' Markets, or terminal markets, are markets where the goods being

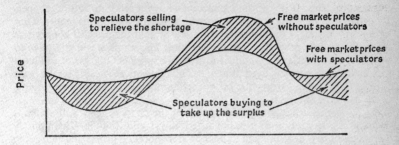

Fig. 45. Damping out fluctuations with speculation

bought and sold are not available yet, but will become available in the future. It is of the greatest importance that 'futures' prices should be firm, both to the buyer and the seller. Since an understanding of 'futures' is essential to our study of markets, let us see why the buyer of copper, or tin, or rubber needs to have firm prices for his goods, even though he does not want them for three months, or six months.

Table 16. How speculation works

How speculation works					
Present time	Action of speculator	Effect of speculation	Future time	Action of speculator	Effect of speculation
Supplies abundant	Buys supplies and holds as stock	Supplies cleared from market	Supplies short	Releases stocks and takes his profits	Shortage relieved
Demand weak		Demand strengthened	Demand strong (as predicted by speculator)		Demand satisfied
Price low		Prices firmer to benefit of primary producers who therefore do not let specific assets waste away	Prices high		Prices eased to benefit of secondary producers who therefore do not let specific assets waste away

The Importance of 'Futures' Prices

(*a*) *To the Buyer.* Imagine a manufacturer who is submitting a tender for the supply of copper piping, radiators, and boilers for a heating installation. The job is to be carried out in July, but tenders must be submitted by March 1. In deciding his price for the job the manufacturer will need to know his raw-material prices. However, these fluctuate day by day. Today's price will not do for the basis of the contract, unless the manufacturer can actually buy the copper today and keep it. This would tie up his capital and present him with storage problems. If he can find someone who will sell him 'future' copper, for delivery in July at a firm price, he will be able to submit his tender. That tender will include a profit on the contract. Should the price of copper rise above his 'future' price it will not affect him. The supplier will still have to supply at the agreed price. Should the price of copper fall, the buyer will have to honour his agreement, even though he could buy more cheaply on the open market. This will not worry the buyer, because he will still earn a reasonable profit from the contract.

(*b*) *To the Seller.* Suppose the supplier of the copper mentioned above is the selling organization of a nationalized industry in Zambia. The industry has wages to pay, development to finance, transport and processing charges to be met. It will feel happier if some at least of its eventual output is sold already. To sell 'futures' at firm prices gives the industry a guaranteed market for some of its output. The chief worry facing producers is the prospect of a fall in the world price of their goods. If the 'bottom falls out of the market' the producers may face serious losses. It is for this reason that they are willing to accommodate buyers anxious to insure against a rise in price.

A futures contract is essentially a transaction between two parties who require to cover themselves against opposite risks, one fearing a rise in price, the other a fall.

(7) Hedges—Shelter from the Bitter Economic Winds

The buyers and sellers mentioned above are willing to buy and sell 'futures' at firm prices so that some of the risk is taken out of their specialist trades. It is inconvenient, however, for them to look for one another, for they are busy with their proper occupations. This is where the speculator, whose proper occupation is to bear the risks of price fluctuations, plays his part. The buyer of copper and the seller of copper make their contracts with the speculator. Such contracts are called 'hedging' contracts. There are many different types of 'hedges', but all are designed to protect the contracting party against some business risk. Examples are:

(*a*) *A manufacturer buying raw cotton which he hopes to manufacture into cotton cloth and sell at some future time at a profit, hedges by selling 'futures' at present prices.* He is afraid that raw cotton may fall in price, and he will be unable to sell his cloth with the expected profit, because competitors who bought later at cheaper prices will undercut him. His 'futures' contract safeguards his profit; for if he is forced to accept a smaller profit on his manufactured goods it will be compensated by a profit on the hedging transaction. The profit on the hedging transaction will exactly equal the reduction in his main business activity. Fig. 46 illustrates this transaction.

(*b*) *A manufacturer who is going to need stocks in the future hedges by buying 'futures' at present prices.* By contrast, the merchant who bought 'futures' from the manufacturer was expecting to need cotton in the future, and had probably tendered for a contract based on the 'spot' prices. He feared a rise in price. If prices remain steady he obtains his cotton at the price on which his tender is based, and will make a normal profit. If prices have fallen he must still pay the former price, but he does not mind doing so. The important thing to him is that he does not want to pay more than the price he used to calculate his contract. In real life the parties do not actually supply the cotton, but 'undo the hedge' paying any balance due to the other party and he who needs the cotton buys it in the open market. The reader is now invited to consider what the manufacturer's position is if prices have risen when the future time arrives.

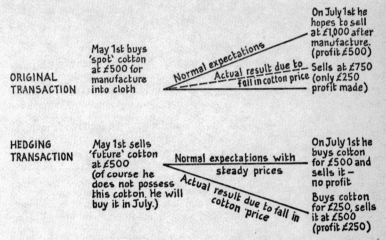

Fig. 46. How a hedging transaction helps a manufacturer to achieve his fair profit despite a fall in raw-material prices

Note: The same argument, from the opposite point of view, applies where there is a rise in price. The manufacturer makes extra profit on the original transaction, but loses on the hedge.

Settling Futures Contracts

The vast majority of futures contracts are not pressed to maturity. The manufacturer who has hedged disposes of the hedge if and when the risk run on his normal contract comes to an end. By selling the futures contract he liquidates it without physical delivery of the commodity having to take place. Despite the high probability that the contracts will never come to maturity, the risk is always there and the market traders are alert to the need to preserve their good names by ensuring that deals are honoured.

Terminal contracts are therefore registered with the London Produce Clearing House, on standard forms provided by the Clearing House and in accordance with the rules of the Terminal Market concerned. Both buyers and sellers are required to lodge with the Clearing House a deposit which is held until the contract is liquidated. If the price moves against either party, so that the deposit would not be great enough to buy him out of his difficulty, he must increase the deposit by paying in a 'margin', which is reclaimed if prices recover in his favour.

Like all clearing houses, the London Produce Clearing House eliminates intermediate buyers and sellers to establish who is finally dealing with whom. These actual contracting parties will be involved in the final settlement.

(8) The Economic Status of Speculation

One of the most difficult subjects facing the student of economics is the status of the speculator. Is the speculator a valuable member of the community, shouldering burdens others are unwilling to bear? Or is he a secret manipulator, creating market situations which will be profitable to him? Let us consider the points for and against speculation.

Points in Favour of Speculative Activities

Middlemen are to be found in various fields of activity; many of the functions they perform are beneficial to the community, and would have to be performed by someone even if the middleman did not exist. These functions include:

(a) *The Holding of Stocks.* This is a highly specialized activity. It involves carrying goods through time, against the ravages of Nature, their own inherent vices, and the criminal or negligent activities of human beings. Nature attacks with microbes, insect pests, vermin, damp, desiccation, fading by sunlight, electrolytic action, and in many other ways. Inherent vices include chemical decomposition, disease and death of livestock, susceptibility to spontaneous combustion, etc. Accidental damage, negligence, embezzlement, pilfering, and robbery are the commonest human causes of loss of stock values.

(b) *The Breaking of Bulk and the Marketing of Goods.* These two activities go hand in hand. The middleman often removes from the manufacturer the burden of marketing his goods. He often handles the transport side of the operation. He buys in bulk, and breaks the consignments down to the needs of the eventual retailer. By dealing with many manufacturers he presents a variety of goods which retailers can select, so that the total volume of transactions is reduced. 100 retailers dealing personally with 100 manufacturers requires 10,000 transactions. The middleman can reduce this to a mere 200 transactions: 100 between the retailers and the middleman, 100 between the middleman and the manufacturers.

(c) *The Carrying of Risks.* Speculators in many fields carry risks which the ordinary manufacturer or private citizen is unwilling to bear. That these risks are serious ones can be seen by the onerous qualifications for entry to the organized markets. A member of Lloyd's requires a personal fortune of £75,000 before entering, and his affairs are then subject to a compulsory audit of the utmost stringency every year. Unlimited liability is also a feature of many of these institutions. The carrying of speculative risks promotes business activity generally, benefiting not only the parties making use of the facilities but also the general public. The level of employment is raised by the greater confidence businessmen have that enterprises will be profitable. The increased scale of business thus made possible means cheaper goods for everyone.

(d) *Speculation is a specialist function.* If specialization is a good thing in general (remember Adam Smith found it to be the source of the wealth of nations), then the performance of risk-carrying functions by specialists is *prima facie* desirable. We have seen that in perfect or near-perfect markets the operations of these specialists provides a residue of dealers so essential to the creation of a market at all. There must be someone always willing to buy, or willing to sell, if the ordinary members of the public are to be able to obtain supplies when they require them, or dispose of surpluses when they have them to spare. Such activities are in the interests of all.

(*e*) *Speculative profits are the result of high prices, not the cause of high prices.* When a speculator makes profits it is because the ordinary movement of supply and demand has caused prices to rise. In these circumstances his accumulated stocks can be disposed of at more than normal profits. He is not the cause of the shortage, but the only person trying to relieve it. In the process of doing so he hopes to earn good profits which compensate him for losses on other transactions. Since speculation is a competitive business, free entry to those envious of the profits earned is available.

These are the defences put up by speculators to justify their activities, and there is a good deal of truth in them. We could unhesitatingly support these claims if in fact speculators always acted absolutely honourably.

Points against Speculative Activities

(*a*) *Market responses are speculator-induced.* The fact is that speculators do, to some extent, influence the market. In particular, many of the responses of the market are induced by speculators for their own advantage. The 'bear' who sells stocks in expectation of a fall in price induces the very response that he is hoping for. The sales he makes force market price down, and create a pattern of nervousness on the market which is to the disadvantage of the general public if personal circumstances force them to sell at this time. The 'bear' who buys back what he originally sold at a cheaper price has profited at the expense of an 'innocent' victim of market forces. It is made worse by the fact that the 'bear' may not have had any shares to sell in the first place. There is something unsavoury about a system in which a person is able to profit by selling shares he does not own to the detriment of a genuine investor. Similarly, there is something unsavoury about a 'stag', who does not want to invest in a company, applying for a large number of shares in the hopes of selling them at a quick profit. He may get a big allotment of shares, while a genuine investor is refused any shares because his application is too small.

(*b*) *The market must follow the least scrupulous speculator.* Even when strict codes of conduct are laid down and everyone is paying lip service to the maintenance of high professional standards of behaviour, the market is powerless when external forces or the pressure of events are mounting. In some recent foreign-exchange crises this has been apparent. International pressures have been pushing the revaluation and devaluation of currencies in certain directions. There is always someone with less scruples, or more to lose, than the next man. When this happens the flood barriers are down and speculative pressure mounts to promote the very events which are considered undesirable. To be left behind in such a race is to court disaster. It is difficult for the individual speculator to go against the main stream of activity. Indeed, he must often join in and swim with the current to preserve his financial position. Only a central bank with virtually limitless resources can hope to swim against the tide.

Today the worst abuses of speculation have been contained and controlled in most countries—partly by legislation, partly by taxation aimed at creaming off super-profits for the benefit of the mass of the people, and finally by a proper sense of self-discipline and the establishment of codes of conduct. At the same time the borderline between legitimate protection of one's own financial position and activity to take advantage of the market is a fine one about which it is difficult for a panel of investigators to agree. In the last analysis the choice lies between a free-enterprise society and a controlled economy.

(9) Summary of Chapter Eleven

1. A market is a place where buyers and sellers are in contact with one another to fix prices.

2. A wide variety of highly organized markets exists to fix prices for the major commodities of the world. There are similar markets for insurance, sea and air cargo space, money and stocks and shares.

3. The methods of dealing in these markets are designed to promote perfection in the market by ensuring homogeneity of products, common knowledge of prices, and elimination of friction and discriminatory dealings. The number of buyers and sellers is large, to promote competition.

4. The specialists in these markets have expert knowledge and large resources; they operate within a code of conduct which is designed to promote fair dealing on behalf of the general public. In particular, the activities of speculators on these markets, while generally beneficial and a major buttress of economic activity, must be supervised by codes of behaviour or legislation.

(10) Suggested Further Reading

Grebby, J. K., and Warson, R.: *Modern Business Training*. Macdonald & Evans: London, 1967.

Paish, F. W.: *Business Finance*. Pitman: London, 1968.

Whitehead, G.: *Commerce Made Simple*. W. H. Allen: London, most recent edition.

Exercises Set 11

1. What is a highly organized market? What is a perfect market? Discuss whether (a) The Stock Exchange or (b) The London Metal Exchange fits both descriptions.

2. 'A free market in diamonds is desirable.' Discuss the implications of this statement for: (a) a Sierra Leone citizen working diamonds outside the control of his Government; (b) a diamond producer inside the present controlled arrangements; (c) a retired actress reluctantly having to sell diamonds given to her when she was 'the toast of London'.

3. How does a 'futures' market help the manufacturer in his pursuit of ordinary business?

4. Speculators are less active in a market where the goods on sales are insusceptible to standardization. Why is this? Give examples of both types of market.

5. What do you understand by 'hedging'? What is the effect of a hedging contract taken out by a manufacturer who feared a fall in prices, if in fact prices rise?

6. 'Speculators reduce fluctuations in market prices.' 'Speculators exacerbate fluctuations in the market, so that frenzied selling, or frenzied buying occurs.' Are both these statements true? Explain each of them.

7. What is meant by a 'minimum contract'? How would such a minimum prevent an ordinary person from dealing on a market?

8. Market price is determined by the interaction of demand and supply. Explain

how this would take place in a market conducted by 'open outcry'. Can it also be true of markets conducted by 'private treaty'?

9. 'A perfect market has many buyers and sellers. The general public may not deal with underwriters at Lloyd's. Therefore Lloyd's is not a perfect market.' Do you agree? Discuss these statements.

10. 'Middlemen perform functions others prefer not to perform.' What are these functions? Are they necessary, and what rewards do middlemen receive?

CHAPTER TWELVE

PRICE DETERMINATION UNDER MONOPOLY CONDITIONS

(1) What Is Monopoly?

Monopoly means supply by only one person or firm. It can exist only where the product being supplied has no close substitutes and the supplier, for some reason, is able to exclude other firms from producing it.

It may arise in the following ways:

(a) Personal supply by a specialist or talented individual. Examples are concert violinists, hair stylists, and fashion designers.

(b) Supply under patent right or copyright. Legal force is given to the rights of inventors, authors, and composers to enjoy for some period of time the fruits of their labours.

(c) Natural monopolies: control of natural resources such as coal mines, oil wells, or mineral deposits; or the control of expensive capital assets which it is socially undesirable to duplicate. It is uneconomic to take water into houses through several pipelines for the sake of competition in the industry, or to lay two railway lines between towns when one is adequate for the traffic.

(d) Monopoly through the economies of scale. When large-scale enterprises exist in an industry it is difficult for competitors to enter that industry, for to do so they must be comparable in scale with the efficient firms already established. This grouping of a few large firms is called *oligopoly*. It is very similar in its effects to monopoly. It may even be socially unwise for new firms to enter, because it would be introducing excess capacity into the industry, which is a waste of capital. It leads to price wars, and reduced standards of quality which can imperil public safety. To avoid these evils we often find a group of suppliers co-operating to supply at fixed prices, instead of competing with one another. This is a form of monopoly, and occurs most often in industries with expensive specific assets where little product differentiation is possible. Cement rings are an example.

From Adam Smith onwards classical economists have held that monopoly was prima facie bad, and the uncontrolled behaviour of monopolists and oligopolists did much to support this view. When the first commercial television companies were formed in Great Britain extremely high returns on capital invested were achieved by some companies. Even if monopolists are in a position to exploit their monopoly, they do not always do so, as was proved in the case of cement rings, and in most countries reasonable controls have effectively restrained those who do. The first thing to notice about monopolists is that they are subject to the authority of the consumer.

(2) Monopolists are Subject to the Authority of the Consumer

A monopolist can dictate either price or quantity, but not both. One half of the decisions to be made will still rest with the consumer. Thus a monopolist who decides to produce a new type of family car may say that he is prepared to market it at a price of 2,000·00. It will be up to the body of consumers to say how many they are prepared to buy at that price. Alternatively, he may decide to make 100,000 models of the car. In that case consumer demand will decide what price to pay, let us imagine 950·00. What the monopolist cannot usually do is say, 'I will make 100,000 cars and you will buy them at £2,000·00. He is still subject to the authority of the consumer, even if he is a monopolist. The exception to this rule is where the goods concerned are a necessity of life and must be purchased by consumers.

(3) The Demand Curve and Marginal-revenue Curve of a Monopolist

In pure competition the demand curve for an *individual* supplier is a line parallel to the *X* axis, for it is an infinitely elastic demand. If an *individual* supplier in perfect competition cuts his price, however slightly, he will be inundated with orders, since his output is trifling compared with the demand of the market. The monopolist is not so fortunate. He can sell more only if he cuts the price, so the demand curve (price line) slopes down towards the right.

For example, a monopolist supplying 10 units at 1·00 each earns a total revenue of 10·00. If he increases output to 11 units, but has to cut the price to 0·99 each he will now earn $11 \times 0·99 = 10·89$. The extra unit has resulted in an extra revenue of 0·89, although it was sold at 0·99. This is because 0·01 was lost on each of the 10 units sold previously. The marginal revenue of a monopolist is therefore less than the average revenue per unit.

Because he is the only supplier of his product, the monopolist's demand curve is a market demand curve. We would therefore expect it to slope downwards to the right as explained above. The marginal-revenue curve slopes down to the right even more steeply, for, as the example shows, the marginal revenue is less than the price at which the items are sold. Fig. 47 illustrates the situation graphically.

(4) Where will a Monopolist Cease Production, and hence Determine Price?

Once again production will cease at the point where marginal cost equals marginal revenue, but the situation under monopoly is quite different from the situation already described on page 89 under perfect competition. Fig. 48 illustrates the situation.

(5) The Monopolist and the Elasticity of Demand

On page 108 we saw that when demand is elastic it will pay a firm to increase output, since total revenue will rise. When demand is inelastic a *reduction* in output will force price up, and raise total revenue. It follows that a monopolist, the sole supplier of his commodity, is best placed to exploit his monopoly when the demand for the goods is inelastic. If the goods are a necessity of life which people must buy, or if it is a habit-forming substance, they will be unable to reduce demand when price rises. Restriction of supplies in this case may force prices up to the benefit of the monopolist.

Total revenue is not the only factor affecting the output of a monopolist, of course; costs also decide whether one output is more profitable than another. If a monopolist can reduce supplies and force prices up, without at the same time raising unit costs, he will find it profitable to do so.

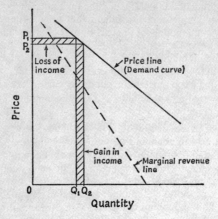

Fig. 47. The marginal revenue of a monopolist

Notes:

1. At P_1 the monopolist sells Q_1 articles.
2. If he increases output by one unit to Q_2 he will receive a lower price because of the downward-sloping demand curve.
3. The whole quantity ,Q_2, will be sold at the price, P_2, bringing in an average revenue of P_2 to the monopolist.
4. The marginal revenue (i.e. the increase in total revenue to the monopolist from the sale of the extra unit) is not P_2, but P_2 less the loss in income sustained because of the lower price on all the other units.
5. The reader should now work out for himself the effect on a monopolist's total revenue in the following cases.
    (*a*) A decision to increase output from 100 to 101 units, if price has to be lowered from 1·00 to 0·99 per unit.
    (*b*) A decision to increase output of record players from 10,000 to 12,500 if price has to be lowered from 30·00 each to 27·50 each. In this case calculate what each extra record player actually earns for the monopolist.

(6) Monopolistic Competition

In real life monopoly is relatively rare, for there are few suppliers in sole control of raw materials, and patent rights exist only for limited periods. It is therefore difficult for suppliers to keep other suppliers from entering the industry to compete with them. The more usual situation is that elements of monopoly exist alongside elements of competition. This type of market situation has been called 'monopolistic competition'. The industry consists of several firms making almost identical products, each an almost perfect substitute for the other. The small differences between them may be real or imaginary. Usually there is some subtle difference which enables the product to be 'branded' with a brand name which makes it different from similar products. Examples of brands which do represent real differences may be found in foods like jam and marmalade, prepared from special recipes.

Sometimes the differentiation is justified by the service provided. For example, dried fruits like currants and sultanas are washed, cleaned, and packed in convenient and attractive packaging. Salt is supplied in convenient packs, with an additive to make it 'run' freely, and with a pourer which is designed to prevent it spilling. In patent medicines subtle differences between products can be contrived, as in the various products, basically aspirin, which act as analgesics. More artificial is the difference between 'pink' and 'blue' paraffin.

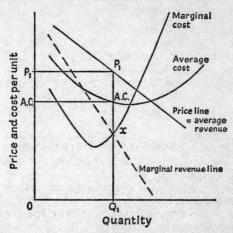

Fig. 48. Price determination in monopoly conditions

Notes:

1. The marginal-cost curve cuts the marginal-revenue curve at x, and well below the price line. Output ceases at this point with an output of OQ_1.
2. Price will be decided by the point where a line from Q_1 parallel to the price axis cuts the price line, at price P_1P_1.
3. The entrepreneur will earn revenue of $OQ_1P_1P_1$ at a cost (including normal profit) of OQ_1, *A.C.*, *A.C.* He is therefore earning super-profits of *A.C.*, P_1, P_1, *A.C. BUT these super-profits will not be competed away, as they would in competitive conditions, because the lucky man is a monopolist.*

(7) The Characteristics of Monopolistic Competition

The chief characteristics are as follows:

(*a*) *The product is not homogeneous*, but differentiated by 'brand names' into a number of 'different' products, each of which is not quite a perfect substitute for the other. Because the products are 'different' the producers can charge different prices and still sell the dearer items. The elasticity of demand for different brands is reduced, that is, the demand is less responsive to price changes because some buyers are convinced a particular brand is better and worth the extra money. Even so, the demand curve is not very inelastic. When the price is only slightly higher than the price of competitive brands customers will continue to buy their favourite brand, and demand will be inelastic. The farther apart the prices move, the greater the elasticity of the highly priced alternative, or the greater the advertising costs of maintaining inelasticity of demand. Either way the supplier is losing his super-profits.

(*b*) *There are several suppliers and entry to the industry is still possible.* The number of suppliers is still sufficiently great for quite severe competition be-tween products. In industries where large-scale operation is essential for technical reasons oligopoly (a few firms in the industry) is the usual rule; examples are the detergent industry and the oil industry. In industries with less specific assets entry is easier, and the competition can be fierce. Examples are the fashion trades, knitwear and hosiery, and prepared foods. Pharma-ceutical products are an intermediate case.

(c) *Heavy expenditure on advertising.* This is a feature of brand promotion. There are two kinds of advertising: informative advertising and persuasive advertising. Informative advertising makes clear the availability of the product, its uses and advantages, its price, quality, and terms of sale. There can be no serious objection to informative advertising. In a specialist world we are all too busy to investigate products for ourselves. The variety of our lives is enhanced by being informed about products which would otherwise escape our attention.

Persuasive advertising does not just inform, it uses subtle techniques to persuade, and even delude, the public into buying. At best it is unnecessary. It may be misleading, wasteful, and even harmful if it makes antisocial be-haviour appear desirable.

The reason why advertising is such an important feature in monopolistic competition is that firms are not content to take market price as fixed and uncontrollable (whereas the individual firm in perfect markets has to do). Because of the differentiation between products they are able to some extent to vary prices to maximize profits. In other words, they have some of the advantages of monopolists who can reduce output and force prices up so long as the demand for the product is inelastic.

Example. Certain goods are in great demand at festival times of the year. The housewife must have them whatever the price. The demand therefore is inelastic. If sellers of such goods raise prices at these times they will make excellent profits. After the festival is over housewives will not demand the same goods nearly so much, but they may do if the price is low. In other words, the demand is elastic. The entrepreneur who lowers prices will sell the product, but not quite so profitably.

We therefore find retailers following policies aimed at maximizing profits: lowering prices when demand is elastic and raising them when demand is inelastic. At one time the advertising emphasizes the low price; at the festival time it emphasizes the product's appropriateness for the festival.

(8) Determination of Prices under Monopolistic Competition

In perfect competition the low-cost firm enjoys super-profits in the short run, but in the long run new firms entering the industry will lower the price and compete away these super-profits. With monopoly conditions the monop-olist is able to maintain his short-run position into the long term because he can prevent new firms from entering the industry. With monopolistic com-petition the supplier of branded goods cannot prevent new firms entering the industry, but they cannot enter it and sell his particular brand. The decision of a supplier about the output he should produce is illustrated in Figs. 49 and 50. Before considering these the reader should note that, as with monopoly, the demand curve for a supplier in monopolistic competition slopes down towards the right. It is a market-demand curve, and the supplier can increase sales only by lowering price.

It follows that marginal revenue is again less than price, and the short-run position of a firm in monopolistic competition is therefore similar to a firm in monopoly conditions.

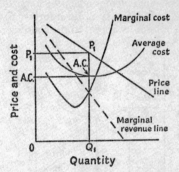

Fig. 49. The short-run position of a supplier in monopolistic competition

Notes:

1. The supplier in Fig. 49 is making super-profits with his brand equal to *A.C.*, P_1, P_1, *A.C.*
2. New firms will be attracted into the industry, selling the same goods in a differentiated form. The new supplier or suppliers will have to be aggressive in advertising and pricing policies if they are to make inroads on the market of the established brand, and to the extent that they are successful there will be a change in the conditions of demand (see page 63).
3. The demand curve for the supplier of the established brand will move to the left, a decrease in demand.
4. The marginal-revenue line will also move to the left, and some of the entrepreneur's super-profits will be competed away.

Sooner or later the competition of other brands may move the demand curve so far to the left that all the super-profits will be competed away. At this point the price line will just be touching the average cost curve. The ultimate position, at which entry to the industry by other competitors will cease, is illustrated in Fig. 50.

(9) Conclusions about Monopolistic Competition

Increasingly monopolistic competition is becoming the characteristic feature of free-enterprise market economies as far as the consumer is concerned. While perfectly competitive markets persist to facilitate the bulk handling of primary commodities, fewer and fewer of such primary products reach the ultimate consumer. The preparation of foods in hygenic pre-packed branded forms, the elimination of personal service in retail trade, the increased standardization of products, and the indifference of affluent people to minor price differences all give monopolistic competition great advantages as a method of production. We should note the following points:

(*a*) *The aim of the competitive monopolist is always to preserve his monopoly position.* The final position of the supplier shown in Fig. 50 with all his super-profits competed away is plainly a situation to be avoided at all costs. If a supplier does get to that position he will have lost the point of 'branding'. The solution is to find an endless succession of real, or imaginary, improvements in his product. This may mean the addition of unnecessary foam to household cleaners, or a change in the length of cigarettes and cigars or the endless re-designing of external trimmings on motor vehicles to make them 'new' models. This otherwise pointless activity puts off for a further few months, or years, the time when a product loses its appeal to the consumer.

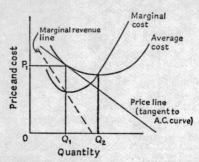

Fig. 50. The long-run position of a supplier under monopolistic competition

Notes:

1. The demand curve has moved, owing to the changed conditions of demand, so far to the left that it has become tangential to (only just touching) the average-cost curve.
2. At this point all super-profits are competed away and the firm is making normal profits only.
3. There is excess capacity in the industry; the supplier could increase output to the optimum level of minimum average cost at OQ_2 and decrease unit costs by doing so, but the marginal revenue would decrease *even more*, leaving him worse off. It is therefore a feature of monopolistic competition that excess capacity exists in the industry in the long run.

At the same time it may lead to genuine improvements which are beneficial to the public. New types of tyres, braking systems, better lighting, and design features which improve safety, economy of operation, comfort, and convenience have been introduced by motor-vehicle manufacturers as part of the process of presenting an old vehicle in a new form.

(*b*) *The industry will usually be operating at less than the optimum.* This is the same as saying that there will always be excess capacity in the industry. It would be possible, but it would not be profitable, to lower the unit cost. This excess capacity must not be exaggerated though. It is at its greatest when the firms are in such strong competition that they have reached the situation shown in Fig. 50. If the entrepreneur is active in differentiating his product the demand curve for his product will not move so far to the left, and he will be able to operate nearer the optimum while still enjoying super-profits.

(*c*) *Non-price competition must be a feature of monopolistic competition.* If the only requirement for high sales was that the goods should be cheap, i.e. value for money, then price competition would be the usual form of competition. Unfortunately a certain amount of informative advertising is indispensable, and some persuasive advertising inevitably follows. The cost of laying down production lines is so great that it is essential to exert every effort to recoup these costs with a reasonable return on capital invested as well. This can be achieved only by varying the demand for one's product by successful advertising.

(10) Summary of Chapter Twelve

1. Monopoly means supply by only one person or firm. The commodity must have no close substitutes, and the monopolist must be able to exclude other firms from its production.

2. Monopolists are still subject to the authority of the consumer, for they cannot compel the public to buy the quantity manufactured at the monopoly price. Consumers may elect to do without the goods altogether unless they are essential to life itself.

3. The demand curve for a monopolist's product slopes downwards to the right, like any market-demand curve.

4. The marginal revenue of a monopolist is always less than his average revenue.

5. The monopolist will never exceed that output where marginal cost equals marginal revenue. At this price he will earn super-profits, which will not be competed away from him because he can exclude other firms from the industry.

6. It will often pay a monopolist to reduce output to the point where the demand for his product becomes elastic.

7. Monopolistic competition is a situation where elements of monopoly exist alongside competition from other firms. This is the situation where 'branded' articles are being sold. Advertising is used to differentiate between products which are basically similar and therefore in competition with one another.

8. In the long run, monopoly profits would all be competed away by rivals entering the industry in monopolistic competition. The supplier's aim is to avoid this situation by 'new' versions of his product. This is often achieved by packaging or altering the exterior appearance of the product, while its basic structure is left the same.

(11) Suggested Further Reading

Cyriax, G.: *Monopoly and Competition.* Longman, 1970.

Lee, D. Anthony V., and Skuse, A.: *Monopoly.* Heinemann, 1969.

Lipsey, R. G., and Stilwell, J. A.: *An Introduction to Positive Economics.* 3rd. Edn. Weidenfeld & Nicolson: London, 1971.

Robinson, E. A. G.: *Monopoly.* Nisbet: 1941.

Robinson, Joan: *Economics of Imperfect Competition.* Macmillan: London, 1933.

Exercises Set 12

1. What is monopoly? In what different ways may monopoly arise? In what circumstances can monopolists dictate both prices and output?

2. 'The price line for a monopolist slopes downwards towards the right. The price

line for a firm in pure competition is horizontal.' Explain. Now explain what would be the marginal revenue in each case.

3. How is price determined in pure competition and under monopoly conditions? Illustrate your answer with fully labelled diagrams.

4. The monopolist will find it profitable to restrict output as long as the demand for his product is inelastic. Discuss.

5. What is monopolistic competition? In your answer refer to any industries you know which operate in these conditions.

6. 'Advertising promotes prosperity.' 'Advertising is wasteful.' Discuss these alternative views.

7. 'The purpose of advertising is to alter the demand curves for products, so that they continue to earn super-profits.' Explain.

8. 'In the short run suppliers under monopolistic competition are monopolists. In the long run they are the marginal firms in competitive industries.' Explain, with diagrams, the short-run and long-run positions of suppliers under monopolistic competition.

9. 'The monopolist cannot sell his product at any price he likes.' Comment on this statement, bringing out the way in which prices of goods supplied by monopolists are decided.

10. What is meant by the term 'excess capacity in an industry'? Why is this capacity not used?

CHAPTER THIRTEEN

FURTHER ASPECTS OF DEMAND AND SUPPLY

(1) Interrelated Demands

(a) Joint, Complementary, or Derived Demand

Sometimes two commodities may be so related that the demand for one affects the demand for the other. They may be in **joint demand,** with one commodity complementing, i.e. completing, the other. Common examples of goods in joint or complementary demand are knives and forks, strawberries and cream, whisky and soda, or bread and butter. Sometimes the joint nature of the demand is a **derived demand,** one of the commodities being a dominant commodity, the demand for which calls forth a demand for the second commodity. The motor car is strongly demanded, but as it will not run without petrol, the demand for petrol is derived from the demand for motor transport.

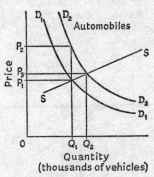
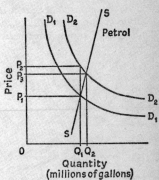

Fig. 51. Joint demand: motor cars and petrol

Notes:

1. The change from D_1 to D_2 represents a similar proportional increase over D_1, in each case.
2. For the purpose of this example, vehicles are imagined to be in elastic supply but the supply of petrol is inelastic. Consequently, the change in demand affects the price of the two goods differently.
3. Both products eventually settle at a price of P_3 and a quantity of Q_2. Because of the different elasticities of supply the price of vehicles rises by one-ninth, but the price of petrol increases by about half.

Joint, complementary, and derived demands are similar, in that an increase in the demand for one product leads to an increase in the demand for the other. What effect such a change in demand has on the price of the commodities depends on the conditions of supply. In Fig. 51 the supply curves have been drawn at different slopes to indicate different elasticities, but readers are reminded that slope is *not* the same as elasticity.

The reader is now invited to think for himself what would be the effect on the price of petrol of a change in the conditions of *supply* of motor vehicles. Imagine that a major vehicle manufacturer has restructured his plant to lower prices, i.e. to give a new supply curve for cars. What will be the effect of this on the demand for vehicles and on the demand for, and price of, petrol? No similar change in the conditions of supply of petrol has occurred.

Derived Demand—a Special Case. A special case of derived demand is the demand for the factors of production, which is derived from the demand for 'utilities' to satisfy 'wants'. If entrepreneurs are to produce, they must have land, labour, and capital. The demand of the motor-car manufacturers for land, premises, plant and machinery, raw materials, labour, and power is derived from the need to produce motor vehicles to satisfy the strong demand for them.

(b) Competitive Demand of Substitutes

Sometimes one commodity is a substitute for another, and an increased demand for one will lead to a reduction in demand for the other. An obvious example is margarine, which is a substitute for butter. Similarly, modern artificial fibres are excellent substitutes for natural fibres. An increased use of fluffy synthetic fibres will lead to a decline in the demand for wool. But the effect is the opposite of the situation with joint demand: an increase in demand for one commodity reduces the demand for the substitute. In Fig. 52 the conditions of supply have been assumed to be similar.

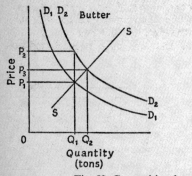 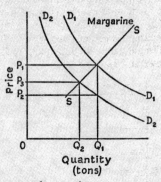

Fig. 52. Competitive demand: butter and margarine

Notes:

1. Owing to some change in the conditions of demand, butter is more strongly demanded. The price of butter rises from P_1 to P_2, settling at P_3 as the quantity supplied extends from Q_1 to Q_2.
2. Margarine is now not demanded so strongly, since butter has been substituted for it. Price falls from P_1 to P_2, but recovers to P_3 as supply contracts from Q_1 to Q_2.

(c) Competitive Demand—the Need to Choose

Substitution takes place not only when the qualities of the substitute are almost identical with those of the goods it replaces but also when the purchase of one commodity prevents the purchase of the other. To this extent all goods are in competitive demand, and especially where a particular product is expensive. The family buying its first motor car finds it must give up many other items it previously enjoyed, and a young couple with a large mortgage may postpone having a family temporarily.

This type of competitive demand affects the total demand for any particular class of goods, and explains why prosperity in particular industries is often accompanied by a decline in business elsewhere. It illustrates again the idea of 'opportunity cost': that having selected one opportunity, the other opportunities which we might have chosen are lost to us.

(*d*) *Composite Demand*

Many commodities are non-specific, that is they may be used for a variety of purposes. Steel may be used to build ships, lay railways, store fuel oil, make consumer durables like washing machines and refrigerators, or form the framework of hospitals, hotels, and office blocks. The demand for steel is the sum of all these varied demands. Such a demand is said to be a **composite demand.**

(2) Interrelated Supply

(*a*) *Joint Supply*

Some products are in joint supply, that is, one cannot be produced without the other. We cannot increase the supply of hides without producing beef, or the supply of wool without increasing mutton. In the extraction of petrol from crude oil profitable disposal of the many by-products is essential if costs of the main process are to be reduced. By skilful use of petrochemical technology, the oil industry uses the majority of its derivatives, but not without affecting the price of any commodities with which they compete.

Simple cases of joint supply, like hides and beef, may be illustrated as shown in Fig. 53.

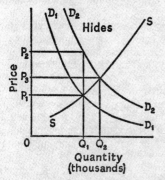 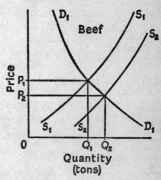

Fig. 53. Joint supply: hides and beef

Notes:

1. A change in demand for leather goods increases the demand for hides. Demand moves from D_1D_1 to D_2D_2 and supply extends to Q_2. Price settles at P_3.
2. The increased output of hides throws more beef on the market. The supply of beef therefore changes from S_1S_1 to S_2S_2, but there has been no increase in demand. This means that the price of beef must fall to P_2. As it does so, demand extends to consume the extra output.

(b) Competitive Supply—Choice of Output

The supply of certain goods follows naturally from circumstances beyond man's control. A Canadian fur-trapper, for example, cannot suddenly decide to grow bananas or coffee beans. More often we choose what we will produce, and to this extent the alternative outputs are in competitive supply.

If we plough up grazing land to sow wheat the supply of milk and beef will be reduced, while that of wheat increases. In manufacture entrepreneurs choose between different products; in service trades they make different facilities available.

On a broader view, the competition between entrepreneurs for factors (land, labour, and capital) makes choice essential. We must choose not only between individual products but also between broad alternative policies. Shall we have more material goods or more leisure, more education or more food, more travel or more defence? Since the factors we possess are limited, we cannot have everything.

(3) The Revealed Preference Theory

This theory holds that the preferences which a household has already revealed will give a clue to its behaviour when prices change, and explain what quantity or range of quantities it will demand in the new situation. This readjustment to a new basket of goods can be explained by dividing the effect of the price change into two different parts: the **substitution effect** and the **income effect**. The substitution effect will encourage the household to substitute the cheaper commodity for other goods if a fall in price has occurred; or other goods for the dearer commodity if the price has risen.

The income effect arises because a change in the price of goods always affects the **real incomes** of households, i.e. their income in terms of what can be bought with their money. A fall in prices increases real incomes, and a rise in prices reduces real incomes.

It can be shown that the substitution effect is always 'non-negative', by which is meant that it always does what is expected. It leads a household to buy more of a cheaper product, and can never lead it to buy less. It leads a household to buy less of a dearer commodity, and can never lead it to buy more.

The income effect, by contrast, may be positive or negative. When real incomes rise we tend to buy more of most commodities, but with some commodities increased income will enable us to change our way of life, alter our diet, etc., so that less of some goods are now demanded. These are the so-called 'inferior goods' (see page 71). Fig. 54 explains the theory in non-mathematical terms.

(4) The Theory of Choice—Indifference-curve Analysis

Another useful technique for considering how consumers choose between alternative satisfactions is **indifference-curve analysis**. For this technique we build up a pattern of indifference curves, each recording a chain of choices between alternatives which yield equal satisfaction.

Consider a simple case of two commodities M and N which are being weighed against each other. The consumer may make the initial decision to

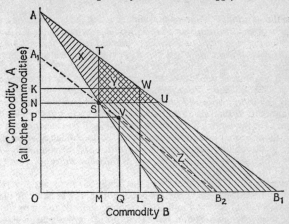

Fig. 54. The substitution effect and the income effect of a change in price

Notes:

1. Commodity *A* represents all other commodities except commodity *B*.
2. The household under consideration can buy any combination of *A* and *B* which it likes. It can buy anywhere inside the triangle *AOB*, but it cannot move beyond the line *AB*, which is the limit of combinations of commodity *B* and all other commodities which this household can afford. This line is therefore called the household's budget line. If it bought *OB* of commodity *B* its entire budget would be spent and it could buy no other goods at all. If it bought *OA* it would spend its entire income on other goods and not buy any of commodity *B* at all. Let us imagine it buys at the point *S* on *AB*, i.e. *OM* of commodity *B* and *ON* of all other goods.
3. When the price of *B* falls the household is now able to buy a larger basket of goods, its real income has risen because all the possible points in the shaded area are now available to it as alternatives. To get maximum satisfaction it should move to some point on *AB₁*, its new budget line. But which point will it choose?
4. First notice that in the shaded area *X* it will only be getting smaller quantities of commodity *B* than *OM*. It is unlikely to choose to change its purchases to any point between *A* and *T*, because it has already revealed a preference for having *OM* of commodity *B*, even when it was expensive. Now it is cheap it will, if it is behaving logically, buy more of commodity *B* because it will substitute commodity *B* for other goods. The only thing that could make it move its purchases into the shaded area *X* would be if the increased real income led to a *negative income effect*, i.e. if commodity *B* were an 'inferior good' and no longer attracted this household since it had become more affluent.
5. Similarly, in the shaded area *Z*, purchases include larger quantities of commodity *B*, but smaller quantities of other goods. The household will therefore be unlikely to choose any point on the budget line between *U* and *B₁*, for it has already revealed a preference for having *ON* of other goods. Only if the substitution effect was very strong indeed, leading to a large increase in consumption of commodity *B*, or if the income effect was so excessively positive that other goods were abandoned from a desire to purchase commodity *B* (which would therefore be 'goods of ostentation') would a family shift its purchases to such a point.
6. The most likely position is somewhere between *T* and *U*. (cont'd)

7. To see the *substitution effect* we must imagine that there is no income effect at all, which involves imagining that as real income rises (due to the fall in price of B), money income is reduced to keep the household only as well off as it was before. This involves sliding the budget line AB_1 parallel to itself until it passes through the original preference point S. The household is now able to afford the basket of goods it was buying previously. But will this now be a sensible basket of goods, or should it rearrange its purchases somewhere along the dotted line A_1B_2? Clearly anywhere between A_1 and S would not be sensible, since it involves less of commodity B than its already revealed preference, and commodity B is now cheaper. The household, if it is acting logically, will purchase more of commodity B. It will therefore move somewhere along the dotted line SB_2. Let us suppose it moves to the point V, substituting a quantity MQ of commodity B for other goods, which are reduced to OP. MQ is the *substitution effect* on this family's demand for commodity B.

8. However, in fact the real income of the family has risen, and it is really able to afford baskets of goods on the budget line AB_1. The most likely place for it to choose is a point between T and U. This point will be W, found by sliding the new budget line A_1B_2 and the point V out to its proper position again at AB_1. We now have the household enjoying OL units of commodity B and OK units of other commodities. QL units of commodity B is the *income effect*.

9. Remember that had the income effect been negative, as it would have been for a poor family subsisting on inferior goods, the income effect could have moved demand for commodity B down to lower levels, somewhere between T and W, leaving the household enjoying a more satisfying basket of goods.

10. It follows that for most goods the demand curve will slope downwards to the right, since the substitution effect will increase demand for the commodity as it becomes cheaper, and so will the income effect, if the income elasticity of the commodity is greater than zero. If the income elasticity of the commodity is negative, then the income effect will counteract the substitution effect, and if it is sufficiently great to cancel out the substitution effect altogether the household will be seen to buy less of commodity B, which must therefore be an 'inferior good'. The demand curve in such a case will be regressive.

11. To conclude, in this example we have:

   (*a*) a substitution effect of MQ extra units of commodity B being purchased;
   (*b*) a positive income effect of QL extra units of commodity B being purchased; and an extra amount NK of other goods;
   (*c*) a total extra consumption of ML units of commodity B and NK units extra of other goods.

have four units of M and seven units of N. Suppose now that he decides that one unit of M is equal to two units of N, then a change either to $5M$ and $5N$ or to $3M$ and $9N$ will not affect his total satisfaction, in other words, he will be *indifferent* between them. What about a change to $2M$ and $11N$? This might also be acceptable to *this* consumer, because there are millions of different consumers, all of whom will have different preferences, but more likely the increasing utility of M to the average consumer, and the decreasing marginal utility of N as he gets a larger supply, will leave him demanding greater quantities of N for each succeeding unit of M surrendered. Therefore $2M$ and $12N$ is more likely to leave him as satisfied as he was before. A full table of 'indifferences' might be as shown in Table 17, where the original choice is shown in a box.

When shown graphically this results in a diagram like Fig. 55.

Suppose now that the original choice had been $5M$ and $8N$. This would have given our consumer greater satisfaction, since he would have had more of both commodities. The indifferences resulting from this new position are displayed in Table 18.

Table 17. Indifference choices

	Other acceptable choices					First choice	Other acceptable choices		
Units of commodity M	16	12	9	7	5	4	3	2	1
Units of commodity N	1	2	3	4	5	7	9	12	16

(Note: It is assumed that the combinations of M and N shown above yield *this* consumer equal satisfaction.)

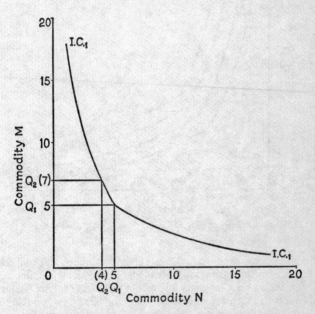

Fig. 55. An indifference curve

Note: At any point along this curve the consumer will be equally satisfied. At Q_1 he will purchase 5 units of M and 5 units of N. At Q_2 he will purchase 7 units of M and 4 units of N. He is indifferent to which he has, for his satisfaction is the same in either case.

Table 18. Further indifference choices

	Other acceptable choices					First choice	Other acceptable choices			
Units of commodity M	16	13	10	8	6	5	4	3	2	1
Units of commodity N	2	3	4	5	6	8	10	13	17	22

(Note: It is again assumed that *this* consumer derives equal satisfaction from all these possible combinations)

Similarly, further groups of choices at higher levels of satisfaction could be drawn up to give a pattern of indifference curves, as shown in Fig. 56.

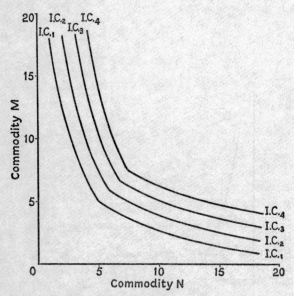

Fig. 56. Pattern of indifference curves

The question now is which of these possible choices will our consumer actually pick? Naturally the consumer would like to select a choice on one of the indifference curves a long way away from the origin O, since the farther he is from O, the greater the quantities of both products he will be able to enjoy, and the greater the satisfaction to be achieved. However, his income is limited, and the portion of it to be spent on these two commodities is even more limited. We can discover the actual choice made by imagining that the total sum to be spent on these two commodities is actually spent on one of them. Suppose it would just buy 20 units of commodity M. Alternatively, if it was all spent on commodity N it would just buy $8N$. A line joining $20M$ to

8*N*, the budget line of the consumer, is shown as *PQ* in Fig. 57 and indicates the possible combinations of *M* and *N* that can be afforded. He can spend this amount of money in any way he likes, but the way that is going to yield him the greatest satisfaction is the point on the line *PQ* which touches the indifference curve farthest from *O*. This is the point *R* on IC_2. His actual choice will be 10 units of *M* and 4 units of *N*. This is shown in Fig. 57.

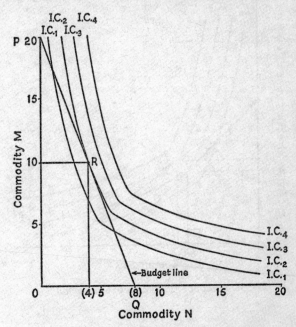

Fig. 57. Buying to achieve maximum satisfaction

What Is the Point of Indifference-curve Analysis?

Indifference curves enable us to explain the behaviour of an individual balancing two commodities one against the other. The marginal-utility theory requires us to believe that the individual can measure in money terms the satisfaction to be derived from an additional unit of a commodity. Advocates of 'indifference' analysis maintain that it is much more sensible to imagine individuals weighing up the satisfaction to be obtained from different combinations of two commodities. If we wish to imagine him weighing up the satisfaction to be derived from different combinations of many commodities we can make one of the axes in the diagram represent money, i.e. all other commodities.

In an elementary textbook it is inappropriate to go deeply into this analysis, but some illustrative examples of the application of indifference curves are given in Figs. 58–61.

(a) The Effect of Changes in the Prices of Commodities.

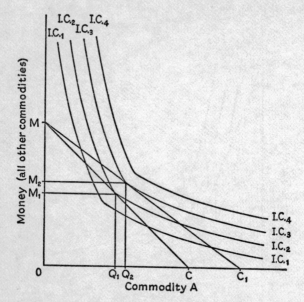

Fig. 58. Effect of a fall in price of a commodity

Notes:

1. The total money available is M. If all this is spent on the commodity at the starting price it will buy OC of the commodity. The indifference curve IC_2 indicates that the consumer would like to have any combination of money and goods on that curve, but as can be seen, his budget line indicates only one possible choice: he can have OQ_1 of the commodity and OM_1 of money—the rest of the money M_1M being spent to buy the commodity.
2. When the price of the commodity falls the money is now sufficient to buy OC_1 of it. The line MC_1 touches the third indifference curve IC_3. The consumer will buy more (OQ_2) of the now cheaper commodity, and keep OM_2 of the money. Since the indifference curve IC_3 is farther from the origin, it is clear that the consumer has increased satisfaction from both his purchases and the extra money left.
3 The reader is now invited to draw a similar diagram showing the effect of an increase in the price of a commodity.

(b) The Effect of Inflation (a Fall in the Value of Money)

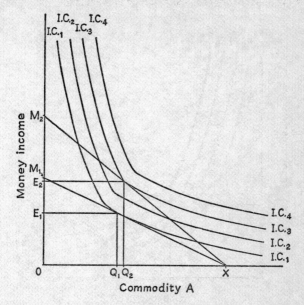

Fig. 59. The effect of inflation

Notes:

1. In inflation the income earned by the factors of production rises as fast as, or even faster than, the price of goods. This effect is discussed fully on page 329. For the purpose of this diagram let us imagine that higher incomes are being received, but prices rise proportionately so that only the same quantity of goods and services can in fact be purchased if total income is spent.

2. Money incomes have risen from M_1 to M_2, but outputs of goods and services have not risen, so that prices have altered to equate monetary demand and the supply of utilities. As a result, M_1 and M_2 are both used to purchase OX of commodity A.

3. The higher income is a tangent to indifference curve IC_3. Although real incomes are not higher, because the money incomes will buy only the same quantity of real goods, the consumer is deluded into: (i) buying more of A, because the extra money in his pocket has less utility than formerly; (ii) thinking that the larger residue of money (OE_2 in the diagram as against OE_1) is 'more' in real terms.

4. He therefore experiences more satisfaction in both real and psychological terms.

5. The reader is now invited to draw a similar diagram to show what happens to consumer satisfaction in a deflationary period.

(c) The Effect of a Rise in Income.

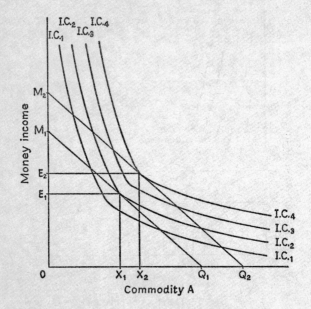

Fig. 60. The effect of a rise in income

Notes:

1. With income of M_1 the consumer can buy Q_1 of commodity A. In fact, he will buy OX_1 of commodity A, for a total expenditure of E_1M_1, retaining the balance of money. This gives him the maximum satisfaction.
2. When he experiences a real increase in income to M_2 he can now purchase Q_2 of commodity A, but will again purchase that quantity which maximizes his satisfaction. This point is to be found on the indifference curve IC_4, when he will purchase OX_2 of commodity A for a total expenditure of E_2M_2.
3. As can be seen, the satisfaction achieved has been increased, which is to be expected when incomes rise.
4. Readers are now invited to draw a similar diagram showing how the choice of a consumer will be affected by a fall in income, and what effect it will have on his satisfaction.

(*d*) *The Income and Substitution Effects with Indifference Curves.* When the price of a commodity falls we have two effects: (i) a **substitution effect** as the consumer substitutes the cheaper commodity for other goods; (ii) an **income effect** as the consumer's real income is increased by the change in prices. These effects have already been noticed in the revealed preference theory (see page 143).

The same effect can be shown by combining Figs. 58 and 59 into one diagram as in Fig. 61.

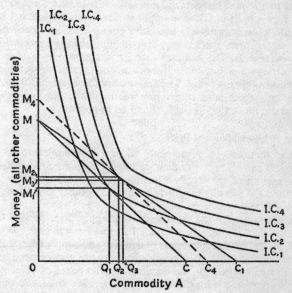

Fig. 61. Income and substitution effects on the change in price of a commodity

Notes:

1. The price of commodity *A* has changed so that more can now be bought of it with the same income.
2. Instead of buying OQ_1 of the commodity and keeping OM_1 money, the consumer now buys OQ_3 of the commodity and keeps OM_3 of money.
3. Imagine that his income had changed enough to buy him the same satisfaction (indifference curve IC_3) as he is now able to enjoy. This involves sliding out from the budget line MC a new budget line, M_4C_4, parallel to MC. This budget line is a tangent to the indifference curve at a point M_2Q_2. Therefore the *income effect* is a change from Q_1 to Q_2 and from M_1 to M_2, while the *substitution effect* is a change from Q_2 to Q_3 and from M_2 to M_3.

(5) Price Controls

The price mechanism decides what goods shall be produced and to whom they shall be supplied. It is a self-regulating mechanism which calls on to the market supplies large enough to satisfy the demand. If all markets were perfectly free the price mechanism would be a very satisfactory system for distributing 'scarce' supplies among consumers. The fact is, however, that not all markets are perfectly free. Many goods are put on the market that would not be demanded at all if people were left alone. Such goods have to be forced on buyers by persuasive advertising. Critics of the price mechanism hold that the creation of artificial 'wants' in this way is undesirable, and diverts scarce resources, which could be more usefully employed in other ways, into the production of unnecessary goods. Other sources of complaint against the price mechanism are the anti-social overtones of a system which is incapable of responding to anything but demand and supply. If addicts demand heroin the market will supply it; but Society ought to have a say in such matters.

In real life, Governments and legislative bodies interfere a good deal in the free play of the price mechanism, and manipulate the market to achieve desirable social ends. The weapons used are taxation, which raises effective prices; subsidies which lower effective prices, and price controls, which dictate maximum and minimum prices. The first two are discussed in Chapter Twenty-nine. The last, sometimes called physical controls, have interesting side effects, and are illustrated in Figs. 62 and 63 opposite.

(6) Market Price and Normal Price

Sometimes these two terms are confused, and as they relate to very similar situations, it is as well to clarify their meaning. Prices are fixed in the market by the interaction of the forces of supply and demand. Both the quantity demanded and the quantity supplied are affected by the price, and are brought into balance at the equilibrium price.

Market price refers to the short-term equilibrium price decided from day to day in the market-place as a result of short-term influences. Where conditions are stable, i.e. the conditions of demand and supply are not changing, the industry settles down to a point where supply and demand are nicely matched. For example, if on the demand side the prices of other goods are not changing particularly, or the income of buyers is stable, or changes in the number of buyers and their scales of preference are not great, then the entrepreneurs will produce what is necessary to meet demand. On the supply side, the entrepreneurs must not be faced with changes in the conditions of supply; international prices of raw materials must be steady and wages and interest rates reasonably stable too. If short-term fluctuations are not exerting much influence the industry settles down to the point where the supply is nicely adjusted to demand, and the rate at which the commodity is consumed exactly equals the rate at which it is produced. Price will now be stable, and this long-run equilibrium price is called **normal price**.

(7) Supply Curves

The Supply Curve of a Single Firm in a Perfectly Competitive Market

We have already established the following rules:

(*a*) No firm will produce at all unless its total revenue exceeds its total variable cost. This is because it will prefer to shut down and produce nothing. That way it suffers losses equal to its total fixed costs. To produce at prices so low that total revenue does not even cover total variable cost would be to add variable losses to fixed losses.

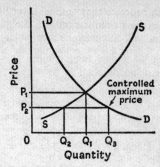

Fig. 62. Maximum price controlled: rationing

Notes:

1. Market price is P_1 and the quantity supplied is Q_1.
2. For some reason, perhaps because the commodity is a basic food in wartime and the market mechanism is enabling the rich to eat while the poor starve, the Government fixes a maximum price of P_2.
3. At this price quantity Q_2 is distributed by the suppliers, but the people would like to buy quantity Q_3. This means that there is a serious shortage. Unscrupulous shopkeepers will keep supplies under the counter for favoured customers.
4. The only fair way to solve the problem is to introduce a rationing system.

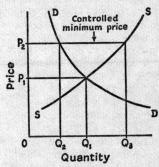

Fig. 63. Minimum price controlled: State stockpiling

Notes:

1. Market price is P_1 and quantity supplied is Q_1.
2. For some reason, usually to guarantee farm incomes, the Government decrees that prices cannot fall below P_2.
3. At this price people only wish to buy Q_2 of the commodity, but suppliers insist on turning out Q_3.
4. Since the public will not buy the commodity, the Government has to do so, and vast stockpiles of food and raw materials are built up which have been purchased with taxpayers' money. Sometimes quite ridiculous situations develop, with hungry people unfed while granaries are bursting. The United States has at times been in great difficulties because of such stocks, and has had to adopt the 'soil bank' scheme. This pays farmers when they *don't* produce, leaving the ground to gain in fertility by lying fallow. The Common Market countries similarly from time to time have huge reserves of farm products, butter mountains and wine lakes.

(*b*) It will pay a firm to produce that output where marginal cost rises to equal marginal revenue. At any point before this the marginal unit will cost less than its sale price, and will therefore be profitable.

If we now consider Fig. 64 we see that the supply curve is the same as the marginal-cost curve once it has risen above average variable cost.

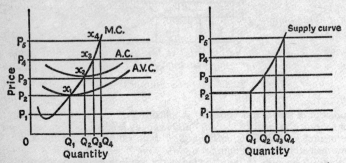

Fig. 64. The supply curve of an individual firm in a competitive market

Notes:
1. At a price of P_2 with an output of Q_1 the total revenue ($OQ_1x_1P_2$) exactly equals the total variable cost ($OQ_1x_1P_2$). A firm that is not already in the industry would not come in at this point because it would be losing its fixed costs. A firm already in the industry, but closed down because of low prices, would now find it worth while to start up production.
2. At each successive price P_3, P_4, P_5 the firm is prepared to supply more, i.e. Q_2, Q_3, Q_4, because it will be profitable to supply until the marginal cost rises to equal the marginal revenue, i.e. the price per unit.
3. *For the individual firm in a competitive industry the supply curve is the same as the marginal-cost curve above the minimum average variable cost.*

The Supply Curve of a Competitive Industry

An industry consists of low-cost firms, medium-cost firms, and high-cost firms. At low prices only the low-cost firms will supply; as prices rise medium-cost firms will find it possible to produce at a profit and will start up, while at very high prices even the high-cost firms come in with some supplies to the market. The supply for a competitive industry must be the sum of the quantities supplied by the individual firms. Taking the supply curve in Fig. 64 as an example, and adding a second firm with higher costs as in Fig. 65, the supply curve of this two-firm industry is the horizontal addition of the individual supplies.

Is there a Supply Curve under Monopoly Conditions?

A supply curve is essentially a pictorial representation of the quantities of goods supplied by the industry at certain prices. In monopoly conditions the sole supplier is not bound by any automatic relationship between supply and price, indeed, he is able to manipulate price by varying supply if the goods he produces are in inelastic demand. The supply is therefore subject to the whim of the supplier. While he still equates marginal cost to marginal revenue, and will therefore never produce a unit if it means a decline in total profit, he is able to choose how much he will produce. Of course, he will choose to maximize profits usually, so that he will produce that output which equates marginal cost and marginal revenue, but he may settle for less than maximum profits if he likes.

It follows that there is no unique relationship between price and supply under monopoly conditions, i.e. there is no relationship which follows automatically from a change in demand.

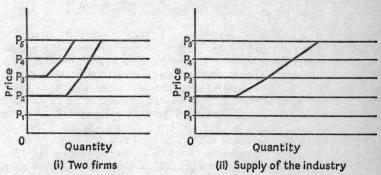

(i) Two firms   (ii) Supply of the industry

Fig. 65. The supply curve of an industry in a competitive market.

Notes:

1. The individual supply curves of two firms are shown in (i) above. Of course, in real life there would be many such firms.
2. The supply curve of the industry is the horizontal addition of the outputs of all the firms. Two firms' outputs have been added in (ii) above, but in practice there would be many such firms, whose outputs (supplies) are decided by the shape of their marginal-cost curves (above minimum average variable cost).

(8) Discriminating Monopoly

Sometimes a monopolist can sell the same product at different prices to different customers. For example, a suit sold in a well-to-do area may fetch a better price than a similar suit sold in a less fashionable area. Cement manufacturers often sell bulk cement at a very much lower price than they sell to retail customers, even though the sacks are identical. Railways often charge special rates to certain customers or charge the traffic what it will bear. Surgeons often supply the same services free to poor patients as they charge expensively to the accounts of rich patients. Obviously price discrimination cannot take place under perfect market conditions; some element of monopoly must exist if the discrimination is to succeed.

Consumer Surplus and Price Discrimination

In perfect competition there is only one market and only one market price for each product. In monopoly or monopolistic competition there are a whole series of prices, represented by the demand curve shown in Fig. 47. If goods are sold at a price of 1·00, because that price is the only price at which the monopolist's output can be sold, it does not alter the fact that some people buying the goods at that price would have been prepared to pay 1·10 or 1·20 or even 2·00. Economists say that such a consumer is enjoying a **consumer's surplus**, i.e. a bonus of satisfaction which results from the monopolist's decision to lower his price and sell a bigger output.

Clearly a consumer's surplus represents a loss to the monopolist. If he could strike a bargain with every customer, and get that customer to pay what the commodity is worth to him, instead of the market price, he would improve his profits. This he can do when he is able to sell to different customers at different prices.

In order to do this the following conditions must be fulfilled:

(a) *It must be possible to keep the 'markets' apart.* Sometimes markets are separated by physical barriers like frontiers. Sometimes they are separated by high transport costs, so that it will not benefit a consumer to buy in the remote market, even though prices there are cheaper. Sometimes contractual separation may be achieved, by requiring the customer supplied at the cheap price to enter into an agreement not to resell to anyone at less than the open-market price. Such restrictive practices have to be registered under the Restrictive Trade Practices Act as far as Great Britain is concerned, but are not prohibited if they are found to be in the public interest.

(b) *The elasticity of demand in the two markets must be different.* There will be no point in offering two different prices if the elasticity of demand of the two groups of customers is the same. It is the refusal of the favoured customer to buy unless terms are made favourable to him that makes the monopolist offer the cheaper rate. In other words, the favoured customer has a more elastic demand than the unfavoured customer. For example, a large industrial user of gas might make special arrangements for a preferential rate in return for using this fuel rather than coal or oil. Cheap-rate electricity at off-peak hours for domestic heating attracts householders into installing electrical storage heaters rather than other heaters using alternative fuels.

The result of these discriminating policies is a larger volume of output, which reduces the excess capacity in the monopolist's undertaking and brings him nearer to the optimum position at which a competitive industry works.

The discriminating monopolist now has the problem of equating the marginal cost of his entire output with a marginal revenue made up of two parts: the marginal revenue to be earned from the consumers in the normal market (called Market I in Fig. 66), and the marginal revenue to be earned from the privileged customers (Market II in Fig. 66). Of course, there could be several such privileged customers. The results are shown in Fig. 66.

(9) Summary of Chapter Thirteen

1. Joint or complementary demand occurs when two goods are used or consumed together, e.g. bread and butter.

2. Derived demand occurs when the use of one of the two goods which are in joint demand follows from the use of the other; e.g. petrol is demanded by motorists for their cars.

3. A special case of derived demand is the demand for factors, which are demanded because of the demand for 'utilities' to satisfy 'wants'.

4. Competitive demand occurs when goods are substitutes for one another; e.g. butter and margarine.

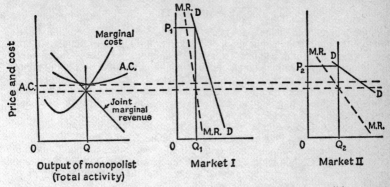

Fig. 66. The output of a monopolist when discrimination is possible

Notes:

1. The entrepreneur expands output until marginal cost equals total marginal revenue.
2. That level of cost is carried over into Markets I and II, and in each case cuts the marginal revenue lines 1 and 2 at points which indicate outputs of Q_1 and Q_2.
3. As a result, OQ_1 of the output will be sold at price P_1, output OQ_2 will be sold at a price of OP_2.
4. The monopolist is making super-profits in each case, but more in Market I than in Market II. His discrimination in favour of the market where demand is more elastic depends upon his ability to keep the two markets separate.

5. Since household incomes are limited, all goods and services are in competitive demand with one another, and the housewife must exercise choice between them.
6. Where the price of a commodity changes, the household will vary its purchases to take account of the change in price. The change in demand can be divided into two parts: a substitution effect and an income effect. The substitution effect is always non-negative; the income effect may be positive or negative.
7. Another technique for examining the preferences of and choices made by customers is indifference-curve analysis.
8. Price controls interfere with the market. Maximum prices lead to a shortage of goods, which means that rationing must be introduced. Minimum prices lead to excessive supply, with the need for Government purchase of the surplus.
9. Market price is the short-term equilibrium price on the market. Normal price is the long-term equilibrium price achieved when an industry has settled down in stable conditions of demand and supply.

(10) Suggested Further Reading

Boulding, K. E.: *Economic Analysis*. Harper & Row: London, 1966.

Hanson, J. L.: *A Textbook of Economics*. Macdonald & Evans: London, 1970.

Lipsey, R. G., and Stilwell, J. A.: *An Introduction to Positive Economics*. 3rd. Edn. Weidenfeld & Nicolson: London, 1971.

Exercises Set 13

1. What are the likely effects of a rise in the price of wool on the following: (*a*) the price of Harris Tweed; (*b*) the price of blankets; (*c*) the price of mutton; (*d*) the demand for fluffy synthetic fibres; (*e*) the price of sheepskins; (*f*) Australian incomes?

2. Explain why a rise in the price of cars might lead to a fall in the price of petrol. Refer in your answer to the specific nature of the assets used in oil refineries.

3. What would you expect to be the effect of an increase in the demand for hides on: (*a*) the price of beef; (*b*) the price of pork; (*c*) the price of plastic handbags; (*d*) the price of wool; (*e*) the price of shoes; (*f*) the rent of grazing land.

4. 'An increase in the price of petrol makes paraffin cheaper.' Do you agree? Support your answer with reasoned economic arguments and diagrams.

5. 'When a commodity becomes cheaper it effectively raises the real incomes of all who use it.' Explain what the author of this remark meant. What changes in expenditure may reasonably be expected as a result of the reduction of the price of goods in strong demand?

6. What is the effect on (*a*) farm outputs, and (*b*) taxation, of a decision never to allow the price of wheat to fall below 2 dollars per bushel.

7. What disturbances in the market will be caused by a Government decision to keep food prices low by a maximum-price policy?

8. Why does the electricity supply industry offer different rates to different classes of consumer? How can they prevent the markets mixing?

9. 'Do not worry, madam, your son's operation will be performed free. Miss Jones, double the bill you typed out this morning for Sir Joshua's son, will you?' Explain the economic implications of these two sentences, spoken by a leading surgeon.

10. In what circumstances is it (*a*) practicable, and (*b*) profitable, for a firm to practise differential charging?

CHAPTER FOURTEEN

EXCHANGE AND MONEY

(1) Specialization and Exchange

Specialization and **exchange** have been described as opposite sides of the same coin. Every economy depends on specialization, and in advanced economies specialization is fully developed by automation and computerization to produce a flood of 'surplus' goods. By 'surplus' we mean surplus to the requirements of the particular group who produced the output under consideration. This group of producers then wishes to trade its surplus output with other workers who have produced surpluses in *their* particular fields of activity. In a similar way some of these workers will wish to exchange some of their surplus goods for personal services, since not all specialists produce an end product. The personal services rendered by employees in tertiary production have also to be 'paid for' by surrendering to them some of the goods produced in primary and secondary production. We must now examine the problems of exchange.

Even the very start of such an examination of exchanges is blurred by the intricate nature of advanced economies. Readers will immediately think of objections to the statements in the previous paragraph. How can one talk about workers in the petroleum industry exchanging the surplus petrol they manufacture with the employees in the building industry? The petrol belongs to the owners of the oil refinery, and the surplus houses erected are the property of the developers who organized the project. These objections are very real, and yet they do not destroy what has been said. Because of an ancient economic device called 'the money system', the basic exchanges which are taking place are hidden by a 'money veil'. The main purpose of this chapter is to examine how 'the money system' works. Before doing so we must consider exchanges arranged without a money system.

(2) Exchange by Barter

Until a full money system has been developed, trade is usually carried on by barter. This is the exchange of goods directly for other goods, and it presents quite serious problems to the parties trading. These problems are not a real handicap when trading is an unusual event, for example in simple tribal societies practising autarchy (self sufficiency). To people growing their own food, keeping their own cattle and weaving their own cloth, the occasional bartering activity can usually be resolved fairly easily. The purchase of a knife or an axe, at an annual fair, or from the visiting pedlar, is an event to which due time can be given.

Trade is not the only activity of mankind, however. Marriage and revenge are older practices still and appear to have played a considerable part in the development of money. Bride-price and blood-price are ancient institutions, and are often reported among primitive people. Compensation for a man's death is a sum equivalent to what his father paid as bride-price for the dead man's mother a generation before. These two activities, and barter, are matters to which due time can be given, especially by peoples largely self sufficient in ordinary bread-and-butter matters

When we live in a community where specialization is the rule, so that every single thing we need has to be obtained by exchange, the difficulties of barter become so onerous that a 'money' system has to be developed.

Even today it is sometimes necessary to use barter. The collapse of a currency system, such as occurred in Germany at the end of the Second World War, meant that barter took place on an extensive scale, and eventually cigarettes acted as money. Bartering agreements at national level have also been arranged between some of the countries of the Communist Bloc and Western nations in the last few years. Bilateral trade of this sort is discussed on page 289.

The Disadvantages of Barter

The disadvantages of barter are (*a*) the need for a coincidence of wants, (*b*) the difficulty of deciding equal values, and (*c*) the indivisibility of large items.

(*a*) *The necessity for a coincidence of wants.* It is impossible to barter unless *A* has what *B* wants, and *A* wants what *B* has. Sometimes this difficulty can be overcome by holding one half of the transaction over until a later time, but this requires trust and a sense of honouring obligations. It is made easier if the respective parties can read and write, so that the debt can be recorded. The records of citizens of the early United States include many such entries. Independence had ended the use of British currency before the United States was ready to provide a dollar system. 'I owe Nathanial Hawke 1 coil of rope length 20 yards', runs a typical entry.

(*b*) *The difficulty of deciding equal values.* Even when each party wants what the other has it does not follow they can agree on a fair exchange. Is a decorated pot worth a plump hen? A good deal of time can be wasted sorting out such equations of value.

(*c*) *The indivisibility of large items.* If a cow is worth two sacks of wheat, what is one sack of wheat worth? Once again we may need to carry over part of the transaction to a later period of time. This is not very easy even in a settled community; with nomadic peoples it is very difficult indeed.

For these reasons the barter system is discarded by societies which develop beyond autarky to more specialized methods of production. For such peoples a money system is essential.

(3) The Functions of Money

Money is (*a*) a medium of exchange, (*b*) a measure of value, (*c*) a store of value, (*d*) a standard for deferred payments, and (*e*) it facilitates one-way payments.

(*a*) *A medium of exchange.* This is the chief function of money. It overcomes the need for a coincidence of wants, since everyone 'wants' money, which represents a claim against any goods or services which will yield satisfaction. It does follow, though, that money must be generally acceptable. In earlier times this general acceptability was achieved by using metals which were themselves valuable: the coinage metals gold, silver, and copper. Today all coins are 'token' money only, that is they are acceptable because we all agree to accept them as being worth a certain claim against goods and services. This general acceptability is supported by a declaration by the law-making body that the tokens do constitute 'legal tender'.

(b) *A measure of value.* This function overcomes the difficulty of equating a decorated pot with a plump hen. We exchange the hen for what is agreed to be a fair quantity of money—now called the price of the hen. We then see whether it is sufficient money to buy the decorated pot. If it is not, we must save the price of the hen until we have enough other money to put with it to buy the pot. Thus the money is also useful as a store of value.

(c) *A store of value.* This store of value can also help us to overcome the disadvantage of barter, that some items are indivisible. The farmer with only one sack of wheat cannot buy half a cow, but he can save up the money he has obtained in exchange for his wheat in the hope that before long he will be able to afford a cow.

The use of money as a store of value only applies when individuals are storing it; a whole nation could not do so. Robinson Crusoe on his island found a box of gold coins which proved useless to him until he returned to civilization. If a whole nation stored up its money and then retired simultaneously they would all starve for lack of current production. Money is only a claim against the real goods and services which have utility. It is of no use unless the wealth is being created which yields satisfaction of wants.

(d) *A standard for deferred payments.* Money is a useful unit of account, and accounts are records of debts to businesses. It follows that the money system provides a standard for deferred payments, enabling us to record debts and eventually collect them either in one payment or in a series of payments on the instalment method. It is important here, however, that the value of money is stable over reasonably lengthy periods of time.

(e) *One-way payments.* Some payments are not made in exchange for goods or services directly enjoyed. The benefits of peaceful existence, freedom from riot and civil disturbance are enjoyed in return for one-way payments called taxes, or rates if they are levied locally. Such one-way payments are inconvenient without a money system. In the Middle Ages the Court of England moved around the country, consuming the taxes in kind levied on the shires of England. As a result the King's Council, the forerunner of Parliament, was sometimes to be found elsewhere than at Westminster, and some famous Acts bear the names of towns where they were enacted. The Provisions of Oxford, 1258, is a well known example.

(4) Exchanging Surpluses through the Money System

Exchange is essential if indirect production is a general feature of the economy. The surpluses produced by specialization have to be exchanged if all are to enjoy a balanced diet and adequate satisfaction of other needs.

Fig. 67 illustrates the part money plays in promoting these exchanges. Everyone, rich or poor, strong or weak, contributes in some way to the production process. It may be by work of a skilled, semi-skilled, or unskilled nature, or by displaying entrepreneurial ability. It may be by a person providing natural resources which for some reason he controls, or by providing

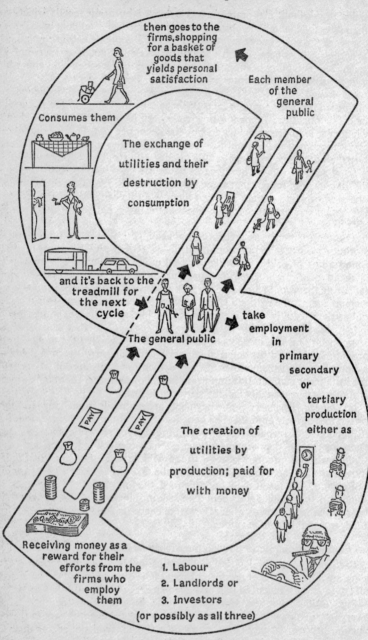

then goes to the firms, shopping for a basket of goods that yields personal satisfaction

Each member of the general public

Consumes them

The exchange of utilities and their destruction by consumption

and it's back to the treadmill for the next cycle

The general public

take employment in primary secondary or tertiary production either as

The creation of utilities by production; paid for with money

Receiving money as a reward for their efforts from the firms who employ them

1. Labour
2. Landlords or
3. Investors
(or possibly as all three)

Fig. 67. The money system

capital he has accumulated. In other words the **factors of production** are put to work, and rewarded by a money payment. The rewards paid to these factors are discussed in the next few chapters; they are paid to, and received by, every member of society. There are no exceptions, but special arrangements have to be made for that tiny section of the population who are unable to work, such as the chronically sick, the aged and infirm. A few unscrupulous or anti-social elements may also obtain support by fair means or foul. Everyone receives some share of the **National Income.** Whether it is a fair share or not is discussed later. Here we are concerned only with *what* happens. Each of these individuals then purchases a 'basket of goods and services' to his personal taste and satisfaction.

A simple illustration of the process is the purchase of a packet of tea by a housewife whose husband is a minor clerk in a Government department. He has been performing his useful, but routine, services on behalf of—let us say —the Ministry of Agriculture and Fisheries. His duties concern the licensing of slaughter-houses and the supervision of their sanitation (a matter of public concern), for which he receives an average wage. His wife uses some of this wage to purchase a packet of tea which was grown in Ceylon on a plantation financed by joint British–Cingalese capital. It was shipped to the United Kingdom in a box lined with metal foil produced in Canada from ore smelted at Kitimat, in British Columbia. The transport was in a British liner manned by an Indian crew. The cargo was auctioned in Mincing Lane, London, and purchased by a blender who eventually packed it in cartons made from pulp produced in Labrador. The blender then wholesaled the tea to the retailer who sold it to the housewife.

At the time of the purchase the housewife's sole thought was that she had enough money for the tea, but would have to postpone until pay day the tin of instant coffee she had also hoped to purchase. Yet, behind the veil of money that obscured what was really going on, an army of people all over the world in a hundred specialized occupations were attending to her needs in return for her husband's supervision of the sanitary arrangements in British slaughter-houses.

(5) The Characteristics of Money

Money must be (*a*) generally acceptable, and stable in value, (*b*) durable and rustproof, (*c*) difficult to imitate, (*d*) portable, and (*e*) divisible into small units.

(*a*) *General acceptability.* This has already been referred to on page 160. There is no difficulty where coins have an intrinsic value of their own; but when that is the case, debasement of the currency may occur if people are tempted to clip precious metal from the edges of coins. Where coins are merely 'token money', i.e. the metal in the coin is worth less than the coin's so-called value, general acceptability is a matter of confidence in the coinage. Where devaluation of a currency is threatened, foreigners are unwilling to accept the coinage or notes of the country in question because they have no confidence that such tokens will keep the value they are supposed to have.

Often new coins are not popular with the public, who take some time to accept the idea of an unusual shape or new metal. The British public resisted the 50-pence piece when it was first introduced in place of the ten-shilling note. Similarly, Scottish bank-notes, although acceptable throughout Britain, are so rarely seen by English and Welsh shopkeepers that the production of one in a supermarket is sure to cause delay while managers are consulted.

(b) *Durability*. Coins and notes are expensive to produce. Most coins have a life of about 50 years, whereas notes last about three months. As a result the United Kingdom has recently changed over to a 50-pence cupro-nickel coin in place of a note of the same value. It is also important that the metal used should not react chemically with the air, or with water. Such 'rusting' would reduce the life of the coin, and its value if it had intrinsic value. The noble metals, gold, silver, and copper are good in this respect, though silver tarnishes and copper does oxidize slowly. Aluminium alloys, being light and therefore portable, are widely used for coinage, but are less durable than cupro-nickel.

(c) *Ease of imitation*. Where coinage or notes are imitated, the coiner or forger obtains a claim against the available consumer goods and services. But the counterfeiter is clearly not entitled to such a claim, for he has not himself joined in any useful productive activity at all. The money system is designed to make exchanges easier between the producers of useful goods and services. Any outsider, any non-producer, who shares in the wealth created must therefore do so at the expense of honest workers who have contributed real wealth to the pool of utilities created. Counterfeiting is most likely to occur when token money is in daily use. It has sometimes been used as an instrument of policy. During the Second World War vast quantities of £1 and £5 notes were manufactured by the Germans with a view to undermining the British economy. Every effort has to be made to make coins and notes difficult to imitate. Supplies of special paper for bank-notes are strictly controlled and the destruction of dirty notes is carefully supervised.

(d) *Portability*. Money must be portable. One of the disadvantages of gold for coins is that it is so heavy. Notes are a great improvement in this respect.

(e) *Divisibility*. It is highly desirable that money should be capable of paying for the smallest transactions of everyday life. This is only possible if small units of money are available, which provides another reason why token coins have replaced coins of intrinsic value. The impossibility of making gold coins small enough to be worth a penny led to the use of copper and even less valuable metals. It has been suggested that coins should be made of plastic, which is light, durable, and very cheap. The ease with which they might be imitated is the major drawback here.

(6) Types of Money

Originally money was in the form of coins, made from the coinage metals, copper, silver, and gold. The face value of the coins and their real value were the same. If the kings who issued coins debased them, i.e. mixed inferior metals with the coinage metals, merchants simply reduced the value of the coins in their transactions. They also weighed coins if they feared they had been 'clipped'.

Gresham's Law. This law, incorrectly attributed to Sir Thomas Gresham, the Elizabethan finance minister charged with the task of restoring confidence in the currency after Henry VIII's debasement of it, states that *bad money drives out good*. If debased coins are issued of a nominal value greater than their intrinsic value as metal, it will pay anyone with one of the older coins to melt it down and use the metal to buy more than the same quantity of debased coins. No doubt this is not easy for everyone to do, especially if there are penalities for tampering with the coinage, but there is some truth in the 'law', which like most economic laws is not an inevitable occurrence but refers to something that tends to happen. When people become sufficiently mature financially to recognize that money is merely a medium of exchange, the token nature of money becomes so generally recognized that attempts to profit in this way are less frequent.

The chief types of money in use today are:

(a) *Token coins.* These are coins made from metals whose real value is less than the face value of the coin. Because they are generally acceptable and because they are given the validity of 'legal tender', they enable exchange to take place on a basis of confidence in the currency. *Legal tender* is any method of payment which we are forced by law to accept as adequate settlement of a debt. For instance, Bank of England notes are legal tender to any amount in the United Kingdom.

(b) *Paper money.* Printed money is more convenient than coins, being lighter to carry and easier to handle in large quantities. The denominations of notes can be arranged to suit price levels in common use.

(c) *Bank deposits.* Deposits at a bank are the same as money. Originally they are paid into the bank in coin or paper by the depositor, or they may be created by the banker in a way which is explained on page 223. These deposits can then be transferred from one person to another by means of cheques. Cheques are not therefore money, but only *orders to pay* money. The quantity of bank deposits transferable today is so great that coins and notes have become the 'small change' of the money system, most big payments being made by cheque. Table 19 shows the April, 1977 figures, for Great Britain.

Table 19. Money in circulation in Great Britain, April 1977

Form of money	£ millions
Coins	485
Bank notes	7,368
Bank deposits	37,633
Total	45,486

(Source: *Bank of England Quarterly Bulletin,* June 1977)

(7) Convertible Currencies

In former times when money was either made of precious metals or was in the form of bank-notes which were backed by gold reserves in the banker's vaults, all token money was **convertible**, i.e. it could be exchanged on demand for precious metals. This was the case in the United Kingdom before 1914. We were on the gold standard. It is not the case today as far as British citizens are concerned. The promise on Bank of England notes which reads 'I promise to pay the bearer on demand the sum of one pound' only refers to some alternative paper security—for instance, a Government security or an entry in the Post Office Savings Bank. Gold is now going through a gradual process of de-monetarization. Even the International Monetary Fund is selling off one third of its gold reserves. As far as foreign businessmen are concerned they can convert sterling to any other world currency or to gold if preferred. This makes them more willing to take sterling, and thus promotes international trade.

Fiduciary Issues. A fiduciary issue of notes was one not backed by gold, and whose basis is trust (*fiducia* is the Latin word for 'trust'). The Bank Charter Act of 1844 sanctioned a fiduciary issue of £14 million. Mainly on the grounds that at any given time some proportion of the note issue was temporarily out of circulation, it was deemed permissible to issue more notes than the actual value of gold in the reserves. The aim of this move was to finance the maximum volume of trade. Today the fiduciary issue is over £7,325 million; even so, the use of bank deposits transferable by cheques to finance transactions, still leaves Bank of England notes as only the 'small change' of the modern money system.

The large fiduciary issue today reflects the enormous volumes of goods and services produced in an advanced nation like Great Britain. If the note issue was linked to the gold reserves as it once was, the value of gold would have had to rise many times since 1914. This would have benefited those countries in which gold is mined. Modern money systems are backed not by the gold reserves, but by the trust that can be placed in a nation to produce goods and services to honour its obligations to foreign holders of its money. The more goods and services it is able to produce the more notes it is entitled to issue; there is no financial crisis unless falling productivity, strikes, civil disturbances, or war threaten to interrupt prompt supplies of goods and services to these foreign creditors.

(8) The Value of Money

Money is a medium of exchange and as such is continuously being traded for countless commodities. It is highly desirable that the value of money should remain stable over the years, otherwise its functions cannot be performed properly. This is particularly true of its use as a standard for deferred payments. For example, if money falls in value over the years, a person borrowing money is made better off because the money with which he later repays his debt is less valuable than the money he borrowed. The person from whom he borrowed the money receives back the devalued currency and has therefore lost on the transaction. To overcome this decline in the value of money, interest rates rise in such times, so that those who lend money receive in interest some of the capital losses they are inevitably going to suffer when repayment time comes. Nineteenth-century businessmen earned $2\frac{1}{2}$ per cent interest and were well pleased; 5 per cent interest was an excellent return on capital. Today many bank loans are being made at 12 per cent, and hire-purchase loans are repayable at about 25 per cent.

(9) An Index of Prices

Changes in the value of money can be followed by using an index of prices. In preparing such an index, a base date is chosen and a suitable selection of prices is taken on that date and regularly thereafter. It may be necessary to weight the index according to the particular behaviour of the group about which we are hoping to collect evidence. In considering the value of money it is probably the average householder we have in mind. How has the changing value of money affected him? To discover the answer to this question we must first find out the pattern of spending of such a householder. This will involve a survey of the spending habits of a random sample of householders. If 10 per cent of the income of an average householder goes on basic foods, these foods must be weighted in the index to give due influence to this important group of purchases. If the average householder never buys platinum cigarette cases, this commodity need not be included in the calculations that lead to the index.

When a suitable selection of goods has been arrived at, the prices of these goods are noted and the total cost becomes the 'base' point from which the index will be measured. It is usually called 100. Suppose this collection of goods costs £20 in January of one year, but a year later it is costing £21. The index has risen from 100 to 105, since this is a 5 per cent increase. *The real value of money for the average householder has fallen and, unless his income has been increased to compensate for the change in prices, his standard of living has been eroded.*

The Index of Retail Prices prepared in Great Britain shows the following changes in recent years (*Source: Monthly Digest of Statistics Nov. 1975*):

	1962	1967	1971	1975 (Sep.)
Retail Prices	100	119·4	153·4	261·2

Clearly the value of the £1 to the average householder has fallen considerably over this 13-year period, and especially between 1971 and 1975.

(10) Summary of Chapter Fourteen

1. People practising specialized production must exchange their outputs of goods and services with one another.

2. Goods may be bartered for other goods and services, but barter has certain disadvantages. The chief of these are the need for a coincidence of wants, the difficulty of equating values, and the indivisibility of large items.

3. Money is a solution to the problems of barter, because each commodity or service can be exchanged for money, which can then be used by the new owner to purchase a balanced supply of utilities.

4. Desirable characteristics of money include general acceptability, portability, and cleanliness in handling.

5. The commonest types of money are token coins, notes, and bank deposits.

6. Some currencies are convertible into gold; others are not convertible. Willingness to accept non-convertible currencies depends on world confidence in the economies of the countries issuing the money, since it represents a claim on these economies for real goods and services.

7. An issue of notes and token money not backed by gold reserves is called a fiduciary issue, i.e. one based on trust.

8. It is important that the value of money should be held steady if its use as a basis for deferred payments is to be fulfilled properly. The changing value of money can be studied by using an index of prices.

(11) Suggested Further Reading

Einzig, P.: *Primitive Money*. Pergamon Press: London, 1966.
Hawthorne, J.: *All About Money*. W. H. Allen: London, 1970.
Morgan, E. V.: *A History of Money*. Penguin: 2nd. Edn., 1969.

Exercises Set 14

1. Why is specialization desirable? Why does money become an essential medium of exchange when specialized production is adopted to provide the goods and services needed in a community?

2. Money need not be valuable in itself, so long as it is generally acceptable. Explain.

3. What are the disadvantages of barter? Why are these disadvantages of less importance to primitive people than to advanced nations?

4. Records show that one of the methods used to force primitive people to accept paid employment in mines or factories was to impose taxation on the head of the family. Suggest why this policy succeeded where persuasion had failed.

5. What are the functions of money? Why are these functions less effectively performed if money changes in value?

6. Gold is intrinsically valuable. Token money needs the support of a legislative declaration that it is 'legal tender'. Explain, referring in your answer to the legal tender of your own country.

7. All nations have laws against counterfeiting. What is wrong with counterfeiting, and why does it strike particularly at economies where token money is in use?

8. What is a fiduciary note issue? Why is it possible for the Bank of England to keep such a large fiduciary issue in circulation today?

9. If money falls in value it helps debtors. Explain.

10. An Index of Wholesale Prices for Great Britain shows the following:

$$1967 = 100, 1968 = 104, 1969 = 106.$$

Comment on these figures with regard to the value of money over the period shown. To what extent could changes have been caused by (*a*) a rise in overseas prices; (*b*) a cut in insurance rates; (*c*) a fall in productivity in certain factories?

CHAPTER FIFTEEN

THE DISTRIBUTION OF WEALTH—REWARDS TO FACTORS

(1) The Importance of 'Distribution Theory'

Adam Smith drew attention in 1776 to the change that had come over production methods in his lifetime. Almost in a generation Britain had become an industrial society. Fortunes were being made in iron works, coal mines, heavy engineering, cotton and woollen manufacture, and the pottery industry. Canals, ports, roads, bridges, aqueducts, and coastal shipping were opening up areas of the country previously uninhabited. A flood of cotton goods, ironware, brassware, porcelain and china, woollen cloth, knitwear, craft and carriages, ships' gear and farm equipment, building material and furniture poured out of the ringing workshops and was forwarded to the four corners of the earth by shippers, insurance brokers, carriers, and financiers. Yet amid all this plenty the paradox that puzzled economists, capitalists, and workers alike was the enduring poverty of the majority of ordinary people. The book that inquired into *The Nature and the Causes of the Wealth of Nations* had nothing to explain the poverty of the working class. Driven by the Enclosure Acts from the land that had previously sustained them, they fought a hard struggle for survival in the shanty towns and overcrowded slums of industrial cities. The great successors to Adam Smith were Thomas Malthus (1766–1834), David Ricardo (1772–1823) and John Stuart Mill (1806–73). Malthus is chiefly famous for his *Essay on Population*, written in 1798 (see page 190). It was this essay that earned economics the nickname of 'the dismal science'. Ricardo was the first economist to recognize that the poverty of ordinary people was simply due to an unsatisfactory distribution of wealth. John Stuart Mill carried the discussion further, to state quite clearly that this was a matter which man could solve by wise policies. No inevitable natural economic forces were at work to defeat him.

The writings of these two great economists are so much a part of the background of modern economics that it is worth while pausing for a moment to consider their influence.

(2) David Ricardo

David Ricardo (1772–1823) wrote about the distribution of wealth in his *Principles of Political Economy and Taxation*, published in 1817. Writing forty-one years after Adam Smith's *Wealth of Nations*, his picture of the economic scene was painted in dark colours. Darker still were the interpretations placed on his book by readers who found its gloomier phrases suited to their own moods. Reaction to the revolution in France, to the unrest after the Napoleonic wars, and to the continued existence of poverty despite wealth had made Britain's leaders hostile to any pressure for reform. They seized on Ricardo's wages theory (see page 191), ignored its hopeful and optimistic phrases, and repeated its gloomy forebodings about the inevitability of future poverty.

This brilliant son of a Dutch Jewish stockbroker was a financial genius who specialized in arbitrage (see page 273). Estranged from his family because of his marriage to a Quaker, Ricardo was reduced to poverty. Borrowing from friends he quickly amassed a huge fortune and turned his leisured activities towards the study of economics, currency, and politics. The main feature of his *Principles* was the emphasis he placed on the distribution of wealth, which John Stuart Mill was to develop.

He is most famous for his definition of rent as 'that portion of the produce of the earth which is paid to the landlord for the use of the original and indestructible powers of the soil'. Ricardo here is quite clear that money is not of any real importance in the payment of rent. The landlord does not want money for the use of his land, but a portion of the produce of the earth: meat and fish, and bread and wine and manufactured goods. We can all accept this lucid and straightforward definition.

Ricardo died suddenly at the age of fifty-one, in 1823. The genuineness of his concern for the evils of the existing system, and his acute statements on economic principles have been obscured by their misrepresentation by others. Along with Malthus he came to be regarded as one who held a gloomy view of the prospects for ordinary people. His definition of rent survives in popular knowledge as clear and meaningful.

What followed from it was not so easy to understand, but it was to become a major point in the theory of distribution which unlocked many riddles that puzzled economists. This was the concept of 'economic rent' (see page 176).

(3) John Stuart Mill

John Stuart Mill (1806–73) was a boy genius whose father, James Mill, was a follower of Jeremy Bentham, the practical philosopher of the Industrial Revolution. His father took personal care of the boy's education from an early age. He began to learn Greek when he was only three, and Latin shortly after. At the age of twelve his studies included philosophy, political economy, and logic. By the age of sixteen he had founded the Utilitarian Society, whose members supported Jeremy Bentham's political theory of 'utility'. This theory held that the standard by which we must judge all the actions of men, institutions, and Governments was the yardstick of human happiness. The action that promoted the well-being and happiness of the greatest number of people was the right one. It is an idea that still commands widespread respect.

Mill did not overthrow the ideas of Adam Smith, Ricardo, or Malthus. He moved their ideas on a short step in a more optimistic direction. He agreed with them that production of wealth was a bitter process, subject to harsh, inexorable laws like competition. 'But,' he says in his *Principles of Political Economy*, 'it is not so with the Distribution of Wealth. That is a matter of human institution solely. The things once there, mankind, individually or collectively, can do with them as they like.'

And, no doubt, what mankind did with the wealth they had created was to be judged from the standpoint of the greatest good to the greatest number. It was an idea that shook a sleeping world awake, and led eventually to the type of managed prosperity which is such a feature of the second half of the twentieth century.

Mill defined economics as 'the practical science of the production and distribution of wealth'. Not only must man produce wealth, he must distribute it more reasonably. Too great a believer in the advantages of competition to advocate Government intervention himself, Mill sowed the seeds of State interference on many 'exceptional' grounds. One of these was that he thought the State should introduce compulsory education; another was that the State should compel factory owners to obey the legislation Parliament had enacted, even though it raised costs. He died in 1873, during Gladstone's great Parliament of 1868–74, when a great burst of legislative activity on education, public health, electoral law, control of corruption, and control of monopolies was passing through the British Parliament.

(4) Rewards to Factors

The money system involves two equal and opposite flows, which are shown diagrammatically in Fig. 68.

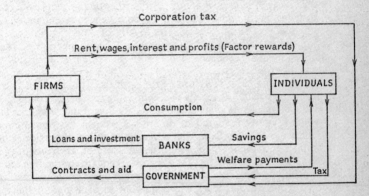

Fig. 68. Flows round the money system

These flows will be discussed more fully in later chapters, but the flow from firms to individuals is the one that interests us at present. It is in this flow of money incomes from firms to individuals that the distribution of wealth is made.

Note, first, that the entire proceeds after tax of the activities of firms are given to individuals, who are the owners of the factors employed. The landlord receives his **rent**, the worker his **wages**, the investor his **interest** and **profits**. The flows into industry consist initially of capital flows; these are paid out to landlords and workers in the form of rent and wages for the initial creation of capital assets like buildings, machinery, and fixtures. Later a different form of flow into the firms takes place: the capital flow is replaced by current-account flows, i.e. payments for the goods and services supplied by the firms once production has started. These inputs are again paid out to the landlords for continued use of their land and to the workers for their labour—but this time not to construction workers but to a different class of labour employed in the production activities of the firm. Now, too, the investors of capital begin to draw rewards for their efforts: interest payments as a reward for postponing their personal consumption while the firms constructed the plants; profits as a reward for running the risks of the enterprise. The entire receipts are paid out to individuals. What, the astute reader will ask, about profits which are not redistributed to the shareholders, but are 'ploughed back' into the firm? Of course all such amounts are paid out to more construction workers to extend the plant and layout of the firm, returning eventually as even bigger profits, or even more growth.

Profit is the residual balance of the activities of firms. The amount of this residue of profit depends on the extent to which the other payments to factors can be increased or decreased. For example, if rent is raised, profits will be lowered; if wages are forced up, profits will be forced down; if interest rates are lowered, profits will be higher. It also varies with the price that can be obtained for the goods and services sold by the firms.

The endless controversy between labour and capital arises from the conflict of interests that exists between them. Today, when we regard entrepreneurs as only another class of labour, it seems peculiar that there should be a conflict between them; but in fact labour is not a homogeneous commodity, for it is split into many different grades. The loyalty of entrepreneurs to the profit motive is linked to their activity as agents for the investing public. Their rewards, and continuation as agents, depends to some extent on their success in achieving good profit records.

The distribution of wealth therefore depends on the willingness of entrepreneurs, in their capacities as agents of the investing public, to concede an increased share of the fruits of production to landlords and workers. The extent to which they are prepared to do so is explained by the **marginal-productivity theory of factor prices**. Alternatively, the ability of landlords and labour to compel entrepreneurs to yield a larger share of the fruits of production enters the 'distribution' picture. When workers are strong, or occupy a bottleneck position where they can easily interrupt production, concessions will be forced from entrepreneurs which amount to a change in the distribution of wealth.

(5) The Market for Factors

A market is a place where buyers and sellers are in contact with one another to fix prices. Just as markets exist for the purchase and sale of commodities, a market may be said to exist for the purchase and sale of factors. There is the 'capital market' where financiers willing to make loans are to be found by those wishing to borrow money. There are estate agents and property dealers with premises, sites, farms, and mines available if the price is right. There are employment bureaux and labour exchanges willing to find jobs for workers and workers for jobs.

The entrepreneurs enter these markets in order to purchase factors. Like all consumers they are price conscious and the basis of their activities is their estimate of the likely productivity to be achieved by employing a factor. As usual in economics it is not a question of an absolute choice between having labour or not having labour. All productive activities require some labour. The choice is a marginal one. Shall I have more labour and less land and capital, or more land and less labour and capital, etc? The basis of his demand for factors is the entrepreneur's estimate of their marginal productivity.

The marginal productivity of a factor is defined as *the increase in total revenue to be derived from the employment of one extra unit of the factor*.

On the supply side the individuals offering land, labour, or capital are concerned to achieve the best price possible for their services. Once again it is usual for economists to consider a perfect market, where free flows of factors take place to the point in the market where the best rewards are being offered. David Ricardo, writing at a time when some of the factor markets were much more perfect than they are today, observed that

> 'Whilst every man is free to employ his capital where he pleases, he will naturally seek for it that employment which is most advantageous; he will naturally be dissatisfied with a profit of 10 per cent if by removing his capital he can obtain a profit of 15 per cent.'

Today there are many imperfections in the factor markets, but even against the friction-producing activities of strong trade unions and organized employers the free play of the market is still influential.

(6) The Demand for Factors—a Derived Demand

The price of a factor is fixed like all other prices by demand for, and supply of, the factor. Factors are demanded by entrepreneurs, and this demand is a derived demand which arises not because the factors are wanted for themselves, but for what they can create in the way of 'utilities' to satisfy 'wants'. It follows that if a unit of a factor is going to provide more in the way of created 'utilities' than its cost to the entrepreneur, he will buy it; if it is not going to create as much wealth as it costs, it will not be purchased by the entrepreneur.

It is for the entrepreneur to demand factors according to his ideas of what will achieve the 'optimum' firm for him. He plans the enterprise, mixing his factors according to the dearness or cheapness of each. If labour is dear he will use more machines, i.e. more capital. The demand for factors is derived from the demand for the goods and services factors can make available.

(7) The Marginal-Productivity Theory of Factor Prices—the Demand Side

The marginal-productivity theory attempts to explain how factor rewards, i.e. the price of factors, are decided. It assumes perfect competition in the market for factors, and looks at the market from both sides. There is the point of view of the buyers of factors: the demand side. It is this point of view that gives the theory its name. The other point of view is that of the suppliers of the factors: the landlords, workers, and investors. These, the theory holds, obey the rule of **maximum net advantage** moving to the point where the best rewards are offered.

Let us look at the demand side first. The marginal-productivity theory of factor prices says that a factor will be rewarded well, or ill, according to the contribution that it makes to the total product, or revenue, of the firm. The theory is concerned with *the addition to output and income of the firm resulting from the employment of an additional unit of the factor*. The marginal unit of the factor is the unit the entrepreneur has just hired, in an expanding industry; or is about to discard in a contracting industry.

The increase in output is often called the **marginal physical product**, and the increase in income the **marginal revenue product**.

The imaginary figures given in Table 20 illustrate the marginal physical products and marginal revenue products of successive employees taken on by a firm in perfect competition. In these circumstances wages are fixed at the market price for that particular class of labour, so that there is nothing the entrepreneur can do to alter wages. His personal demands are very tiny compared to total demand. Fig. 69 shows the same information in diagrammatic form. Table 20, Fig. 69 and the notes below it should now be studied.

Table 20. Marginal physical product and marginal revenue product in perfect competition

Number of men	Units of output	Marginal physical product (I.e. output of extra man)	Marginal revenue product (i.e. extra man's output in money terms)	Wage (in currency units)
1	5	5	25·00	20·00
2	12	7	35·00	20·00
3	22	10	50·00	20·00
4	33	11.	55·00	20·00
5	43	10	50·00	20·00
6	50	7	35·00	20·00
7	55	5	25·00	20·00
8	59	4	20·00	20·00
9	62	3	15·00	20·00
10	64	2	10·00	20·00

In rather similar ways we can show that the entrepreneur's use of land will depend on the marginal productivity of the land, and his use of capital will depend on the marginal productivity of capital. If the revenue produced by the land is likely to be greater than the cost of the land, the entrepreneur will demand its use; if not he will look elsewhere for land at a cheaper price. If the likely revenue to be earned from the use of capital will exceed the rate of interest (i.e. the charge for borrowing the capital), the entrepreneur will go ahead with the project and borrow the money. If not, he will postpone the project until capital is cheaper.

(8) The Marginal Productivity Theory of Factor Prices—the Supply Side

From the point of view of the factor owners, their willingness to supply depends on the achievement of *the maximum net advantage* to them. The term *net* advantage involves a deduction from the rewards of the agreement of any losses inevitable in the bargain. These may be monetary losses or nonmonetary losses. Many a worker offered employment at higher wages elsewhere does not take it because his wife will not be near her mother, or the children will need to change schools. If the advantages of the bargain outweigh the disadvantages, factors will move between firms and industries. These movements clearly reflect the derived nature of the demand for factors, for it is the elasticity of demand for the ultimate output which controls the ability of the entrepreneur to pass increased factor costs on to the ultimate consumer; and hence his willingness to make concessions. If a change in taste or fashion makes a product highly desirable to consumers, the marginal productivity of factors can be maintained even if factor costs rise; the entrepreneur simply raises the price of the product. If a change in taste or fashion makes the product less desirable the entrepreneur must either yield concessions which he knows will mean lower profit margins, or stand firm and see labour migrate from the industry. One way he loses capital, which flows away from the industry, the other way he loses labour. Of course the various vested interests may do their best to reduce these flows, but in the long run they are unable to stop a declining industry from declining or a developing industry from developing.

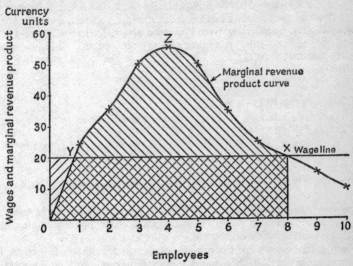

Fig. 69. Deciding how many men to employ

Notes:

1. Marginal revenue produced increases at first, and reaches a maximum at the point Z when four employees are engaged.
2. The fifth worker produces an increase of 50·00 currency units, which is less than the fourth worker's marginal product but it is still worth while employing him for his wage is only 20·00.
3. When the marginal revenue product falls below the wage line at the point X (eight workers employed) it is not profitable to employ any more.
4. The total wage is shown by the area 08X20 = 160·00.
5. The total revenue is the shaded area under the curve 0YZX8, and is equal to 295·00 (the sum of the marginal-revenue products).
6. The reader should note that the rewards to the other factors can also be seen from the diagram. They are the area under the curve YZX minus the area of the triangle 0Y20.

(9) Criticisms of the Marginal Productivity Theory

Although there is obvious truth in the statement that entrepreneurs will not buy a factor if it is going to cost more than it produces, this theory has been much criticized. One criticism is that it is all too theoretical, that entrepreneurs cannot know what any one worker's contribution to revenue is. In fact, of course, they don't; but this does not alter the fact that when the entrepreneur maximizes his profits he does so by paying the factors what they deserve according to their marginal-revenue products. The theory does not require that the entrepreneur knows, only that he pays in such a way as to maximize profits. Another criticism is that the theory leads to peculiar conclusions. For example, it might suggest that high wages are the cause of unemployment, because if wages were lower more hands would be taken on. In fact the theory has little to say about the causes of unemployment, which it is generally recognized lie in the region of total monetary demand for goods and services. If the demand for goods and services is generally weak, the derived demand for factors will be weak too. To draw from this the conclusion that lowering wages will raise employment would be quite wrong, for to lower wages at all would only decrease still further the monetary demand, the low level of which is already causing the difficulty. A full discussion of this is to be found on pages 317–33.

(10) The Rewards to Factors

The rewards accruing to the factors are termed respectively rent, wages, interest, and profit.

Rent is that portion of the produce of the earth which is paid to the landlord for the use of the original and indestructible powers of the soil (David Ricardo).

Wages are that portion of the produce of the earth which is paid to the worker for the use of his labour.

Interest is that portion of the produce of the earth paid to the investor for the postponement of his own consumption, and the placing of his claims against resources at the disposal of the entrepreneurs.

Profit is that portion of the produce of the earth paid to the investor for bearing the risks of losing his capital. It is a residual amount left after rewarding the other factors.

Early economists found great difficulty in explaining the rewards to factors, and the definitions given here are the result of more than a century of discussion. For example, the poor rewards paid to workers in the coal mines seemed quite out of proportion to the rewards paid to university lecturers or the rewards paid to professional actresses. A major clue to explain these apparently illogical rewards was the doctrine of 'economic rent'. The name is confusing, since it would appear to refer to land only; but although this idea developed from David Ricardo's view of rent, it is now recognized that 'economic rents' are earned by all factors.

(11) Economic Rent—How the Idea Started

Imagine a country where there is plenty of land, all of good quality and not inhabited by any indigenous people. Some African countries are like this today. There is plenty of good land, and anyone can carve out a smallholding for himself. In these circumstances would anyone pay rent? Of course not, for free land is to be had for the asking. Ricardo said,

'It is only, then, because land is not unlimited in quantity and uniform in quality, and because in the progress of population, land of an inferior quality or less advantageously situated is called into cultivation, that rent is ever paid for the use of it.

When in the progress of society, land of the second degree of fertility is taken into cultivation, rent immediately commences on that of the first quality, and the amount of that rent will depend on the difference in the quality of these two portions of land.

When land of the third quality is taken into cultivation, rent immediately commences on the second, and is regulated as before, by the difference in their productive powers. At the same time the rent of the first quality will rise.'

The point here is that land is not uniform in quality, and as population rises more and more marginal land must come into use. The high costs of production on the most marginal land will decide the price of grain. The better land, yielding a higher return, must earn rent. The rent payable on good or conveniently situated land, as distinct from inaccessible marginal land of poor quality, was a payment to the landlord for the use of its peculiar and indestructible powers.

It was at this point that the difficulty arose. A major controversy during the Napoleonic War period until 1815 had been the high rents of farms. These high rents were due to the high prices for corn resulting from the war. Some politicians, and most ordinary people, blamed the landlords' rents for the high price of bread. Ricardo defended them, proving that the high price of bread was causing the high rents: in other words, *rents were price-determined, not price-determining*.

As this controversy developed, simplification of the argument led to the adoption of two basic premises: (*a*) that land is in short supply, (*b*) it will only grow corn. If it doesn't grow corn, then it will not be used. If it does grow corn, then the rent that it earns is a payment to the factor land over and above what is necessary to keep it in its previous employment, namely lying idle. This rather muddled thinking led to the conclusion that the whole of 'rent' was a surplus payment to landlords for being the fortunate owners of a factor which was in fixed supply and strongly demanded. The stronger the demand, the higher the 'rent'.

The meaning of economic rent, often simply called 'rent', is much wider today, and the idea that rent for land is entirely 'economic rent' has been rejected on the grounds that land does have alternative uses. Vilfredo Pareto, an Italian economist, defined 'rent' as 'a payment to a factor over and above what is necessary to keep it in its present employment'. If a factor, whether it be land, labour, or capital, is not sufficiently rewarded in its present occupation, then it will move out to seek a better reward elsewhere. We must therefore pay the factor at least as much as its 'transfer' earnings. **Transfer earnings** are the amount the factor would earn in its best-paid alternative employment. To use an earlier term, transfer earnings are the 'opportunity cost' of the factor.

A few examples may help. Imagine a lady teacher who has taught in a school for many years and is attached to the village, its people, and her own status in the community. Suppose she earns 60·00 per week. Would she leave the school if they cut her salary to 50·00? Probably not. Would she leave at a salary of 40·00? Possibly not. Would she leave at 30·00? Well, yes, she might. Then 30·00 is her transfer earnings, and she is earning 30·00 'economic rent'.

Consider a baker selling bread and pastries in a country area. He can charge more or less what he likes for cakes, and earns a comfortable living from the business of, say, 60·00 per week. A multiple firm starts to operate in the area selling from mobile shops. The baker is forced to cut prices. When his earnings fall to 34·00 per week he is seriously considering giving up the business. Obviously the 26·00 was 'economic rent'.

Table 21 shows the normal rewards to factors, and the names given to their particular forms of economic rent.

Table 21. Normal and abnormal rewards to factors

Factor	Normal reward	Economic rent
Land	Commercial rent	'Situation rent'
Labour	Wages	'Rent of ability'
Capital (i) (For foregone consumption)	Interest	—
Capital (ii) (For taking risks)	Profit	'Monopoly rent' or 'super-profits'

Notes:

1. Interest does rise above normal sometimes, but because money is 'hot' (able to flow quickly round the system from places where interest is low to places where interest is high) the economic rent it earns is short-lived.
2. Examples of situation rent are the high rents of properties in London's Oxford Street, or Fifth Avenue, New York. Because shoppers in these fashionable areas are prepared to pay high prices, and the number of shop fronts is limited, premises earn more than normal rent. Doctors seeking premises in Harley Street similarly bid up the rents of surgeries in this fashionable area.
3. Rent of ability is the name given to the 'rent' element in wages. There are many examples. A pop singer earning £10,000·00 per week would as willingly sing for £1,000·00, and probably a short while before he reached his sudden popularity was doing so for £20·00. If the best price he could earn in any other occupation is £50·00 per week, then £9,950·00 of his earnings is economic rent.
4. When a monopolist, or a supplier of branded goods, earns more than normal profit, the super-profits earned are often referred to as 'monopoly rent'. Normal profit is that portion of profit which just keeps the entrepreneur in the industry. Monopoly rent, like all economic rent, is a payment to the factor capital over and above what is needed to keep it in its present employment.

(12) Rent, Quasi-Rent, and Elasticity of Supply

If a factor earns more than normal rewards it is because the free flow of factors around the market is interrupted by some sort of economic friction. The ability of some trade unions to exclude non-members from entering an industry is an example of such friction. It enables the union's members to earn more than normal rewards for their labour. Similar 'rents' may be earned by the fortunate possessors of skills which are in great demand and are either the result of natural talent or long training. Both opera singers and computer programmers are able to command economic rents: the first because their natural talents are rare, the second because the supply of trained personnel is inelastic. Dentists and doctors earn more than normal rewards because of the long training required; labourers are often poorly paid because their skills can be quickly acquired.

In deciding the rewards to factors, elasticity of supply is of great importance. If supply is inelastic, factors will be able to command economic rents, and the more fixed the supply the greater the proportion of the reward paid that will be economic rent. If supply is completely fixed, and no alternative use is possible, the price of the factor depends entirely on the demand. An example is the rent of property in a parade of shops. Such land cannot be returned to corn growing or market gardening, and its price is largely economic rent fixed by the demand for its services as shop property. Fig. 70 illustrates the change in rent that follows an alteration in demand.

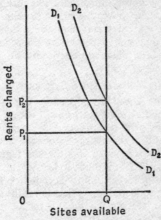

Fig. 70. Economic rent for shop sites

Notes:

1. When demand is D_1D_1 the rent charged is P_1. Probably this rent is 'economic rent' already, because this land has no alternative uses—it is stuck in the middle of a parade of shops.
2. When demand rises to D_2D_2 the rent rises to P_2. Clearly the whole of this increase is 'economic rent', arising from the demand for this type of shop property which is in inelastic supply.

Mark Twain tells an amusing story about the wages of pilots on the Mississippi River steamboats in the nineteenth century. The pilots' union had fixed wages at \$240 a month, but in hard times when there were unemployed pilots about, the steamship owners forced down wages because pilots were in elastic supply. One pilot was forced to sign on for \$100 a month and promptly took his ship up the centre of the river against the full force of the current. Fearful that fuel supplies would run out, the captain sent his compliments and suggested that better speeds could be achieved if the pilot would steer closer to the bank, where a notoriously slow vessel was overtaking them at the moment. Back went the pilot's compliments to the captain, but he could not be expected to know as much as a man earning \$240 a month. The supply of pilots, now that the vessel had left the quayside, was very inelastic indeed, and 30 seconds later the ship was shaving the bushes near the bank, while a pilot on full pay earning his 'fair' share of economic rent was showing the rival steamship what a compound engine could do.

The confusing use of the same word 'rent' to describe things as different as the payment for farm land and the wages of violinists or operatic sopranos, led Alfred Marshall, an eminent Victorian economist to adopt the term 'quasi-rent' for rent earned by the other factors. The Latin word *quasi* means 'as if', and the term quasi-rent therefore indicates a close connection between these abnormal earnings and situation-rent earned by some types of land. The general acceptance of 'rents' as being a reward to any factor over and above what is necessary to keep it in its present employment has led to a change in the use of the term quasi-rent. It is now often used for temporary rents, which will eventually be eliminated by competition. The fortunate owner of stocks of food at a time when, owing to weather or industrial disputes, an area is cut off by transport dislocations, may earn temporary quasi-rents. Similarly, a shortage of computer programmers may lead to higher salaries being earned temporarily by such workers. These are quasi-rents of ability.

(13) Are Rents Price-Determining or Price-Determined?

Ever since Ricardo wrote about rent, discussion has persisted as to whether rents are price-determining or price-determined. Ricardo held that rents are price-determined and not price-determining; in other words that the high price of land was the result of the high price of corn and not the cause of it. The cause of the high price of corn was the shortages due to war and a succession of bad harvests. There is much to be said for this argument. It has already been pointed out in the section on speculation (see page 126) that a speculator selling stored produce at high prices is not the cause of the shortage, but the only person who is doing anything to relieve it. His efforts are not forcing up the price, but tending to reduce it.

By contrast, the high situation-rents paid to landlords in fashionable areas are the result of competition between those in search of property or sites which are in inelastic supply. To the multiple-shop proprietor seeking a site in the West End of London countless sites are available for his particular purpose, even though sites in general are in inelastic supply, so that the whole of the payments he makes are transfer earnings and he certainly includes them in the calculations of the prices he will charge for goods. Such payments therefore form part of the costs of production, and are price-determining. The debate seems likely to continue.

To the extent that rents are the result of the fortunate situation of the individual who benefits, they can be taxed away for the benefit of the general public without the factor being withdrawn from service and without prices being increased. If this is done, the public who have in fact contributed to the rents earned, recoup them through the tax net. It seems highly desirable that this should be so, but it is a political rather than an economic decision.

(14) Summary of Chapter Fifteen

1. The problem of the continued poverty of masses of people, when wealth was being created in great quantities, led the early economists to turn their attention to the distribution of wealth.

2. The entire proceeds of production flow in the form of money payments to individuals who are either landlords, workers, or investors.

3. The proportions in which the wealth is shared depend on the demand for, and supply of, factors.

4. The demand for factors is a derived demand which arises from the demand for utilities to satisfy wants.

5. The entrepreneurs who demand factors will not pay more for them than the marginal-revenue productivity of the factor.

6. The suppliers of factors, landlords, workers, and investors will not supply the factor to any entrepreneur if they can earn a better reward elsewhere, so that factors flow around the factor markets to equalize, in the long run, the net advantage to factor owners.

7. Part of the rewards to factors, which arises when free flow around the markets is interrupted for some reason, is economic rent, a reward paid to any factor which happens for the moment to be in inelastic supply.

(15) Suggested Further Reading

Harvey, J.: *Intermediate Economics*. Macmillan: London, 2nd. Edn., 1971.

Lekachman, R.: *A History of Economic Ideas*. Harper and Row: London, 1965.

Lipsey, R. G., and Stilwell, J. A.: *An Introduction to Positive Economics*. Weidenfeld & Nicolson: London, 3rd. Edn., 1971.

Stonier, A., and Hague, D.: *A Textbook of Economic Theory*. Longmans: London, 1964.

Exercises Set 15

1. 'The production of wealth is one thing; distribution of wealth is another.' What is the importance of the distribution of wealth and how is it arranged in market economies?

2. What is rent? What is economic rent? What is quasi-rent?

3. Explain why a miner might earn £30·00 for a week's work underground, while a television personality earns £1,000·00 for a two-hour programme.

4. Consider the proportion of earnings which are economic rents in each of the following cases:

(*a*) a lady teacher, salary £25·00, who could never dream of taking up any other vocation.

(*b*) A refuse collector earning £20·00 per week, who is thinking of taking employment as a road-haulage driver, for £25·00 per week.

(*c*) A folk ballad singer earning £300·00 per week who used to be a clerk at £17·00 per week.

(*d*) A trade union official, formerly earning £2,700·00 per annum chosen by the Prime Minister to be chairman of a nationalized industry at £25,000·00 per annum. He would be prepared to take on the post even for £5,000·00.

(*e*) A midwife earning £18·00 a week in a British hospital who rejects an offer of a post at a salary equivalent to £60·00 a week in an American small town.

5. What are transfer earnings? What will be the effect on an entrepreneur who refuses to pay this amount to a skilled employee?

6. Distinguish between 'normal profit' and 'monopoly rent'. Can monopoly rents ever be justified?

7. What is the marginal-productivity theory of wages? How far does it explain wages in the real world?

8. What economic forces help to determine the rewards paid to (*a*) a plot of land in a city centre, (*b*) a talented actress, (*c*) a semi-skilled assembler in an electronics factory?

9. This Table shows the number of shirts made in a factory and the number of staff employed. Copy it out and complete the table. Each shirt is worth 0·50.

Women employed	Output of shirts	Marginal product (in currency units of 1·00)
1	24	
2	54	
3	86	
4	116	
5	140	
6	150	
7	158	

How many women will be employed if wages are (i) 10·00, (ii) 15·00?

10. This Table shows the profit earned by a travel agency operating a head office and a number of branches. Each branch costs £10,000 to set up, and a 15 per cent return on capital invested is required. All branches are equally profitable. What is the maximum number of branches that the head office should operate? Copy out and complete the Table.

No. of establishments	Capital used (units of 1·00)	Profit earned (units of 1·00)	Marginal product
Head Office	20,000	4,000	
H.O. + 1 branch	?	6,200	
+ 2 branches	?	8,100	
+ 3 ,,	?	9,800	
+ 4 ,,	?	11,400	
+ 5 ,,	?	12,900	
+ 6 ,,	?	14,000	
+ 7 ,,	?	14,900	
+ 8 ,,	?	15,500	

CHAPTER SIXTEEN

REWARDS TO FACTORS—RENT

(1) Rent—The Reward to Land

Land consists of the resources of the earth made available by Nature. Some of these resources are free goods, like the air and the sunshine. Some are not quite free, but are in abundant supply so that they are relatively cheap, like water and marginal land. Some are in short supply and the fortunate owners of such resources are able to command payments for their use, called rent.

In everyday language, rent is a sum of money paid for the use of landed property. Everyone needs a geographical 'territory', some place that he can call home. He must therefore buy a piece of land and build a house on it, or buy an existing piece of property, or rent a home from someone (called a landlord) who does have such a property surplus to his own requirements. As we have already seen, the meaning of the word 'rent' has become confused, and the terms **economic rent** and **commercial rent** have come into use to differentiate between the special sense in economics and the ordinary commercial meaning. When a tenant pays his rent to a landlord, be it a private landlord, a local council, a New Town Development Corporation, or perhaps a Government department, he is said to be paying 'commercial rent'.

Where the payment is for use of a deposit of natural resources, such as an iron-ore concentration or a bed of gravel or sand, the rent is usually paid in the form of a royalty per ton of mineral extracted. It is often arranged that the royalty owner will be paid at least a minimum sum per annum for the use of the deposit, whether the mining company manages to extract that quantity or not. When this is the arrangement the minimum payment agreed on is called the **minimum rent**.

The word 'rent' is also used in connection with payment for a television set or a motor vehicle. Today we can hire these from firms with names like 'Rentacar' or 'Rentaset'. The 'rents' paid are not, however, payments for a factor, but payments for some product or service supplied on a temporary basis.

The rent of land is decided by the interaction of supply and demand. If demand is strong, or suitable land is in short supply, prices will be high. If demand is weak or land is plentiful, prices will be low.

(2) The Demand for Land

The demand for land is derived from the demand for the satisfaction of the basic wants of shelter and geographical territory. Demand is strong when population is rising, and weak when population is declining. Demand is strong when incomes rise and weaker when incomes fall.

Demand for land is said to be 'price-elastic' when it changes more than proportionally with a change in price. The elasticity of demand for land depends on a number of factors. If the demand for the product to be grown or produced is elastic, the demand for land on which to produce it will be elastic too. If the demand for the product is inelastic, the demand for the land is inelastic too, and it will continue to be demanded despite changes in price. The demand for land in fashionable shopping areas is inelastic because it is very unlikely that customers for fashion goods will ever cease to regard shopping in these areas as a desirable and pleasant way to spend their time and money.

Where substitution with other factors is a possibility the entrepreneur will use less of an expensive factor and more of an inexpensive factor. Thus skyscrapers (capital) in New York are built higher and higher, and a year or two ago considerable discussion occurred in the Press as to the desirability of allowing Buckingham Palace to be overlooked by the London Hilton Hotel. If land is expensive, the addition of extra capital may reduce rents to reasonable proportions. The expensive site costs in great cities are reduced by putting taller buildings on them, which are then rented off as apartments.

(3) The Supply of Land

Early economists were impressed with the shortage of land, which is limited to what Nature has supplied. As they were mostly British, and the land in Great Britain has been completely owned since Norman times, this view is understandable. Perhaps more important, the influential writings of Thomas Malthus on *Population* had led them to expect an early 'population explosion' which would fill the earth with people. In fact changes in both population and in methods of production have slowed down the complete occupation of land, and only in our own time has this problem begun to look serious. Even today it is more a matter of poisoning the world with effluent than a shortage of land for agricultural or industrial purposes.

For many purposes land is in plentiful supply, and activities such as reclamation from the sea and slum clearance in the centres of large cities are even increasing the supply of land. Despite this, shortages do exist in particular areas, or for particular types of land, and both commercial rent and economic rent are everywhere demanded. A particularly interesting example of land shortage is the situation currently facing the authorities of the Port of Rotterdam, in Holland. Not only is land reclamation an important activity for the port authority, but it is vital that the areas made available should be utilized to the full. Applications for land received from industrial and commercial firms are therefore considered very carefully. Plant density is a crucial element in the decision to grant permission to an industrial user, for only the very intensive industries using bulk-carrier shipping to supply very large plants are likely to be economic in the long run. Other industries can be accommodated in less vital areas farther inland or along the canals linking Holland with the Rhine.

The early economists did not envisage the intensive use of land as we know it today. Extensive agriculture is very wasteful of land, and in times past has ruined in a matter of years the fertility built up by millions of years of natural activity. Intensive agriculture, by contrast, preserves and even enhances the fertility of the soil. Intensive housing reduces the spread of urban areas and offers economies in sanitation and other social assets. This has made possible very dense concentrations of population in such areas as Hong Kong and Singapore. In Britain about 10 per cent of land is urban and about 80 per cent agricultural.

When goods are in demand, a higher price calls forth a larger supply. It is less easy to produce extra supplies of land, but land for a particular purpose, such as housing, can always be obtained at a price, provided that planning authorities do not interfere. The supply of land is inelastic, but the supply of land for a particular purpose is much more elastic, and if intensive use is made of it, whether for agriculture (for instance by using greenhouses) or for housing (by building skyscrapers) or for industry (by using dense plant concentrations), it is probably very elastic indeed.

(4) The Price of Land

How much an entrepreneur will pay for the factor land depends on his estimate of the marginal productivity of the land to him. He will not pay more for a cubic yard of sand than he will earn for it from a builder who requires it. He will not pay more for an acre of arable land than he can earn from the best crop he can grow on it. Similarly the landowner will only part with the ownership of a yard of gravel or a ton of ore if he feels that he is being offered a fair price for it. He will only rent an acre of land to a farmer if he feels sure he cannot get a better price for it from some other user of the land. In other words he will always try to obtain the maximum net advantage from the use of his land.

The price of land is fixed as a result of the interaction of supply and demand, the supplier of land attempting to achieve the maximum net advantage from it, and the entrepreneurs demanding it only if its marginal product is likely to exceed the rent payable.

(5) Elasticity of Supply of Land—Rent of Situation

If the price of a commodity rises it will generally call into the market an increased supply of that commodity. If the price of land rises, it may or may not be able to call forth an increased supply of land. For example, an increase in the price being offered by hill farmers may increase the quantity of land available for sheep rearing. An increase in the price of land at the junction of Piccadilly Circus and Haymarket in London cannot produce any increase in the sites in that area. It is this inelasticity of supply which leads to 'economic rent' being paid for land, i.e. 'rent of situation'. Where an entrepreneur is indifferent as to situation he will not pay economic rents, but will set up his enterprise in a cheaper situation elsewhere. Where he is bound to choose a particular site, because the advantages of location outweigh the disadvantages of high cost he will continue to demand land and pay 'situation' rent.

Poor rural land therefore only earns commercial rent; better land earns 'economic rent' as well. For instance, if wheat-growing land is currently fetching 100·00 an acre and entrepreneurs are thinking of planting hop gardens they will have to pay at least the transfer earnings of 100·00 to rent land for hops. If the profitability of hops is such that the demand for land for hops forces up the rent to 140·00 the hop growers as an industry are paying 100·00 as transfer earnings and 40·00 as economic rent.

Urban land, by contrast, is in inelastic supply and its situation is of paramount importance. Whatever the price, its supply cannot be increased, and a large part of its earnings must be 'situation' rent. Entrepreneurs who set up businesses in fashionable areas cannot avoid paying high prices for land.

These high prices are the result of strong demand, and are not a payment for the 'original and indestructible powers of the soil'.

The Location of Offices Bureau, a British Government Commission set up in 1963 to ease the congestion in the Capital by helping firms find premises outside London, give some interesting statistics on rents in the London area compared with other areas. Rents in London are as high as £18 per square foot per year for office accommodation. As each employee requires 120 square feet of space (irrespective of canteen and car-parking space), the cost per worker may be as much as £2,160 per year, when rent, rates, lighting, and heating have been taken into account. Comparable rents are shown in Table 22.

Table 22. Rents in the United Kingdom, 1974

Place	Average cost per sq. ft. per annum	Approximate annual. cost per employee
London	£9 – £18	£1,080 – £2,160
Bedford	£2·00	£240
Colchester	£1·60	£192
Leicester	£1·45	£174
Southend-on-Sea	£2·25	£270
Harrogate	£1·10	£132
Liverpool	£3·00	£360
Edinburgh	£1·60	£192

(6) Summary of Chapter Sixteen

1. Land consists of the resources made available by Nature. In most countries rent is charged for land. If the land is a resource the rent payable is often determined as a royalty per ton of the resource extracted.

2. Commercial rent is payment for the use of landed property.

3. The price of land is the result of the interaction of demand and supply.

4. The demand for land is derived from the demand for agricultural and mineral products.

5. If the price of land is high, substitution of other factors may occur. Thus intensive methods may be adopted in agriculture, or high-rise blocks of flats may be erected on sites to spread the cost of land over a large number of apartments.

6. The entrepreneur demands land as long as its marginal product exceeds the cost price, i.e. the rent payable.

7. The landowner will rent out land to the highest bidder, so as to get the maximum advantage from his land.

8. Where land is in inelastic supply, as with urban land in fashionable areas, the strong demand will raise rents so that the land earns 'situation' rent.

(7) Suggested Further Reading

Hanson, J. L.: *A Textbook of Economics*. Macdonald & Evans: London, 1970.
Lipsey, R. G., and Stilwell, J. A.: *An Introduction to Positive Economics*. Weidenfeld & Nicolson: London, 3rd. Edn., 1971.

Stonier, A., and Hague, D.: *A Textbook of Economic Theory*. Longmans: London, 1964.

Exercises Set 16

1. What is land to an economist? Is land a free commodity? Is it fixed in supply?

2. A cinema owner is looking for a site in the heart of a large city. Consider the rent he might have to pay, and discuss whether it is economic rent.

3. Point out the similarities and differences between the following:

(*a*) the charge to rent a 50-acre farm from an estate owner in a rural area;

(*b*) the charge to rent a site for a supermarket in a new town;

(*c*) the charge to rent a television set;

(*d*) the charge to rent a theatre in London's West End.

4. Explain the following:

(*a*) rent is the price of accommodation;

(*b*) rent is a surplus.

5. Suggest why the opening of a motorway leads to an increase in rents in the areas around access points to the motorway.

6. 'The cost of reclaiming this land from the sea is high. We suggest therefore that the location of the Wheaty Biscuit Company on this site will be unsatisfactory, in view of the high rents; the site should therefore be reserved either for the James Watt Engineering Co., or the Mogul Oil Co.' Discuss.

7. 'Consult us when you choose your industrial site. Government grants available' (Development Area New Town Corporation). What are the rent implications of this advertisement?

CHAPTER SEVENTEEN

REWARDS TO FACTORS—WAGES

(1) Wages—the Reward to Labour

Labour has been defined as the supply of human resources, both physical and mental, which is available to engage in the production of goods and services. The reward paid for labour is wages, though some prefer the term salaries. To an accountant there is a difference: the term 'salaries' is generally used to designate the pay of office or supervisory staff, and this forms part of overhead expenses rather than part of prime costs. To the economist wages and salaries are merely alternative names for the reward earned by the factor labour.

Labour is not homogeneous, for it is a human resource. Labour may be intelligent or stupid, skilled or unskilled, enthusiastic or work-shy, co-operative or resentful. An industry may have a history of bad labour relations over a long period, so that men are embittered by years of low wages and repressive management. Such was the situation in the mining industry in Great Britain before nationalization in 1947. By contrast many employees develop such loyalty to their firms that they do not change to more rewarding employment, enjoying instead non-monetary satisfactions.

In these circumstances economic theory can never be precise, and the more extensive the field under discussion the broader the terms we have to use. This chapter draws attention to some of the major influences at work in the determination of wages.

(2) Wage-Rates and Earnings

Wage-rates are the price of labour, which entrepreneurs are prepared to pay for the use of a man's physical or mental skills. They may be expressed in units of time: so much an hour, so much a week, or month. They may be piece-rates: so much per unit of production. In free competition entrepreneurs would vary the rates they offer according to the marginal net product of the worker. In practice these rates are often the subject of negotiation between the representatives of labour and management, and cannot be varied according to economic theory.

Earnings means the actual sum of money earned. They may be the agreed weekly or monthly wage; or the product of the hourly wage rate and the hours worked; or the product of the piece-rate and the number of pieces produced. A bespoke tailor paid 12·50 per coat who makes seven coats in a week has earnings of 87·50. The following points are of interest when contrasting time-rates and wage-rates.

Time-rates

Time-rates are more satisfactory when:

(*a*) Output cannot be easily measured. For example, in teaching, most professional employments, or police work.

(*b*) The employment itself is the incentive, so that there is no need to devise incentives to higher productivity. This is true in many professional and near-professional employments, in clerical work of many sorts, and supervision posts in factories.

(*c*) Where high speed is impossible, or might be harmful, as in transport services, hospital services, repair work of many sorts.

Sometimes time-rates are unsatisfactory, especially if overtime is regularly worked. There is a temptation to go easy during the day so that plenty of overtime will be available. This means supervision of workers is essential. With time-rates, the work output may become that of the least-willing worker. The energetic and enthusiastic man receives no direct reward for his extra effort, and may even be looked upon as someone who is trying to spoil things for the rest. Such situations are less likely to develop with a piece-work system.

Piece-rates

The advantages of piece-rates are:

(*a*) Productivity is raised, because there is no bar to the hard worker earning a reward for his extra effort. The worker is keen to reach work, keen to start work, and reluctant to stop work.

(*b*) A different kind of spirit develops, with workers devising new methods of work which raise output.

(*c*) Capital costs are lowered, for the machinery is used more intensively so that machine failure precedes obsolescence, and the subsequent re-tooling with modern equipment raises output to new levels.

At the same time piece-work has disadvantages. It turns men into money-making machines, causing them to overwork. It leads to resentment by the less nimble and less efficient of their more active or more successful fellow workers. One remedy is to change to team piece-rates, where the extra product is shared evenly among the team. This reduces friction, but may lower productivity if the more active reduce their efforts now the incentive has gone.

Piece-work causes difficulties when new rates have to be negotiated, and causes unrest when agreements in one field of activity enable workers to earn more than workers in other parts of the plant, or industry. Sometimes piece-work rates are regressive, i.e. less is earned per unit on higher outputs. This reduces the worker's incentive to work hard.

(3) Money Wages and Real Wages

Money wages refers to the actual money earned by the worker. *Real wages* refers to the actual 'basket' of goods and services which he can purchase with his money wages. In periods of rising prices workers may be conceded wage increases by employers, but may find that their increased money wages have not enabled them to buy as many goods and services as before. Like Alice in Wonderland, they have to keep running desperately hard just to keep where they are. Conversely, in times of falling prices, workers who are forced to accept a cut in salary may still find themselves better off, because their reduced money incomes have not fallen as much as prices have fallen. When the massive slump between the two world wars lowered prices to very low levels, schoolteachers who were forced to take a very serious cut in salary found that in fact they had suffered no real hardship.

The index figures (Jan. 1970 = 100) in Table 23 illustrate the changes in the United Kingdom in earnings and retail prices.

Table 23. Average earnings and prices, 1970–76

Source: Monthly Digest of Statistics	1970	1973	1974	1975	1976
Average earnings	100	153	180	228	261
Retail prices	100	128	149	185	215

Notes
1. Average earnings rose, surging upwards in 1974–5.
2. Retail prices rose steadily, but not by quite as much.
3. It follows that although the average citizen is not as well off as the rise in money earning would indicate, he has made some advance in real terms. He is actually able to enjoy 21 per cent more actual goods than he could afford in 1970.

(4) Early Theories about Wages

Reference has already been made to the difficulties early economists experienced in explaining the unequal distribution of wealth and the continuing poverty of the masses of the people. It was the meagre wages of the poor which caused their miserable share of the world's produce, and the economists did little to improve their lot. Economic theory furnished excellent excuses to the capitalist classes for the perpetuation of low wages, and led Thomas Carlyle to call political economy a 'dismal science'. The chief of the excuses for keeping wages low was advanced by Malthus in his *Essay on Population*, which appeared anonymously in 1798. Let us pause to consider its influence.

Thomas Robert Malthus (1766–1834) and the Subsistence Theory of Wages

Thomas Malthus was the son of a country squire, who became a parson for a short while after leaving university where he read mathematics and philosophy. The climate of thought at the time, when the French Revolution had not yet turned ugly and revengeful, was optimistic. Progress was in the air: it was an Age of Reason. Tom Paine's book of that name was just about to appear, and the development and perfection of a better society, with better men to live in it, was optimistically forecast. Malthus was sceptical, and when the mood in France changed, he pondered on the forces acting against the improvement of mankind. He decided that population pressure was the chief cause of poverty, and his *Essay on Population* described, without real evidence of any kind, the 'inevitable' nature of the forces at work.

Briefly, the *Essay on Population* held that population tended to increase in geometrical ratio, e.g. 2–4–8–16–32–64 etc., with world population doubling every twenty-five years. By contrast, land was limited in area and could only be improved by heavy capital investment. The likely improvement in food supplies was at best an arithmetic progression, e.g. 2–4–6–8–10–12. The difference between the two ratios made poverty inevitable unless the passion between the sexes could be controlled. Why, then, had mankind survived thus far? Because natural checks were exerted to redress the balance between population and food supply. These checks were of two sorts. Self-restraint, displayed chiefly by the rich and prosperous, was used to reduce the size of families for fear of poverty or decline in the social scale. Marriage was postponed until later in life, and the size of families was limited voluntarily to maintain the standard of living of the family.

For the poor, with no motive for reducing sexual appetite, nature had devised positive checks. Infant mortality, infanticide, diseases, epidemics, plagues, unwholesome foods, dangerous occupations, and even famine which 'with one mighty blow, levels the population with the food of the world'.

His theories were at once siezed upon and expounded by the leaders of society of his time. The spokesmen of the poor reviled the essay and its author, but were powerless to defeat arguments which fitted so well with the established political and economic framework of the times. Why pay higher wages when the only result would be an increase in sexual appetite and a new generation to eat the parents down to the poverty level again? Why envisage safer working conditions, better housing, and better sanitation when these checks and balances were but a natural device to prevent famine from stalking the land? Well might William Cobbett, the radical writer, say 'Parson! I have during my life detested many men; but never anyone so much as you'.

Although respectable opinion took up his arguments, and Malthus himself was much listened to throughout his lifetime, the world has escaped until now the dire calamities he foretold. The opening up of the American prairies, the Ukraine, Australia, New Zealand, and Argentina proved capable of supporting mankind for a century or two. Whether Malthus might yet be proved right is a different matter, discussed later in this chapter.

The germ of Malthus's ideas came from the French 'physiocrats' who held that it was in the nature of things that wages could never rise above a bare subsistence level. When wages did for a time rise much above the bare necessities of life, the illusion of prosperity produced larger families, and the severe competition among workers was soon at work to reduce wages again. In a world where child labour was the rule, it was only a few years before the children forced unemployment upon the parents, and all were reduced to poverty. Such was the **Subsistence Theory of Wages.** The working classes were eventually to prove it wrong. With the gradual growth in the complexity of work and the scale of enterprise, the demand for labour began to exceed the supply. The subsistence theory speaks only of the supply of labour, it does not take any heed of the demand side. As demand grew, labour was able to exact its due rewards. That it had grown bitter in the process was, perhaps, regrettable. Much of that bitterness came from fear of the workhouse—an enduring monument to Malthus's effect upon the times in which he lived.

David Ricardo and the 'Wages Fund' Theory of Wages

While chiefly remembered for his ideas on rent (see page 170), Ricardo's theory of wages is also of interest. He held that, like any other commodity, the price of labour depended on supply and demand. On the demand side, the capital available to entrepreneurs was the sole source of payment for the workers, and represented a 'wages fund' from which they could be paid. On the supply side, labour supply depended upon Malthusian arguments about population. The intense competition of labourers one with another, at a time when combinations of workers to withdraw their labour from the market were illegal, kept the price of labour low. The fraction

$$\frac{\text{Total wages fund } (capital\ available)}{\text{Total population}}$$

fixed the wages of working men.

Here was a second theory which was seized upon by the employing classes to justify the continuation of low wages. Despite some optimistic suggestions by Ricardo tending to modify the severity of the 'iron laws of wages' (such as his suggestion that subsistence level might mean different things in different countries), advocates of the theory used it to justify the abolition of the Poor Laws. Even Ricardo argued that any interference with market forces was bad, because it prevented the mass of the people from experiencing that grinding poverty which alone could teach them not to have more young ones. The Poor Law system of that time, devised by the magistrates of Speenhamland in Berkshire, was to levy rates in support of the poor, and to subsidize the wages of low-paid workers by giving them public assistance to support their families. Ricardo's theory holds that such action must be wrong, because in raising rates (i.e. local taxes) from the rich of the neighbourhood, you must reduce their ability to save; and it is the savings of the rich which provides the capital for the wages fund. If you reduce the wages fund there is less for the workers to receive as wages.

Ricardo held that if population could be restrained, so that wages could be increased to the point where workers could enjoy high wages for a few years, the experience of plenty would convince working people how much better prosperity was than large families. Education could not of itself convince people, only that most efficient of educators, experience, both bitter and sweet.

Today we reject the idea that capital is the sole source of wages; there is no 'wages fund' as Ricardo envisaged it. Not only do the banks 'create' capital by multiplying up the savings deposited with them, but the current earnings of firms form part of the rewards to labour. It is not capital alone, but the whole National Income, which is the source of rewards to factors.

Before leaving this section about early theories of wages, it is appropriate to consider the life and writings of one early writer and thinker whose ideas still command a wide following.

Karl Marx (1818–83) and the 'Full Fruits of Production' Theory of Wages

Karl Marx was a scholar, philosopher, journalist, and revolutionary extraordinary who spent much of his life in dedicated poverty reading in the British Museum library. His impressive series of books, and those of his great collaborator Friedrich Engels, are read more widely today than they were in his own times and have been translated into every language. His fundamental philosophy of 'dialectical materialism' rejects religion and holds that human progress is the result of interacting and opposing forces in the real world. His labour theory of value held that a commodity's worth was directly related to the hours of work that had gone into making it, under the normal conditions of production and with the average degree of skill and intensity prevalent at the time. Because only labour created value, the worker was entitled to the full fruits of production. Those sums distributed as rent, interest, and profits, which Marx called surplus values, were stolen from the worker by the capitalist class. He prophesied that the increasing rapacity of the capitalist class and the increasing misery of the masses of the people would inevitably lead to a revolutionary overthrow of the system, in which the capitalists would themselves be expropriated. The socialization of the means of production, distribution, and exchange would restore to the masses the full fruits of their activities.

Marx's enduring appeal lies in the emotional idealism he inspired. To bring a heaven upon earth within the reach of the world's starving masses is everywhere deemed an acceptable aim. That later Capitalism has proved less demanding and rapacious than Marx envisaged is perhaps only a reaction to the widespread support his ideas received. That Communism has proved largely unable to achieve the aims in real life which its founders envisaged is a measure of the weaknesses in Marx's economics.

(5) The Marginal Productivity Theory of Wages

This theory has already been explained on page 175. It holds that entrepreneurs will only purchase the factor labour when its price (i.e. wages) is less than the marginal product of an additional unit. Labour, on the other hand, moves between various employments to achieve the maximum net personal advantage. Wages, the price of labour, are fixed by the interaction of the demand for labour and the supply of labour.

The Demand for Labour

We have seen that the demand for each factor is a derived demand, arising from the demand for the goods and services the factor makes available. In the case of labour, this results in a demand curve which slopes off towards the right in the usual way: more labour will be demanded when the price is low, provided that other things remain unchanged. As shown in Fig. 69 (page 175) the demand curve for labour is the same curve as the marginal-revenue productivity curve. How far out from the origin of the graph will such a curve be? This depends on the marginal productivity of labour, which varies either with the price of the goods or the productivity of the workers. A change in price might occur through a change in demand for the product being considered. If the price of the product increases it will raise the marginal-revenue productivity of labour, and entrepreneurs will be prepared to employ more workers. If the price of the product remains steady but the productivity of workers is increased so that costs per unit of output are lowered, this will again raise the marginal revenue produced and will encourage entrepreneurs to employ more workers. Thus a trade union like the Electrical Trades Union might well support an advertising policy encouraging the householder to adopt electrical storage heaters as a method of domestic heating, while at the same time urging its members to abandon some practice which reduced output. The first would shift the demand curve for labour to the right by increasing demand for the product; the second would shift it to the right by making the industry more profitable. Either way the effect is to increase both wages and the number of men employed (see Fig. 71 overleaf).

The Elasticity of Demand for Labour

The elasticity of demand for labour is also of great importance in the fixing of wages. If the demand for labour is elastic, entrepreneurs will be able to withdraw easily from the market and it will therefore be difficult for labour to secure wage increases.

The demand for labour will be elastic when: (*a*) the demand for the final product is elastic; (*b*) the labour can be replaced by other labour; (*c*) other factors (particularly capital) can replace the labour; (*d*) labour costs represent a high proportion of total costs.

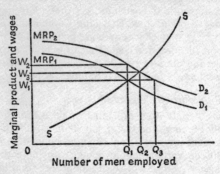

Fig. 71. The effect on wages and employment of a change in marginal productivity of labour

Notes:

1. The marginal-revenue product curve is the same as the demand curve for labour.
2. When the marginal revenue produced rises the curve moves to the right to MRP_2.
3. The possibilities are now as follows:

   (*a*) The present workers Q_1 will earn higher incomes, wages rising to W_2.

   (*b*) If extra workers are able to come in the supply of labour extends to Q_2 and wages rise only to W_3.

   (*c*) If there was unemployment in the trade so that the supply curve was infinitely elastic, employment would increase to Q_3 and the wages would remain at W_1 since the supply curve would be horizontal.

(*a*) *Elasticity of demand for labour and the demand for the final product.* The supplier who concedes a wage increase must raise prices to the consumer. This means that a smaller supply will be available at every price, and a change in the conditions of supply has occurred. The different effects on the sales of products which are in elastic demand, and on those in inelastic demand, is shown in Fig. 72.

(*b*) *Elasticity of demand for labour which is unskilled.* The most likely substitute for any particular class of labour is other labour. It follows that unskilled workers find it difficult to secure wage increases in the face of determined entrepreneurs, for other workers can easily be substituted for them. Provided that the demand for the product that he can make is strong, the demand for a skilled worker's services will be inelastic. Consequently his bargaining position will be a strong one, since he can always move to a position of greater net personal advantage. Immigrant labour is often unskilled labour, since the most mobile form of labour is peasant labour, moving from peasant communities to towns. This movement of unskilled labour is a feature of present-day populations, not only from the new Commonwealth countries to Great

Britain, but from the Mediterranean lands to the Common Market countries, from African villages to the towns, and from the rural areas of South America to the cities of the coastal regions. Some of the opposition to this type of immigration comes from unskilled workers fearing its effect on their standard of living.

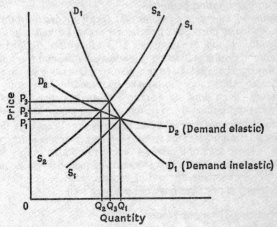

Fig. 72. The effect of elasticity of demand on sales after a price increase

Notes:

1. Owing to an increase in wages the supply curve has moved to the left.
2. The price of the product which is in elastic demand rises a little, and demand contracts a great deal, to Q_2.
3. The price of the product which is in inelastic demand rises a great deal, but demand only contracts a little to Q_3.
4. It follows that a supplier whose product is in elastic demand will resist wage increases more than a supplier whose product is in inelastic demand. If wage increases are forced upon him he will reduce the demand for labour.

(c) *Elasticity of demand for labour which can be replaced by machinery.* Elastic demand might be found where it was possible to substitute other factors, particularly capital, for labour. Aggressive wages policies by labourers might result in the purchase by contractors of mechanical earth-shifting equipment which reduces the demand for labour considerably. The demand for labour will be more elastic if such aids are cheap. *In purchasing a balanced assortment of factors an entrepreneur will select them until their marginal products relative to their prices are equal.*

(d) *Elasticity of demand for labour where labour costs form a high proportion of total costs.* In these circumstances any increase in labour costs means a considerable increase in the sale price charged for the ultimate product, and a reduction in profit margins if the demand for the product is at all elastic. The granting of such wage increases will therefore mean serious reductions in the marginal-revenue productivity of labour, and the entrepreneur will therefore reduce demand for it at the higher prices he must now pay.

The Supply of Labour

The supply of labour depends on several features of the society under discussion. First there is the population structure. Then there are the prevailing customs and laws about education and employment, the willingness of labour to work for the wages and other incentives offered to it, and the degree of emigration or immigration permitted.

The **mobility of labour** is an important factor in deciding the supply of labour for particular purposes or particular areas. Labour tends to be most mobile when it is young, or unmarried. It is difficult for labour to flow from one area to another unless housing is made available, and the social costs of providing this may be great. Labour is also very immobile where retraining is required, because the supply can only be increased by fairly long courses of training during which time the worker is non-productive. If mature adults with family responsibilities are to be retrained, for example because their unemployment is *structural* (caused by a change in world demand), the costs will be great. Such retraining is often resisted by workers in the industry for which they are to be trained, since it involves an increase in the supply of their type of skilled labour which results in a reduction of their bargaining power. Such retraining is therefore best directed at growth areas of industry where traditional trade-union practices have not yet appeared.

(6) The Bargaining Theory of Wages

Some economists argue that the only appropriate theory of wages for the second half of the twentieth century is one that recognizes that decisions about wages are made by two groups of monopolists. The organized trade unions are monopolist suppliers of labour; the organized employers are monopolist (strictly speaking, 'monopsonist') buyers of labour. Most wage bargains are struck between these two organized groups, who are therefore the important operators in the wages market. If we accept that there is some truth in this idea, then we must also recognize that the Government is a third important operator on the labour market. First, the Government is often holding the economy at a satisfactory level by techniques developed to manage the economy, so that the bargainers can only operate in the climate of market activity which prevails. Secondly, the Government has a part to play in preventing the erosion of the standard of living of the unorganized part of the community, the pensioners, the young, and the poorly organized workers. Whether it does this by an openly discussed **Incomes Policy** or by more subtle measures, it is 'holding the ring' for the rest of the people to ensure that neither group of monopolists exploits its position. A full discussion of Incomes Policy is given on page 356. Here we must consider what is meant by collective bargaining.

Collective Bargaining

The worker is at his most vulnerable when he is not represented by any organization. He has small reserves and must find employment quickly. He has an imperfect knowledge of the market, and cannot know where to offer his labour for the best reward. If there is surplus labour available, workers may compete with one another to their mutual disadvantage and to the benefit of the employer. Workers have therefore formed trade unions to represent them in any bargaining that is to take place. The advantages of collective activity are also appreciated by the entrepreneurs. If wages are agreed throughout the industry, the fierceness of competition is reduced. Rival employers cannot cut costs by cutting wages, and hence price competition is reduced.

Functions of Trade Unions. From among the varied functions of present-day trade unions we may pick out the following:

(*a*) Securing an adequate reward to members for their efforts in the employment concerned. The adequacy of this reward may depend on the extent to which social provision is made for education, health, unemployment relief, and sickness benefit: if these are socially provided, the wage demanded will be reduced. If the employee has to provide these things for himself he will need a higher level of wages.

(*b*) Securing an improvement in working conditions. These include safer systems of work in hazardous employments like mining; provision of special clothing and protective equipment where dirty or dangerous materials are in use; reducing hours of work and extending holiday periods etc.

(*c*) The provision of educational, recreational, and social amenities. Particular emphasis is placed on adequate training for apprentices and new workers.

Besides these major activities, trade-union opinion is becoming increasingly influential in all sorts of policy-making activities. Government committees, quasi-judicial inquiries and tribunals, nationalized boards etc., all have trade-union representation as a matter of course.

Conditions Favourable to Wage Increases

Generally speaking, a trade union will be able to obtain concessions from employers which result in wage increases in the following circumstances:

(*a*) Where the demand for goods is strong, so that the entrepreneurs are likely to be able to pass on the increased wages to the consumer in the form of increased prices. This has an inflationary effect on the economy, and is discussed on page 329.

(*b*) Where the increased wages can be justified on the grounds of increased productivity. This means that a promise of higher outputs per worker will be made, so that the increased wages need not cause an increase in prices but can be spread over the larger volume of stock that is manufactured. Such increases in productivity are achieved by abandoning restrictive practices directed against new machinery or new methods of work.

(*c*) Where too large a labour force exists in the industry. If labour can be persuaded to retire from the industry, taking some sort of severance pay as compensation, the fewer workers left in the industry can then enjoy higher wages. Recently the dock labour force in the Port of London has accepted a very considerable reduction in the register of port workers in return for substantial wage increases to the remainder of the labour force. Wage increases are accepted at the expense of employment.

(*d*) Where entrepreneurs are earning 'economic rents', and the trade union can bring sufficient force to bear on their employers to make them yield up some of these profits.

(*e*) Where the employer is a low-cost employer, whose low-cost position is being partly achieved by the exploitation of the workers, i.e. by paying them a smaller wage than the marginal net product. In such circumstances there is a strong incentive for the workers to organize, and such an organization may compel concessions. Workers exploited in this way are sometimes difficult to organize, however. They may be scattered in many small firms, or live in areas where unemployment is abnormally high. They may be immigrants, who do not speak the language, or refugees fearful of deportation.

(7) 'Economic Rent' and Wages

Labour is very diverse and the rewards paid to workers vary greatly. There is very often some element of economic rent in wages: some payment to the worker over and above what is necessary to keep him in his present employment. This is called 'rent of ability'. Common examples are the high fees earned by professional musicians and vocalists of international reputation. Former trade-union officials appointed to lucrative posts at the head of public corporations are earning economic rents; so are employees in industries with strong trade-union restrictions on the entry of apprentices. Professional bodies who make examinations artificially difficult to pass so that the profession will not become overcrowded secure 'economic rents' for their members; so do shop stewards who negotiate agreements permitting the addition of overtime hours to wage claims, even though the overtime is not in fact worked. It must be admitted that the term 'rent of ability' seems inappropriate in some of these examples. Perhaps a better name is 'scarcity rents'.

(8) Summary of Chapter Seventeen

1. The reward paid to the factor labour is called wages.

2. Wages are often different from earnings, because of the inclusion of payments like overtime money and bonus money.

3. The common ways of calculating earnings are 'time' rates and 'piece' rates.

4. Money wages are not the same as real wages. An increase in money wages will not mean an increased standard of living if prices are rising as fast as incomes.

5. Among early theories of wages, the Subsistence Theory held that the mass of the people would always be poor because any increase in living standards was counteracted by a rise in population. The Wages-Fund Theory held that taxation of the rich to help the poor was self-defeating; it only reduced the savings of the rich, whose contributions to the fund of capital out of which wages were paid were thereby decreased.

6. Modern theories of wages include the Marginal-Productivity Theory and the Bargaining Theory. The latter holds that wages are decided by the bargaining of two sets of monopolists: the organized trade unions and the employers' organizations.

7. 'Rent of ability' is the economic rent earned by the factor labour.

(9) Suggested Further Reading

Dobb, M.: *Wages*. Nisbet: 1956.
Hanson, J. L.: *A Textbook of Economics*. Macdonald & Evans: London, 1970.
Lekachman, R.: *A History of Economic Ideas* (Chapters 7 and 9). Harper & Row: London, 1965.

Lipsey, R. G., and Stilwell, J. A.: *An Introduction to Positive Economics.* 3rd. Edn. Weidenfeld & Nicolson: London, 1971.

Exercises Set 17

1. What are 'wages' to an economist? Distinguish between money wages and real wages.

2. What sorts of employment could best be rewarded by a 'piece-rate' wages system? What are the advantages of piece-rates from the point of view of (*a*) workers, (*b*) entrepreneurs?

3. What is the elasticity of demand for labour? Is the demand for machinists in the garment trades likely to be elastic or inelastic? Give reasons.

4. Discuss whether the supply of labour will be increased or decreased by the following. In each case indicate the likely effect on wages.

(*a*) The reduction of apprenticeship periods from seven years to five years owing to changed educational achievements prior to the commencement of the apprenticeship.

(*b*) Prohibition of immigration from less developed areas of the world.

(*c*) Institution of a lump-sum premium on entry to all professional occupations.

(*d*) Institution of 'degree entrants only' qualifications for the teaching profession, simultaneously with a fully professional scale of rewards to teachers.

(*e*) Abandonment of educational entry requirements for lawyers' clerks.

5. 'The market for labour is very imperfect, yet competition is fierce.' Discuss.

6. Distinguish between money wages and real wages. If money wages rise by 50 per cent and prices rise by 25 per cent, what increase has the worker achieved in real terms?

7. What do you understand by the Malthusian Doctrine? Why did it have such a profound effect upon the early nineteenth century?

8. Why are wages generally lower in India than in Great Britain?

9. What do you understand by the term mobility of labour? In your answer consider the following cases:

(*a*) A French peasant whose farm is suffering from soil erosion who hears of cheap land in Canada.

(*b*) A teacher devoted to her pupils in the primary school who is offered a post at a secondary school 300 miles away.

(*c*) A skilled engineer offered a post as research technician in a university department at a slightly lower wage than his present one.

(*d*) A young machinist of limited intelligence. She has just been praised by her employer for completing a dozen garments without a single reject for the first time since she took employment.

10. What is 'collective bargaining'? What economic circumstances favour the employers in such bargaining?

CHAPTER EIGHTEEN

REWARDS TO FACTORS—INTEREST

(1) Interest—the Reward to Capital

We have already discussed (see page 23) some aspects of capital. In economics the word 'capital' has several meanings. It refers first to **liquid capital**, funds available in money form which are not required for consumption purposes but can be set aside by consumers for the use of entrepreneurs as factor capital, to be engaged in production. **Fixed capital** refers to the solid assets created by the entrepreneurs from some of the liquid capital made available to them. They may be buildings, plant, machinery, furniture, motor vehicles etc. These then become part of either **private capital**, which is a stock of assets owned and controlled by firms or individuals for private purposes, or **social capital**, a stock of assets owned and controlled communally for the benefit or enjoyment of the citizens as a whole. The rest of the liquid capital may be used as **working capital**, to buy stocks and pay wages in the actual production of consumer goods.

Liquid capital is really a claim against the goods and services produced in the previous production period, which the recipient of the money income decides to save. If I earn 40·00 per week but my needs are satisfied with an expenditure of 32·00 per week, the remaining 8·00 can be saved. I will postpone consuming this further share of the world's goods to which I am entitled, and make it available to any entrepreneur who wishes to borrow it, provided that I feel sure I shall be able to regain it when required, and that he will pay me something for postponing my consumption. This payment for postponing consumption is called **interest**.

Interest is the payment made for a loan of liquid capital. It is usually paid at an agreed rate per cent.

The entrepreneur who receives the use of the money then uses it to employ other factors (i.e. land and labour) either to create consumption goods or non-consumption goods, in other words to create capital goods. In this way the liquid capital is turned into fixed capital, a stock of producer goods which will be available in the future for producing an increased supply of consumer goods. Thus liquid capital employed to produce an oil refinery results in increased supply of petrol for many years to come, while liquid capital used to build a theatre or an opera-house provides entertainment for future generations.

(2) Collecting Capital—the Institutional Investor

If I decide to save 8·00 per week, as suggested above, I shall need to feel sure that I can regain my funds at any time should I require them. I may have decided to save for a specific purpose, like a holiday or a new car. I may have simply decided to save in case some unfortunate event occurs, like an illness or an accident. Everyone likes to have some reserves 'against a rainy day'. As very few of us are experienced enough, or have enough time, to judge whether an entrepreneur's schemes are sound or not, it is quite common to leave these problems to a specialist such as a banker. Most ordinary people therefore save money with a bank or building society, where funds are absolutely safe and a reasonable rate of interest is earned, and leave it to the institution to direct it where it is required.

Some of the savings made available each week are used for short-term loans to businessmen, local authorities, and Government agencies, who for some reason have temporary need of money. People, for example, pay taxes in an uneven way, so that sometimes the Government is short of cash, while at other times it has funds to spare. This type of short term loan is arranged on what is called the 'Money Market', a general term for many different kinds of financial specialists who supply certain types of loans. There are Discount Houses, Merchant Bankers, Accepting Houses, Commercial Banks, Finance Houses, Mercantile Credit Bankers etc.

The rest of the savings made available may go into more permanent forms of loan, which are designed to be used in producing fixed capital assets, like buildings and plant. This more permanent type of investment is handled rather differently by what is called the 'Capital Market'. This again consists of a number of firms acting in different ways. Some of the commoner types are Unit Trusts and Investment Trusts, Issuing Houses and Building Societies; the Stock Exchange provides a special market where those who have saved in the past but now wish to regain liquidity may do so by selling their investments for cash.

Since many of these institutions spread their investments and loans over a wide field of industrial and commercial activity, in other words develop *balanced portfolios of investments*, they may be found operating in both the capital market and the money market.

The small saver, by lending his money on agreed terms to a bank or building society, or perhaps to an insurance company, achieves a reasonably secure investment without having to bother about the safety of the money he has saved. The institution to whom he has lent his money will take on the responsibility of checking the security of the investment. These institutions and their activities are described in Chapter Twenty. (See page 220.)

(3) The Supply of Loanable Funds

(*a*) *Savings by Individuals.* The ability of individuals to save varies with their personal incomes and personal situations. Some individuals have a high **propensity to consume.** They may have families to support, or need expensive medical treatment and care. They may have carefree personalities which give no thought to tomorrow, and be prodigal in their behaviour. Others have a high **propensity to save**, counting thrift a great virtue and abhorring waste of economic resources, however trivial. Generally speaking the income of the individual affects his propensity to save. A poor man, earning a wage of 25·00 per week will find it difficult to pay his way in the world and may even need welfare payments from the State to help him meet his most elementary needs. He has a high propensity to consume—more than 100 per cent of his earned income. A rich man, earning 500·00 per week, may spend 100·00 on current requirements per week—four times more than the poor man—yet be said to have a low propensity to consume and a high propensity to save, because he is only spending 20 per cent of his income. Clearly the terms 'propensity to consume' and 'propensity to save' are relative terms: they are meaningful only when related to income. The 25 of the 'spendthrift' poor man is much less than the 100 spent by the 'thrifty' rich man.

(*b*) *Savings by Corporations or Companies.* Corporations save on a very large scale, retaining in their businesses profits which have been earned in the course of their activities. These profits really belong to the shareholders, who might prefer that they should be distributed as dividends, but the distribution of dividends is a matter of company policy. Cautious directors may prefer to retain profits as reserves to meet future contingencies. Sometimes Governments require them to do so, and impose a policy of 'dividend restraint'. While it is probably desirable in many cases for firms to retain adequate reserves, so that the business can be expanded, there are disadvantages too. One disadvantage is that the large, well established firm is never short of capital, and its directors may be led to spend these reserves on less essential assets. Splendid executive suites contribute little to higher productivity. If the same funds had been returned to their true owners, the shareholders, they might have been employed more usefully—for example in helping struggling inventors to exploit bright ideas.

(*c*) *Savings by Governments.* Governments frequently save, sometimes on a grand scale. Since a Government is by definition a law-making body employing forces to impose the law among its citizens, it can impose taxation and compel the payment thereof. This enables it to make people 'save', if it seems desirable to do so, by taxing away their incomes. There are many occasions when the existence of excess spending power in a country's economy is liable to produce an inflationary situation. Such a situation would benefit no one and do many people harm. Inflation is discussed on page 329.

In 1968 the Chancellor of the Exchequer withdrew from the British economy by special taxation an extra sum of £934 million. This very severe Government 'saving' was an example of **budgeting for a surplus**, i.e. taxing people by more than the Government really needs, to enforce 'savings' from the population. Conversely, on April 1st, 1977, the United Kingdom foreign currency debt stood at $11·5 billion, while nationalized industries and other public sector bodies had borrowed a further $10·7 billion, a truly staggering example of dis-saving, or **budgeting for a deficit.**

(4) The Demand for Loanable Funds

Funds are required by the same three groups that make funds available: individual citizens, corporations or firms, and the Government. Individuals and firms are numerous, and some can be saving while others are borrowing. Government agencies are also numerous, and may be carrying out different activities at different times. For example, when the Treasury is busy collecting funds, other departments may be disbursing funds; temporary loans called 'Ways and Means Loans' may then be arranged for particular departments when required.

(*a*) *Individuals* demand loans for a variety of purposes, of which house purchase and hire purchase of consumer durables (e.g. television sets and motor cars) are the most important. In February 1977 total hire purchase debt in the United Kingdom stood at £2,661 million. Much of this was provided by finance houses, but as Table 24 shows, the banks provided them with £541 million.

At the same time almost £9,000 million was on loan from banks to manu-facturing industries, and another £4,000 million to agriculture, forestry and mining enterprises. The banks had also lent over £4,000 million to individuals and £11,000 million to service industries like transport, wholesalers and retailers. Total bank advances exceeded £35,000 million.

Table 24. Classification of bankers' loans

	Feb 1977			Feb 1977	
	£'s m	%		£'s m	%
Manufacturing			**Services**		
Food, drink and tobacco	1,431	4	Transport and communications	1,553	4·5
Chemicals etc.	1,484	4·5	Public Utilities, national and local		
Metal manufacturing	542	1·5	government	3,250	9·5
Engineering, ship-building & vehicles	3,078	8·5	Distribution	3,737	10·5
Other manufacturing	2,177	6	Other services	2,666	7·5
Total manufacturing	8,712	24·5	Total services	11,206	32·0
Other production			**Financial**		
Agriculture, Forestry and fishing	1,161	3·5	Hire purchase, finance houses	541	1·5
Mining and quarrying	1,308	3·5	Property companies	2,793	8
Construction	1,624	4·5	Other financial	3,608	10
Total other manufacturing	4,093	11·5	Total financial	6,942	19·5
Personal					
House purchase	1,353	4			
Other personal	2,913	8·5			
Total personal	4,266	12·5	Total advances	£35,219m	100%

Source:
Midland Bank Review, May 1977

(*b*) *Firms and Corporations* demand funds for both fixed and working capital. The whole prosperity of society is dependent on adequate capital being made available to create the producer goods that are necessary to create the 'utilities' that satisfy 'wants'. In a free-enterprise society the majority of such activities are undertaken by firms and limited companies who appeal to the public, both privately and publicly, for funds. As the classification of bankers' advances (Table 24) shows, the banks are active in providing such funds.

The demand by firms is intensified these days by the pace of technological advance. Research and development generate an increasingly wide variety of products and processes which need to be followed up with capital investment if they are to prove fruitful. Whole ranges of new materials have appeared in the last 30 years, rendering older materials obsolete.

(*c*) *Government and local-government* demand for funds centres on the need to provide socially desirable assets. The whole infra-structure of town and countryside is of increasing importance as denser populations have to be supported. Sanitation, education and retraining, communications, traffic control etc. have great economic contributions to make. The nationalized industries provide essential services to firms as well as individuals, and the contributions they make to industry may be of crucial importance to economic efficiency. If such industries are starved of capital the effect on the economy may be very serious.

(5) The Rate of Interest

It is difficult to give a clear picture of how the rate of interest is decided, for the decision is affected by so many different influences. No theory can explain all aspects of a situation where many people who save behave illogically, or where expert financial manipulators are operating to balance profitable investments against less profitable ones, risky investments against safe ones, sophisticated savers against naïve ones, and so on. Even more, the Government or the Central Bank of any country often controls interest rates in an effort to achieve the management of prosperity or the fulfilment of national aspirations. Such activities make absolute nonsense of any sort of 'cast-iron' theory of interest rates.

It is therefore best to look at some of the savers and at some of the borrowers to see what motivates them in their lending or borrowing. We will then examine some of the major theories of interest and discuss the pros and cons of each.

Types of Savers

(a) *The naïve members of the public.* Many simple people save money regularly in quite tiny sums. When they keep it in a stocking hidden under the mattress, this is called 'hoarding', and the money is lost to the economic system. Such claims against the goods produced in the period when the income was earned are not put to use by entrepreneurs, and never become capital at all. If money keeps its value the claims against goods may eventually be enjoyed by the saver, or more likely by his heirs. But if money loses its value the claims may simply be wasted. There is a story of a Polish miser who saved all his life, living frugally and denying himself many essentials. He carried his hoard in a belt around his waist, and lived in fear of robbery. When the Polish currency collapsed at the end of the Second World War he exchanged his entire hoard for one bread roll.

Even when money is saved in some institution, it does not necessarily follow that it earns a proper rate of interest. For example, many people leave their savings in accounts which are not earning an adequate rate of interest. The best example today is the money left in Post Office Savings Bank Accounts, which earns $3\frac{1}{2}$ per cent—a very low rate of interest. The balances left in the current accounts of commercial banks formerly carried no interest, and gave the banks a very valuable source of profit at no cost. This led during 1974 to a general reduction in bank charges to those leaving balances in their accounts.

(b) *More sophisticated individual savers.* Less naïve savers may decide to invest their savings in a variety of ways, according to the degree of risk run. The saver who wants to avoid any risk at all will lend his money on **savings accounts,** or **deposit accounts** to banks or building societies. These institutions collect money from savers for the purpose of lending it out to borrowers; they assume virtually all the risks but pay quite reasonable rates of interest to savers. Building societies, for example, pay rates of interest very close to Minimum Lending Rate. *Minimum Lending Rate (MLR) is the rate at which the Bank of England will discount first-class bills of exchange.* Since May 1978 it has been determined by the Treasury, in the light of the Government's need to meet its monetary targets for domestic credit expansion. Before 1972 MLR was called Bank Rate. In 1972, when it was first introduced, MLR was set by a market mechanism based on a formula related to the Treasury Bill rate set every Friday. This idea proved impracticable and was abandoned. The commercial banks pay 2 per cent less than the Minimum Lending Rate to depositors (but often arrange special rates for firms depositing large sums). This is not as good a rate as the building-society rate, but building societies are designed to help house purchasers and are not intended for large investors. There is usually a limit set to the amount that may be invested in such societies.

The more sophisticated saver, then, lending his money to such institutions, runs no risk at all and earns a reasonable rate of 'pure' interest.

(*c*) *Sophisticated saving—the institutional investor.* Some investors are more prepared to run calculated risks, if the reward to be earned is higher. Other investors, the institutional investors, combine risk-free investments (earning 'pure' interest only) with rather more speculative investments earning higher rates of interest. Such institutions might be ordinary banks, or insurance companies with large pools of premiums collected from the insuring public. From these pools of reserves the relatives of deceased insured persons and the unfortunate members of society who are injured in accidents, or taken ill on holiday, or suffer the loss of premises through fire or flood damage, will be compensated. Trade unions similarly collect subscriptions from members to be used when sickness, unemployment, or industrial disputes arise.

What rates of interest do such institutional investors hope for? The answer is that they hope to achieve a rather better rate of interest than the 'pure' interest rate earned by the ordinary citizen. Their activities are dominated by two opposite motives: the desire to earn a reasonable interest rate and the

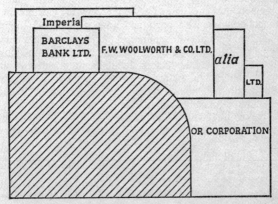

Fig. 73. A balanced portfolio of investments

desire to keep reasonable reserves of liquid assets to meet claims when they arise, e.g. after storms, fires, or strikes. The method adopted is the 'balanced-portfolio' method.

Short-Term and Long-Term Rates of Interest

Some of the investments made by sophisticated savers are short-term loans to the Discount Houses and other specialist operators on the Money Market. 'Short-term' loans are loans made for a period of less than three months, and the rate of interest earned will usually be something less than Bank Rate. They are not therefore very profitable loans, but they have the advantage of being more liquid than long-term loans. Many short-term loans are very short indeed, for instance loans 'at call' are repayable immediately on request. Loans 'at short notice' are usually repayable within one to three days of being asked, though some may be 'seven days' loans. Who uses such short-term loans? The majority are used by firms or Government departments temporarily short of funds. Businessmen who are engaged in profitable transactions which will be concluded in the short-term period will often find it profitable to finance the venture on the Money Market by means of a **Trade Bill**. This is a Bill of Exchange, an interesting commercial document which gives security for a short-term debt. Those readers who are unfamiliar with trade bills will find a description of their use in *Commerce Made Simple*. A **Treasury Bill** is a similar bill issued by the British Treasury. The Radcliffe Report, which examined various financial institutions, found that many businessmen are not at all concerned with the rate of interest they pay, for it represents only a small fraction of the profits made on trade. If a particular transaction, say the purchase of 10,000 tons of wheat, is to yield eventually a 40 per cent profit, the manufacturer financing it with a Bill of Exchange will care little whether it costs him 10, $10\frac{1}{2}$, or 11 per cent. He is going to clear a very useful profit margin whatever happens.

Many savers like to lend on a short-term basis, but many borrowers wish to borrow for longer periods. The rate of interest for long-term borrowing is usually greater because the advantage of early liquidity is lost, and the risks of non-payment of interest, or non-repayment of capital are increased. Banks lend considerable sums to personal borrowers and to firms, taking whatever **collateral security** they can. The title deeds to property, or debentures secured on fixed assets or stock are acceptable forms of collateral. Interest rates will usually be 2–3 per cent above Minimum Lending Rate. Such rates of interest may again be of little interest to businessmen making good profit margins, but undoubtedly personal loans to individuals are sensitive to interest rates. High interest rates may cause many persons to postpone purchase of items whose utility has to be weighed against the repayments envisaged.

Hire purchase of consumer durables is usually arranged over at least a full year, often two or three years. The person lending to such borrowers not only has to wait longer than three months, but also has to accept repayment in small sums over the whole of the period. This requires the keeping of records of payments, and perhaps the sending of reminders to slow payers. It also involves considerable risks of non-payment, especially where the asset is worn out before the repayment period is over. Loans of this kind are usually made by specialist firms called **finance houses**. They set up the necessary bookkeeping systems and employ specialists in repossession and debt collection.

The rate of interest charged is much higher than Bank Rate, and may even be excessive in many cases. It is one of the more speculative fields of loan activity, and is subject to stringent legal control over documentation procedures. Even so, the activities of finance houses are of great importance to poor people needing extended credit periods. Hire-purchase rates of interest are rarely less than 20 per cent, and often exceed 30 per cent, but because of technical procedures in the repayment system rarely appear to the unsophisticated purchaser to be as high as they in fact are. The movement of the commercial banks into the hire-purchase field by their links with the finance houses is a desirable development which is now taking place. For a full description of hire purchase the reader should refer to *Commerce Made Simple*.

Very long-term investment of capital is arranged under a rather different system. The saver, lending his money to the Government or to an industrialist, buys bonds or shares which represent a relatively permanent investment in the firm or industry concerned. The liquidity of that capital is lost completely for many years, but can be regained by the investor through the Stock Exchange, which is a market for stocks and shares. By selling his security to another investor, the original investor is restored to a liquid position. This leaves the original fixed capital still in the industrial firm or public enterprise, but its ownership has changed hands at a price that was appropriate for the time when the bargain was struck. All such investments earn interest or dividend, but because liquidity is easily regained the rate of interest will be less than hire-purchase interest rates. Dividends do include an element of profit however, so that it is sometimes hard to see exactly what 'pure' interest is being earned on industrial or commercial shares.

We therefore see that interest rates range from about 2 per cent below Minimum Lending Rate on short-term investments to about 25–30 per cent for speculative hire-purchase loans. Most exorbitant rate of interest of all is the moneylenders' rate of 4% per month, controlled by the Consumer Credit Act, 1974. It is difficult to see an economic pattern in these interest rates, but many of them are not truly 'interest' in the economic sense of that word. We must distinguish the following elements in any 'interest' payment:

(*a*) *'Pure' interest*—payment for postponing consumption and making loanable funds available.

(*b*) *'Service' charges*—charged by the lender for the trouble of keeping accounts and collecting payments.

(*c*) *'Profits'*—the rewards for running the risks that interest may not be paid, nor capital repaid, in due course.

Strictly speaking, profits are a separate reward from interest, and if we remove this section (*c*) from the picture, to be discussed in the next chapter, we can simplify the study of interest a good deal.

(6) The Loanable Funds Theory of Interest

This theory is often called the Classical Economists' explanation. The term 'Classical Economists' is applied to the main stream of economic thought which developed in Britain, Europe, and the United States of America after 1870. Alfred Marshall was its most original mind, and marginal analysis was its changed approach. The economics of Smith, Malthus, Ricardo, and John

Stuart Mill was transformed into a more mathematical, diagrammatic demonstration of the forces at work in the economy. Let us pause a moment to consider Alfred Marshall as the typical classical economist.

Alfred Marshall (1842–1924)

Alfred Marshall was the son of the cashier of the Bank of England. His father intended him to enter the Church, and gave him a strictly classical education, but eventually the young man rebelled. Instead of going to Oxford, he went to Cambridge to study mathematics and physics. Here he became an agnostic, but true to his basic philosophy never spoke against religion. Marshall disliked controversy, and claimed little originality for himself. He held that the great economists who had preceded him, Smith, Malthus, Ricardo, and Mill had developed techniques which were appropriate for their times, and which held within them the new approach he and others had developed. His great work, *Principles of Economics*, did not appear until 1890, having been twenty years in preparation. His ideas were thus later in publication than those of some of his contemporaries, but it was in Marshall's nature to rewrite and refine until he had a definitive work.

Most of the main-stream ideas of modern economics are to be found in Marshall's *Principles*. The ideas of internal and external economies of scale, of marginal utility, elasticity of demand and supply, downward-sloping demand curves, and discriminating monopoly are either explicitly or implicitly included.

Marshall's work was greatly appreciated in the United Kingdom. The Victorian era was always ready to give recognition to a finished great work, even if Continental critics might justly claim that most of the ideas had already been published in lesser volumes. Marshall was optimistic about Capitalism; he wanted economics to uplift the ordinary man and, after ending his poverty, lead him on to a noble life. There would be many ordinary men today who would hold that it has done so.

To return to the loanable-funds theory, the Classical Economists held that the rate of interest equated the demand for loanable funds with the supply of loanable funds. If the demand for funds for investment purposes rises, the rate of interest will rise and will encourage more individuals to postpone consumption and save money. This money will then be lent to the entrepreneurs, placing the forgone consumption at their disposal. The rate of interest therefore keeps savings equal to investment. A change of interest does not generate any increased income in the money system, it merely reduces personal consumption by encouraging individuals to save. Fig. 74 illustrates the situation simply.

What is wrong with this theory? The chief objections are as follows:

(*a*) It assumes that the interest rate can fluctuate freely. In real life these days the rate tends to be influenced by the Central Bank.

(*b*) It assumes that both investment and consumption are 'interest-elastic', responding to the interest rates freely. In fact we have already seen that interest rates affect many businessmen very little: in other words, investment is inelastic with respect to interest. Also there is a good deal of evidence to suggest that savings are more strongly affected by expectations than by interest rates. Thus when slump times are coming people save more, even though interest rates are falling, while in prosperous times they save less even though interest rates are high. These are formidable criticisms. They lead us on to consider the work of a celebrated twentieth-century economist, John Maynard Keynes.

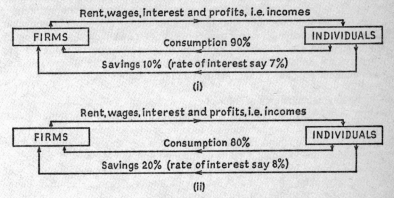

Fig. 74. The 'Loanable Funds' theory of interest

Notes:

1. In (i) the public are consuming 90 per cent of their incomes and saving 10 per cent of them, receiving interest at the rate of 7 per cent.
2. In (ii) they have reduced consumption to 80 per cent of income because they are attracted by the higher interest rates now offered on savings.
3. Since the savings made available have been used by the entrepreneurs to expand their firms there has been no change in the total demand for goods and services.

John Maynard Keynes (1883–1946)

John Maynard Keynes has been called the greatest economist of the twentieth century. One has to go back to Malthus and Ricardo to find economists who influenced their own times as greatly as Keynes. His ideas were not all new, but he altered those he borrowed, and constructed an economic model of the capitalist system that pinpointed age-old weaknesses. His theory of interest, which we shall examine shortly, held that savings disturbed the economy. Thrift in the early days of capitalism had been a good thing, because the postponer of current consumption was only doing so in order to invest in industry. As the capitalist system developed, the functions of saving and investment have been separated. The entrepreneur of today is not himself a saver, but an invester only, investing other people's savings. This means that the thrift of those postponing current consumption will affect the level of activity in the economy if the entrepreneurs are unwilling to invest. Nervous expectations about the prospects of profitability can lead to a reduction in business activity and a depression, or slump.

With one simple idea Keynes had solved the mystery of the capitalist system: the occurrence of business cycles which cause unemployment and poverty amidst plenty. Cycles of business activity are caused by an imbalance between savings and investment. Low levels of activity, and underemployment, are caused by a lack of demand in the economy. To cure unemployment encourage spending; down with thrift.

For 30 years economists advised just that, and the spectre of mass unemployment was lifted from the market economies of the advanced nations. More recently, since the mid-seventies, it has returned, but in rather a different form. Today unemployment does not mean grinding poverty; welfare programmes ensure that the unemployed secure a reasonable share of the economy's resources. Though presumably unemployment can never be a totally enjoyable situation, it is more easily borne than formerly. It seems likely that the name of John Maynard Keynes will be remembered with affection by mankind. He threw back Thomas Carlyle's criticism of economics as the 'dismal science'. His managed prosperity has produced a more gracious society.

(7) The Keynesian Theory of Interest

The major part of Keynes's work deals with the level of activity in the economy and the management of prosperity. This is discussed later (see page 317), but he found that investment is the key to the prosperity of an economic system because it controls incomes and employment. The rate of interest is one of the factors deciding investment, the other is the prospect of profitability. What then decides the rate of interest? Keynes held that there are two elements in interest. These are:

(*a*) The available stock of money in existence. This stock of money, which is either cash or bank credit, is an actual fact. Ordinary people can do nothing about it, though Keynes was to show that Governments can.

(*b*) The desire of people to hold money, and keep their wealth in liquid form. This is not an unchangeable fact of life; it is a subjective point of view taken up by every individual and changing from day to day and hour to hour. Some people have a high liquidity preference, and others have a low liquidity preference. Generally speaking, poor people have a high propensity to consume and a low propensity to save. Give a beggar a pound note and he will rush into a cafe for a meal. Give a millionaire a pound note and he will save it to buy shares in a profitable venture. The desire to hold money is governed by three attitudes to money, to which Keynes gave names as follows:

(i) *The transactions motive.* Money is needed for everyday use, to buy goods and services. The poor person holds all his wealth in liquid form, for it is only sufficient to support life for a few days.

(ii) *The precautionary motive.* Money is needed as a reserve against unforeseen events. These emergencies require people to keep their assets in liquid or near-liquid forms. Thus the private citizen leaves certain balances as credits in the banks, and the banks, for fear it is demanded suddenly, must be cautious about preserving adequate cash reserves.

These two motives are fairly stable, and do not cause much fluctuation in either the rate of interest or the level of activity in the economy. When these two motives have been satisfied, the person who still has some liquid funds available is now able to consider investment. He is therefore able to indulge the third, speculative, motive.

(iii) *The speculative motive.* When the other motives are adequately provided for, the rich person or the institutional investor will now only hold money if expectations of future events seem to make it desirable. A speculator is one who makes profits out of his judgement of future events. If it seems likely that to invest now will yield a good rate of interest, but delay will mean a less rewarding contract in the future, he will press ahead and invest now.

If he feels that by withholding investment now he will be able to reach a better agreement in the future, he will keep his assets in liquid form.

Interest may therefore be defined as *the reward for surrendering liquidity*. The rate of interest is *that rate which equates the demand to hold money with the available stock of money*. Fig. 75 illustrates the situation.

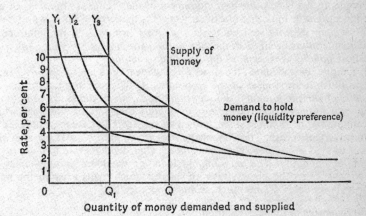

Fig. 75. Determination of the rate of interest

Notes:

1. The stock of money, OQ, is in fixed supply at any given time.
2. The lines Y_1, Y_2, and Y_3 indicate different demands to hold money (i.e. different liquidity preferences). At Y_1 the distribution of income is such that the demand for cash is low. Consequently there is a large share of the supply of money available for investment and the rate of interest is low: only 3 per cent. A few rich people have most of the available supply of money; the mass of the people cannot consume.
3. At Y_2 and Y_3 larger demands to hold money indicate that there is a more equal distribution of income in the economy. As incomes rise so does the propensity to consume and consequently greater liquidity preference is displayed. The result is that less funds are available for investment and the rate of interest rises to 4 per cent and 6 per cent, respectively.
4. If the supply of money was reduced to Q_1, say by Government action, the interest rates at each level would be forced up to 4, 6, and 10 per cent, respectively.
5. The shape of these curves is explained as follows. When rates are high, prices of stocks are low, and many 'bulls' on the Stock Exchange will have bought them hoping for a rise in price if interest rates fall. (The reader who cannot follow this must realize that a 4 per cent Stock of 100·00 par value falls to 50·00 when 8 per cent is the current rate of interest; and rises in value as interest falls back, say to $7\frac{1}{2}$ per cent or 7 per cent.) Therefore at high rates of interest liquidity preference is low as speculators prefer to have stocks. When interest rates fall, speculators take their profits and liquidity preference rises, i.e. it moves farther out from the vertical axis of the graph. At about 2 per cent no one will surrender liquidity for such a meagre reward, and the three lines tend to merge—liquidity preference becomes infinite.

(8) The Structure of Interest Rates

As a result of Keynes's influence the advanced countries with market economies have changed out of recognition in the lifetimes of most people. Interest theories have changed too, and must now include the concept of the rate of interest as a monetary tool to be manipulated by the Government in the interests of the people. Profound changes in the influence of important ministers have followed from this ability to change the economic life of the people. In the U.S.A. the aggrandizement of the President's office is not unconnected with the belief of ordinary citizens that a chief duty of presidents is to keep them in well paid jobs. In Great Britain even the influence of Parliament has declined in the face of the patronage of the Prime Minister, whose policies are crucial to business and social life.

Despite these changes, the structure of interest rates underlying investment still illustrates the ideas of the economists. Differences in interest rates are closely linked to liquidity: the very liquid loan, which can easily be retrieved in cash form, carries a lower rate of interest than the 'illiquid' loan which cannot. The marketable share, quoted on the Stock Exchanges, can be easily reconverted to cash. The unquoted share, which must be sold privately if it can be sold at all, usually commands a higher dividend rate to compensate for its illiquidity. The very illiquid loan, or the loan without collateral security, earns the highest rates of interest. Such loans exist in the more speculative fields of hire purchase and moneylending.

(9) Summary of Chapter Eighteen

1. Interest is the payment made for the loan of liquid capital. It is usually paid at an agreed rate per cent.

2. Since the loan of money is subject to risk, it is usual for these risks to be assumed by specialist firms called institutional investors.

3. Loanable funds may be made available by individuals, firms, or Governments.

4. The demand for capital is made by different individuals, firms, and Government agencies.

5. Rates of interest paid vary widely with the naïvety or sophistication of lenders and borrowers. Borrowing on short term is cheaper than long-term borrowing.

6. The loanable-funds theory of interest holds that the rate of interest equates the demand for loanable funds with their supply.

7. The Keynesian theory of interest holds that the rate of interest reflects the degree of liquidity preference shown by the holders of money.

8. Since the adoption of Keynesian and monetarist policies, interest can also be regarded as a monetary phenomenon—a tool used by the monetary authorities to shape the nation's economy.

(10) Suggested Further Reading

Harvey, J.: *Intermediate Economics*. 2nd. Edn., Macmillan: London, 1971.
Lekachman, R.: *A History of Economic Ideas*. Harper & Row: London, 1965.
Lipsey, R. G., and Stilwell, J. A.: *An Introduction to Positive Economics*. 3rd. Edn., Weidenfeld & Nicolson: London, 1971.
Marshall, A.: *Principles of Economics*. Macmillan: London, 1961.

Exercises Set 18

1. What is interest? Who receives it, and why does it vary?

2. 'The Government has decided to offer a higher rate of interest to regular savers, who are prepared to leave their savings untouched for a period of at least six months.' Explain the economic justifications for the higher rate of interest mentioned in this announcement.

3. 'Initially capital was saved by individuals and used by them to promote their enterprises. Today the functions of saving and investment have been largely separated.' Explain.

4. 'Capital is accumulated by self-denial.' 'Capital is a surplus that is not required for everyday purposes.' Discuss the truth of these statements, and their economic implications.

5. Why, at any given time, are there several rates of interest? What kinds of loan earn these different rates?

6. Who was J. M. Keynes? What were his ideas on liquidity preference?

7. Bankers advances show the following classes of borrower:

Type of borrower	£ million
Manufacturers	4,500
Farmers	800
Householders	900
Tertiary services	1,500
Foreigners	2,300

(*a*) State: (i) the total of bank advances; (ii) the percentage of total advances going to each class of borrower.

(*b*) Discuss the likely considerations entering into a banker's decision to lend money to (i) manufacturers, (ii) foreigners.

8. What is a balanced portfolio of investments? Suggest classes of share suitable for a balanced portfolio for a trade union which has to meet the following future commitments: (*a*) pension funds for members likely to retire in twenty years' time; (*b*) strike payments to a small number of members in one particular industry where industrial unrest is likely to occur very shortly.

9. What is likely to be the effect of a rise in basic lending rates of 2 per cent on the following?

(*a*) An industrialist proposing to buy a machine which will reduce labour costs by 40 per cent.

(*b*) A schoolteacher who has budgeted that he can just afford a holiday in Spain if he borrows 100·00.

(*c*) A sole trader in a competitive industry who has been considering whether to borrow funds at 8 per cent for a project which will yield him an estimated 12½ per cent.

10. Expectations affect liquidity preference. Consider the effect on American citizens' desire to hold cash for the following events:

(*a*) A Russian decision to install missiles in the West Indies.

(*b*) A downturn in the economy promising fewer employment opportunities.

(*c*) Economic expansion due to an intensification of the space programme.

(*d*) A reduction in taxation leaving the majority of citizens more wealthy.

CHAPTER NINETEEN

PROFIT—THE REWARD FOR BEARING UNCERTAINTY

(1) Uncertainty

In controlled economies the State initiates all enterprise, and private enterprise is discouraged. In economies which produce utilities to satisfy the wants of mankind by a free-enterprise system, someone has to take the decisions to produce. Free enterprise is shown by entrepreneurs, who employ and co-ordinate the factors of production. In simple cases the entrepreneur personally supervises the activities, deciding what to produce and in what quantities, and marketing the eventual output in exchange for money. This involves a variety of risks. There are some risks, called **insurable risks**, which can be predicted with reasonable accuracy. For example, the chances of a hailstorm flattening a wheat crop are known with considerable accuracy, for records have been kept for many years. Similarly the chances that my chimney-stack will be struck by lightning, or that the father of a family will suffer a fatal heart attack can be calculated mathematically. These risks can be covered by insurance.

Other risks, called non-insurable risks, cannot be covered by insurance, for they are insusceptible to statistical calculation. What is the probability that I shall prove to be a good businessman? How likely is it that the furniture I propose to manufacture will prove popular? No insurance company will cover me for these sorts of uncertainty, for there is no accumulated evidence to help it predict the probability that the event will take place. Such uncertainties must be borne by the entrepreneur, and the number of bankruptcy proceedings and winding-up resolutions passed by companies shows that success is by no means certain.

(2) The Risks of Business

Enterprise consists in producing goods and services in anticipation of demand. Even where demand is highly probable it is never quite certain, and since modern business situations are dynamic (in other words, they change continuously) the uncertainties of production are increased. Business risks come under three main headings: marketing risks, obsolescence risks, and political risks.

(*a*) *Uncertainties in market conditions.* An entrepreneur cannot feel entirely confident that his product will sell. Public taste and fashion is unpredictable and the demand for many goods is elastic outside certain price ranges. If an entrepreneur tools up an expensive factory layout only to find that world prices of his raw materials have risen in the meantime, pricing him out of the market, his efforts have been in vain. New products may or may not catch on, and promotion costs can be very high. Good **market research** beforehand should inform the businessman of many predictable influences at work on the market, such as trends in employment, patterns of income, unfavourable reactions of certain age-ranges etc. which might influence his publicity. So enormous are the present-day costs of laying down complex production lines that entrepreneurs dare not be wrong, and have to spend a fortune on persuasive advertising to ensure that the product sells.

(*b*) *Uncertainties due to rival products and changes in technology.* Obsolescence renders an existing piece of equipment uneconomic before it is worn out fully, because more efficient new products replace it. In present dynamic business conditions scientists and technologists produce an unending series of new materials, designs, and patterns. There is a well known saying to the effect that 'if a man builds a better mousetrap, the world will beat a path to his door'. Every nation is engaged in the process of innovation and the rewards are very great. The Atomic Energy Authority, in a recent development for marketing radioactive products, announced its estimate of the potential market as £1,000 million. New techniques constantly improve production methods, to the chagrin of those who have just invested expensively in the old ones. New materials with greater strength, heat resistance, weatherproof qualities, adhesive properties etc. quickly replace traditional materials to the discomfiture of workers and entrepreneurs.

(*c*) *Financial, legal, and political uncertainties.* This class of risks which businessmen must bear arises from the financial, legal, and political framework in which we all live. The national interest must take preference over personal interests in many cases. Contracts are frequently frustrated by the outbreak of wars, by the declaration that proposed products or services are illegal, by the refusal of financial permission to export capital or buy foreign exchange, by the development of social disorders or withdrawal of labour.

The compensation for running these risks is profit, the second reward to the factor capital. Interest is the other reward to capital, as we have seen in Chapter Eighteen.

(3) The Reward for Bearing Uncertainty

Profit is the reward paid to the entrepreneur for risking the loss of his capital. We have already discussed the difficulty of deciding who is the entrepreneur in modern advanced economies. There are, of course, many sole traders and partners engaged in small-scale enterprises who still provide their own capital and are entitled to the profits of the enterprise. They also, of course, suffer the losses. We agreed, however, that hundreds of thousands of such small-scale firms are relatively insignificant compared with the 15,000 public limited companies in Great Britain alone. One such firm, with several hundred million pounds of capital, probably does as much business every year as all the small-scale enterprises put together.

In these enterprises there are no old-fashioned entrepreneurs, only paid employees who also own a few shares to comply with statutory requirements. The twenty-seven directors of the National Westminster Bank of London who held shares in the bank on 31 December 1977 owned between them only 61,127 of the bank's total of 224,815,000 shares. We see therefore that the entrepreneurs of this world-famous bank own a negligible fraction of its capital; 0·03 per cent to be precise. This is typical of the modern position. Who then are the entrepreneurs? In a property-owning democracy we are all shareholders. Everyone who insures his life, or his car, or his house; every trade unionist who joins a welfare scheme, every pensioner with a few trust units is a shareholder in countless enterprises. The profits from these enterprises, paid for running the risks of losing the capital, provide the insurance funds, pension funds, and welfare funds of our society.

From the economic point of view profit is different from the other rewards to factors. The chief differences are:

(a) *Profit is a residue of business activity.* Unlike rent, interest, and wages, it has no certain contractual basis. It is uncertain, depending on the degree of success in predicting demand, and the good fortune of the entrepreneur in not meeting competition, political disturbances, or legal or financial restraints.

(b) *Profit may be negative,* i.e. a loss may be sustained. This is implicit in its residual nature. The loss sustained eats into the contributed capital, reducing the worth of the business to the shareholders who own it.

(c) *Profit fluctuates in dynamic conditions.* When 'boom' times come the entrepreneur is able to make good profits, which rise faster than wages, rent, or interest. When a 'slump' arrives the reverse is true. Wages cannot be reduced immediately. Rent is usually tied to a lease with a certain life. Interest is a contractual matter which remains fixed until the contract is discharged. Profits therefore decline as falling demand reduces turnover.

(4) Elements of profit

Profit to the accountant is the difference between the sale price of an article and its total costs of production, using the word 'production' in its economic meaning to include manufacture, distribution, and marketing costs. Economists cannot accept this as the true profit in economic terms, because we include in costs the alternatives foregone. We notice the following elements in profit:

(a) *The wage of the entrepreneur.* Where the entrepreneur is just another worker his salary is included in the overhead costs of the enterprise. Thus the fees of part-time directors and the salaries of full-time directors of limited companies are included in the costs charged to the profit-and-loss account when profits are being calculated. Small-scale enterprises where the entrepreneur is self-employed do not include any remuneration for the entrepreneur in these calculations. Thus a shopkeeper whose profits are 2,500·00 per year could probably be earning 2,000·00 as the manager of some other enterprise. He cannot therefore disregard this in his calculations of the value of the enterprise. Deducting this 'alternative cost' from the profits of the enterprise leaves 500·00 as his true return from it.

(b) *Normal profit.* The second element in profit is **normal profit**, already defined as an acceptable return on capital invested (see page 78). Every enterprise must earn a reasonable reward for the capital invested in it, otherwise the capital will leave the industry and go to some alternative employment where the rewards for bearing uncertainties are better. In perfect conditions this free flow of capital will eliminate any element of 'economic rent' in the profits earned by firms, and leave all firms achieving 'normal' profits. In real life this does not quite happen. Some firms have better entrepreneurs than others, who keep ahead of competitors even in the long run. We must therefore recognize a 'rent of ability' as accruing to such entrepreneurs.

Another point is that normal profit is not uniform between industries, because some industries are particularly susceptible to uncertainties and consequently require a higher rate of normal profit to attract capital.

We may therefore recognize in normal profit several elements. First there is the interest element which is not really profit at all. Then there is an element of true profit—the reward for bearing risks—which will be larger in some industries than in others. Finally there is an element of 'rent of ability' earned by the best entrepreneurs.

(c) *Quasi-rents.* Quasi-rents are abnormal profits over and above normal profit, which are enjoyed by an entrepreneur temporarily because competitors cannot enter the industry. This may be because there is a shortage of skilled workers, or because plant takes time to construct. Quasi-rent is an extra profit earned on factors which happen to be fixed in supply for some reason.

(d) *Monopoly rents.* These are economic rents enjoyed by entrepreneurs who are able successfully to exclude competitors from the industry. This may be done by patent rights, copyrights, sole ownership of natural resources, or the artificial branding of products.

(5) The Functions of Profit in a Free-enterprise System

The profit motive is viewed very differently by people of different political and economic persuasions. Some denigrate profit as the 'immoral earnings' of the capitalist class. However true this view was in the early days of capitalism, today nearly everyone lives to some extent on such 'immoral' earnings. Others praise the profit motive as a truly dynamic force in society, which has solved the problem of creating utilities to satisfy wants. Working as it does through the enterprise of individuals, it must lead to disparities of wealth, but there are means of redistributing such disparities. The tax system redresses the inequalities of income continuously, while Capital Transfer Tax returns to the people the bulk of the wealth to which they have contributed. By arranging to do so at the least painful moment, when the accumulator of the wealth has died, his natural resentment is avoided. These matters of policy are more appropriate to the study of Applied Economics than to the present volume. For our purposes it is sufficient to answer the question, What does profit do in a free-enterprise economy? The main functions of profit may be summarized as follows:

(a) *Profit motivates enterprise.* Enterprise alone produces utilities to satisfy wants. The prospects of profitability encourage men to bear uncertainties. The normal profit is the minimum reward that will coax them to surrender liquidity now for increased consumption at some future date.

(b) *Profit permits growth.* Not only does mankind wish to satisfy his elementary wants, he hopes to enjoy progressively more sophisticated satisfactions. These require higher and higher levels of industrial and social investment. Profits are the major source of such investment, especially abnormal profits. They can be ploughed back into the same industry, or on distribution to shareholders can be reinvested in new industries. They enable higher rewards to be offered to factors, to encourage them to move to the newer and more profitable industries, away from declining or obsolete trades.

(c) *Profits often indicate efficiency.* Since the general rule is that a firm with low costs is more profitable, the profitability of a firm is some indication of its efficiency. It might equally indicate unscrupulous behaviour, for example by monopolists. In general though, it is profit by others that encourages new firms to enter an industry or to imitate the successful firm. Moreover, the competitive power of the low-cost firm eventually drives the high-cost firm out of business. Its resources are transferred elsewhere. By showing where expansion should occur, since profits indicate higher prices caused by strong public demand, they redistribute industry to take account of changes of taste or fashion.

(6) *Abuse of the Profit System*

It would be ridiculous to suggest that the profit motive is never abused, and that individualism is bound to operate for the collective good. At the same time the collective good is inseparable from the individual good. It does appear that there is less incentive to reduce costs and practise economy if no personal loss or gain is involved. A sound framework of law can correct the worst abuses of the profit system. The less serious abuses appear to be a price we must pay for freedom.

(7) Summary of Chapter Nineteen

1. All business activities incur risks. Risks which cannot be covered by insurance must be borne by the entrepreneur.

2. The chief non-insurable risks are market risks, risks of competition due to rival products, risks due to changes in technology, and financial, legal, and political risks.

3. Profit is an unusual reward to factors. It is a residual reward; it fluctuates with changing circumstances and it can even be negative, i.e. losses can be made.

4. The elements of profit are entrepreneurial wages, normal profit, quasi-rents, and monopoly rents.

5. The function of profit is to reward the factor capital for bearing uncertainties, to redistribute capital where it is most effective in producing profits and to expand production in the directions most desired by the public so as to maximize satisfactions.

6. Abuses of the profit system are best controlled by legislation, or taxation may be used to redistribute incomes.

(8) Suggested Further Reading

Knight, F. H.: *Risk, Uncertainty, and Profit.* Harper & Row: London, 1966.
Lipsey, R. G., and Stilwell, J. A.: *An Introduction to Positive Economics.* 3rd. Edn., Weidenfeld & Nicolson: London, 1971.
Stonier, A., and Hague, D.: *A Textbook of Economic Theory.* Longmans: London, 1964.

Exercises Set 19

1. What is uncertainty? What types of uncertainty must be borne by entrepreneurs?

2. 'I am not in business to make profits. I am in business to make shoes.' Discuss these statements critically.

3. 'Profit is not contractual like other rewards to factors; it is residual.' Explain.

4. 'I created this business using techniques I have patented myself. As a result it has been impossible for others to compete with my products. I earn £10,000·00 a year, but must expect some change in this when the patents expire in five years' time.' What elements of profit would you discover in an analysis of this entrepreneur's reward? What do you expect will happen when the patents expire?

5. What are monopoly rents? Explain clearly the following aspects of them: (*a*) How they arise; (*b*) whether they are permanent or impermanent; (*c*) what economic factors are at work to keep them reasonable; (*d*) how they may be controlled; (*e*) how they may be recouped for the benefit of ordinary people. (If necessary re-read Chapter Twelve on monopoly conditions.)

6. A retail tobacconist tells you that his total profit is a mere £700·00. He used to earn £1,200·00 as a civil servant. He has invested £1,000·00 in his business, and now asks your opinion about his profit position. Advise him, giving reasoned economic arguments.

7. An American publisher is about to produce paperback books which sell well in the U.S.A. for the British market. What uncertainties are involved in this project?

8. 'In boom times profit margins are good. In slump times profit margins are bad.' Explain.

9. In what circumstances does capital move from one industry to another? What effect does this have on (*a*) profit margins, (*b*) consumer satisfaction, (*c*) the mobility of labour?

10. 'You could buy debentures at a steady 7 per cent, or you could buy ordinary shares. They have paid 20 per cent for the last three years, but are rather speculative in this industry' (stockbroker to client). Clarify this information, bringing out the economic implications for the client.

CHAPTER TWENTY

THE FINANCIAL INSTITUTIONS

(1) Introduction

The private-enterprise system is one where specialization flourishes, particularly if the operations to be performed are of an intricate or technical nature. It follows that many institutions have been developed to promote particular activities where enterprise can achieve economies. These institutions are like an intricate pattern filling in the fabric of our economic life, with old institutions dying away and new institutions arising as they are required.

Nowhere is this specialized collection of institutions as fully developed as in the financial field, for money is the key that opens all doors. Some of these institutions have premises which are known to everyone, like the Bank of England in Threadneedle Street, or the Stock Exchange in Throgmorton Street. Others exist in a multitude of small offices linked through the telephone and Telex systems. The 'money market', for example, is a general term used to describe all the activities of central banks, commercial banks, merchant banks, discount houses, and finance houses which deal in money. You cannot visit the Money Market, for there is no such meeting place.

The true study of these institutions is Commerce, and a full description of the major institutions is given in *Commerce Made Simple*. A brief description of these operators in the financial field is essential if the next field of study, **macroeconomics,** is to be understood. Macroeconomics is the study of the whole economies, rather than of individual buyers, sellers, and firms. The study of such small units is called **microeconomics.** As we move from the study of microeconomics to the study of macroeconomics we enter the field of public economic policy. The institutions studied in this section are some of the most important organizations through which Governments can implement policies.

(2) The Bank of England

The Bank of England was founded in 1694, to lend money to the Government. It was given a monopoly of joint-stock banking and became the Government's bank. It was at that time not a nationalized institution but a private bank which wielded great influence partly because of its close relationship with the Treasury. Just over a century later Sheridan, the dramatist, described the Bank as 'an elderly lady in the City, of great credit and long standing'. Possibly this description of the Bank led James Gillray, a caricaturist of the day to depict the Bank in a famous cartoon called 'The Old Lady of Threadneedle Street in Danger'. It showed Prime Minister Pitt attacking the Bank to obtain money for the Napoleonic Wars. The old lady was putting up a spirited resistance. The nickname stuck, and has been in popular use ever since.

In 1844 the Bank Charter Act reorganized the Bank of England, splitting it into two parts: the Banking Department and the Issue Department. The

Banking Department dealt with banking operations as they affected the Government, the commercial banks, the money market, and the few private firms who bank with the Bank of England. The Issue Department was charged with seeing that bank notes were issued as required by the public within the limits set by the gold reserves and a small fiduciary issue of £14 million (see page 166).

In 1946 Parliament brought the Bank of England within the control of the Government. The Governor, Deputy Governor, and sixteen directors who form the Directorate are appointed by the sovereign on the recommendation of the Prime Minister. No longer can it be claimed, justifiably or otherwise, that the Bank prevents the implementation of desirable social policies. The Treasury is able to implement Government policies through the Bank's control over the extent to which the commercial banks may lend money.

The Functions of the Bank of England

The Bank of England is a central bank, or national bank, charged with the control of the banking system in the interests of the nation. In the last 25 years the key functions of Governments have been the management and control of prosperity. Most nations are preoccupied with these activities, and an indispensable requirement is a 'central bank' which can control the general activities of the ordinary banks.

The chief functions of the Bank of England are to act as the Government's bank in the widest possible sense, anticipating where possible the banking problems that may arise and examining those that do arise. It then undertakes the appropriate operations in the money, capital, and foreign-exchange markets. A full list of activities includes the following:

(a) The Bank's role as banker

(i) Banker to the Government.

(ii) Banker to the banks and the money market.

(iii) Banker to foreign central banks and international organizations.

(iv) Banker to a residue of private customers.

(v) Manager of the note issue for the British Isles.

(vi) The registrar of Government stocks, and the servicer of the National Debt.

(vii) Operator of the exchange-control system to protect the foreign exchange reserves.

(b) The Bank's operations in the markets

(i) The implementation of Government policy to control the economy by controlling the money market for short-term loans.

(ii) The implementation of Government policy in both the long- and short-term loan markets by raising or lowering Minimum Lending Rate.

(iii) To meet the Government's long-term borrowing requirements by open-market operations on the Stock Exchange; this may also influence the lending policies of the commercial banks.

(iv) Managing the exchange rate to protect the pound. In these days of a 'floating' pound exchange rate management is a more residual action than formerly—but it is still important.

(c) *The Bank's influence on policy*

(i) Because of its influential position in the financial affairs of the country, the Bank is able to give useful financial advice to the Treasury and to assist in forecasts of the economic situation and the balance-of-payments position.

(ii) It often advises on capital structure and the finance of companies.

(iii) It participates in the international activities of such bodies as the International Monetary Fund and the International Bank for Reconstruction and Development.

A detailed description of all these activities is impossible here, and the reader who is not familiar with them is referred to *Commerce Made Simple*, pages 180–196.

(3) The Money Market

The Money Market is a general name for a whole complex of firms handling different aspects of the financial transactions necessary in advanced societies. A full list includes the following:

(a) The commercial banks, which handle ordinary banking affairs for the general public.

(b) The merchant banks, sometimes called 'accepting houses', which specialize in financing foreign trade by accepting bills of exchange for less well known merchants.

(c) The discount houses, which operate the market for short-term loans.

(d) The foreign exchange market, in which a few authorized bankers exchange pounds for foreign currencies.

(4) Commercial Banks

A bank is defined as an institution which collects surplus funds from the general public, safeguards them, and makes them available to the true owner when required, but also lends sums not required by their true owners to those who are in need of funds and can provide security.

The basic functions of a bank are:

(a) The collection of surplus funds from the general public.

(b) The safeguarding of such funds.

(c) The transfer of these funds from one person to another, without their leaving the bank, by means of the **cheque** and **credit-transfer** systems.

(d) The lending of surplus funds not required by the present owner to other customers who are in need of funds, in return for interest and collateral security. The interest is shared between the bank (a reward for its services) and the true owner (a reward for not using his money).

The English banking system is a tripartite system like a three-layer cake. The three parts are:

(a) The Bank of England, á 'State bank' or 'national bank'.

(b) Specialized banking institutions, such as the discount houses and merchant banks, which deal only with special customers providing funds for special purposes.

(c) The commercial, or joint-stock banks, which deal with the general public, but are also active in most financial fields.

Development of Commercial Banks

In the eighteenth century the banking system developed as a means of providing the capital for the agricultural and industrial revolutions. Not only goldsmiths, but merchants, landowners, and other well-to-do people practised banking as a sideline and gradually developed the necessary expert knowledge.

Since a single banker was limited by his personal capital, the idea of partnerships in banking was adopted from an early date; limited liability came much later. It soon became clear that a bank that was too small and localized in its connections was likely to go bankrupt if hard times hit that particular area. For instance, banks in a farming area might be bankrupted if all the depositors withdrew their funds at the same time to replace cattle, machinery, and fencing lost in a severe flood. This led to the amalgamation of banks in different localities to give a broader base to the bank.

The advantages of amalgamations, both with regard to the stability of the banking system and economical operation in other ways has reduced the number of banks over the years, so that by the 1920s England had only the 'Big Five' and six smaller banks. This process is continuing even at the present time. An amalgamation of National Provincial and Westminster to form the National Westminster Group has reduced the Big Five to a 'Big Four': National Westminster, Barclays, Lloyds, and Midland. Similarly the six smaller banks have tended to move more within the sphere of the large banks; Coutts & Co. for example have joined the National Westminster Group but have not completely lost their individual identity. Coutts & Co. is one of the oldest names in banking. To let that name pass into history on a mere amalgamation would be a great pity.

The place of the commercial banks in the British economy is a particularly important one. They stand at the very centre of business activity and can promote prosperity or deflate the economy into unemployment. For this reason the banks are closely controlled in their credit policies by the Bank of England, which is itself influenced and controlled by the Treasury. This is dealt with later (see page 328), but a preliminary understanding of how bank credit operates to inflate or deflate the economy is desirable.

An example of Credit Creation

Fig. 76 concerns a deposit of £100 made by Mr. A to the credit of his account. The banks know from experience that on average a depositor will not ask for more than 8 per cent of his deposit to be refunded in cash. Before 1971 they kept a **cash ratio** of 8 per cent available to meet this demand from depositors, but in September 1971 the Bank of England introduced new arrangements requiring the banks to keep a **minimum reserve ratio** of $12\frac{1}{2}$ per cent. A simple view of banking would be one that suggested that bankers must therefore keep a reserve of £12·50 for every £100 deposited. If Mr. A should require its return, this would be available, leaving £87·50 to be loaned to customers. A more sophisticated view is taken by bankers, who regard the £100 cash deposits as a minimum reserve of $12\frac{1}{2}$ per cent for total deposits of £800. With £100 of Mr. A's cash in the tills the bank can repay $12\frac{1}{2}$ per cent to depositors of £800. Mr. A is a depositor of £100, and if the bank lends £700 to some needy customer he will spend it and the recipient will at once deposit the cheque back with the bank. This new depositor will only withdraw 8 per cent but in any case the bank have 12½ per cent available, i.e. £87·50 of Mr. A's money. They therefore feel free to loan out £700 to customers.

This the bank does to customers like Mr. B, in Fig. 76, opening up for him two accounts; a **current account** which has a credit of £700 which Mr. B is free to spend, and a **loan account** in which Mr. B is debited not only with the sum loaned but also with interest on the amount. Mr. B promptly goes out to buy a car, giving a cheque for £700 to the garage owner Mr. C. Mr. C at once deposits the cheque with the bank in his account. As far as Mr. C is concerned it is perfectly good money, he has no idea that the bank has created it out of thin air; in other words has **created credit**.

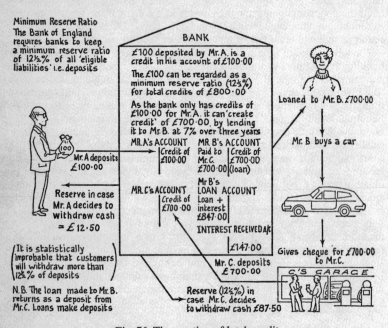

Fig. 76. The creation of bank credit

The reader should now notice the following points:

(a) The bank has made a **loan** to Mr. B, which became a **deposit** from Mr. C. *Loans make deposits.*

(b) The statistical probability is that Mr. C will ask for 8 per cent of his deposit back. That is all right, for the bank has a minimum reserve of up to 12½ per cent (£87·50) available.

(c) The amount of money in the economy has been expanded by the banks from £100 to £800. With such a very large increase in spending power it is perhaps not surprising that the central bank sometimes finds it necessary to apply a credit squeeze.

(d) As Mr. B repays the loan the bank will receive £147 interest. Banks usually pay depositors 2 per cent less than Minimum Lending Rate, and charge borrowers 2 per cent more than Minimum Lending Rate. In this example Minimum Lending Rate is assumed to be 5 per cent. The interest will therefore be shared out as follows during the three year period.

Mr. A receives £9 (interest at 3% on £100 for three years).
Mr. C receives £63 (interest at 3% on £700 for three years).
The bank retains £75 (profit for running risks).

(e) In fact this example is a *little* biased because the bank would hesitate to lend out the whole £700 of imaginary money on illiquid loans like this one to Mr. B. It would lend out some of the money to more liquid borrowers such as the discount houses. This will be explained more fully later (see pages 226 and 227).

The Problem of Inter-Bank Settlements

As there are in fact several commercial banks, it is quite likely that Mr. C will deposit his cheque in some bank other than the one which made the loan to Mr. B. If this happens, at the end of the day Mr. B's bank will have to pay Mr. C's bank a large sum of money which it has only invented. It follows that the system can only work satisfactory if other customers from Mr. C's bank deposit an equal value of cheques with Mr. B's bank. Provided that the major banks keep their credit policies going along similar lines, then by an averaging process they will all receive deposits of the required amounts. But if one bank pursues more generous credit policies than the others it will lose cash to them, and will be forced to reduce its activities. This explains why when one bank manager refuses you a loan it is not much use going to another bank. They are all in the same situation as far as credit policy is concerned.

The Minimum Reserve Ratio

On 16th September, 1971, the Bank of England introduced new arrangements for the control of credit, to replace the former system of an 8 per cent cash ratio and a 28 per cent liquidity ratio. In future the banks will observe (day by day) a uniform **minimum reserve ratio** of $12\frac{1}{2}$ per cent of all **eligible liabilities**. In addition the Bank may call from time to time for additional **Special Deposits**. These will be placed with the Bank of England, and will earn interest at the **Treasury Bill Rate**, but the withdrawal of these amounts from the bank's liquid assets will cause them to reduce their loans to the public. This will reduce business activity in inflationary times, while the refund of special deposits will encourage expansion in deflationary periods. The calls or refunds of Special Deposits will take place whenever the Bank of England deems it desirable.

Eligible liabilities are defined as the sterling deposit liabilities of the banking system as a whole, excluding deposits having an original maturity of over two years, plus any sums obtained by switching foreign currencies into sterling.

Eligible reserve assets will comprise balances with the Bank of England (other than Special Deposits), Treasury Bills, moneys at call with the London Discount Market, gilt edged stocks with less than a year to run to maturity and any local authority or commercial bills eligible for re-discount at the Bank of England. **Till money is not included.**

Liquidity versus Profitability

Bankers earn a living by lending money at interest, and also by charging for certain services that they perform for their customers. In lending money the banks have to balance their natural desire to make a good profit with the necessity to play safe and maintain a good minimum reserve ratio. Liquidity and profitability are opposites; one cannot have both at once. A banker who lends money for long periods will earn a lot of interest, but if he lends so much that he has to stop his customers getting their money out when they want it he will be very unpopular.

Fig. 77 shows diagrammatically the important divisions of bank assets. The whole structure is an inverted pyramid poised on the till money. If the general public eat into this cash base by withdrawing funds unexpectedly from the bank, even for the most worthy reasons, the whole unstable edifice of banking could come crashing down, and with it the economy of the nation.

At the beginning of both World Wars the British Government's first act was to close the banks. They feared that while people were worried and agitated about their own and the country's situation, they might withdraw funds which would ruin the banking system. In a few days, when the public had grown accustomed to the idea of being at war, the banks reopened without any serious effects on their cash ratios. Successful banking depends on confidence—confidence in the political and economic stability of the whole country.

The structure of bank assets reflects the anxiety of the banks to achieve a balance between profitability and liquidity. About one-fifth of all funds are kept in cash or near-cash form, so that only the most extreme conditions could possibly affect the bank's ability to repay depositors. A further fifth of bank assets is kept in relatively liquid gilt-edged securities which could be sold fairly easily (though this might involve some capital loss). The other half of the bank's assets are loaned to customers, repayable over relatively short periods of about two years on average. These loans are repayable at regular intervals with interest, so that even with these relatively illiquid loans some funds will be returning to the banks for redeployment every week of the year.

Limitations on Bank Credit Policy

Although it might appear that the creation of bank credit places unlimited resources at the disposal of the banks, in fact there are some severe limitations on their creation of credit. These are:

(*a*) The need to maintain liquidity in a system based almost entirely on confidence.

(*b*) The need to ensure security for the loans. A high proportion of bad debts would cut into the profitability of loans as a whole, since absolute safety must be given to depositors who have entrusted funds to the bank. Very often banks will not give loans unless adequate security called **collateral** (literally 'side by side') **security** is available. The deeds of property are usually good security, for land and buildings nearly always have some value. A life-assurance policy is often offered as security, but it is less acceptable because, apart from its surrender value, if any, the policy will not be paid unless the borrower dies. Gilt-edged securities are acceptable collateral, as are shares in reputable firms, but the best guarantee for any bank is the known integrity of the customer. Where risks are taken they are calculated risks; good reliable loans are balanced against less worthy ones, and the principles of a 'balanced portfolio' of assets are followed.

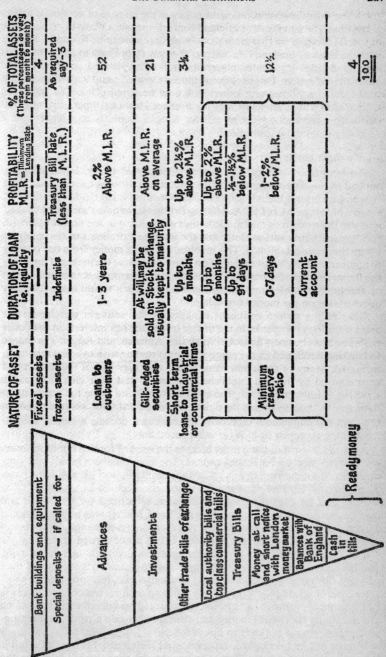

NATURE OF ASSET	DURATION OF LOAN i.e. liquidity	PROFITABILITY M.L.R. = Minimum Lending Rate	% OF TOTAL ASSETS (These percentages do vary from month to month)
Fixed assets			4
Frozen assets	Indefinite		As required say-3
Loans to customers	1-3 years	2% Above M.L.R.	52
Gilt-edged securities	At will may be sold on Stock Exchange, usually kept to maturity	Above M.L.R. on average	21
Short term loans to industrial or commercial firms	Up to 6 months	Up to 2½% above M.L.R.	3½
	Up to 6 months	Up to 2% above M.L.R.	
Minimum reserve ratio	Up to 91 days	½-1½% below M.L.R.	12½
	0-7 days	1-2% below M.L.R.	
	Current account	—	
			4⁄100

Bank buildings and equipment
Special deposits — if called for
Advances
Investments
Other trade bills of exchange
Local authority bills and top class commercial bills
Treasury Bills
Money at call and short notice with London money market
Balances with Bank of England
Cash in tills

Ready money

Fig. 77. The structure of a bank's assets: liquidity versus profitability (*c*) The third limitation on credit policy is the climate of economic affairs at the time. The new Bank of England controls include a week-by-week review of special deposits, so that large slices of bank funds can be frozen as deposits with the Bank of England if necessary. The new rules apply to all the financial institutions, not just the commercial banks. The justified complaint made under the old system, that banks were unfairly treated compared with merchant banks, finance houses and others has now been redressed. The minimum reserve ratio will be slightly lower for Finance Houses (10 per cent only) but the Bank reserves the right to call for Special Deposits at a higher rate if necessary from these institutions.

(5) Merchant Banks

The term 'merchant banker' is very widely used today, but is properly applied to the sixteen members of the Accepting Houses Committee. These sixteen City houses include such famous names as N. M. Rothschild & Sons, Samuel Montagu & Co. Ltd., and Baring Brothers. The name 'merchant banker' refers to their origin as mercantile houses specializing in the export of British goods, particularly cotton cloth, and the import of products of the countries where they were established. This involved remitting money from one country to another, and the bill of exchange on London became the means of financing the import and export trades. The merchants concerned became well known as absolutely reliable firms whose signature on a bill would make it readily discountable on the money market.

Some of the sixteen merchant bankers are still active as merchants: one owns subsidiary companies in the timber trade; one has interests in the coffee trade; one has business houses in Australia, America, and Africa. The change to banking developed as the number of firms trading with overseas territories increased. Many of these new firms found that they lacked the respect and trust enjoyed by the well established houses, so that their bills of exchange were less readily discounted. The solution was found to be the accepting of these traders' bills by one of the older established firms, for a consideration in the form of commission. Gradually the merchant became a banker specializing in the accepting of bills for other merchants.

A second interest of these firms became the issue of foreign bonds for overseas Governments who lacked capital. The issue of these bonds was only possible if the names of famous houses appeared in association with the issue. The merchant bankers arranged for a quotation on the London Stock Exchange, and handled the issues which were subscribed for by British and overseas investors. The London Foreign Bond Market was an international market and a source of 'invisible earnings' of foreign exchange. For balance-of-payments reasons the issue of foreign bonds is not carried on today.

The Acceptance Houses are still the specialist financiers of foreign trade, and the acceptance of bills of exchange drawn on London is still one of their primary functions. Alongside the use of foreign bills has grown up a widespread use of inland bills. This growth in inland business has occurred because of the more competitive rates of interest charged on bills of exchange, which are essentially short-term money and therefore provide a ready, and reasonably priced, source of funds to businessmen.

It must not be overlooked, however, that the essential feature of a bill is its self-liquidating nature. That is to say, by the time the bill falls due, the

THE COMMERCIAL BANK LTD.

Balance sheet (simplified and annotated) as at Dec. 31st 1971

Current liabilities	£ millions	£ millions
Notes in circulation	3	
Dividends due	7	
Creditors	17	
Amounts owing to depositors and other classes of customer	4,021	4,048
Provisions		
For taxation	40	
For pensions	17	57
Preference shareholders' interest in the bank		14
Ordinary shareholders' interest in the bank		
Capital contributed	91	
Reserves ploughed back in past years	240	331
		£4450

	Comments	% of total assets	Likely profit margin	£ millions
Liquid assets				
Till money and items in course of collection	Minimum reserve ratio	4%	0%	178
Balances at Bank of England		12½%	Average 1½% below Minimum Lending Rate	556
Money at call and short notice (loaned to discount houses)				
Local authority and other first class bills of exchange		3½%	Up to 2½% above M.L.R.	156
Other trade bills of exchange				
	Total liquid assets			890
Investments (nearly all in gilt-edged securities)	Held to earn income, but could be sold on the Stock Exchange	21%	A little above M.L.R.	935
Illiquid assets				
Advances to customers	Loans made to earn income, repayments coming in regularly of course	52%	2-3% above M.L.R.	2,314
Frozen assets				
Special deposits	By order of Central Bank	say 3%	1% below M.L.R.	153
Fixed assets				
Premises and equipment	Never likely to be realized in cash form	4%	0%	178
		100%		£4450

Note: Banks usually publish their balance sheets in the order of liquidity, i.e. the most liquid assets are named first

Fig. 78. Balance sheet of a typical commercial bank

trading venture it was designed to finance should have been completed and should have provided the funds for settlement of the bill. Bills are not intended to form a long-term financial alternative to bank loans or overdraft facilities. They are simply a method whereby the exporter receives his payment and the importer enjoys a period of credit, while the goods are in transit, being unloaded, going through customs formalities, etc.

The merchant banks carry out many other functions, of which the issuing of new securities, activities as a confirming house for overseas orders, and the handling of bullion are the most important.

(6) Discount Houses

The 'discount market' consists of eleven firms who are members of the London Discount Market Association. They specialize in **bill broking**, i.e. the provision of short-term money by way of discounting bills to borrowers who require funds which they expect to be able to repay within three months (in fact many borrowers will repay within 24 hours). This is a specialized form of banking. The discount houses provide a market-place where those who have surplus money, the use of which they are prepared to sell, can be put in touch with those prepared to buy the use of this money. The smallest unit for money on the market is £10,000, but occasionally lower amounts are used.

Today the savings of the nation are increasingly concentrated in the hands of institutional investors, such as banks, insurance companies, and building societies, who assume the responsibility of caring for and earning interest on the savings of the ordinary public. As this is a competitive world the institutional investors are becoming more and more sophisticated in their outlook. Money is not allowed to lie idle, but is loaned out to earn interest when it is not required for the main activities of the institution which has collected it. Even 'overnight' interest can be earned from banks anxious to meet their daily minimum cash reserve requirements. Every institutional investor has a 'balanced portfolio' of investments of different types. Some of the short-term investments in the portfolio will have been purchased from the bill brokers of the London Discount Market Association. The commonest short-term investments are Treasury Bills, Bank Bills, Trade Bills of Exchange, Short Gilt-Edged Securities, Corporation Stocks and, more recently, Sterling Certificates of Deposit. Some houses also deal in Dollar Certificates of Deposit and Foreign Currency Bills.

Bill-Broking

Bill-broking may be defined as dealing in money: taking it from those who have a surplus and distributing it to those who have need of it. When we take money from people we must pay interest on it in due course, so that if we lend it out to people who have need of it we must clearly lend at a higher rate of interest than we are to pay to the person from whom it was obtained. The difference between the borrowing rate and the lending rate is the source of the profits of the discount house.

If this profit margin is to be kept competitive there is no room for expensive paper records of transactions. Almost all the deals are by word of mouth only, but, once given, the discount banker's word is his bond. In a single day as much as £1,500 million may be handled by the market, with very little fuss or formality.

Flexible behaviour is absolutely essential to the bill broker. Changes in prices on the commodity markets or rates of interest anywhere in the world may lead to a strong demand for money, or cause a glut of money to be available. These trends must be reflected in changed interest rates or a lot of money will be lost. Now that the Treasury has assumed control of Minimum Lending Rate (May 1978) it proposes to announce changes at noon on Thursdays. This type of formal announcement is one type of fluctuation. Others are less formal, and result from the changing demand for, and supply of, short-term funds. The discount houses must remain ever alert to possible changes.

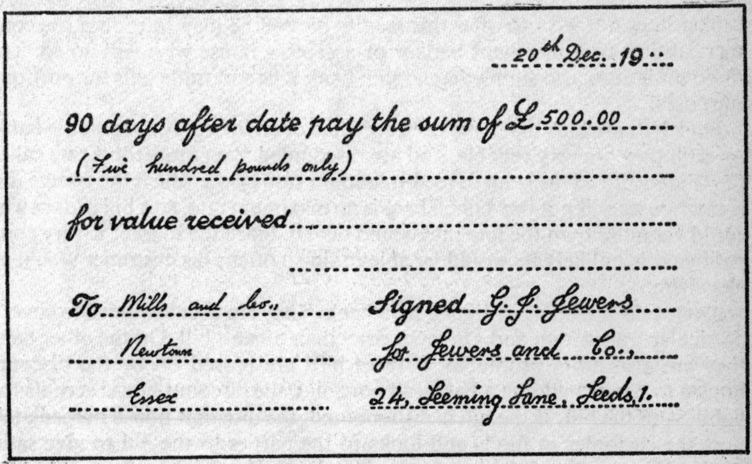

<figure>
20th Dec. 19...

90 days after date pay the sum of £500.00......
(Five hundred pounds only)......................

for value received..............................

To Mills and Co.,   Signed G. F. Jewers
    Newtown   for Jewers and Co.,
    Essex   24 Leeming Lane, Leeds 1.
</figure>

Fig. 79. An Inland Bill of Exchange

Services of the Bill Brokers to the Lending Sector

Bill brokers are prepared to borrow money from anyone who has a surplus and they agree to repay it as required. Money that is to be repayable on demand is known as 'call' money because it is on call at any time. 'Short-notice' money is usually repayable in a few days.

To the banks, bill brokers offer a secure outlet for liquid funds, which can still be regarded by the banks as part of their reserve ratio. The basic rate of interest is about $1\frac{1}{8}$ per cent below the Minimum Lending Rate, but the actual rate depends on supply and demand and the Treasury Bill tender. It is therefore quite profitable to the banks to lend this money at negligible risk. The brokers also buy from the commercial banks those bills of exchange which the banks have discounted for customers and do not wish to keep to maturity. Such bills are promises to pay made by commercial firms, and re-discounted by the banks to the money market.

To commercial firms wishing to lend money the discount houses offer the clearing-bank deposit rate, usually 2 per cent less than the Minimum Lending Rate. This is very useful to firms which have money to spare, but do not wish to put it on deposit because they will have to give seven days' notice of withdrawal. If firms are prepared to leave it at seven days' notice they can earn $\frac{1}{4}$ per cent above the clearing-bank deposit rate.

Services of the Bill Brokers to the Borrowing Sector

To the Government, the discount houses offer the loan of the short-term money they need; assuming an informal responsibility for underwriting the whole of the Treasury Bill issue every Friday. It is this conventional understanding which enables the Bank of England to control to some extent the economy of the country (see page 233).

To commercial firms, the discount houses offer direct loans by discounting trade bills. These are bills given to the commercial firm by a customer who promises to pay later. By discounting these bills the commercial firm is able to obtain the money at once, less a certain rate of interest. If a discount broker does not wish to offer this facility himself he may introduce the commercial firm to a merchant banker or accepting house who will do so. The discount houses also supply banks with bank bills and trade bills for portfolio purposes.

Bank bills are bills that have been accepted or endorsed by a reputable bank. As such they are very reliable, and are discounted at a competitive rate called the 'Fine Rate'. This is an agreed minimum rate below which the twelve discount houses will not buy bills. There is no maximum rate, so a bill broker who could get more than the fine rate would take it. Since the market is very competitive it is unlikely he would be able to do so often; his customer would go elsewhere.

Trade bills are bills not signed by a bank. They are usually drawn to cover a particular transaction and are more risky than a bank bill. On the other hand they are also more profitable. If these bills are passed on by the discount houses to banks building a balanced portfolio, the discount house accepts full liability on the bill. If the bill is dishonoured, the discount house immediately puts the customer in funds and looks to the parties to the bill to give satisfaction. It may therefore be said that the discount houses lend respectability to many commercial transactions and thus oil the wheels of commerce. One point about these trade bills is that they are usually for small amounts, mere hundreds or thousands of pounds. Usually the smallest unit in the discount market is £10,000, but the discount houses do handle trade bills for quite small sums. There is no limit on the size of a bill, whose reliability is judged by the names on the bill and their credit-worthiness.

How the Discount Market Operates

The portfolio of investments that a firm in the discount market owns is earning interest at varying rates. Gilts earn more than Minimum Lending Rate, bank bills just below, and the trade bills somewhere between $\frac{1}{8}$ and 2 per cent above this rate. At the same time the discount market itself has borrowed the money from the banks, at rates varying between Minimum Lending Rate and $1\frac{5}{8}$ per cent below, or from commercial firms at 2 per cent below this rate, i.e. the commercial-bank deposit rate. Naturally, like any other borrower from the bank, the discount house has to provide collateral security, hence large parts of its portfolio of investments are actually lodged as security with the banks to whom they are in debt.

If this situation continued for a few months or longer the profits earned by the money-market firm would be the difference between the interest they earn and the interest they have to pay out. In fact the situation never stays static for even one day. First, the discount houses have promised to lend the Government money every day, by buying Treasury Bills for which they tendered the previous Friday. Next, the banks always 'call' money in the mornings to pay out the sums they have agreed to lend to the public, the commercial firms, and the Government, and also to pay tax moneys paid to them which they now have to hand on to the Treasury. If the banks do this it makes the discount houses very short of cash in the morning. Later in the day the banks will probably have cash to spare because depositors have paid in money during the day. The discount houses have to telephone round desperately to get the cash they need before 2.30 p.m., which is the closing time for borrowing from the Bank of England. Great excitement develops as they try to obtain the funds they need, ringing round on their private switch-boards to raise the money: there is no time to ask a telephonist to get them a number, seconds might mean that someone else will get half a million pounds first.

At 2.30 those bankers whose attempts to raise cash have been unsuccessful must present themselves at the Bank of England to borrow what they need. They have been 'forced into the Bank', and if the Bank is anxious to raise interest rates all round it will charge them Minimum Lending, or even more. This is sad for the discount houses since they have already loaned the money to someone at less than this rate, and are therefore going to make a loss. Suppose a discount house had borrowed cash from a commercial bank at $5\frac{7}{8}$ per cent and agreed to loan it at 6 per cent to a metal broker. On being forced into the Bank it is up to the Bank whether it will charge the discount house a penal rate. If the Bank is satisfied with the present level of the economy it might not penalize the discount house, but if it wishes to discourage credit it may charge Minimum Lending Rate, or even more. A discount house, forced to pay a penal rate, loses 2 per cent on the sum borrowed. On £100,000 this amounts to a £500 loss on a '3 months' bill. The bill brokers will be charging more for loans next day, and credit will be discouraged.

Recent Developments in the Discount Market

The history of bill-broking is a history of adaptability to changing conditions in the money market. In the early days of the Industrial Revolution inland bills were a major source of currency, and bill brokers earned a steady living by helping to sort out uneven situations in the money market. As branch banking developed these uneven situations were adjusted by the head offices of the big banks, and the bill brokers turned to foreign bills, i.e. bills drawn on London to settle international indebtedness. During this period the saying grew up that 'a good bill should smell of the sea'.

In recent years there has been a considerable increase in the use of inland bills to finance internal trade and provide working capital, particularly in the more profitable, but more speculative, hire-purchase field. This has increased the part played by the bill broker in developing the economy of the nation. A succession of credit squeezes has made loans and overdrafts from the ordinary banks more difficult to obtain. Businessmen have had to turn elsewhere to secure funds, and the inland bill of exchange has been one way to obtain them.

Another recent development is the issue by local authorities of short-term bills and bonds with a life of one to four years. These enable the local authorities to fund some of their short-term debts, against the security of the rates. The time chosen, one to four years, lies conveniently between the three-month Treasury and trade bills and the five-year period usually chosen for short-term Government bonds.

The Economic Significance of the Discount Market

If the discount houses had an entirely free hand in borrowing funds from savers and lending them to spenders the economy might at times get too active. Control over the economy is partly established by controlling the discount houses. This is achieved by an informal undertaking by the discount houses to subscribe for the full amount of Treasury Bills offered each Friday by the Bank of England. By setting the size of this tender sufficiently large to keep the discount houses rather short of money, the Bank of England keeps control of them. They are sure to get into difficulties (and be 'forced into the Bank') if their rates are too low, so that firms are encouraged to borrow. If they are in difficulties the Bank of England can lend to them, as 'lender of last resort' (direct assistance) or lend to banks and other borrowers to ease the pressure on them (indirect assistance). If the Bank of England is satisfied with the economy it will lend cheaply and the discount houses will be able to balance their books, and make a profit on their deals. If the Bank is worried about the economy and thinks that the discount houses are causing the economy to inflate, it will charge them a 'penal rate' and they will make losses. They will have to recoup these losses by raising interest rates next day.

(7) The Foreign-Exchange Market

This is another market which has no central market-place, but operates through the general offices of the banks concerned with overseas trade. The main preoccupation of the foreign-exchange dealers is to secure supplies of foreign currency as required to finance international trade. The price of foreign currencies, like all prices, is determined by the demand for that currency and the supply of it. The demand for the currency depends on the demand for that country's goods and services by foreigners, and the supply of the currency depends on how many overseas goods and services its home nationals wish to buy. Capital movements can also affect the exchange rate by making supplies of a currency available on long-term loans or investments.

A fuller discussion on exchange rates is given on pages 268–87.

(8) The Capital Market

The Capital Market is another general name, like the name Money Market, which refers to a field of general activity rather than a particular place where buyers and sellers meet. Capital is required for many purposes, and specialized institutions have developed to provide it. The influence of these institutional investors has grown in the last thirty years, since a more equal distribution of wealth has been achieved. The high levels of taxation prevent rich people from accumulating large supplies of capital as in former times. Capital now has to be collected in relatively trifling sums from vast numbers of people, by special institutions.

A full list of these institutions includes, apart from the banks, the following:

(*a*) Issuing houses, which take on the work of issuing new shares or debentures for firms wishing to expand their activities.

(*b*) Building societies, collecting funds for those who wish to buy their own houses with loans financed through a mortgage.

(*c*) Finance houses, dealing in the more risky, but more profitable, hire-purchase fields for financing the purchase of consumer durables and cars.

(*d*) Investment Trusts and Unit Trusts, which specialize in collecting small sums from a great number of investors for the purchase of a balanced portfolio of shares. In this way they provide the fixed capital required by industry.

(*e*) Insurance companies are very active in the capital market. They have large sums to invest every week as premiums are received from the insuring public.

(*f*) Finally the Stock Exchange has an important part to play in the raising of long-term capital. Besides its chief function of providing a market-place for existing stocks and shares, it now plays some part in the raising of capital by granting a quotation to a new issue of shares. These shares are then 'placed' by the issuing house with one or two large purchasers of shares, insurance companies, or investment trusts.

(9) The Stock Exchange

A stock exchange is a highly organized financial market where bonds, stocks, and shares can be bought or sold. The London Stock Exchange is situated in Throgmorton Street within a few yards of the Bank of England, and at the centre of the financial affairs of the City. It is a respected and valued national institution, but it is not alone. There are independent groups of stock exchanges in other large cities, while members of the Provincial Brokers' Stock Exchange also carry on business in numerous smaller towns.

Stock-market business is world-wide, and New York, Johannesburg, Melbourne, Tokyo, Calcutta, Paris, Amsterdam, and Brussels are all famous centres of stock-exchange activity.

The function of a stock exchange is to put those who wish to sell stocks or shares in touch with those who wish to buy, so that investments can change hands in the quickest, cheapest, and fairest manner possible.

When a member of the general public invests his savings by lending them to the managers of a company, he does not intend that the company shall have the use of his money for ever, for he does not know when fate may knock on his door and present him with problems. The investment as far as the investor is concerned is a purely temporary one, depending on his good luck to some extent. If the fates are kind the investment may last for years; if the fates are unkind he, or his heirs, may wish to withdraw the investment in cash form, just like withdrawing money from a bank.

From the point of view of directors of the firm the matter is quite different. They regard the investment as a permanent one, for they spend the invested money on land and buildings, plant and machinery, transport and other equipment. They cannot possibly return the money, for they no longer have it. They have turned it into assets, and in the process it becomes 'fixed'. Fixed capital is capital tied up in fixed assets, which have been purchased for permanent use in the business.

It follows that a shareholder cannot withdraw his money as if it was cash deposited in a bank. He must sell the shares on the Stock Exchange to someone who has cash and wishes to invest it in the firm concerned. The price at which the exchange takes place will reflect the estimates by the two parties of the value of the share in the company which it represents. It may therefore involve the seller in some **capital gain** or **capital loss**, according to whether the price is above or below the cost price of the share when he bought it.

The company whose shares are being bought and sold has little interest in the matter at all, but it will register the transfer of shares in order to keep its list of shareholders up to date. The company merely pursues its lawful activities, as laid down in its Memorandum of Association, leaving the specialist dealers on the Stock Exchange to arrange matters when the public wish to buy or sell securities.

Buying and Selling Securities

The investor who wishes to purchase stocks or shares must approach a stockbroker who will undertake the purchase for him. The Stock Exchange is another type of highly organized market, already referred to in the chapter on Markets (see page 115). Only experts may deal on such markets, for the ordinary member of the public would not know the procedures to be followed, and would almost certainly make a bad bargain. Only the expert with experience of the market can judge what is a fair price for a share.

There are two classes of experts: (*a*) brokers, and (*b*) jobbers who are also known as dealers. The broker buys and sells shares on behalf of the general public, or he may deal on his own account. When acting for the public he is an agent employed to deal at the most favourable price obtainable. Brokers are paid by the client, the charge usually being in the region of 1¼ per cent. Brokers also give their clients advice in connection with investment affairs. They are forbidden to advertise.

Brokers execute their clients' orders by dealing with the jobbers. The jobber is a wholesaler of stocks and shares. A broker wishing to sell shares on behalf of a client will sell them at a fair price to the jobber who will add them to his store of securities. A broker wishing to buy shares on behalf of a client will obtain them from the jobber at a fair price. The difference between the jobber's buying price and the price at which he sells is the 'jobber's turn' (see page 237). As the market is highly competitive, it is unlikely that the profit will be excessive, especially when the risks of loss are taken into account.

Because the Stock Exchange today lists more than 9,500 different securities, jobbers cannot be expert dealers in them all. A jobber or firm of jobbers will concentrate on certain classes of shares and make a special study of them. There are always a number of jobbers dealing in each group of securities; they compete for the business brought to them by brokers, and so a competitive 'market' is created.

Often jobbers who deal in the same types of shares will stand close to one another on one part of the floor of the Stock Exchange. Thus all those who deal in Government and similar stocks will be found in the 'gilt-edged' market; and the dealers in shares of engineering firm's will be found grouped together in the 'Industrials' market. However, this does not always happen, and the jobbers in bank, shipping, oil, property, and brewery shares are scattered about the floor of the Stock Exchange. It is the existence of this competitive market which ensures that the public gets a fair price for shares sold on the Exchange.

This type of highly organized market does not evolve overnight. An unbroken succession of business activity since the seventeenth century has developed the customs, rules, and controlling council of the Stock Exchange, ensuring that the public's affairs will be conducted efficiently, cheaply, and quickly.

How a Bargain is Struck

As in any market a deal takes place only when the price is right. If one party thinks the price wrong he will hesitate, and if the other senses this hesitation in any way he will alter the price if he thinks he can still make a profit by doing so, or if he thinks he should cut his losses by selling at once. If he has quoted a rock-bottom price anyway he will not lower it further. As prices on the Stock Exchange vary with world business activity, the brokers and jobbers are continually balancing in their heads the business trends throughout the world. Success or failure of firms whose shares are being dealt with, or of other firms in the same line of business; wars and rumours of wars; natural disasters; economic crises; Government activities restricting or encouraging the flow of raw materials, manufactured goods, or capital around the world; all these affect the present value of a share on the market.

Fig. 80 illustrates how the system works. The floor of the House, to which only brokers and jobbers have access, is shown with some of the main 'markets'. These markets consist of groups of jobbers, specializing in particular fields, and prepared to buy or sell as required.

Outside the Exchange, but of course free to enter at any time, are the stockbrokers operating from their private offices where they are available for advice and help to the general public.

A member of the public, Mrs. A, wishing to sell £500 'International Industries' shares, asks her stockbroker to act for her in selling them at the

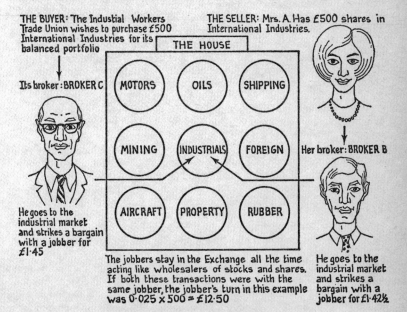

Fig. 80. How the Stock Exchange works

best possible price. The broker enters the Exchange and proceeds to the 'Industrial' market where he approaches one of the jobbers dealing in this type of share. He may not reveal whether he is a buyer or a seller, for this would enable the jobber to vary the price to suit the transaction and make it more profitable to himself. The jobber now quotes two prices, using fractions that go down to $\frac{1}{8}$th of a new penny, say £1·42½–£1·45. The lower price is the 'bid' price at which he is prepared to buy. The upper price is the 'offer' price at which he is prepared to sell.

Since Mrs. A's broker is trying to sell shares he may reply 'I'll sell you 500 at £1·42½.' Each will then make a note of the bargain struck in his 'bargain book'. If the broker feels that a better price than £1·42½ is possible he will ask the jobber 'anything else'. The jobber may then say '£1·041'. This is a worse price than before for a broker trying to sell shares. He will therefore move on to another jobber, looking for a better bargain. In this example we will pretend he is satisfied with £1·42½ and sells at that figure.

When a bargain has been struck a note is made of it in the 'bargain books' of the jobber and broker. Having agreed to deal at this price a jobber will always honour his bargain, for the proud motto of the Stock Exchange is *Dictum Meum Pactum*, 'My Word is my Bond'.

The Economic Significance of the Stock Market

In a free-enterprise society, capital has to be collected from individuals. In today's egalitarian society where wealth is more evenly divided than ever before, this capital is spread so thinly that special institutions are needed to collect it. These institutions are not investing capital permanently, but only incidentally as a sideline to their main occupations. Thus the bank's main occupations are safeguarding moneys and facilitating payments for their clients. The insurance companies' main occupation is to cover risks. Trade unions exist to further industrial action and the welfare of their members. For all these institutions managed liquidity is essential. Their investment policies are designed to achieve a balance between profitability and liquidity. The Stock Exchange provides the means whereby liquidity is regained, and also the means whereby a portfolio rendered unsafe by changes in the positions of Governments and businessmen may be adjusted to yield greater security. Of course these services are available for individuals too, but the really significant investors today are the institutional investors.

Among the institutions of modern society central and local governments are some of the most important. In an increasingly complex society administrative control of defence, health, and education extends to cover major national monopolies like fuel and power, transport, atomic energy, and even certain types of land. This **public sector** of the economy requires finance too. The activities of the Government broker ensure that such funds will continue to be made available through the gilt-edged market.

The gilt-edged market is an active market in Government stocks. The sale of these stocks is used to finance the long-term borrowing of Government departments and nationalized industries. The 'trustee status' of such stocks assists the market in maintaining an active interest in gilt-edged securities. The main object of the Bank of England's activities here is to promote the sale of long-term stock and keep the market healthy so that this type of long-term loan will always be available to the Government.

All purchases and sales are made through the Government broker and are largely authorized by the Bank's Issue Department. From time to time the Bank's portfolio is restored by new issues of stock. Most of these new issues cannot be sold at once to the general public but are taken up by the Issue Department. Funding is a chief aim of the Issue Department. It may be defined as persuading citizens and institutions to lend money on a long-term basis (creating a fund) instead of only for a short term.

Like all highly organized markets the activities of jobbers and brokers on the Stock Exchange are involved, and the general public cannot hope to understand what the specialist is doing. It follows that his activities may abuse his privileged position. The Stock Exchange Council exercises a supervisory control over members, and its Code of Dealing indicates acceptable standards of behaviour by dealers. It is also represented on a Panel, composed of representatives of banks and other institutions, whose 'Takeover Code' attempts to supervise the behaviour of bidders trying to gain control of companies. This code has been much criticized, on the ground that it does not ensure equal treatment for all shareholders. It certainly takes time for such Codes to close all the loopholes which can be devised by astute and expert specialists, but the worst abuses of speculative activities have gradually been controlled by the Panel and Council, and it seems likely that these improvements will continue.

The result of the activities of the Stock Exchange is the collection of a vast amount of capital for both private and public enterprises. This capital is not collected through the Exchange, rather it is collected *because* of the Exchange. It encourages the investor to invest, because he knows liquidity can be regained. This investment enables capital projects to go ahead, employment opportunities to be provided, and unit costs to be reduced as economies of scale are achieved. It even provides, by its published prices, the yardstick on which estates, inheritances, and compensation (in nationalization procedures for example) are valued.

(10) Summary of Chapter Twenty

1. Financial institutions are of great importance in developing and controlling economies.

2. The Bank of England, like all central banks, is used to implement Government policies by promoting expansion or contraction of the economy as required.

3. The 'Money Market' is a general name for all banks and financial institutions who are active in making liquid funds available, to promote the activities of industry and trade.

4. The commercial banks provide a wide variety of services for the ordinary public, and are also very active in making funds available to the discount houses and other specialist operators. In particular their activities in making loans available to customers create deposits to the credit of customers. This creation of credit is an active influence on the economy of the country.

The banks retain a minimum reserve ratio of $12\frac{1}{2}$ per cent of all 'eligible liabilities', either as cash reserves with the Bank of England or as call money and short term money on the London markets. They also have about 4 per cent of their assets as cash in their tills.

Bankers are continuously involved in choosing between liquidity and profitability. Their credit policies are dominated by the need for liquidity and security, and by the influence of the central bank.

5. Merchant bankers promote foreign trade by accepting bills of exchange for less worthy business houses.

6. The Discount Market is the market for short-term loans. It is the medium through which the Government influences rates of interest and controls the level of activity in the economy.

7. The Foreign-exchange Market is the market where the currencies of the world are compared and prices are fixed for pounds, dollars, francs, D. marks etc.

8. The Capital Market consists of a wide variety of institutions collecting capital from the public and making it available to various kinds of entrepreneurs. Most important are the issuing houses, insurance companies, investment and unit trusts, building societies, finance houses, and the ordinary banks.

9. The Stock Exchange is the market for existing securities, where those wishing to regain liquidity, by selling their shares in firms or their Government stocks, may be put in touch with those wishing to surrender liquidity in favour of fixed assets.

(11) Suggested Further Reading

Clarke & Pulay, G. *The World's Money. How it Works*. Allen & Unwin, 1970.
Sayers, R. S.: *Modern Banking*. Oxford U.P.: London, 1967.
Whitehead, G.: *Commerce Made Simple*. W. H. Allen: London, 1974 Edn.
The Radcliffe Report on the Working of the Monetary System. H.M. Stationery Office: London, 1959.

Exercises Set 20

1. Define a bank. What are its basic functions and how does it perform them?

2. What is the 'minimum reserve ratio' of a bank? What influence does it have on the activities of bankers?

3. 'Loans make deposits'. Explain this statement, and the importance of the creation of bank credit in the economy of a country.

4. The banks are preoccupied with achieving liquidity, profitability, and security. Explain the importance of each of these to the banker. How does he achieve all three at the same time?

5. 'Bankers can only lend what is lent to them by others'. Discuss.

6. 'Discount houses render great service to bankers and businessmen alike.' What services do they render, and what reward do they get for these services?

7. 'A financial market is just like any other market-place.' Explain, referring in your answer to (a) the Discount Market, and (b) the Foreign-exchange Market.

8. The Bank of England is Great Britain's Central Bank. What are its chief functions?

9. What is a Stock Exchange, and how does it serve (a) the general public, and (b) the business community?

10. Mrs. A. has decided to sell 1,000 shares in General Electric to buy her son a car as a graduation present. The Motorists' Insurance Co. had decided to buy 1,000 shares in General Electric as part of its portfolio. How will the two parties be dealt with so that the needs of both are satisfied?

CHAPTER TWENTY-ONE

INTERNATIONAL TRADE

(1) Why Trade with Foreign Countries?

Nations trade with one another for several reasons. First, Nature has been haphazard in the way she has distributed resources around the world, so that some nations possess natural ores and chemical deposits in excess of their own personal requirements, while other nations have no supplies. Britain has large coal reserves but lacks copper, South Africa has gold but lacks oil (although she is still prospecting). Kuwait has vast oil deposits but little else. The exchange between nations of such resources is an obvious solution to the shortages.

Secondly, climate plays a large part in the production of many natural products. Jungle hardwoods will only grow in tropical climates. The natural habitat of the fur-bearing animals is in the cold regions of the world, while citrus fruits require a Mediterranean climate. Tobacco will grow in the United Kingdom, but cannot be properly cured in the British climate. Only very large countries like the U.S.A. and the U.S.S.R. embrace within their borders all the climatic regions of the world. Such nations may achieve some degree of success in practising self sufficiency. Other nations must trade.

Thirdly, it sometimes happens that a nation, despite efficient production, has such vast demands that she must supplement home production with imports. For example, Britain grows wheat very efficiently, but not on a scale large enough to support her entire needs. India grows rice, but Burma has been for centuries the 'rice-bowl of India'.

Even when a nation is able to produce all the goods it needs there may be reasons for not doing so. For strategic reasons the United States is deliberately husbanding its own oil resources while it can obtain cheap supplies from Venezuela and the Middle East. Similarly, Great Britain has allowed her own cotton industry to run down in order to assist the people of Hong Kong and other territories whose economic well-being is linked for historical reasons with the United Kingdom.

Trade also takes place when it is to the economic advantage of the nations concerned to specialize in particular activities. For example both Britain and Sweden can make steel, but much Swedish steel is used in British industry because of its high quality and unique properties. Sweden buys many British cars even though Swedish cars are world famous. The explanation is to be found in the **Law of Comparative Costs**, which is the main feature of this chapter on the theory of international trade. Before we examine this law let us consider two basic economic ideas: the principle of comparative advantage and the idea of alternative costs.

(2) The Principle of Comparative Advantage

Consider two men, Prof. Splitit an atomic physicist, and Bill Greenfingers a gardener. The professor is a highly educated scientist, earning in his normal employment 4·00 per hour. He is also a keen gardener, and because of his scientific training is actually a better gardener than Bill Greenfingers; twice as good in fact. Bill Greenfingers is a good gardener, and earns 0·50 per hour at his employment. So we have:

	Professor S.	*Gardener B. G.*
Normal hourly earnings	4·00	0·50
Earnings as a gardener	1·00	0·50

Notice that the professor has an absolute advantage in earning power over Bill Greenfingers both as an atomic scientist and as a gardener. But at which job has he a *comparative* advantage? Clearly, the ratios of 4·00 to 0·50 and 1·00 to 0·50 show that he as a 4:1 advantage in his specialist occupation.

Suppose the professor gives up an hour of his earning time to weed the garden. The garden will receive in this one hour the equivalent of two hours' gardening by Bill Greenfingers, for the professor is twice as good a gardener as Bill. If Prof. S. specializes in his own employment and earns 4·00, he will then be able to pay Bill Greenfingers to do eight hours' gardening. The garden will therefore look four times as tidy as if the professor had tended it personally.

Economists say that it will, generally speaking, be advantageous for mankind if people specialize in those occupations at which they have the greatest comparative advantage, or the least comparative disadvantage, leaving others to produce the goods and services for which they have little aptitude. This principle of comparative advantage is the basis of specialization into trades and occupations, and it is of great importance in the theory of international trade.

(3) The Idea of Alternative Costs

'Alternative costs', also called 'opportunity costs', have been discussed earlier on page 5. Any nation has certain factors (land, labour and capital). These factors of production are available to produce goods and services. It can move its factors into or out of production at will. Suppose we say that a basic group of factors comprising an entrepreneur and twenty men, £10,000·00 capital, and 500 acres of land, are to be devoted to the production of wheat. The result will be an output of a given quantity of wheat, say 1,000 tons.

Had these same factors been employed in other ways, different goods or services could have been produced. They might have raised beef instead, or intensively fed poultry, or they might have made saucepans, or built roads. To move factors over to other forms of production is quite easy, but it usually involves some retraining of labour and modifications to building etc. Such little difficulties are called 'economic friction'. If there is a good deal of friction, changes will not be made easily; if there is only a little friction, changes will take place more readily.

If these factors are put to work in different ways they may turn out 1,000 tons of wheat, or, say 100 tons of aluminium. The 'cost' of the wheat we actually produce is the aluminium we do not produce; or the 'cost' of the aluminium we actually manufacture is the wheat we do not grow. The factors cannot be employed on both at once, so we have to make a choice.

The alternative costs may be displayed as follows:

1,000 tons wheat : 100 tons aluminium
or 1,000 : 100
or 10 : 1

The alternative-costs ratio is therefore 10:1. We can have 10 tons of wheat, or one ton of aluminium, but not both. The cost of 10 tons of wheat is one ton of aluminium, while the cost of one ton of aluminium is 10 tons of wheat.

It is different alternative-costs ratios that give individuals a comparative advantage in one trade or another. If the factors of production (land, labour, or capital) are employed where they have the greatest comparative advantage, or the least comparative disadvantage, output will be at a maximum. Let us now consider how these basic economic ideas arise also in international trade.

(4) The Law of Comparative Costs

The Law of Comparative Costs states that *nations will find it profitable to trade with other nations when (a) they have different alternative-cost ratios, and (b) the international terms of trade lie within the limits set by their domestic alternative-cost ratios.*

This is not an easy law to understand and the reader is urged to study the next page or two very carefully.

(5) An Example of Specialization in International Trade

Imagine two countries: one is a South American republic which we shall call Garibaldia, the other is a western advanced nation (like Great Britain) which we shall call Occidentalia. Each has land, labour and capital available for employment. These factors are employed in many different activities, but we shall consider only a small set of factors comprising some land, some capital, and some labour, including an entrepreneur. This set can be employed in either beef production or aluminium production. The figures given in Table 25 show the alternative costs of these two products.

Notice that, as stated in the Law of Comparative Costs, these two countries *do have different alternative-cost ratios.* The cost of a unit of aluminium in

Table 25. Comparative advantage in beef production

Country	Garibaldia		Occidentalia	
Products (In units of 1,000 tons)	Aluminium (1,000 tons)	Beef (1,000 tons)	Aluminium (1,000 tons)	Beef (1,000 tons)
Output of a given set of factors	4 : 10		9 : 11	
Alternative cost ratios	1 : 2·5		1 : 1·2	
Effect of changing factors over from one product to another	Giving up 1 unit of aluminium	Enables this country to produce 2·5 units of beef	Giving up 1 unit of aluminium	Enables this country to produce 1·2 units of beef
Country with a comparative advantage in beef production	Garibaldia has the advantage		———	

Garibaldia is 2·5 units of beef. The cost of a unit of aluminium in Occidentalia is 1·2 units of beef. For every unit of aluminium production she gives up, Garibaldia can have 2·5 units of beef, whereas Occidentalia can have only 1·2 units of beef. It is clear that if one country is going to specialize in beef production it ought to be Garibaldia, because she has the comparative advantage.

Table 26. Comparative advantage in aluminium production

Country	Garibaldia		Occidentalia	
Products (In units of 1,000 tons)	Beef (1,000 tons)	Aluminium (1,000 tons)	Beef (1,000 tons)	Aluminium (1,000 tons)
Output of a given set of factors	10 : 4		11 : 9	
Alternative cost ratios	1 : 0·4		1 : 0·82	
Effect of changing factors over from one product to another	Giving up 1 unit of beef	Enables this country to produce ·4 units of aluminium	Giving up 1 unit of beef	Enables this country to produce ·82 units of aluminium
Country with a comparative advantage in aluminium production	—		Occidentalia has the advantage	

In Table 26 this information has been rearranged to show the same figures the other way round. We now see that if one country is proposing to specialize in aluminium it ought to be Occidentalia, because she has the comparative advantage in producing this product. For every unit of beef Occidentalia gives up, she will produce 0·82 units of aluminium. For every unit of beef Garibaldia gives up she will produce only 0·4 units of aluminium. Clearly then, Occidentalia ought to be the one that produces aluminium as its special product.

Now let us examine what happens to the total wealth of the world if these two countries specialize. For the sake of simplicity we shall pretend that the world consists of these two countries only.

Table 27. 'World' output before specialization

World output before specialization		
Country	Beef	Aluminium
Occidentalia	120 units	100 units
Garibaldia	110 units	60 units
'World' output	230 units	160 units

Table 27 shows the situation before either country specializes. Since these countries have different factor endowments to start with, there is no connection between their outputs before specialization commences. Let us assume that at this time Occidentalia produces 120 units of beef and 100 units of aluminium, whereas Garibaldia produces 110 units of beef and 60 units of aluminium.

Each country is producing for its own use, and world output is 230 units of beef and 160 units of aluminium.

Before proceeding further let us be quite clear about the fact that Occidentalia has an **absolute advantage** in both beef and aluminium production. 'Absolute advantage' is defined as a situation where a country, with a given input of factor resources, produces more of a commodity than another country using a similar set of factors. Thus in Table 25 equal sets of factors in the two countries produce 4 units of aluminium in Garibaldia (against 9 units in Occidentalia), and 10 units of beef in Garibaldia (against 11 units in Occidentalia). Occidentalia has an absolute advantage in both commodities, but her comparative advantage is in aluminium production.

In order to see what happens when these countries decide to specialize in the things they do best, we need to consider the 'production possibility schedules' shown in Table 28. In each case present production is shown by an arrow and a heavy 'box' round the figures.

Note carefully what happens as successive sets of factors are moved out of one industry and into the other. As Garibaldia changes over to specialized beef production her output of aluminium declines 60, 56, 52, 48 etc., while her beef output rises 110, 120, 130 etc.

In the same way, as Occidentalia moves factors into specialized aluminium production her output of beef declines 120, 110, 100, 90 etc., but her output of aluminium rises 100, 108, 116, 125 etc.

The final result, supposing each country specialized completely, would be 'world' outputs of 260 units of beef (by Garibaldia) and 198 units of aluminium (by Occidentalia). These outputs are made clear in Table 29.

As a result of each country specializing in the industry at which it has a comparative advantage, the world is richer by 30,000 tons of beef and 38,000 tons of aluminium. How is this extra wealth to be shared between Occidentalia and Garibaldia?

One country is now producing all the beef, and the other all the aluminium. They are now about to engage in international trade, but on what *terms* will they trade? The **terms of trade** will be decided by the international demand for and supply of the products concerned. If the demand for beef is strong while the demand for aluminium is weak, the terms of trade will be favourable to Garibaldia. If the demand for beef is weak, and the demand for aluminium is strong the terms of trade will be favourable to Occidentalia.

Returning to the Law of Comparative Costs for a moment, we recall that 'nations will find it profitable to trade with other nations when (*a*) they have different alternative cost ratios'.

We have seen that these two countries do have different alternative cost ratios. These are

Garibaldia	*Occidentalia*
Beef : Aluminium	Beef : Aluminium
2·5 : 1	1·2 : 1

The law continues: (*b*) the international terms of trade lie within the limits set by their domestic alternative cost ratios'. What exactly does this part of the law mean?

Supposing the terms of trade are favourable to Garibaldia. There is a strong demand for beef, and her farmers are in a good bargaining position. Suppose

Table 28. Moving factors over into specialized production

PRODUCTION POSSIBILITY SCHEDULE – GARIBALDIA

(Present output shown by arrow)

Units of beef	260	250	240	230	220	210	200	190	180	170	160	150	140	130	120	110	100	90	80	70	60	50	40	30	20	10	0
Units of aluminium	0	4	8	12	16	20	24	28	32	36	40	44	48	52	56	60	64	68	72	76	80	84	88	92	96	100	104

Moving into specialized beef production →

← Moving into specialized aluminium production

PRODUCTION POSSIBILITY SCHEDULE – OCCIDENTALIA

(Present output shown by arrow)

Units of beef	240	230	220	210	200	190	180	170	160	150	140	130	120	110	100	90	80	70	60	50	40	30	20	10	0
Units of aluminium	2	10	18	26	34	43	51	59	67	75	84	92	100	108	116	125	133	141	149	157	166	174	182	190	198

her trade representatives offer to buy one unit of Occidentalian aluminium for 1·85 units of Garibaldian beef. This would be a very kind offer on their part, since they are taking up a position exactly half way between the two alternative costs 2·5 and 1·2. Since they are in a strong bargaining position they are much more likely to say 'one unit of your aluminium for 1·5 units of beef, or 1·4, or even 1·3 units of beef'. Occidentalia will have to give in to the hard bargaining because the terms of trade are against her. But if the Garibaldian traders get really greedy and demand one unit of aluminium for one unit of beef they will find that Occidentalia loses interest. She can produce her own beef by moving factors out of aluminium production and get 1·2 units of beef, so there is no point in buying from Garibaldia at a lower price than 1·2. The limit is set by her domestic alternative-cost ratio.

As the Law of Comparative Costs says, it ceases to be profitable to trade if the international terms of trade move outside the limits set by the domestic alternative-cost ratios.

Table 29. Increased 'World' output as a result of international specialization

Country	World output after specialization	
	Beef	Aluminium
Occidentalia	—	198
Garibaldia	260	—
'World' output	260	198
Rise in 'World' output	30	38

Conversely, if the terms of trade favour Occidentalia she will be able to demand more beef for her aluminium. If she demands 1·85 units, or 2·0 units, trade will still continue; but if she greedily tries to demand 2·5 units or more, the Garibaldian negotiators will refuse to trade. It would be cheaper to move factors over to aluminium production and make the metal at home.

Tables 30 and 31 (overleaf) make these matters clear, and show how the extra wealth is shared up between the two countries.

Remember that what decides how the extra wealth is shared is the international terms of trade.

(6) Reasons why Nations never Specialize Completely

To keep the explanation simple in the above examples certain assumptions were made which were not necessarily true-to-life. Let us examine each of these assumptions in turn.

(a) *The 'world' has only two countries.* This does not need us to modify the original argument very much. Instead of specialization taking place just between two countries, all the countries of the world are involved. Of course many countries grow wheat and make steel, but many countries that could make steel prefer to buy it from the nations with comparative advantages in steel production. At the same time it is very true that complete specialization may never occur even when it is economically advantageous. For strategic reasons Britain continues to support home farming, although in some respects it is uneconomic. For psychological reasons many developing countries have

Table 30. Sharing the extra output: terms of trade favourable to Garibaldia (i.e. beef is dear, and aluminium is cheap—say 1·5:1)

Country	Garibaldia		Occidentalia	
Commodity	Wealth before specialization	Wealth after specialization	Wealth before specialization	Wealth after specialization
Beef	110 units	Say 128 units	120 units	Bought from Garibaldia 132 units
Aluminium	60 units	This leaves 132 units of beef to sell. With terms of trade 1·5:1 Garibaldia buys 88 units of aluminium	100 units	For this 132 units of beef Occidentalia pays Garibaldia 88 units of aluminium. This leaves her 110 units
Total units enjoyed	170 units	216 units	220 units	242 units
Share of extra output (68 units)	46 = 18 beef + 28 aluminium		22 = 12 beef + 10 aluminium	
Conclusion:	Garibaldia is getting the lion's share			

Table 31. Sharing the extra output: terms of trade favourable to Occidentalia (i.e. beef is cheap, and aluminium is dear—say 2:1)

Country	Garibaldia		Occidentalia	
	Wealth before specialization	Wealth after trading	Wealth before specialization	Wealth after trading
Beef	110 units	Say 128 units	120 units	Bought from Garibaldia 132 units
Aluminium	60 units	Selling 132 units of beef at 2·0:1 Garibaldia buys 66 units of aluminium	100 units	For this 132 units of beef Occidentalia pays 66 units of aluminium. This leaves her 132 units
Total units enjoyed	170	194	220	264
Share of extra wealth (68 units)	24 = 18 beef + 6 aluminium		44 = 12 beef 32 aluminium	
Conclusion	Occidentalia is getting the lion's share			

airlines although they can't afford them, don't need them, and could get better service from foreign airlines. Specialization will never be complete even when it makes economic sense if it makes national, strategic, or social nonsense.

(*b*) *The existence of perfect competition between nations.* We have assumed that if cheap aluminium from Occidentalia floods into Garibaldia the Garibaldian aluminium industry will not attempt to stop it, because it has made up its mind to go out of business anyway. Similarly the farmers of Occidentalia will not object to cheap Garibaldian beef flooding the country, for they have all decided to become aluminium workers and exchange their saucepans for foreign beef. In fact this is an unlikely situation, and the chief difficulty about international trade is how to overcome the opposition of 'vested interests', i.e. entrepreneurs who have sunk capital and effort into relatively unproductive home-based industries. This is a second reason why complete specialization between nations rarely occurs.

(*c*) *The assumption that all units of factors are equally efficient.* As Garibaldia moved successive units of factors out of aluminium production and into beef production we assumed in our 'production possibility schedules' that aluminium production fell by 4 units and beef production rose by 10 units. We imagined that all the sets of factors were equally efficient. In fact of course this would not be the case. The first set of factors to be taken out of production would be those that were of least use to the aluminium industry. Probably they would also be particularly keen to change over to beef production. As the process continues, with more and more factors moving out of the aluminium industry, the factors changing over will be better and better factors for aluminium production and worse and worse factors for beef production. There will thus be twin forces at work to stop complete specialization. The very best aluminium workers will resist strongly any suggestion to move them out of aluminium production, while the economic arguments in favour of doing so will be reduced because of their manifest unsuitability for beef production.

The same forces will be at work in Occidentalia. The very best beef farmers will resist any attempts to move them into saucepan factories, while their manifest unfitness for the work will be a strong argument against doing so on economic grounds.

The crucial point in the process is where native production is more efficient than the foreign competitor notwithstanding his comparative advantage. There must come a stage where the very best Garibaldian aluminium smelters are better than the least efficient Occidentalian aluminium plants; or where the very best Occidentalian farmers are more efficient than the laziest and most incompetent Garibaldian cowboys. At this point specialization between nations will cease. Increasing returns on one side and decreasing returns on the other bring the process to an end before it reaches its theoretical limits.

(*d*) *Transport costs.* Transport costs also interfere with the simple picture discussed, because of course such costs are inseparable from specialization. If nations are to specialize they must transport goods and raw materials around the world. The effect of transport costs is to narrow the limits between which it will prove profitable to trade. Instead of it being profitable to trade when the international terms of trade lie within the limits set by their domestic alternative-cost ratios, it will only be profitable to trade in a rather narrower band with the transport charges being added to the domestic-cost calculations of both countries.

(*e*) *Demand must be strong enough to justify complete specialization.* Suppose in the example chosen total 'world' demand for beef had only been 245 units. With this production everyone who wants beef can obtain it. Clearly there would be no point in specializing to the point of producing 260 units of beef.

Specialization is limited by the extent of the market, just as it is in home trade. Thus the Pitcairn Islanders, descendants of the mutineers from H.M.S. *Bounty* make excellent souvenirs, but they do not concentrate exclusively upon production of these, since world demand is relatively limited.

(*f*) *Absence of tariffs or quotas*. The last assumption was that no artificial barriers to trade have been erected, such as tariffs or quotas. Where such barriers exist, the full competitive effect of specialization cannot come into play, and world output will rise by a smaller amount than it should.

For all these reasons nations may not specialize completely in the real world.

(7) The Terms of Trade

We saw in the section on comparative costs that the rate at which goods are exchanged betwen nations must lie *within the limits set by the domestic alternative-cost ratios*, otherwise it will pay a nation to move its factors out of specialized occupations and produce the goods itself.

What determines the exchange rate for goods is the international demand for and supply of any particular commodity. The usual market forces operate internationally and the resultant rate of exchange represents the **terms of trade** between any two countries. At any given time they may favour one country or the other, but if they become too unfavourable to one nation that nation will move factors over to new employments and trade will cease. We must now consider some of the influences on the international demand for, and supply of, goods.

The Demand for Goods in International Trade

Demand for goods is affected by the following:

(*a*) *Wars, and rumours of wars*. Any signs of political disturbance make entrepreneurs and nations nervous about the possible interruption of supplies; or that demand for their products will increase at times when raw materials are not available. They therefore begin to stockpile raw materials, and this alters the terms of trade in favour of the primary producing nations. Stockpiling raises prices, and moves the exchange rate for goods farther away from the domestic cost level of the primary producer and closer to the cost level of the advanced secondary nations.

(*b*) *Population and income changes*. Growth in population increases the demand for primary commodities and benefits the primary producing nations. This is particularly true where increased population is accompanied by high income levels, as happened with the bulges in the birth-rates of advanced nations after the Second World War. Growth of population in the developing nations is less influential, since they practise self sufficiency to a great extent, but it may alter the pattern of trade by reducing the quantities of primary products they can supply for world markets. Thus increased population and incomes in South America reduced the quantity of Argentine and Uruguyan beef reaching world markets after 1945.

(*c*) *Depressions and booms*. Managed prosperity in the advanced nations tends to keep demand strong, to the benefit of primary producing nations. Depressions in economies which are less well managed cause serious cuts in world prices, particularly where the supply of products is inelastic. Thus rubber plantations cannot cut back production when prices fall as easily as, for example, factories. Therefore price of rubber fluctuates more than the prices of products (e.g. secondary manufactured goods) which are in elastic supply.

(*d*) *Actions by influential buyers.* Some users of commodities are so influential that they can affect the prices of goods on the world markets. The chief of these are the stockpiling agencies of the United States Government. American stockpiles are so vast that a temporary rise in world prices can be prevented by the release of reserves which have been accumulated when prices were lower. This type of activity is like speculation on a vast scale: it smooths out fluctuations in world production and keeps prices and profit margins steadier for the benefit of both producers and consumers.

The Supply of Goods in International Trade

Supply of goods is affected by the following:

(*a*) *Wars, civil disturbances, and strikes.* Any sort of military or civil disturbance affects the supply of goods. First, the actual production regions may be over-run, like the Nigerian oilfields in the Eastern Region during the Nigerian Civil War. Secondly, the means of transport may be interrupted, ships commandeered, bridges blown up, railway networks dislocated, or air routes closed. An example of the intricate transport network is afforded by the present-day airfreight system. Every night planes arrive at London Airport from Helsinki, Oslo, Stockholm, Berlin, Frankfurt, and the other major Continental airports. Their cargoes are transferred to America-bound flights for New York, and from these to Chicago-bound and California-bound aircraft. Because of the speed of modern planes and the rotation of the earth, goods freighted from Helsinki at 5.00 p.m. one day can be on sale in the streets of Los Angeles by 9.0 a.m. next morning. Such long-haul networks are easily interrupted by any sort of civil or military disturbance.

(*b*) *Changes in technology.* The supply of goods in international trade is greatly affected by technological advances, and by the spread of technology to more and more countries. Synthetic rubber has affected the terms of trade to the disadvantage of the natural-rubber producers, and the invention of artificial fibres has drastically affected the wool-producing, cotton-producing, and silk-producing countries. New manufacturing nations, which enter production with the most modern plants and without the encumbrances of established labour organizations, can reduce prices to the detriment of established nations whose terms of trade become more unfavourable.

Measuring changes in the Terms of Trade

Favourable changes in the terms of trade benefit the citizens of a nation, because they can purchase with their produce a larger share of the world's goods. This means that of the extra wealth resulting from the international specialization of labour a larger share is now going to them.

These changes can be measured by comparing the average price of exports with the average price of imports. The easiest way to do this is by index numbers. The United Kingdom index of export prices and index of import prices are compiled using 1961 as the base year. The fraction

$$\frac{Index\ of\ Average\ Export\ Prices}{Index\ of\ Average\ Import\ Prices} \times 100$$

gives an index for the terms of trade. Thus in 1961 when both the export and import indices were defined as 100, the terms-of-trade index was 100. A year later, in 1962, the export index stood at 101 and the import index at 99. The terms-of-trade index was then

$$\frac{101}{99} \times 100 = 102$$

indicating an improvement in the terms of trade in favour of the United Kingdom. A list over the 21 years 1957–77 is given in Table 32.

Table 32. United Kingdom Terms of Trade Index 1957–77

Year	Index of exports (1)	Index of imports (2)	Terms of trade (1) ÷ (2) ×100
1957	100	111	90
1959	98	102	96
1961	100	100	100
1963	104	103	101
1965	110	108	102
1967	118	117	101
1969	127	126	101
1970	135	131	103
1971	148	134	110
1972	158	142	111
1973	170	183	93
1974	220	285	77
1975	268	322	83
1976	325	393	83
1977	385	459	84

The higher the index the more favourable the terms for the United Kingdom. Significant changes occurred in the earlier years, in favour of the advanced nations. For nearly a decade the index remained around the 100 mark, but then world demand altered the terms of trade, again in favour of the advanced nations. Suddenly in 1973 world prices altered, and the terms of trade turned heavily against the United Kingdom.

(8) The Volume of World Trade

If world trade is not restricted in any way, countries will specialize in those industries where they have a comparative advantage and as a result of this specialization output will increase. The world will be richer, and production will take place in the most economic location. The volume of world trade will rise and the whole world will be wealthier; but this will not necessarily mean that all the peoples of the world will benefit equally. The terms of trade will decide who gets the lion's share of the increased wealth.

Just as individuals tend to do what is best for them, nations tend to advocate free trade when they are in a strongly competitive position and are likely to profit by an expansion of world trade. When their situation is an uncompetitive high-cost situation, they tend to be 'protectionist'. This means they set up tariff walls to shut out foreign products, unless they are prepared to pay a duty on entry. For example, in the eighteenth century the infant cotton industry of Lancashire and Glasgow was a relatively high-cost industry and objected strongly to the importation of cheap Indian cotton goods. Technological advance raised productivity in the cotton mills, and by 1811 the cry of the cotton masters was for free trade: let India sell her wares freely in this country, and let Lancashire export to India in return. The resulting penetration of the Indian market by cheap Lancashire cottons brought prosperity to Lancashire. Eventually the erection of cotton mills in India and Hong Kong enabled these countries to compete again with Lancashire. Then the cotton manufacturers raised a cry for protection. Similarly America, which is now the strongest advocate of free trade, pursued a highly protectionist policy throughout the nineteenth century, and still protects many industries today.

How Home Industries are Protected

Home industries may be protected by (*a*) embargoes, (*b*) quotas, (*c*) tariffs, (*d*) currency restrictions, (*e*) 'prior-to-import' deposits.

(*a*) *Embargoes* prohibit the import of particular commodities, or the goods of particular countries.

(*b*) *Quotas* limit the import of particular goods, or the import from particular areas, to a permitted quota. Thus a system of quota licences has to be organized and imports must not exceed the quota. This may be a quota by volume, say 100,000 articles, or a quota by value, say to a limit of £100,000.

(*c*) *Tariffs* impose a duty on goods entering the country, which raises the price at which they can be sold on the home market. This means that they will be less competitive than they otherwise would be. Sometimes 'most-favoured-nation' treatment, i.e. a preferential duty rate, is accorded to the products of particular countries. This diverts trade into particular directions and interferes with the strictly economic pattern which would otherwise develop. Zambia, for example, in January 1970 gave measures of protection to her industries in the metal, plastic piping, refrigeration, clothing, and printing industries. Ghana imposes tariffs on television sets, electrodes, bolts, nuts, screws, containers, motor vehicles, and textiles. Kenya imposes protective duties on pulp and paper to protect the Broderick Falls pulp and paper mill.

(*d*) *Currency restrictions* work through the foreign-exchange market, limiting the import of goods from areas whose currency is difficult to obtain for some reason.

(*e*) *'Prior-to-import' deposits* require the importer to deposit a percentage of the purchase price of proposed imports into a special account. By varying the percentage rate it is possible to limit imports very effectively (e.g. a small deposit for imports deemed to be necessary, but larger deposits for non-essentials). Chile has imposed import deposits of 10,000 per cent in some cases.

The effect of all such methods is to reduce the international specialization of labour and decrease total world wealth. They perpetuate the continuance of production in uneconomic areas and prevent the maximum achievement of the economies of scale in the efficient areas. They result in a lower standard of living for the people of the protected country: the general body of the citizens has to bear as a social cost the expense of subsidizing the inefficient home industry. Economically this type of restriction in free trade is unjustifiable, and many attempts have been made to remove such barriers. The most successful have been relatively local free-trade areas, of which the European Common Market (E.E.C.), now enlarged to nine countries, is the best known.

Economic Arguments in Favour of Protection

(a) *Protection of infant industries.* Most nations seem to accept that where a country is attempting to establish a new industry she will inevitably erect tariff barriers to protect it. This amounts to forcing her own citizens to buy an inferior and more expensive product made at home instead of better imported products. The justification for this is that, without such protection, her people cannot acquire the skill and knowledge which alone will result eventually in well made goods of improved design. There are many examples of efficient industries established in this way, but almost as many examples could be quoted of industries which started behind a tariff wall and have continued behind it, never reaching really viable status in world markets. *The same resources, devoted to other ends, might have proved more beneficial to the country.*

(b) *Prevention of 'dumping'.* Dumping is the export of goods to countries where they are sold at a lower price than they fetch on the home market. This discrimination in favour of foreigners may be practised in order to earn foreign exchange, or it may be made possible by increased economies of scale which would be lost if only the home market was supplied. Either way it represents serious competition to the importing country, whose own industry may be ruined by it. Where the competition is the result of efficiency it is legitimate; but where it is the result of a discriminatory policy, possibly even designed to ruin the industry of the importing country so as to remove it as a competitor in world markets, the importing country is justified in imposing tariffs to prevent this unfair competition.

(c) *Temporary protective measures.* These may be imposed for short periods. For example in 1964 the British Government imposed a 15 per cent tariff surcharge on imports, and gave tax rebates on exports to correct a very severe adverse balance of payments. In August, 1971 the American Government imposed a 10 per cent import surcharge as part of a package of measures to reduce the pressure on the dollar. These measures were greeted by strong protests from other nations, since they were contrary to international agreement. They were removed in December, 1971 after devaluation of the dollar.

Non-Economic Arguments in Favour of Protection

(a) *Strategic reasons.* Many countries continue to produce goods, even though they could buy them more cheaply from abroad: to give up production of the goods would be unwise for reasons of national security. Great Britain continues to grow agricultural produce despite the comparative disadvantages of her small-scale agriculture. Experience in two world wars has convinced her it would be dangerous to give up farming completely.

A less well-known example is the situation that Britain found herself in during the early years of the Second World War. There was at this time a period called the 'phoney-war', when no battles were fought—except in Finland—and when some people doubted whether Britain was really serious about fighting Hitler. In fact she was having very great difficulty because some important industries, particularly the ceramics industries, had been allowed to decline to vanishing point. Many essential components, like electrical insulators, had previously been imported from Europe. The sudden removal of this source of supply led to desperate shortages of components for military equipment. A whole ceramics industry had to be built up from nothing before the war could be pursued.

Most nations protect their aircraft, ship-building, and other crucial industries.

(*b*) *Social reasons.* Industries deemed to be desirable on social grounds may be continued after they become non-competitive. For example, declining industries like cotton have been protected to a limited extent to prevent undue hardship in the cotton towns of Lancashire, while compensation for mill owners prepared to shut mills has gradually reduced the industry and improved its efficiency.

The British coal industry has been given considerable support in recent years while rationalization is being introduced. For several years the National Coal Board has been closing a mine every week, and in many cases these mines have been the sole source of income for isolated villages which grew up around the pit in its prosperous days. The resulting changes in the life of former miners and their families can be imagined. Mining is a tough and dangerous job, which breeds men of courage and character. You cannot suddenly expect such men to become assemblers in light electrical trades, or similar work. Their physique is unutilized and they feel and become demoralized. Mineworkers are an excellent example of specific labour, difficult to resettle in other work. Some measure of protection must be given, especially to older men.

(9) Summary of Chapter Twenty-one

1. Trade takes place between nations because resources are unevenly distributed, climate varies, and the people of some areas have natural advantages over the people of other areas.

2. When discussing advantages, comparative advantage is more important than absolute advantage. Men, and nations, should specialize in those occupations at which they have the greatest comparative advantage or the least comparative disadvantage.

3. When factors can be put to work doing either one thing or another the two alternative occupations are said to be alternative costs. Thus the cost of the wheat we decide to produce is the aluminium we decide *not* to produce.

4. The student should memorize the Law of Comparative Costs (see page 243).

5. The 'terms of trade' are the relative prices of exports and imports. A country whose exports are dear relative to her imports has favourable terms of trade. A country whose imports are dear relative to her exports has unfavourable terms of trade.

6. Changes in the terms of trade may be indicated by an index number found by the formula

$$\frac{Index \; of \; Average \; Export \; Prices}{Index \; of \; Average \; Import \; Prices} \times 100$$

7. If world trade is free, nations will only carry on those occupations at which they have a comparative advantage and will obtain other goods by trade.

8. Protection of home industries may be justified in certain cases for strategic or social reasons. Its economic cost is a lower standard of living for the nation's citizens.

(10) Suggested Further Reading

Harrod, R. F.: *International Economics*. Nisbet: London, 1958.
Katrak, H.: *International Trade and the Balance of Payments*. Fontana, 1971.
Lipsey, R. G., and Stilwell, J. A.: *An Introduction to Positive Economics*.
 3rd. Edn., Weidenfeld & Nicolson: London, 1971.
Whale, P. B.: *International Trade*. Frank Cass: London.

Exercises Set 21

1. What do economists understand by the term 'comparative advantage'?

2. 'The cost of the steel we decided to make is the cast iron we decided not to make.' Explain.

3. Outline the gains to be expected from free international trade. How are these gains shared between the trading countries?

4. What are the 'terms of trade'? How may these terms of trade be measured?

5. What is a production possibility schedule? Draw one up for a country considering specializing in beef production, instead of beef and wheat. Take diminishing and increasing returns of production from factors into account.

6. 'We could make whisky, but we buy it from Scotland. Why?' Explain.

7. 'The theory of comparative costs proves that free trade is the best policy.' Criticize this statement.

8. 'Generally speaking it will be profitable for Britain to grow her beef in electronics factories and sow her wheat in automobile plants.' What did the speaker mean by these remarks to a gathering of farmers? Why was the farmers' reply 'Until a war comes along!' a valid retort?

9. Australia and Britain can produce both wheat and cars. A given set of factors would produce the following outputs per day:

	Units of wheat (100 bushels)	Cars
Australia	1,000	200
Britain	1,400	700

(a) Who has the absolute advantage in each of these products?
(b) Who has the comparative advantage in wheat production?
(c) Who has the comparative advantage in producing cars?
(d) Will trade take place when 1½ units of wheat exchanges for one unit of cars?
(e) Will exchange take place when 3½ units of wheat exchange for one unit of cars?

10. Switzerland and Britain can both make watches and electrical transformers. A given set of factors would produce in one day the following outputs:

	Watches	Transformers
Britain	500	250
Switzerland	750	250

(*a*) Has either country an absolute advantage in either of these products?

(*b*) Who has the comparative advantage in watches?

(*c*) Who has the comparative advantage in transformers?

(*d*) What specialization will take place?

(*e*) What will be the rise in 'world' wealth assuming five such sets of factors are at present engaged in each country on each product?

(*f*) How will this wealth be shared assuming one transformer costs 2·6 watches, and each nation requires the same number of transformers as before specialization?

CHAPTER TWENTY-TWO

SETTLING INTERNATIONAL INDEBTEDNESS—THE BALANCE OF PAYMENTS

(1) Introduction

When nations engage in international trade they must pay one another for the goods and services being exchanged. International trade is a complex business, like all trading, and payment presents special problems. First of all there is the question of whether the currency is acceptable. Gold is at present being demonetarized, though it is still widely acceptable. Most currencies are only acceptable in their own territories. In this chapter we shall examine the problems of international indebtedness.

(2) Paying for Imports

Every country has its own currency, and its merchants wish to be paid in that currency or in some currency which is freely convertible into it. For example, a German industrialist selling goods to a Portuguese importer might not be prepared to accept Portuguese escudos; but he would accept Deutschemarks, and he would be prepared to accept American dollars as his bank would freely convert them into Deutschemarks for him. Gold is generally acceptable, but the price fluctuates daily. Certain 'great' currencies are nearly always acceptable. The chief ones are the American dollar, the Swiss franc, the German Deutschemark, the £ sterling and the Japanese yen.

While the actual details of obtaining the particular currency required are arranged by the banks who deal on the foreign-exchange market, their activities do depend on a rough balance being achieved between imports and exports. If the pound is valued at 2·40 dollars, and a consignment of Scotch whisky is being sold to a total value of $240,000, the American buyer will need £100,000 to make the purchase. Suppose a British manufacturer is buying 10 American machine-tools at $24,000 each, he will need $240,000 to complete the purchase. Clearly the dealers on the foreign-exchange market will be happy to arrange both transactions, for each will make the other possible. Exports pay for imports and the result is a **balance of trade**.

Sometimes the goods exported are insufficient to pay for the goods imported, and an adverse balance of trade results. This adverse balance may be corrected by items which are called 'invisible' items, because they are for services rendered, not for actual goods. The chief invisible items are shipping, air transport, insurance, banking, and tourist services; a full list is given on page 259.

Finally, if there is any further imbalance, and invisible items are insufficient to cover it, a nation will either have to pay out of its reserves for the goods and services imported or it may be involved in borrowing capital from overseas. Somehow or other it will have to balance its 'balance of payments'.

(3) United Kingdom Balance of Payments

The balance of payments of the United Kingdom is published in a special form each year, but the interest in the figures is so great that monthly reports about the progress of the accounts are given as well. These results are featured in the Press and on television, and the general public are kept constantly in touch with developments.

The annual accounts are divided into the 'Current Account' and a 'Capital Flow' section. The reader who is familiar with book-keeping will appreciate that the phrase 'current-account item' refers to an item which has to be settled within the current year, whereas 'capital expenditure' refers to expenditure over a period of years. Therefore in these accounts the current account items are all matters of current trading, part of the **balance of trade** or the **balance of invisible trade**. The capital flow items are long-term items which will be repayable over several years, and possibly over many years.

Table 33 shows a set of balance-of-payments accounts, expanded to give a clearer picture than the usual published accounts.

(4) The Balance of Visible Trade

Visible items, as their name implies, are items which have a physical existence and can actually be seen. Raw materials, food, and manufactured goods of all kinds are items of visible trade.

The valuation F.O.B. means 'Free on Board'. It is the value of the goods and transit charges as far as the deck of the ship. It does not include the insurance or the freight charges made by the shipowner.

A typical year's import and export trade for the United Kingdom (see Fig. 81) shows the major headings of goods being bought and sold. Imports consist largely of primary products or semi-manufactures. Only about one-quarter of all imports are finished manufactures, while exports are almost entirely manufactures. In 1976 there was an adverse balance of trade of £3,592 million (adjusted to £3,204 million in Fig. 33 on a Balance of Payments basis). In most years some imports have to be paid for by invisible earnings.

(5) The Balance of Invisible Trade

'Invisible' exports make a very large positive contribution to the United Kingdom's balance of overseas payments. In the years since the Second World War the balance of visible trade has only been favourable in four years: 1956, 1958, 1970 and 1971. The balance of invisible trade has only been unfavourable in one year: 1946. It follows that the prosperity of Great Britain is to a great extent made possible by the earnings of invisible services. What are these services? A list of them reads as follows:

Sea transport	Government services
Civil aviation	Financial and other services
Travel and tourism	Private transfers
Interest, profits and dividends	

Sea transport. At one time almost the entire world trade was carried by British merchant ships. Today the protection granted by many nations to their own merchant fleets and the growth of 'flags of convenience' have reduced the share of trade carried by British vessels. Each year very large sums

Table 33. U.K. Balance of Payments, 1976

Current Account

The Balance of Visible Trade

Debits (Debts to foreigners) £m	Credits (Debts by foreigners) £m
Imports (valued free on board) 28,987	Exports and re-exports (valued free on board) 25,416
	Adverse balance on visible trade 3,571
£m 28,987	£m 28,987

The Balance of Invisibles

Adverse visible balance   3,571

Payments (invisible imports)		Receipts (invisible exports)	
Government services	969	Government services	215
Sea transport	3,206	Sea transport	3,251
Civil aviation	810	Civil aviation	1,051
Travel and tourism	1,008	Travel and tourism	1,628
Financial services (see opposite)	–	Financial services (net of imports)	1,086
Other services	1,584	Other services	2,190
Interest, profits and dividends	2,567	Interest, profits and dividends	3,746
Other transfers	1,528	Other transfers	671
	11,672		13,838
		Adverse balance on Current Account	1,405
£m 15,243		£m 15,243	

Capital Items

Adverse balance on Current Account	1,405	Foreign investment (i) in U.K. public sector	203
Government loans to foreign governments (net)	158	(ii) in U.K. private sector	2,051
		Balancing item	591
Private sector investments in foreign firms	2,100	Adverse over-all balance	3,628
U.K. Bank lending to foreign banks (net) (the euro-currency market)	106		
Withdrawals by foreigners of sterling balances	1,152		
Trade credit given to foreign customers (net)	1,009		
Other short-term transactions	543		
£m 6,473		£m 6,473	

Official Financing

(Monetary movements to finance the deficit suffered)

Adverse balance (deficit to be financed)	3,628	Drawings from official reserves	853
		Borrowing from abroad by public sector	1,791
		Drawings from I.M.F.	984
£m 3,628		£m 3,628	

are earned as foreign exchange but unfortunately nearly as much has to be paid by our merchants to foreign carriers. Table 33 shows the situation as far as sea transport is concerned.

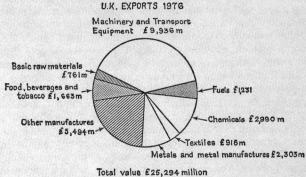

Fig. 81. Visible trade of the United Kingdom, 1976

Civil aviation. Civil aviation is increasingly valuable as an earner of invisible balances. About £30 million per year has been contributed to the balance-of-payments accounts by civil aviation since 1963. With bigger and faster planes like the Boeing 747 and the Concorde, it could well be that this contribution will increase in the years ahead. This is particularly so since a wider under-standing of freight economics is evident among the business community. In particular the idea of taking *total* costs into account when deciding the relative merits of air and sea freighting is leading to increased use of air transport. The high cost of the actual transport is offset by reduced insurance charges, faster transit, and other advantages. Fast and regular services by British planes are therefore attractive to overseas businessmen.

Travel and tourism. The United Kingdom usually suffers adverse balances on travel and tourism, because a large part of her population is affluent enough to holiday abroad. For many countries tourism earns net invisible balances which are a great help to the economy. Again, larger and faster aircraft are likely to expand the tourist market. We could see holidays in the developing

African countries proving very attractive to Europeans. Countries like Tanzania, Malawi, Kenya, Tunisia, and Libya might find this very beneficial. In Table 33 the balance of payments for this particular item can be seen, but the reader should note that tourism is subject to fluctuations from year to year.

Interest, profits, and dividends. The effect of these items on invisible earnings is very great, but it is important to have a clear picture of the difference between capital and current-account items. Suppose Britain lends Ghana £10 million for a hydroelectric power project. This sum would be a capital payment and would represent an adverse item on the balance of payments. Contrasting with this, a decision by an American company to take over a British firm at a purchase price of £50 million would be a capital receipt by Britain and a favourable item on the balance of payments. In due course each of these transactions would result in a succession of repayments in the opposite direction. The interest part of Ghana's repayments would appear as favourable current-account movements in years to come, and the repayment of the capital borrowed will be a favourable capital-account movement. The former British firm, now an American-owned subsidiary, will pay dividends to its American owners which will represent unfavourable invisible payments. In the year under discussion the figures in Table 33 show what the balance of payments was on this particular item, and how important overseas investment is in this respect to an over-all Balance of Payments.

Government services. These include military and civil expenditure in foreign currencies, and represent a considerable loss each year on the balance of payments. Table 33 shows what the actual position was in the year under discussion, most of the expenditure being for military and diplomatic purposes. The E.E.C. has caused these figures to increase in recent years, not always adversely. The full figures are in the Pink Book (Central Statistical Office).

Financial and other services. These services are very valuable, earning substantial balances for Britain. They include banking, insurance, advertising and consultancy charges, and the licensing of foreign firms to use British discoveries and patents. This last item is increasingly important as the less developed nations become secondary producers. They must become protective towards their new industries and exclude foreign competition. Thus if Tanzania establishes a footwear factory she will protect it from competition by British shoes. By contrast she will welcome a licensing system which permits her to use in her shoe factory the latest British inventions in the footwear industry. A former visible trade item, shoes, inevitably declines in export value, but the invisible item may be just as remunerative.

Private transfers. Lastly invisible items include certain movements of funds for private reasons. Thus immigrants bring funds with them which benefit the balance of payments. Emigrants take funds out, to the detriment of the balance of payments. The estates of deceased persons whose relatives live in a different country similarly move in or out as the will is executed.

(6) Currency Flows—Capital Items

Capital items are long-term payments either outwards or inwards. The United Kingdom has for many years invested capital abroad. At one time enormous investments overseas brought in each year a flood of interest and dividend payments on current account, but these huge reserves had to be sold to pay for the two World Wars and only small residual sums are left.

Investments abroad may take the form of direct loans to overseas Governments, or of buying securities on the stock exchanges. Thus a private investor who buys shares in Japanese steel firms is investing in Japan just as effectively as if he had arranged a loan to a Japanese businessman. These investments are partly undertaken by private investors, and partly by the Government. British Government loans to foreign Governments etc. are described in the accounts as 'Official investment abroad'.

A good deal of debate goes on as to the desirability of investing abroad. The protagonists point to the enormous need for capital in the developing nations. The antagonists are quick to retort that it is precisely these nations who do not get the investments; that private overseas investment more often goes to secure and developed nations. One can hardly blame a private investor who does not invest in insecure, unstable areas. Such regions should be helped by official Government agencies who have a greater chance of securing the return of their capital. While private investors can easily be expropriated, Governments have long memories and can usually bring up a failure to repay at some time in the future.

Investments entering the country refer to British firms taken over by foreign investors, or shares and securities purchased by foreign nationals. Much of this foreign investment is excess capital from countries whose interest rates are relatively low. Such money is called 'hot money', because it is very liquid and can flow out just as easily as it flows in. It is a source of speculative pressure at times when the exchange rate of a currency is about to be altered.

(7) Currency Flows—Monetary Movements

We have seen that the balance of trade rarely balances, the balance of visible and invisible items together is occasionally favourable and occasionally unfavourable. Capital items may make the current account balance better, or worse. The resulting surplus, or deficit must be cleared in some way. **The Balance of Payments must always balance.**

To clear a deficit we have the following solutions:

(*a*) Pay the outstanding balances out of our gold and foreign currency reserves in the Central Bank. This is a direct, physical monetary movement of gold and currency, and runs our balances down to lower levels.

(*b*) Sell overseas investments acquired in earlier times. This amounts to living on our capital.

(*c*) Borrow reserves from the International Monetary Fund (I.M.F.), and use these reserves to clear our debts.

(*d*) We can borrow from foreign Governments or private foreign citizens. This usually means leaving the debt unpaid: it amounts to forcing overseas countries to lend us money, by increasing the amount of Sterling balances they hold.

Of course borrowing and accumulating debts by methods (*c*) and (*d*) do not clear up the adverse balance. They simply make the situation in the next accounting period more difficult.

A surplus on the Balance of Payments is cleared in the opposite way:

(*a*) We may collect currency or gold and build up our reserves.

(*b*) We may acquire overseas investments.

(*c*) We may repay any money borrowed earlier from the I.M.F. (see page 276).

(*d*) We may simply become a creditor nation and build up a body of overseas debtors who will pay us in the months ahead.

Either way the balance of payments is balanced as a result of the final book-keeping entries, but there is usually a small **balancing item.** This 'balancing item' is the sum of the errors in all the other figures. It seems large —£6 million—but in fact these errors average out to zero, taking one year with another. This detailed balancing item is slightly different from the global one in Table 35.

(8) A Disequilibrium in the Balance of Payments

A 'disequilibrium' means a failure to achieve equilibrium or balance. The balance of payments will always 'balance', because any deficit on current account will be made up by borrowing on capital account. We may write this process down in diagrammatic form as shown in Table 34.

Table 34. The balance of payments in diagrammatic form

<u>The balance of payments</u>

Import of goods + services received + long-term capital loans to overseas countries (and see note below)	=	Export of goods + services rendered to others + long-term capital loans received from overseas + losses from reserves + amounts borrowed internationally

Note: If the balance of payments was a favourable one the last two items on the right-hand side would move over to the left-hand side and read

+ gains to reserves
+ amounts loaned internationally.

Suppose we have a temporary adverse balance, because we spend overseas more than we earn. Rather like a man with a bank account in which he has deposited some money in case of difficulties, a temporary overspending will not matter. The reserves will just be run down a little; that is what reserves are for. Even a long-term adverse balance does not matter if it is planned. For example, a developing country might plan for a period of ten years to overspend £2 million each year, so that a major project like a hydroelectric power station and a factory complex associated with it could be built. When the power station is built the wealth it creates will be used only partly to give a higher standard of living to the people. The rest of the wealth will be used to repay the adverse balances incurred when it was built. The long-term adverse balance is really only 'temporary'; its correction eventually is envisaged in the long-term plan.

A long-term adverse balance of payments which has not been planned is caused by a country living beyond its means. This really does matter, and will have to be corrected sooner or later. The only way it can be corrected is by lowering the effective price of exports to make them more desirable to overseas customers, and by raising the effective price of imports, to make them less desirable to home nationals.

Table 35 shows the United Kingdom balances from 1967 to 1976. The adverse balances of 1967–8 were corrected and turned into very favourable balances for a few years, but then in 1972 a further period of adverse balances began, which were made worse by the oil crisis of 1973, and world inflation.

Table 35. U.K. Balance of payments, 1967–76 (£ million)

	1967	1969	1971	1973	1974	1975	1976
Visible trade	−557	−143	+285	−2,375	−5,221	−3,195	−3,592
Invisibles	+244	+592	+808	+1,165	+1,841	+1,545	+2,116
Current balance	−313	+449	+1,093	−1,210	−3,380	−1,650	−1,476
Capital flows	−600	−109	+1,853	+1,012	+1,606	+ 354	−2,285
Balancing item	+242	+403	+ 282	+ 408	+ 128	− 169	+ 133
Total currency flow	−671	+743	+3,228	+ 210	−1,646	−1,465	−3,628
Special drawing rights (+)	—	—	+ 125	—	—	—	—
Final balance	−671	+743	+3,353	+ 210	−1,646	−1,465	−3,628
Financed as follows							
Monetary movements (a)	+556	−699	−1,817	—	+1,751	+ 810	+2,775
Official reserves (b)	+115	− 44	−1,536	−210	− 105	+655	+ 853

Notes: In (a) above a + sign means the U.K. increased her debts to the rest of the world.
In (b) above a + sign means drawings out of the official reserves.

(9) Correcting a Disequilibrium in the Balance of Payments by Increasing Exports

One way to correct a disequilibrium in the balance of payments is to make our exports cheaper and our imports dearer. There are two methods of doing this, because there are two elements in the price of exports which are under our control.

The Price of Exports

The price of exports is made up of:

(*a*) *The home costs of the exports*, which means the factor cost per unit of output. To reduce the price of exports we must either reduce the factor costs or raise productivity so that the present costs are shared out among a greater number of units of output. This means we must lower the rewards to factors (i.e. wages, rents, interest, and profits) or we must raise output.

(*b*) *The rate at which the home currency exchanges against foreign currencies.* To reduce export prices we must either let this exchange rate move downwards gradually and find its own level where a balance of payments will be achieved, or we must devalue it in one go to a new figure. The first method is known as the **flexible exchange-rate method**, the second is called the **devaluation method**.

The attack on the home costs of exports involves some sort of deflation of the economy if one cannot achieve higher productivity. This means unemployment, wage cuts, taxation, and 'credit' squeezes to reduce prosperity at home.

The attack on the rate of exchange (part (*b*) above) raises import prices so that home nationals cannot afford foreign goods and lowers export prices so that more goods can be sold abroad to earn foreign exchange.

Either way it means a reduction in the standard of living of home nationals, but this is required to achieve the improvement in the balance of payments.

(10) History of the Balance-of-Payments Problem

The developments have been as follows:

(a) *The Gold-Standard period* up to 1914 and from 1925 until the Gold Standard was abandoned in 1931. This method does not allow the exchange rate to fluctuate, except between very tiny limits called the 'gold points'. The entire problem of managing the balance of payments falls on deflation of the economy, which means unemployment etc. In 1931 this proved quite unacceptable to most countries and the method was abandoned.

(b) *The Flexible-Exchange Rate period* (1931–44). Here the balance of payments was achieved by letting the exchange rate vary. This meant the foreigner suffered rather than the home nationals. The result was a decline in world trade, and world trade became a matter of bilateral agreements rather than multilateral agreements (see page 289).

(c) *The Managed-Flexibility Period* (from 1944 to 1971). In these years, by international agreement made at the Bretton Woods Conference in 1944, balances of payments were achieved by a mixture of both methods. Managed flexibility means that the exchange rate is allowed to vary a little, but when it reaches certain limits the attack on home costs will begin, and any further adjustment of export prices will mean lowering the standard of living of home nationals.

(d) *Floating Exchange Rates.* On 15th August 1971 the 'managed flexibility' system was ended by measures to restrict the convertibility of the dollar, introduced by President Nixon. New parities were agreed on December 17, 1971, but the flexibility of rates had been increased to $2\frac{1}{4}$ per cent either side of par. In June 1972 Britain abandoned these parities, and by March 1973 all currencies were floating freely.

(e) After 1973, when the oil-producing countries increased the *price of oil*, most advanced nations experienced severe balance of payments problems. The U.K. adverse current balance in 1974 was £3,380 million, and in 1976 the over-all deficit was £3,628 million. However, North Sea oil incomes should correct these deficits in the years ahead.

(11) Summary of Chapter Twenty-two

1. Imports must be paid for by exports.

2. The balance of trade is the balance achieved between the import and export of goods, called 'visible trade'.

3. The balance of invisible trade is the balance achieved between the payments for services received and the payments earned by rendering services to others. The chief 'invisible' items are shipping, banking, insurance, travel and tourism, civil aviation, and Government services.

4. The balance of trade and the balance of invisible trade together make up the balance on current account.

5. Capital movements are private or official investments abroad, set against the investments by overseas nationals in this country.

6. The balance of payments is the final result of all these influences. It is bound to balance, because monetary movements take place to settle indebtedness.

7. A disequilibrium in the balance of payments over a long period requires the country to alter its way of life to prevent its reserves becoming exhausted.

(12) Suggested Further Reading

Lipsey, R. G., and Stilwell, J. A.: *An Introduction to Positive Economics*. Weidenfeld & Nicolson: London, 3rd. Edn., 1971.

Manser, W. A. P.: *Balance of Payments 1971*: Longman, 1971.

The student should read the current *Bank Reviews* as they appear, and any official bulletins on the balance of payments issued by the Central Office of Information.

Exercises Set 22

1. Would the following result in a gain or loss of foreign currency to Great Britain?

(*a*) The purchase of 20,000 Swiss watches by a London businessman.

(*b*) The purchase by a British merchant bank of Swiss Government securities on the Geneva Stock Exchange.

(*c*) A visit to England by a party of Swiss schoolchildren.

(*d*) A winter sports holiday by a London youth club.

(*e*) A Lloyd's underwriter agrees to insure a Swiss cable-car company against accidents to passengers.

(*f*) Claims by the relatives of victims killed in the collapse of a Swiss cable-car insured with Lloyd's.

2. During the Second World War all foreign investments owned by British citizens had to be sold to the Treasury for disposal abroad. Why do you think this was done, and how did it help the war effort?

3. The Government has agreed to the purchase of a British motor-car manufacturing firm by an American combine. Not only has the American firm agreed to pay $67 million but they have promised to invest a further $25 million over the next three years. What are the implications of this, (*a*) in the short term, and (*b*) in the long term, for Britain's balance of payments?

4. Would the following result in a gain or loss of dollars to Great Britain?

(*a*) A decision by America to transfer some military bases from continental Europe to East Anglia.

(*b*) A decision by British Airways to purchase Boeing 747 planes for long-haul routes to Australia.

(*c*) The purchase by the U.S.A. of a British-built mammoth tanker.

(*d*) The refuelling of a British tramp ship in San Francisco.

(*e*) A British investor in U.S. stock is paid a dividend of 4 per cent.

(*f*) A successful tour of the United States by British pop-artists.

5. Compile a balance of payments for the country Atlantis from the data given below:

> *Visibles:* exports £A 2,794 m; imports £A 2,540 m.
> *Invisibles:* exports £A 1,455 m; imports £A 1,600 m.
> *Loans from overseas:* £A 230 m.
> Balance was achieved by changes in the reserves of Atlantis.

6. 'The balance of trade rarely balances. The balance of payments always balances.' Explain.

7. How can a nation earn foreign currency to buy from countries abroad those goods that it requires?

8. What are 'invisible items' in foreign trade? List the chief types of invisible items, and consider their relative usefulness in meeting the United Kingdom's overseas needs.

9. Export of goods helps the balance of payments. Export of capital adversely affects the balance of payments. Do you agree? Explain fully.

10. How can a surplus on current account be balanced on capital account?

CHAPTER TWENTY-THREE

CURING A DISEQUILIBRIUM IN THE BALANCE OF PAYMENTS

(1) Introduction

Nations that require goods and services from abroad must make adequate arrangements to pay for them, by exporting goods and services. These exports must be so priced that they represent an attractive proposition to overseas customers. If they do not attract customers it will be impossible to achieve a balance of payments on overseas trade, and special measures will be needed to correct the imbalance. The three methods of correcting an imbalance of payments are:

(*a*) The Gold-Standard method.
(*b*) The Flexible-Exchange-Rate or Floating Currency method.
(*c*) The method of Managed Flexibility (adopted at Bretton Woods in 1944).

Of these three methods the Gold Standard Method was operated up to 1914, and in a modified form during 1925–31. With the recent decision (1975) of the International Monetary Fund to end the system of gold-related currencies the Gold Standard Method is now only of historical interest, but a short account is included here. It is the only system that is self-regulating (provided everyone keeps to the rules). Its abandonment implies that control has been established by Governments over the exchange rates of their currencies, and some degree of manipulation of foreign exchange in the interests of national economies is being practised.

The flexible Exchange Rate Method was practised between 1931 and 1944, and since 1973 has been in use again. Its effects are described later. The Bretton-Woods system of Managed Flexibility was operated from 1944 to 1972, and is fully explained below.

(2) The Gold-Standard Method

(*a*) *All currencies are linked to gold.* When a country is on the Gold Standard its currency can be exchanged freely for a given weight of gold. In 1914 the £1 sterling was worth 113.0016 grains of fine gold, and the United States dollar was worth 23.33 grains. The rate of exchange between two currencies, both of which are on the Gold Standard, is therefore related to the quantity of gold that each is worth, and this is called the **mint par of exchange**. In 1914 the rate of exchange between the £1 and the dollar was a little over $4·86 = £1. To simplify things in the following discussion we will pretend that the £1 is worth four dollars.

(*b*) *Currencies cannot fluctuate because gold will be shipped.* When currencies are tied in this way to gold it is impossible for the value of the currency to fluctuate outside very fine limits (called the **gold points**) because if this was allowed to happen it would pay a businessman to change his money into gold and ship the gold. Consider for example the following circumstances:

(i) £1 = $4 at the mint par of exchange.

(ii) Because British goods are not selling to America and American goods are popular in Britain the price of the dollar is steadily rising: £1 = 3·99; £1 = 3·98; £1 = 3·97 . . . etc.

(iii) It costs 1 cent to ship gold weighing 113.0016 grains to America.

How would a businessman who owes $10,000 to an American businessman pay the money? The following alternatives are available.

(i) Buy dollars on the foreign-exchange market at $3·97 = £1:

$$\text{cost} = \frac{10,000}{3·97} = £2,519$$

(ii) Exchange £2,500 into gold and then pay to ship it:
$$\text{cost} = £2,500 + £6·25 \text{ shipping charges}$$
$$= £2,506·25.$$

Clearly it is cheaper to ship gold, and as gold is not difficult to obtain (unlike today), the businessman would buy the gold and ship it. The result is that a currency cannot fluctuate outside the limits set by the cost of shipping gold. So £1·00 will never fluctuate outside the limits $4·01–3·99. Beyond these points gold will be shipped. It follows that a change in the balance of payments cannot be achieved by altering the exchange rate. The Gold Standard system has its own built-in mechanism for correcting a balance-of-payments disequilibrium and it works through two forces. It also works at both ends of the problem, attacking the weak country's economy to make it stronger, and attacking the strong country's economy to make it weaker.

Continuing to consider the United Kingdom and the U.S.A., Table 36 shows the complete effects of the movement of gold. Bank Rate mentioned in the table is the old term for Minimum Lending Rate.

Table 36. The Gold-Standard mechanism at work

	HOW THE GOLD STANDARD WORKED	
	U.K. balance of payments (Adverse balance)	U.S.A. balance of payments (Favourable balance)
Event 1	Dollars in demand – price rises	Pounds are plentiful – price falls
Event 2	Gold is shipped to U.S.A.	Gold arrives from U.K.
Event 3	Reserves decline – Bank Rate up	Reserves increase – Bank Rate down
Curative effect 1	Hot money flows in, attracted by high Bank Rate	Hot money flows out – repelled by low Bank Rate
Event 4	Other interest rates rise	Other interest rates fall
Event 5	Marginal projects choked off – entrepreneurs uneasy	Marginal projects proceed – entrepreneurs buoyant
Event 6	Unemployment and deflation	Fuller employment – inflation
Curative effect 2	Demand for imports cut	Demand for imports rises
Event 7	British exports now cheaper	U.S.A. exports now dearer
Curative effect 3	Increased demand for U.K. goods from U.S.A.	Decreased demand for U.S.A. goods from Britain
Final result	Equilibrium restored	Equilibrium restored

Advantages of Gold-Standard Method

(*a*) There is no balance-of-payments problem: the whole system is automatic, provided that each country sticks to the rules. These rules are: (i) Deflate when gold flows out; force your citizens to cut their standard of living; exports will grow and the gold will return. (ii) Inflate when gold flows in; permit your citizens to enjoy a fuller economic life; exports will shrink and the gold flow will diminish.

(*b*) International trade is encouraged because absolute confidence exists in the currencies. When a businessman does a deal he expects a certain profit. If the currency rate is a fluctuating one his profit may be diminished, or even vanish altogether. On the Gold Standard, currencies cannot fluctuate beyond the gold points, which is a very tiny fluctuation indeed. International trade therefore proceeds with confidence.

(*c*) Bank-note issues are tied to the gold reserves. **Hyperinflation,** a very rapid decline in the value of money caused by the excessive printing of banknotes, cannot occur, because the obligation to convert notes to gold prevents any excessive manipulation of the note issue.

Despite these impressive advantages the disadvantages of the gold standard led to the abandonment of the system in 1931.

Disadvantages of the Gold-Standard Method

(*a*) It makes every nation stick to the same rules, even if the rules do not happen to make particular sense at that time for that nation at that stage of development. For example, a nation which has already a severe degree of unemployment but happens to be losing gold for some reason, is forced to deflate still further and intensify the misery. A healthy dose of new investment would be inflationary in the short term, but might lead to higher productivity and a better trading balance within a year or two.

(*b*) A more serious objection is the effect on a country with a favourable balance of payments. Why should it be forced to give itself a dose of inflation to help some other nation out of difficulties? Let the sick nation take some medicine, not the healthy nation. For this reason countries often did not stick to the rule about inflating when gold flowed in. They added it to the reserves and let it lie idle there. The result of this refusal to accept the rules of the Gold Standard was that the imbalance of the nation in difficulties continued and intensified. Despite drastic deflationary measures on the home economy, the balance of payments could not be restored.

(*c*) It is really rather ridiculous to tie the level of the activity in an economy to gold. Gold is not a particularly valuable metal except for personal adornment. It owes its position as a coinage metal to the fact that it is fairly rare and does not rust. What have these qualities to do with mankind and his desire to satisfy wants by producing utilities? Nothing at all. It is a disadvantage to nations that do not happen to have gold in the crust of the earth, and an unfair advantage to those that do. In any case world trade is rising faster than gold supply, and why shouldn't it do so?

(*d*) Another serious criticism of the system is that gold can flow in or out for reasons other than an adverse balance of payments. The Gold Standard is particularly susceptible to speculative pressures and financial manipulators do not worry whose economy they are wrecking so long as they make a short-term profit. It is bad enough having to make men unemployed when the state of the nation requires it: to do so when a speculator is trying to make a quick 'killing' is absolutely indefensible.

(*e*) It is not as easy as it sounds to reduce the costs of goods. The rewards to factors are fixed in the short run, especially rents, wages, and interest. It takes time for earnings to decline, and even longer for wages to be cut. Of course workers were not as sophisticated in those days as they are today, but it became increasingly difficult to reduce the home standard of living and force unemployment on the mass of the people—especially as the underlying mechanism was defective because prosperous countries refused to inflate. Even when you have succeeded in cutting costs it does not mean you will necessarily be able to cure the balance of payments if the elasticity of demand for your goods is unfavourable. Suppose a car selling for 2,400·00 is cut to 2,300·00 by the Gold-Standard System. Will you sell more? It depends on the elasticity of demand for cars. If it is inelastic, and you only sell the same number as before you will be worse off, not better off. It is the same with imports. If as a result of the Gold-Standard system they are now more expensive, will we buy less? It depends on the elasticity of demand again. If we can't help buying them, because they are basic requirements like iron ore, or because we are addicted, like tobacco, then we shall have to buy them, and pay more for them. The system could conceivably make us worse off.

In 1931 the Gold Standard was abandoned, and for a few years countries tried a second method of curing a disequilibrium: flexible exchange rates.

(3) The Flexible-Exchange-Rate or Floating Currency Method

We have already seen that a disequilibrium is caused by the high price of exports, which makes them a poor proposition for the overseas buyer. The price of United Kingdom exports is made up of (*a*) the home price in Sterling, and (*b*) the rate of exchange between Sterling and other currencies. The Gold Standard worked by attacking the home price in Sterling, causing deflation at home and inflation abroad. The flexible-exchange-rate method worked by attacking the export price from the other direction: the rate of exchange between Sterling and other currencies. Between the years 1931 and 1944 countries tried to alter their export prices without deflating the home economy, by letting the exchange rate look after the balance of payments. If you allow your currency to depreciate compared with other currencies, your exports will get cheaper and your imports dearer. **Depreciation** is the name given to this drop in exchange value when it occurs in a free market; **devaluation** is the same thing, taken as a result of Government action in a market that is not free. This occurs when we have 'managed flexibility', the system in use between 1944 and 1972. Since 1973 all currencies have returned to the 'floating currency' system, where the exchange rate is settled in a 'free' market, though the system of 'dirty floating' still allows Governments to interfere to some extent. Before examining how this sytem works let us consider the question of foreign exchange rates.

How are Exchange Rates Determined?

Exchange rates are determined in a free-market situation by the demand for, and supply of, a particular currency. The rate of exchange will fluctuate in a free market, with the currency drifting down in value if the demand for it is weak. Between 1931 and 1944 there were no limits on the fluctuations. Sterling could therefore depreciate to lower exchange levels if the supply of pounds was greater than the demand for them or it could appreciate if the supply was smaller than the demand.

Disregarding the historical position for a moment and thinking solely of a free market where the exchange rate has settled at £1 = $2·40, what will cause the exchange rate to fluctuate from this level?

When many U.K. citizens wish to buy American goods or see American films, the supply of pounds will be great. If Americans are not so keen to buy British goods the supply of dollars will be smaller. The dealers on the London Foreign-Exchange Market, which is a world wide market linked by telephone and Telex systems, will have to accept less dollars for each pound if they are to obtain supplies of dollars now that they are scarce. The price of the £1 therefore depreciates: £1 = $2·40, $2·39, $2·38 . . . etc. As it falls British goods become more attractive to American buyers, and American goods less attractive to British buyers. The supply of dollars will begin to rise, and the supply of pounds to fall. Equilibrium will therefore be established.

To illustrate this, consider a British car priced at £1,600. At a rate of exchange of £1 = $2·40, an American customer must give 3,840 dollars for it. If the dollar rises in value to $2·30 = £1, he will only need to pay 3,680 dollars.

Besides the relative prices of goods in the two countries concerned, other important influences on the exchange rate of their currencies include the following:

(a) *The long-term capital movements.* If capital crosses national boundaries it naturally has to be exchanged into the foreign currency. It follows that capital leaving a country must weaken the exchange rate and capital entering a country must tend to raise the exchange rate.

(b) *'Hot'-money flows*, i.e. short-term capital movements, have the same effect as long-term capital movements. As they tend to be connected with the rate of interest that can be earned the effectiveness of such movements can be influenced by Bank Rate, now called Minimum Lending Rate.

(c) *Government expenditures* can also cross national frontiers, for defence purposes, or for economic aid or relief to other nations. These represent a very considerable influence on exchange rates. For example, the present-day weakness of the dollar compared with twenty years ago is to a considerable extent a reflection of American generosity in aid programmes to the rest of the world.

(d) *Speculative pressures*, induced by expectations of future depreciation of the currency can also affect exchange rates. 'Hot' money may of course be speculative, but speculative pressure can involve movements of medium- and even long-term capital. It can also involve changes in payment periods for ordinary business transactions, with U.K. citizens hurrying to pay before the currency depreciates and foreigners delaying payment for British goods until it has done so.

While, therefore, the most influential factor in determining the exchange rate of a country in the long term is the degree of productivity and competitive ability of its industry and agriculture in world markets, many other factors enter into the exchange rate on any particular day.

Arbitrage

To see exactly how the fluctuating exchange rates worked in 1931–44 we must just mention **arbitrage** transactions. On page 170 we referred to David Ricardo making a fortune quickly by his genius in arbitrage. It was somewhat easier in his day than it is today, because arbitrage transactions depend on imperfections in the foreign-exchange market, and the telephone and Telex systems have reduced imperfections of knowledge about reigning prices.

Suppose £1 is worth 2·40 dollars on the London market and also 10 French francs. Suppose on the New York market 2·40 dollars = £1 and 1 French franc equals 0·25 dollars.

A dealer in London could change £10,000 into 100,000 francs. He could then sell his 100,000 francs on the New York market for 25,000 dollars and change them back into Sterling on the London market. This would bring him £10,416. A useful profit has resulted from the transactions.

Naturally this sort of opportunity will not persist for long. Buying of francs on the London market will raise their price and after a while the uneven prices will be eliminated. The name 'arbitrage' refers to this property of arbitrage operations, to *settle* the rate of indirect exchange between currencies. To arbitrate is to settle a matter that is in dispute.

How the Flexible-Exchange-Rate System Worked

Table 37 shows the full working of the flexible-exchange-rate system.

Table 37. How the flexible-exchange-rate system works

HOW THE FLEXIBLE EXCHANGE RATE SYSTEM WORKS		
	U.K. balance of payments (Adverse balance)	U.S.A. balance of payments (Favourable balance)
Initial exchange rate	£1	$ 2·40
Event No 1	Dollars are in demand – so price rises	Pounds are plentiful – so price falls
New exchange rate	£1	$ 2·30
Curative effect	American goods dearer – British cut imports	British goods cheaper – Americans buy British goods
Final position	Balance of payments achieved	Balance of payments achieved

Advantages of the Flexible-Exchange-Rate System

Under the flexible-exchange-rate system, the economy of any individual country was not under the influence of an external monetary force, in contrast to the Gold Standard system. It became possible for the Government to control and influence the economy, and Keynesian economics (see page 322) was just at that time showing how this could be done. An economy with under-employed factors could therefore ignore any call to deflate still further because of the loss of gold. It could inflate the economy by making work available on socially desirable projects, and the resulting spending power multiplied throughout the economy to the benefit of all. This mechanism is explained fully later.

It also became possible to ignore the gold reserves when deciding what note issue was desirable. Increasing wealth occurs without any change in world gold supplies, and there is really not much point in tying the note issue to the stock of gold. This had already been recognized by the Currency & Bank Notes Act of 1928 which raised the fiduciary issue to £260 million. By the late 1970s it was close to £8,000 million.

Disadvantages of the Flexible-Exchange-Rate System

This system, which was operated originally from 1931 to 44, is at present being used again, most currencies having been floated in 1972–3. The disadvantages of the system in 1931–44 are discussed below. They led to the development of the Bretton-Woods System. An appraisal of the 'floating currency' system since 1973 is given on page 284. In 1931–44 the chief disadvantages were:

(a) *It caused a serious decline in world trade*. If world trade is to be profitable to both parties, the exchange of goods and services must take place within the limits set by the domestic alternative-cost ratios (see page 243), and this belt of limits is in many cases quite narrow. It follows that profit margins are often small, and can easily be wiped out altogether by fluctuations in the exchange rate. The flexible-exchange-rate system therefore made foreign business more risky, since the uncertainties had increased. World trade therefore declined, and multilateral trade in particular (see page 289). Nations turned instead to bilateral trading and 'most-favoured-nation' arrangements. Britain turned to 'Commonwealth Preference' and the formation of the Sterling Area.

(b) *Flexible exchange rates invited speculative activities*. When exchange rates are flexible they can be influenced by factors others than the demand for and supply of imports and exports. Capital is also moving around the world and is bound to influence the exchange rates. Some moneys, short-term loans, are particularly 'hot', rushing around in search of the best interest rates with the greatest security. Such money is bound to exert speculative pressure on a currency when the speculators hear that there is a good prospect of it depreciating in value. They will rush out of pounds into any other currency, so that they can rush back in again when it is cheaper. Their sales of Sterling will have precisely the effect they desire: lowering the pound's exchange value.

Even ordinary business transactions are affected by the chances of depreciation. Thus a foreign firm due to buy pounds to pay British exporters for their goods will delay as long as possible if there is a chance that depreciation of the currency will enable it to buy Sterling more cheaply. Similarly a British firm paying for foreign goods will pay as quickly as possible before a change in the exchange rate makes the foreign currency more expensive.

A further defect of the flexible-exchange-rate system is that the exchange rates tended to be manipulated by Governments for domestic purposes. This is particularly true of the level of employment in a country. If the level of employment can be raised even temporarily (e.g. in election years) by manipulating the exchange rate, this may enable the Government concerned to secure re-election.

Two solutions were found for these problems. First, the tying of currencies to a 'great' currency such as Sterling or the U.S. dollar, gave some security to exchange rates. The Sterling Bloc made agreements among themselves not to let currency depreciate too wildly between them, whatever happened to other countries. Secondly, the **Exchange Equalization Account** was developed as a means of stabilizing exchange rates against speculative pressure, while refusing to stabilize them if there really was an imbalance in the balance of payments. This device became much more important after 1944, because it provided the management that is required for 'managed flexibility'. It is therefore very instructive to consider how it was used.

(4) The Exchange Equalization Account—Managing a Currency

To control speculative activities operating against Sterling, a reserve fund of gold and foreign currencies was set up by borrowing against the security of gilt-edged stock and Treasury Bills. When the pound was under speculative pressure (e.g. because short-term money was leaving London and investors wished to sell pounds) the fund would be used to buy up the pounds on offer, releasing dollars or gold instead. The fund had increased its holdings of pounds and reduced its holdings of other currencies, but it had kept the pound steady on the market. When funds were flowing into London and foreign investors wanted pounds, the Exchange Equalization Fund was ready to supply pounds and take in the dollars and other currencies that were being exchanged, ready for the next bout of speculative pressure.

This system of managing the rate of exchange was very adaptable, because the managers of the Fund did not need to use it if the depreciation that was taking place was not a speculative one, but was the result of a genuine imbalance of payments. By refusing to buy pounds in these circumstances they could let the exchange rate depreciate to what they judged to be its true level.

(5) The Move to 'Managed Flexibility'

The experiences of 1931–44 led straight to the system of managed flexibility. In the middle of war, the Allies began to prepare for peace. The climate was one of international understanding. The Atlantic Treaty had placed human rights in the forefront of Allied aims, including the obviously economic aim of freedom from poverty. The achievement of such an ideal was impossible unless some of the barriers between nations could be removed, and barriers to international trade associated with international-exchange problems were among the best recognized. Accordingly a great conference of the Free World's monetary authorities was held in the United States at Bretton Woods, near Washington. It resulted in the Bretton Woods Agreement, 1944, and the General Agreement on Tariffs and Trade, 1947 (see page 288).

(6) The Bretton Woods Agreement

The conference at Bretton Woods in 1944 recognized that some system better than the Gold Standard and better than the flexible-exchange-rate method was necessary. World trade was out of line with the volume of gold to back it, and while gold could have been revalued upwards to get over the difficulty this would have benefited certain nations unfairly. On the other hand, freely fluctuating exchange rates made trade subject to sudden and unpredictable changes which ruined profitability of enterprise, so that merchants would not take the risks. What was needed was a system of 'managed flexibility' so that if a country was suffering from an adverse balance of payments of a permanent nature it could give notice to merchants and devalue its currency, but if it was merely being put under pressure by speculators its reserves could be used for as long as was necessary to 'burn the speculators' fingers'. This phrase needs some explanation.

Speculators are engaged in the foreign-exchange markets for ordinary business reasons, to buy Sterling for the purchase of British goods, for example. Their speculative activities begin when they see a temporary short-term advantage to be gained by refusing to buy Sterling, or selling Sterling which they already have, or even selling Sterling which they do *not* have, in the expectation of buying it later at a cheaper price. Sooner or later, though, the operator must come back to the fact that he needs to buy Sterling to buy British goods. The whole problem of managing speculative pressure is to have bottomless reserves. If, no matter how much the speculator sells, you continue to take it from him cheerfully and give him dollars or gold or whatever else he asks for, his nerve will crack. It is obvious he is not going to win, and he will decide to buy back the Sterling he needs. He is said to 'burn his fingers' when he has to pay more for it than he received when selling it a short while before. That will teach him not to deal in 'hot' money.

How shall we give any nation that wants it bottomless reserves? The answer was found in setting up an International Monetary Fund.

(7) The International Monetary Fund

The agreements made at Bretton Woods for the establishment of an International Monetary Fund were as follows:

(*a*) By an agreed date all members should declare the par values of their currencies. Great Britain declared that the £1 should be equal to 4·03 American dollars, for example. This agreed rate of exchange would be permitted to fluctuate by up to 1 per cent on either side of the agreed parity figure. Because of two devaluations, in 1949 and 1967, the pound last stood at £1 = $2·40. Until August, 1971 it was allowed to fluctuate between $2·42 and $2·38 or 1 per cent of its agreed parity. It follows then that except for very abnormal times, like the devaluations mentioned, a foreign businessman making a contract knew that he was unlikely to lose more than 1 per cent of his contract price by exchange fluctuations. As profit margins are much greater than 1 per cent, the proportion of his ultimate profit at risk was very small. World trade continued to expand under this system in a thoroughly satisfactory way.

(*b*) All currencies should be freely convertible on current transactions within five years. In fact this proved impossible, but by 1958 it had been achieved as far as non-residents were concerned, though even today, U.K. citizens may not change pounds into gold.

(*c*) Changes of exchange rate should not normally be permitted; but if the change was of less than 10 per cent and deemed absolutely essential, a country could depreciate its currency without prior consultation with the Fund authorities. If the devaluation was to be greater than 10 per cent, the Fund authorities must sanction the arrangement.

(*d*) The International Monetary Fund (I.M.F.), following the idea of the Exchange Equalization Account, is a huge reserve of currency and gold collected on a quota basis from all the members of the Fund. Great Britain's original contribution was $1,300 million. This was raised in 1959, and again in 1965. Finally, in February 1970 a further revision raised Britain's contributions to $2,800 million. One quarter of the quota had to be contributed in gold, the other three quarters was contributed in a country's own currency. Since 1976, when the International Monetary Fund decided to phase out the use of gold in its system, the gold contributions are being disposed of—partly by returning them to members and partly by selling them on the open market (at a large profit). This profit is being used to help developing nations with their Balance of Payments problems.

Originally there were 39 members of the Fund. By the beginning of 1970 there were 110 members, comprising almost the whole of the western world. Switzerland is a notable exception.

Use of the Fund when a Disequilibrium occurs

When a country is suffering an adverse balance of payments and its own reserves appear to be inadequate to withstand the speculative pressure, the members may exercise **Drawing Rights** against the Fund, in a series of 'tranches' (*tranche* is the French word for 'slice'). The first slice, or gold tranche, is its own contribution of gold plus any shortage of the member's contribution to the Fund. For example, the U.K. quota was 25 per cent gold and 75 per cent Sterling; suppose some other member, wishing to buy British goods, had borrowed Sterling from the Fund. The U.K. would be entitled to put in enough pounds to take out not only its gold share, but any extra currency it wanted up to the limit of its full quota. The Fund would now hold 100 per cent of the U.K. quota in Sterling, and the United Kingdom would go back to its battle to support the pound armed with these extra reserves. If they proved insufficient it could return for more 'tranches'—four more slices of 25 per cent each of its quota. By this time the Fund would be holding 200 per cent of its quota of Sterling. However, while the gold tranche was available as of right, the successive further tranches would mean more and more stringent guarantees from the borrowing nation that it was really doing something adequate to cure its balance-of-payments problems. A speculation that persisted as long as this must mean some fundamental weakness in the nation's economic affairs (e.g. ridiculously generous welfare arrangements) and the fund authorities may refuse further help unless corrective measures are taken.

Besides these Drawing Rights, there is a further scheme called the **General Agreement to Borrow** (G.A.B.) whereby a group of 10 influential nations agree to provide temporary loans to the Fund when required.

'Managing' a Currency

When a currency is strongly demanded its price tends to rise on the foreign-exchange market. When a currency is not in demand its price tends to fall. If it appeared likely to rise above, or fall below, the agreed limits of 1 per cent of its value, the central bank stepped in to sell, or buy, as required. Thus if Sterling fell close to 2·38 dollars, the Bank of England would start to buy pounds, losing gold and dollar reserves as it did so. If the Sterling Area reserves appeared to be insufficient to withstand the pressure the Bank of England would borrow the gold tranche from the I.M.F. If the situation continued to drain away reserves the Bank's representatives would fly to consult with the I.M.F. authorities and no doubt returned with a further 'tranche'.

It must be remembered that borrowing from the Fund in this way is no cure for balance-of-payments problems. It merely *helps* a country withstand speculation, or fluctuations in business activity, when its balance of payments is fundamentally sound. That is why the questions asked by the Fund authorities get more and more pointed as further 'tranches' are requested. In any case, as a complete stop to borrowing is made when the Fund has double the quota of any currency, it does mean that a country's position must be recouped later in times when it has surpluses of gold and foreign exchange.

Scarce Currencies

It is possible that a currency may become scarce because other nations have borrowed it from the Fund. When the stock falls below 75 per cent of the quota it may be declared 'scarce' under the rules, and the authorities may ration it between applicants or replenish the stock by buying or borrowing it from the member. A persistently favourable balance of payments is likely to result in the currency becoming scarce, and could lead to demands for a revaluation of the currency. Rather like the Gold-Standard mechanism, this is the equivalent of asking a fit nation to take medicine to help an ill nation recover. Germany resisted for several years in the late 1960s the idea of a revaluation; instead she tried to induce her citizens to buy foreign goods and import more to ease the shortage of D. marks. Finally in October 1969 she agreed to revalue at a rate 8½ per cent above the previous figure. In May 1971 she 'floated' the D mark, and it rose a further 5 per cent.

(8) Special Drawing Rights

The first major alteration to the Bretton Woods Agreement came into force on 1 January 1970, with the introduction of Special Drawing Rights (S.D.R.s). These are a new kind of reserve asset. Keynes had suggested at the Bretton Woods Conference that if gold continued to be inadequate as a reserve currency for world trade, a new kind of international currency, for which he suggested the word 'Bancor', should be invented by the world's monetary authorities. Since, as with all banking, the whole money system depends on general acceptability, the general acceptability of 'Bancors' (bank gold) would enable them to finance trade. The world was sceptical, and the idea was not adopted.

In the last few years the world situation as far as reserves are concerned has worsened. World trade has risen far beyond the ability of gold to back it, and although we could revalue gold there are several good reasons why we should not do so. One reason is that the chief nations to benefit would be South Africa and Russia, and justifiably or not there is a good deal of feeling in the world that neither of these countries deserves a bonus. The other beneficiaries would be those who had hoarded gold in the past—precisely the people who have helped keep it in short supply. They have been the least cooperative in helping to make the present system work.

Other reasons for *not* revaluing gold include its inflationary effects on certain countries, and also that it represents a very primitive basis for trade. To continue to use gold to finance international trade, when all that is needed is an internationally accepted medium for payment, is a reactionary solution. Sooner or later the international system has to grow up just as domestic economies have had to grow up.

In view of the shortage of gold the reserves of many nations have had to be increased by keeping **reserve currencies** with their gold, and this usually meant dollars or Sterling. Now if a nation has large stocks of these two currencies in her reserves and she hears that either is likely to be devalued, she is going to get very worried about a possible loss and is going to try to move out of that currency and into gold or some other reserve currency. In other words, the monetary pressure against both the dollar and the pound has increased very considerably since more and more countries began to use these as a reserve currency.

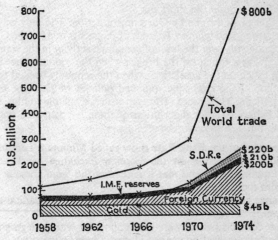

Fig. 82. World trade and world reserves

World reserves (see Fig. 82) have fallen relative to the volume of trade they have to finance, from 57 per cent in 1958 to 40 per cent in 1966, 32 per cent in 1970 (and this includes some of the new reserve assets **Special Drawing Rights**) and to 26 per cent in 1974. From experience we know that a nation with reserves as low as 20 per cent is invariably in difficulties. It is this situation which has led to the development of Special Drawing Rights. They are not quite the same as 'Bancors'; they are designed to extend the present I.M.F. arrangements by giving all members who agree to accept them an allocation. Great Britain's share of the 3½ billion created on January 1st, 1970, was 402 million, each one equivalent to a U.S. dollar. A further 3 billion were created in 1971 and 1972. A country wishing to use Special Drawing Rights will notify the Fund that it wishes to exchange some for usable foreign currency. The authorities will then designate which countries are to make currency available, and take S.D.R.s instead. Clearly they will choose the countries whose balance-of-payments positions are strong. While this has proved to supply some strengthening of reserves, the pace of events overtook the introduction of S.D.R.s. The serious deficits in the British balance of payments led the United Kingdom to 'float' sterling in 1972 and by 1973 all currencies were floating.

(9) Correcting a Temporary Disequilibrium in the Balance of Payments

The remaining problem to be solved under the 'managed flexibility' system was how to correct an adverse balance of payments. The Gold-Standard mechanism automatically corrected an imbalance by deflating the home economy. The flexible-exchange-rate method automatically corrected it by varying the exchange rate. The trouble with 'managed flexibility' was that it could not automatically do either. Apart from a fluctuation of 1 per cent, which might do some good, the exchange rate was fixed. The gold reserves were also fixed except when used to support a currency on the open market to keep the rate up to the agreed figure. This could not really deflate the home economy, at any rate in the short run.

The solution proved to be by Government action. The only way to deflate the home economy and secure a Balance of Payments was for the Government to introduce controls over the level of economic activity in the economy. Like a motorist giving a touch on the brakes when the economy needed to slow down and a touch on the accelerator when the economy needed to speed up, the Chancellor of the Exchequer pursued policies which came to be called 'Stop–Go' policies. There were various measures available to him, which have been listed below. A fuller description of these is postponed until later, to avoid repetition. The measures were:

(*a*) Adjustment of the Bank Rate (now called Minimum Lending Rate).

(*b*) Support for Sterling on the Foreign Exchange Market, using the Exchange Equalization Fund and if necessary the 'gold tranche' and other tranches from the I.M.F.

(*c*) Exchange control measures to prevent the export of capital and reduce foreign travel.

(*d*) Import controls (which were very unpopular with foreign governments and invited retaliatory action against United Kingdom exports).

(*e*) Aid to exporters to encourage exports.

(*f*) Hire purchase controls and other credit squeezes to reduce home demand and induce a certain measure of unemployment into the economy.

All these measures would help a temporary disequilibrium in the Balance of Payments, but naturally they were not popular. While the general well-being was ensured, individuals found that the stop–go measures meant unemployment, or bankruptcy, or uncertainty which made investment in new equipment less advantageous. The confidence inspired by twenty years of Keynesian policies designed to prevent trade cycles was threatened by the need to preserve a Balance of Payments.

What if the disequilibrium was more permanent, and reflected an enduring disinterest of foreigners in United Kingdom exports, which they considered over-priced and poor value for money? For such a serious long-term disequilibrium the Bretton Woods System envisaged 'devaluation'—a change in exchange rates which recognized the permanent nature of the situation.

(10) Curing a Permanent Disequilibrium—Devaluation or Depreciation?

The Bretton Woods system of managed flexibility provided that a permanent disequilibrium in the balance of payments of any country should be cured by a process called devaluation. A permanent disequilibrium means that the value of home goods being demanded by foreigners is much less than the value of foreign goods being demanded by home nationals, and the values are never likely to be equalized unless drastic steps are taken. These drastic steps mean a lowering of the exchange rate between the home country's currency and the other world currencies. This was what 'devaluation' meant— a drastic lowering of the pound sterling against other currencies as far as the United Kingdom is concerned. Under the Bretton Woods Agreement a nation in severe difficulties could devalue its currency by 10 per cent without notice. A devaluation greater than 10 per cent required the approval of the I.M.F. authorities. This would be given within three days, or longer if the proposed devaluation was more than 20 per cent.

The effect of devaluation is to make a country's goods cheaper on the export market, so that foreign countries will find them a more attractive proposition. It also makes imports dearer, so that home nationals will reduce their demands for goods from overseas, turning instead to home-produced goods (this is called import substitution). Devaluation should therefore bring payments into balance.

In 1967 Sterling was devalued by 14 per cent. It was this devaluation which finally led to the collapse of the Bretton Woods system, but at the time it was made this was not expected at all. What had clearly happened was that the United Kingdom economy was in permanent imbalance with the rest of the world, and Sterling was under severe pressure from speculators, who expected it to be devalued sooner or later. 'Hot money' movements were enormous. This means that countries holding Sterling as part of their reserves and banks holding Sterling for future transactions with the United Kingdom sold their Sterling, intending to buy it back cheaper when it had fallen in value. The increased volume of world trade, and the limited amount of gold being mined, meant that much of world reserves were in the reserve currencies, dollars and Sterling. With large Sterling reserves, countries had more to lose by a devaluation if they were caught holding Sterling. Also, very large multi-national companies were very sophisticated about pursuing overall profit-ability, so that financial benefits from changes in exchange rates were actively pursued, while 'leads and lags' influenced the actual dates of payment. A company importing goods into the United Kingdom just before a devaluation will 'lead' with its payment, paying at once while Sterling is high. A foreign customer buying British exports will 'lag' behind with its payment, hoping that Sterling will fall before payment is made. In this sort of situation the Bretton Woods system of devaluation was adopted. Speculators then took their profits, but many genuine supporters of the Bretton Woods system who had refused to join in the 'hot-money' speculation lost 14 per cent of the value of their holdings, and were not very pleased. The imbalance of payments was slow to correct—partly because the elasticities of demand for United Kingdom imports and exports were not favourable. Let us now take a look at this aspect of a devaluation, before considering floating exchange rates i.e. **depreciation of a currency**.

Elasticities and Devaluation

The three elasticities to be considered here are (a) the elasticity of demand for exports, (b) the elasticity of demand for imports, and (c) the elasticity of supply of exports. Each of these will vitally affect the success of devaluation. They are, of course, equally important under the floating exchange rate system prevailing at present. To make the discussion more realistic, reference will be made to the British devaluation of 1967, when a 14 per cent devaluation of Sterling occurred.

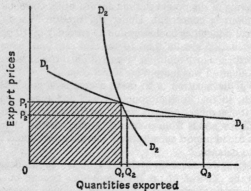

Fig. 83. Effect of the elasticity of demand for exports on the earnings of foreign exchange after devaluation.

Notes:
1. If the demand for exports is elastic the curve may be as in $D_1 D_1$.
2. If the demand for exports is inelastic the curve may be as in $D_2 D_2$.
3. Total earnings (before devaluation) of foreign exchange are shown by the shaded area.
4. In the case of exports where the demand is inelastic, quantities sold rise only to $O Q_2$, less than proportionately, and total earnings of foreign exchange decline.
5. In the case of exports where demand is elastic, quantities sold increase more than proportionately to $O Q_3$, and total earnings of foreign exchange increase.

(a) *The elasticity of demands for exports.* If we are reducing the prices of our exports in order to increase earnings of foreign exchange, it is vital that the demand for our exports is elastic. Suppose we reduce export prices by 14 per cent, and the rise in export sales is exactly proportional, in other words there is unitary elasticity of demand. The result will be that the earnings of foreign exchange have not altered. The greater volume of sales earning foreign exchange will be offset by the smaller amounts earned on each consignment. We will even be worse off in other ways, for we will have had all the extra trouble of shipping larger volumes of goods for the same result.

It will be even worse if the demand for our goods is inelastic. Then our extra effort in selling a slightly larger volume of goods will have been worse than useless, for the smaller earnings in foreign exchange on each consignment mean we will actually earn less total foreign exchange. The balance of payments may even deteriorate. Only if the demand for our exports is elastic, so that greatly increased volumes of sales occur, will the devaluation result in larger earnings of foreign exchange.

In the 1967 devaluation Great Britain's exports, which were mainly manufactured goods, proved to be in elastic demand and from that point of view the devaluation was a success.

(b) *The elasticity of demand for imports.* Here the situation is very similar, but works in the opposite way. A country which is devaluing its currency wishes to correct its balance of payments by increasing exports and decreasing imports. How successful it will be in decreasing imports depends on the elasticity of demand for imports by its citizens. The devaluation will raise the price of imports to them. Will their demand reduce proportionately, more than proportionately, or less than proportionately to the change in price? If the imports are basic raw materials which are essential to production, it may be impossible for the demand for them to decrease at all. Indeed higher export

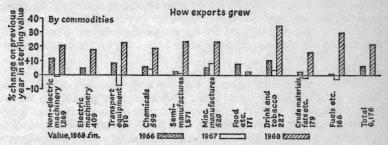

Fig. 84. How exports grew after the 1967 devaluation. (These figures were adjusted later to a total of £6,223 million.)

sales could even require larger imports of basic raw materials. If the imports are non-essentials, or if similar products are produced at home so that home products can be substituted for them, then the decrease in demand may be more than proportional. This situation is necessary if the devaluation is to be successful from the import point of view, but the situation is not quite as crucial as with exports. Since the price of imports has not changed in their own currencies we are not having to pay out more foreign exchange per unit imported, even though the home consumer is paying more for it. Therefore any reduction is welcome, even the small reduction in the demand for goods which are in inelastic demand.

Fig. 85 gives a comparison of visible trade balances in the years after the 1967 devaluation. It shows that while exports rose sharply, showing elastic

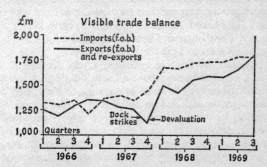

Fig. 85. Closing the trade gap after the 1967 devaluation

Notes:
1. Exports were in elastic demand and increased considerably.
2. Imports were in inelastic demand, and refused to decline at all. As a result, devaluation took a long time to narrow the trade gap.

demand, imports did not fall at all, but indeed continued to increase slowly. The reduction in the visible trade gap was therefore closed by exports, not by imports. The elasticity of exports was favourable for devaluation, the elasticity of imports proved to be unfavourable, and the beneficial effects of devaluation took a long while to take effect.

(c) *The elasticity of supply of exports.* If exports are to be sold in increasing quantities they must be available to sell. This means it may be necessary to reduce home demand for them if the supply of exports is inelastic. Anything we do to reduce home demand will increase the supply of exports. A good deal of the credit squeeze imposed by the British Government after the 1967 devaluation was aimed at releasing goods in this way for the export market.

Floating Exchange Rates

The result of the devaluation of 1967 was a slow recovery of the United Kingdom balance of payments and a total collapse of the Bretton Woods system. The fact is that in the sophisticated state of world economies today any fixed exchange rate is vulnerable, especially if foreign countries are using it as a reserve currency. The United States dollar came under pressure almost at once, for its gold reserves were only 10 billion dollars, and there were 50 billion dollars at large in the world. It has already been said that any country with reserves of only 20 per cent is vulnerable and in August 1971 the U.S.A. was forced to suspend convertibility of dollars into gold.

Managed flexibility was to be given one more try. On December 17th, 1971, an agreement called the Smithsonian Agreement was drawn up in Washington. The dollar was revalued against gold to $38 per fine ounce. New parities were agreed, the Dmark, the Yen and other hard currencies were revalued and even the £ was revalued to £1 = $2·6057. Fluctuations of 2¼ per cent either side of the fixed parity were allowed. This increased the chances that a speculator would burn his fingers, because Central Banks were not obliged to come in and support their currencies so quickly. Britain was unable to maintain its agreed parity and in June 1972 the pound was floated. The correctness of this decision was emphasized in March 1973 when all other major currencies floated against the dollar. The E.E.C. countries, except Britain, Italy, and Eire, floated jointly, keeping their exchange rates fixed with one another. The Agreement thus lasted a mere 15 months. In early 1974 France left the Common Market Joint Float and floated independently, while a free market in gold rocketed gold up to $150 to the fine ounce.

What is the effect of floating exchange rates? Instead of once-for-all devaluation to a new fixed parity position, the 'floating' of an exchange rate allows a currency to change its value in response to the supply and demand position. If the pound is weak and the dollar is strong the pound will depreciate against the dollar, its value sinking enough to achieve an equilibrium price where supply and demand are equal. In fact what we have had since 1972 is not a freely floating situation but what is known as 'dirty' floating. A government which feels that some short-term advantage can be gained by keeping the value of its currency at a certain level may support the currency by buying it on the open market using its reserves to do so. Equally, if it prefers its currency not to rise—perhaps to keep its exports in demand on world markets —it can sell the currency on the market, taking other currencies into its reserves instead. Such interferences with exchange rates occur daily, but in the long run a currency which comes under pressure must fall in value. This may be either because those who have the currency wish to sell it, or because the goods of that nation are so poor that no one wishes to buy them.

Although flexible exchange rates have largely eliminated the sort of speculative pressure that used to occur under the Bretton Woods system, they have disadvantages too. They create uncertainty in international trade, and businessmen who make bargains with small profit margins may find these eaten away by a depreciation of the currency. In general it is better to stipulate contracts in a 'hard' currency which is unlikely to fluctuate. An active forward exchange market, which enables businessmen to get firm prices now for currency to be earned in the future, is also helpful. One recent development is the use of **'currency baskets'** instead of a particular currency for designating the value of contracts. The idea of a currency basket is that an official body designates a **'unit of account'**, which consists of a basket of currencies. The two chief units that are available at present are the E.U.A. (European Unit of Account) and the S.D.R. (the Special Drawing Rights Unit of the International Monetary Fund). The E.U.A. consists of a basket of nine currencies; the S.D.R. is a basket of sixteen currencies. The composition of a unit is trade-weighted, so that each unit reflects the value of international trade carried on by the different nations. Thus the E.U.A. has 0·828 of a Deutschemark in it and £0·0885 sterling. At May 1976 the Dmark element represented 29·4 per cent of the unit, and the £ sterling element represented 14·7 per cent. Now, if a businessman offers to sell a piece of equipment for 100,000 E.U.A., and the value of Dmarks rises, it is almost certain that the value of sterling will fall, so that the value of the E.U.A. will not fluctuate very much at all. The value of the units is recalculated every day, and officially announced, but fluctuations will be much smaller than the fluctuations of a single currency like the dollar, the pound sterling or the Swiss franc. Actual settlement of the debt is made in an agreed **settlement currency**, which will be exchanged at the rate prevailing on the settlement date. To see how this works, consider the businessman selling his machine for 100,000 E.U.A. on a certain date when 1 E.U.A. = £0·60. The price of the machine is therefore £60,000. In three months' time, when payment is to be made, the £ sterling has fallen considerably in value but the E.U.A. is almost the same: 1 E.U.A. now equals £0·68. The businessman will therefore receive 100,000 E.U.A. converted to sterling at 1 E.U.A. = £0·68, i.e. £68,000—the true 'real' value of the machine.

The claim, so dear to opponents of 'stop–go' policies, that flexible exchange rates would eliminate the interference of Balance of Payments problems with the level of activity in the economy, has not been upheld since 1972. It has not proved possible to let the Balance of Payments take care of itself by allowing sterling to depreciate in value against other countries to the point where United Kingdom goods become attractive to foreigners. If demand is not controlled prices of British goods will rise. Sterling then has to decline in value if foreigners are to find British goods attractive—in other words, the home price is made attractive for foreigners by a lower exchange rate. This very decline in value may bring about a downward spiralling collapse of the value of sterling both at home and abroad. If this proceeds to the point where I.M.F. help is necessary, the I.M.F. will insist upon close control of the money supply, using its special definition of money supply called Domestic Credit Expansion

(D.C.E.). This measures the *change* in money supply to the general public in the country concerned, and is explained in Chapter Thirty (see page 361). It applies a particularly tight control of domestic credit, tighter than the controls which were used in traditional 'Stop–Go' policies. Some comparison of 'Stop–Go' policies with the situation in the mid-seventies is of interest here. In 1963 in a bout of Stop–Go activity unemployment rose to a sharp peak of about 600,000 and led to a change of Government. Since 1970 unemployment has only once been below 600,000, and from 1977 to 1978, when the I.M.F.'s rules had to be observed, it has never been less than 1,400,000.

To conclude we may say that floating exchange rates have reduced the general tension in world trading that arose under the Bretton Woods System whenever a particular currency (especially one that was being used by many nations as a reserve currency) came under pressure. The hectic speculation against sterling in particular is much reduced. At the same time national governments are still forced to 'manage' their economies in such a way as to take account of Balance of Payments problems. In this respect it is interesting to read the General Obligations of Members of the International Monetary Fund, which are as follows:

Article IV, Section 1. General obligations of members

Recognizing that the essential purpose of the international monetary system is to provide a framework that facilitates the exchange of goods, services, and capital among countries, and that sustains sound economic growth, and that a principal objective is the continuing development of the orderly underlying conditions that are necessary for financial and economic stability, each member undertakes to collaborate with the Fund and other members to assure orderly exchange arrangements and to promote a stable system of exchange rates. In particular, each member shall:

(i) endeavour to direct its economic and financial policies towards the objective of fostering orderly economic growth with reasonable price stability, with due regard to its circumstances;

(ii) seek to promote stability by fostering orderly underlying economic and financial conditions and a monetary system that does not tend to produce erratic disruptions;

(iii) avoid manipulating exchange rates or the international monetary system in order to prevent effective balance of payments adjustment or to gain an unfair competitive advantage over other members; and

(iv) follow exchange policies compatible with the undertakings under this Section.

The European Monetary System

At the time of going to press a new return to fixed exchange rates between the members of the E.E.C. is being proposed, designed to start on 1 January, 1979. Called the European Monetary System (E.M.S.), it is proposed that member nations should declare a fixed parity with one another's exchange rates, but there will be a common float against the rest of the world. Whether such a system can succeed in the absence of complete political union is very doubtful —such joint floats have fallen apart in the past because national aspirations are less easy to achieve in a straitjacket of fixed exchange rates. Critics argue that for the system to succeed it would require wide-ranging controls of capital, to the disadvantage of other nations and the disruption of activities of the I.M.F. and the World Bank. The creation of a European Monetary Fund (a super-Exchange Equalisation Fund) to fight off speculative pressure on a particular currency is envisaged, and would appear to duplicate the I.M.F.'s role, as well as offering prospects of a speculator's paradise.

Tight control of credit would appear to be inevitable under such a system, and would call for the control of domestic economies in the interest of European exchange rates. While this might be a factor tending towards a larger political union it would meet severe opposition from nationalists of many factions. The system is also likely to put the dollar under severe strain, especially if individual Central Banks are free to enter the market for national —rather than European—reasons, to indulge in dollar intervention. The reader should watch sources of political and economic comment for appreciations of these developments.

(11) Summary of Chapter Twenty-three

1. The Gold Standard achieved equilibrium by deflating the economy of the country losing gold because of its adverse balance, and inflating the economy of the country gaining gold reserves.

2. The Gold-Standard rules were: deflate when you lose gold, inflate when you gain gold.

3. The flexible exchange rate achieved equilibrium by letting the currency depreciate when a balance was adverse, and letting it appreciate when the balance of payments was favourable.

4. Exchange rates are determined by the demand for, and the supply of, a particular currency. To some extent this reflects the relative efficiency of the industries of the two countries, but it also reflects capital movements.

5. In order to prevent fluctuations in the exchange rate caused by short-term capital flows and speculative pressures, the Exchange Equalization Account method of managing the exchange rate was devised. This involved buying pounds on the open market when 'a run on the pound' developed, and selling pounds when the demand for pounds was strong.

6. The Bretton Woods Agreement of 1944 introduced a system of 'managed flexibility'. This involved keeping exchange rates at a fixed parity with other currencies to encourage business confidence in trade. To help manage currencies the International Monetary Fund (I.M.F.) was set up. Also set up was the International Bank for Reconstruction and Development.

7. In a disequilibrium situation where a member's own reserves are insufficient, the member may borrow until the Fund has twice its quota of contributions. In addition, reserves have been increased by the creation of Special Drawing Rights (S.D.R.s).

8. As the 'managed-flexibility' system could not affect either the home economy of the country suffering an imbalance of payments, or its exchange rate, control of the disequilibrium had to be achieved by Government measures. Of these Minimum Lending Rate, hire-purchase controls, tariffs, exchange controls and devaluation were the most effective.

9. Managed flexibility was modified in 1971, and virtually abandoned in 1973, when all currencies floated against the dollar. Floating permits the currency to find its own level in the market.

CHAPTER TWENTY-FOUR

THE FREE TRADE AREAS

(1) Limited Free Trade

From an economic viewpoint free trade is highly desirable, because it brings the advantages of specialization and large-scale production. From national, social, and psychological viewpoints it may have less appeal, because it is likely that the terms of trade will favour the richer and more highly capitalized countries at the expense of the undeveloped countries. The most acceptable free-trade areas therefore tend to be between nations of roughly comparable economic strength, whose citizens have roughly similar standards of living and similar technologies. In these circumstances genuine comparative advantages may still lie with particular areas because of native temperament or accumulated knowledge and experience. Thus the Italian gift for style in clothes, shoes, and cars is likely to prove advantageous, while Germany's engineering skill will make her heavy-industrial equipment competitive within the Common Market. Britain's manufactures will be readily acceptable to Denmark, whose dairy products will compete favourably with British agricultural goods.

Where a limited free-trade area is established the degree of reciprocity in trade is high, and this reduces national, social, and psychological objections.

(2) Bilateral and Multilateral Trade

Bilateral trade means two-sided trade, i.e. trade between two countries only. As will be seen from Fig. 86, the volume of world trade that can be achieved when nations trade bilaterally is smaller than with multilateral, many-nation, trade. During the years 1930–40 a major depression developed in the United States of America and spread rapidly to the rest of the world. To protect home industries nearly all nations put up tariff barriers to keep foreign goods out, and where they traded at all it was on a bilateral basis. The result was a serious decline in world trade with loss of economic advantage to mankind in general. By encouraging international specialization of labour, multilateral trade encourages the best use of resources. This advantage was partially lost in the years under discussion, and the experience led to an international conference at Geneva in 1947 where a General Agreement on Tariffs and Trade (G.A.T.T.) was signed. Before discussing this agreement let us consider Fig. 86, and the notes below it.

(3) The General Agreement on Tariffs and Trade (G.A.T.T.)

Among the major examinations of international monetary and trading arrangements held during and after the Second World War was a convention at Geneva which resulted in the General Agreement on Tariffs and Trade. The agreement was signed in 1947, by twenty-three nations; the number has now reached seventy. The convention's aims had been as follows:

(*a*) To reduce existing trade barriers between nations.

(*b*) To reduce discrimination against particular nations.

(*c*) To promote international confidence in tariff policies by promoting consultation rather than unilateral action as a means of deciding tariffs.

The United States made very generous reductions in tariffs as a result of the 1947 negotiations, and these enabled European nations in particular to penetrate the North American market. This policy of the 'good creditor' enabled Europe to recover from many of its post-war difficulties.

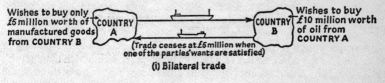

(i) Bilateral trade

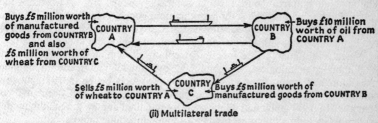

(ii) Multilateral trade

Fig. 86. Bilateral and multilateral trade: (i) Bilateral trade—trade ceases at £5 million; (ii) Multilateral trade—trade rises to £10 million

Notes:

1. With bilateral-trading agreements trade can only continue to the point where one country's requirements have been satisfied. In part (i) of the above diagram, Country *B* would like to import a further £5 million of oil from Country *A* but cannot do so because Country *A* does not want any more of Country *B*'s manufactures.

2. With multilateral trade the desire of Country *C* to buy goods from Country *B* enables world trade to rise in volume. Since Country *A* is willing to buy wheat from *C*, she will sell further oil to *B*, who will pay for it with manufactured goods delivered to *C*, who will pay for them by shipping wheat to *A*.

3. Clearly the more nations involved in world trade the better, and hence a general agreement on tariffs and trade will promote international specialization.

In 1963 President Kennedy persuaded the American Congress to cut American tariffs if other nations would agree to do so by June 1967. This initiated a new round of discussions called the Kennedy Round, which ended in 1967 with massive tariff reductions by the industrialized nations. Some 70 per cent of their dutiable import tariffs were cut, and in two-thirds of the cases the cuts were of 50 per cent. A 'product-by-product' basis was the most successful method of agreeing these tariff cuts; chemicals, pulp and paper, transport equipment, machinery, base metals, and many more commodities had extensive cuts made. The one major flaw in the agreements was the extent to which primary producing countries were unable to gain concessions about agricultural products. Almost all nations have strategic or social reasons for not reducing agriculture. Developing nations tend to be agricultural, but the Kennedy Round did not prove helpful in allowing them to specialize in the activities at which they have a comparative advantage. Instead the refusal of advanced nations to cut back their agricultural programmes has given developing nations an added incentive to diversify and industrialize their economies.

One principle of G.A.T.T. is that the member countries agree to give 'most-favoured-nation' treatment to all members. This means that if Britain cuts her tariff on American-manufactured electrical goods by 10 per cent she will do the same for all G.A.T.T. members. With seventy nations in the Agreement it means that practically the whole world shares in the tariff cut. Such tariff cuts are made much less likely as a result.

A major criticism of G.A.T.T. comes from the seventy-seven members of the Less Developed Countries (L.D.C.s) who object to it as a 'rich man's club'. They have put concrete proposals before the developed nations through the United Nations Organization, for a general system of free and preferential entry of manufactured and semi-manufactured goods from the L.D.C.s to the developed countries. The suggestion was made to the second plenary session of the United Nations Conference on Trade and Development (U.N.C.T.A.D.) at New Delhi in 1967. The idea is to replace aid, which has unsatisfactory emotional, psychological, and political overtones, with trade. A limited programme of unrestricted entry for some products began in 1971, against some opposition. The programme is called the Generalized System of Preferences. In 1974 a United Nations Report called for an extension of the system to include all textiles, leather and agricultural produce.

A new round of G.A.T.T. negotiations, called the 'Tokyo Round', began in 1973 in Tokyo. It is now (1978) taking place in Geneva, and concentrating on 'non-tariff' problems. These include *subsidies* (which help a nation's exporters by paying part of their costs) and *countervailing duties*, which slap a tariff on goods coming into a country if those goods have been helped by a subsidy. In agriculture there are many *administrative devices* (such as the imposition of fierce 'quality' standards to exclude imports) which are a barrier to trade.

The 'World Bank'—the International Bank for Reconstruction and Development

The other major creation of the Bretton Woods Conference in 1944 was the World Bank, or I.B.R.D. for short. This bank receives contributions from members and raises funds by issuing dollar bonds. It has enabled some useful development programmes to go ahead, but its work is currently being reviewed to change its direction from the sponsoring of prestige industrial projects to a more 'grass-roots' level.

The difficulty with development projects is that the fundamental educational level of the less developed countries leaves them unqualified to operate prestige projects which the Bank has formerly tended to sponsor. Also the more sophisticated projects tend to be so advanced that they need little labour, whereas employment is a chief requirement in these countries, especially if basic skills are to be acquired.

The Bank is therefore turning at least some of its efforts towards sponsoring basic training programmes, population-control schemes, and improvements of basic agriculture. These less developed countries are nearly all agricultural nations, yet productivity is so low that they are nearly all net importers of agricultural products. Some $4,000 million worth of food is imported annually by these countries. The World Bank programmes envisage changing this by aid to develop new strains of rice and wheat, and by providing fertilizer and simple agricultural equipment.

(4) The General Pattern of Free-Trade Areas

It has already been said that free trade proceeds best between nations of similar technological status. The major free-trade groupings are the European Economic Community, now closely aligned with E.F.T.A. (the European Free Trade Area), and Comecon, the Communist trading group. Other groupings fluctuate in effectiveness as the developing nations which form them seek to achieve their national and international aspirations. The groupings in Table 38 are the chief trading areas.

Table 38. Free-trade areas

(Proposals have also been made for possible free-trade areas for the Middle East, Central Africa, West Africa, Scandinavia, and the North Atlantic countries.)

Full name	Short title	Total population (Millions)	Countries involved	1970 income per head(£)
European Economic Community	E.E.C.	250	Germany, France, Italy, Belgium, Netherlands, Luxemburg, Great Britain, Denmark, Eire	650
European Free Trade Association	E.F.T.A.	35	Norway, Sweden, Austria, Portugal, Switzerland, Iceland, (Finland is an associate)	680
Council for Mutual Economic Aid	Comecon	340	U.S.S.R., Poland, Rumania, East Germany, Czechoslovakia, Hungary, Bulgaria, Mongolia	Not available
Latin American Free Trade Association	L.A.F.T.A.	220	Brazil, Mexico, Argentina, Colombia, Peru, Venezuela, Chile, Ecuador, Bolivia, Uruguay, Paraguay	168
Central American Common Market	C.A.C.M.	14	Guatemala, El Salvador, Honduras, Nicaragua, Costa Rica	125
Caribbean Free Trade Association	C.A.R.I.F.T.A.	5	Barbados, Trinidad, Guyana, Jamaica, Tobago, Leeward Is., Windward Is.	156
East African Community	E.A.C.	30	Kenya, Uganda, Tanzania	42

The advantages of free-trade areas stem from the increased market which is made available to members. It is not only actual population but purchasing power that is important, so that the strongest areas are those that have affluent populations.

(5) The Sterling Area

Before 1931 all countries had freely convertible currencies, i.e. they were on the Gold Standard and their currencies could be exchanged for gold on demand. Any imbalance of foreign trade was cleared up by the Gold-Standard mechanism (see page 269).

Most countries strongly resented the need to deflate when an adverse balance of payments arose, and in 1931 the Gold Standard was abandoned. The alternative was to let exchange rates fluctuate freely, but this was a deterrent to trade since exporters could not rely on getting their full profits. If the exchange rate moved against them they might find their profit margins reduced, or even wiped out altogether.

A partial solution to this problem was to tie one's currency to a 'great' currency, and the U.S. dollar and the £ Sterling were the obvious ones to choose. A great many nations, including all the Commonwealth countries except Canada, chose Sterling. Their reasons for doing so were as follows:

(a) Most of their trade was done with the United Kingdom.

(b) The banking, insurance, and other facilities of London were already established in their territories, and in particular the major commodity markets of the City were handling their basic produce. At a time when world supplies were reaching 'glut' proportions, with coffee being burned in railway trains in Brazil and crops being ploughed back all over the world, nations with a share in the British market naturally chose to perpetuate it.

It was, however, a purely voluntary association. Its members gave one another 'most-favoured-nation' treatment, keeping tariffs to low levels and keeping exchange rates steady except where absolutely necessary.

1972 saw enormous changes in the Sterling Area, which was reduced in June to the United Kingdom, the Channel Islands, the Isle of Man, Eire and Gibraltar. The link between Sterling and Australian currency was ended in December 1971. In 1972 Malaysia, Singapore, Malta, Hong Kong and South Africa severed their direct links with Sterling as a currency. It seems most unlikely that former Sterling Area countries will receive more favourable terms in financial affairs than our fellow members of the European Economic Community, and as Britain is also pledged to do what she can to reduce the problems of Sterling's role as a reserve currency the Sterling Area as an effective force in world trade has almost disappeared.

(6) The European Economic Community (E.E.C.)

During the Second World War the idea grew up of a Federal Union of Europe. The powers of Europe should be bound together by ties so strong that any further war between them would become unthinkable. Experience of the inter-war years had led people to realize that defeated nations must be helped to their feet again. Any sort of vacuum gave opportunities to a demagogue to persuade people that he knew the answers to their problems. When war ended in 1945 the Allies, with the possible exception of the U.S.S.R. who had suffered more than most, did not exact reparations from the defeated enemy, who in any case had suffered severely, but instead began to rebuild Europe including Germany. The idea of a super-European State, beginning with an economic union and developing into a political union, had been born.

The stages of its early development were as follows:

(a) Three countries, Belgium, The Netherlands, and Luxemburg formed the Benelux Customs Union in 1945.

(b) The rebuilding of Germany, the recovery of France, and the industrialization of Italy all took place. A useful instrument during this period which helped solve adverse balance-of-payments problems for individual countries was the European Payments Union. Undoubtedly American generosity had a lot to do with the rapid recovery of Europe, but the most interesting economic thought for the period was that it is surprising how quickly capital assets can be replaced when the population, even though decimated by war, is sophisticated and trained. Calculations revealed that the entire stock of capital assets of a country like Germany amount to no more than two years of the entire National Income. Of course one cannot save the entire National Income and invest it, or one would starve to death in the process. What did happen was that, with very high savings to replenish capital, Germany rose like a phoenix from a destitute and impoverished nation to an advanced, technological society able to lead the whole of Europe, in a mere ten years.

(c) In 1952 the six nations, Belgium, France, Germany, Italy, Luxemburg, and The Netherlands joined to form the European Coal and Steel Community.

(d) In 1957 the Treaty of Rome was signed, in which the six nations agreed to form the European Economic Community, popularly known as the Common Market. It actually came into existence on 1 January 1958. Its basic ideas were:

(i) Members would still pursue their own economic policies, seeking their own best performance, but the upward harmonization of living standards was to be a major aspect of policy.

(ii) A sufficient degree of co-ordination and co-operation was envisaged to ensure an overall balance of payments.

(iii) In choosing their own business cycle policies (i.e. their use of Keynesian economics to manage prosperity) they should consider the effect of their policies on the other members and not do anything that would harm them.

(iv) Associate members from less developed countries would be considered, who would be granted certain benefits in trade. Turkey, Greece, and several African countries have taken up associate status.

(v) Tariffs should be reduced by 10 per cent per year, and at the same time external tariffs against non-members should be raised, or levelled, to the point where a common barrier was erected to all foreign imports.

This planned programme was fully achieved by 1968 when the tenth and final instalment of tariffs between members was removed, and a common external tariff of about 12 per cent was built up against other nations.

Results achieved by the E.E.C. up to 1973

Very good levels of progress were achieved in the realization of the original objectives of the Community, but problems arose too. The trade of the Community between 1958 and 1970 rose from £10,000 million to £29,500 million. Of this, internal trade with one another rose by 500 per cent from £3,000 million to £15,000 million—a very high growth rate by any standards.

Developments Since Britain's Entry in 1973

On 1 January, 1973, the United Kingdom became a full member of the E.E.C. as did Denmark and Eire. Norway withdrew at the last moment after a referendum. After a few years in which harmonization of tariffs was achieved, full status for the new members was finally reached on 1 July, 1977. Britain's trade with the E.E.C. has improved considerably since membership began,

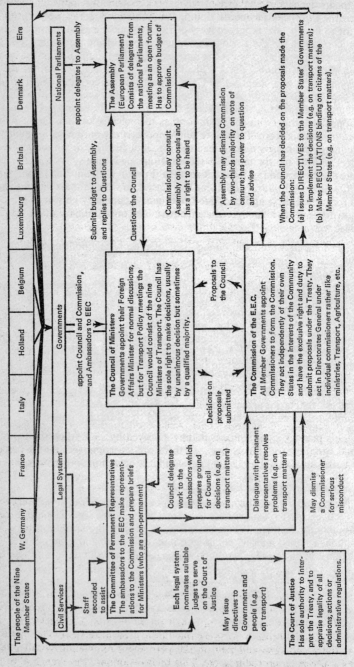

Fig. 87. The institutions of the European Economic Community

from 29·6 per cent of total exports to 36·7 per cent in 1977. With the increasing influence of oil products in this trade the improvement seems likely to continue.

The European Institutions

Fig. 87 (page 294) displays these institutions diagrammatically. There are five of them: the Council of Ministers, the Commission, The European Parliament, the Court of Justice and the Committee of Permanent Representatives. Their organization and functions are as follows:

The Council of Ministers. This consists of one Minister from each of the member states. Generally the Foreign Minister is regarded as the appropriate minister, but on special occasions when particular policies are under discussion the Minister for the Department concerned—say fuel and power, or agriculture—would represent his country. Presidency of the Council is taken in turn for six-monthly periods. The Council takes all basic decisions on Community policy, and is empowered to pass minor matters with a simple majority. On major matters a system of weighted voting is used, and a qualified majority is necessary. The weighting gives 4 votes to major powers, 2 votes to lesser powers and one vote to very small powers like Luxemburg. In practice the Council has usually wrestled with matters until unanimity is reached, since, particularly on new and controversial policies, it is not deemed wise to force policies upon unwilling partners.

The Commission. The Commission consists of two commissioners from each major member and one from smaller powers, chosen by agreement. They are pledged to independence of the governments of their countries, and act in accordance with the powers laid down in the Treaty of Rome. They coordinate activity in particular fields, considering issues from a community point of view independent of national interests or aspirations. Their function is to formulate proposals for decision by the Council of Ministers and to supply information to, and answers to questions from, the European Parliament. They have a staff of Community 'Civil Servants' in Brussels, and provide the day-to-day administration of the Community.

The European Parliament. This consists of 36 representatives of major powers, 14 from smaller powers and 6 representatives from tiny powers. These representatives are chosen from the national parliaments. Their function is to debate all matters of Community policy, to question both the Commission and the Council of Ministers and to supervise the Community budget. It can compel the Commission to resign en bloc by a two thirds majority.

The Court of Justice. Whenever rules and regulations are promulgated they must inevitably be the cause of disputes between parties favourably or adversely affected. It is for the Court of Justice, composed of learned judges from member nations, to interpret and declare the meaning of disputed passages. Governments, firms and individuals as well as the Community authorities have a right of appeal to the Court of Justice if they are aggrieved by the application of any Community rule.

The Committee of Permanent Representatives. This consists of the nine ambassadors to the E.E.C. from the member countries. Their function is to act as permanent watchdogs on behalf of the Foreign Secretaries (or other Departmental Ministers forming the Council of Ministers). The latter are essentially part-time and rely on the permanent representatives to prepare briefs, advise on procedures, etc. This body—Coreper, the French abbreviation—has proved very effective in getting practical agreement on all sorts of detailed matters and then having them ratified by the Council of Ministers without difficulty. A proposal to make these representatives of greater importance is being aired at the moment (1978).

The Community Budget

The Community budget is rather like the British 'estimates' drawn up before the start of the financial year. The Community year is a calendar year, and the budget is prepared in E.U.A.s (European Units of Account), which in 1978 replaced the gold-based unit of account in use since 1972. This new E.U.A. is a 'currency basket' whose value is related to the trade weighted influence of the nine national currencies. Its value is calculated daily. The total value of the budget in 1973 was 4,237 million E.U.A.'s, each unit of account being equal to one U.S. dollar. By 1978 the Budget had risen to 12,400 million E.U.A.'s, each E.U.A. being equivalent to 1·18 U.S. dollars. It has thus grown about 3·45 times in the five years. In 1973 the Budget represented 0·53 per cent of the Community's total Gross Domestic Product. In 1978, although 3·45 times as big, it had only risen to 0·81 per cent of the Community's Gross Domestic Product. Clearly only a tiny fraction of the total wealth created in the Community is controlled by and used by the Community.

The total budget for 1978 shown in Table 38(a) is equivalent to about £8,060 million, and almost three quarters of it goes on the Common Agricultural Policy.

Table 38(a). Community Spending 1978

Appropriations for Payment	*Million E.U.A.'s*	%
Intervention Appropriations		
1. Agricultural sector	9,132	73·87
2. Social sector	559	4·52
3. Regional sector	525	4·25
4. Research, energy, industry, transport	295	2·39
5. Developmental cooperation	381	3·08
Operating Appropriations		
6. Staff	387	3·13
7. Administration	106	0·85
8. Information	13	0·11
9. Aids and subsidies	45	0·36
Reserves	5	0·04
Reimbursements to Member States from own resources	689	5·58
Total 'Commission' budget	12,137	98·18
Budgets of other institutions	225	1·82
Grand total	12,362	100·00

(7) The European Free Trade Area (E.F.T.A.)

The E.F.T.A. states have all established individual agreements with the E.E.C. which preserve the free trade formerly established with the U.K., Eire and Denmark.

(8) 'Trade-Diverting' Effects of Free-Trade Areas

An important aspect of free-trade areas is their tendency to divert trade from traditional channels towards 'internal' sources of supply within the Free Trade Area.

(9) Summary of Chapter Twenty-four

1. Free trade tends to be practised today within limited groupings of countries of similar living standards and levels of development.

2. Generally speaking, multilateral trade permits a larger volume of world trade than a series of bilateral trading arrangements.

3. The General Agreement on Tariffs and Trade is an international body that attempts to promote world trade by arranging for tariffs to be reduced.

4. The group of seventy-seven Less Developed Countries (L.D.C.s) attempts through the United Nations Conference on Trade and Development (U.N.C.T.A.D.) to secure a larger share of trade for its members.

5. The main free trade areas of the world are the European Economic Community, the European Free Trade Association, the Council for Mutual Economic Aid, the Latin American Free Trade Area, the Central American Common Market, the East African Community, and the Caribbean Free Trade Area.

6. The Sterling Area formerly consisted mainly of Commonwealth countries, held together in a loose association by the advantages of trading in the British market and by the facilities for finance through the City of London.

The Sterling Area has now been reduced to the British Isles, the Channel Isles, the Isle of Man, Eire and Gibraltar.

7. The European Economic Community, or Common Market, is a grouping of nine major European countries pledged to secure economic and even political union. The nine countries with their 'Associates' form a market of about 300 million people.

(10) Suggested Further Reading

Harrod, R. F.: *International Economics*. Nisbet: London, 1958.
Swann, D. *The Economics of the Common Market*. Penguin: 1970.

Exercises Set 24

1. What is a free-trade area? What advantages are likely to be achieved by joining such an organization? Are there any disadvantages?

2. Distinguish between bilateral trade and multilateral trade. Which is more beneficial, and why?

3. What was the 'Kennedy Round'? What advantages did it bring in international trade? What criticisms have been made of it by less developed countries?

4. A proposal to develop a Common Market of West Africa has been put forward. Examine the economic, social, and political implications for the West African nations of such a suggestion.

5. What is the Sterling Area? How did it come into existence and why has it largely disappeared today?

6. 'Britain has abandoned the Sterling Area and assumed a leading European role.' What problems does this pose for (*a*) New Zealand, (*b*) France?

7. What was the Treaty of Rome? How successfully have the plans made there been achieved?

8. What were the aims of E.F.T.A.? Why has Britain left the organization?

9. 'No nation, least of all Great Britain, can remain an island unto itself.' What major factors require Britain to form, join, and trade with free-trade areas?

10. The largest, and most desirable, free-trade area would be a North Atlantic Free Trade Area in which the U.S.A., Canada, and Europe joined. What (*a*) advantages and (*b*) disadvantages for Great Britain are implicit in the idea of N.A.F.T.A.?

CHAPTER TWENTY-FIVE

WHAT IS MACROECONOMICS?

(1) Introduction

Adam Smith thought that free enterprise and free trade would produce all the progress that was possible. The task of the economist was to display how man created wealth, but not to direct or guide the economy unnecessarily. Two centuries later there is scarcely a country in the world where the politicians and the economists are not banded together to direct and guide the economy. In most countries, in different ways perhaps, the greatest good of the greatest number is the justification for their activities. We live in an age of the concensus: 'what does everyone think should be done?' It might be claimed that it works at least as well as *laissez-faire* worked in the nineteenth century.

'Macro' is derived from the Greek word *makros* meaning 'large'. We sometimes talk of the universe as a 'macrocosm'. We say a thing is 'macroscopic' when we can see it with the naked eye, in contrast to microscopic things invisible to the naked eye. We now approach macroeconomics, the economics of whole societies, after a great many chapters about microeconomics, the economics of individual consumers, individual firms, and individual industries. Macroeconomics considers the whole economy from a national point of view.

In studying macroeconomics we turn our attention to the major forces acting and interacting within the economy. What forces are at work in the economy? What levels of activity are being achieved? What levels of activity are desirable? How shall we achieve them when we have decided? These are absorbing problems, made even more interesting because the whole economy stands or falls by what is achieved for the individual. If *I* am not prosperous, what use is it to me that society as a whole is prosperous? What satisfaction do I get, when I am poor, to know that others are rich? If I am unemployed, high levels of general employment do *me* no good, and what use is the general security if I am insecure?

The central problem of economics in the second half of the twentieth century is the management of prosperity to maximize individual and general welfare.

(2) The Problems of Macroeconomics

In the chapters which follow we have to study a number of problems which face the Government of any country, for macroeconomics is concerned with what actions Governments can take to achieve desired ends. In former times, and in a very few countries perhaps still today, the free play of market forces was left to decide the level of national income, and the rate of growth of the economy. As a result of this policy of *laissez-faire* ('let the thing work itself out') the economy tended to grow in spiral-like movements of business activity. Years of furious expansion, called 'booms', were followed by years of consolidation and slower progress, called 'slumps'. The economy was always growing, but it suffered from cycles of activity spiralling upwards. The more exposed members of society, the poor, and the immigrant, suffered great misery. A cry went out for more conscious control of business activity, and eventually Keynesian economics showed the way to achieve it. More recently, after a quarter of a century of Keynesian economics the 'Monetarist School' calls for monetary measures to manage the economy.

Under this final group of studies, then, we must consider:

(a) The national income; what it is, how it may be increased, and how it may be fairly shared.

(b) Business cycles; their causes and cures. This involves a study of deflation, inflation, and equilibrium levels of activity in the economy.

(c) Problems associated with full employment, structural unemployment, and regional under-employment.

(d) The public sector of the economy; its conflict with the private sector and their reconciliation with one another.

(e) Public finance.

(f) The balance-of-payments problem, already discussed in Chapter Twenty-two, presents itself mainly at macroeconomic levels.

(g) The international implications of national policies and co-operation with other countries.

Exercises Set 25 (Revision Questions on Microeconomics)

Before proceeding to macroeconomics a set of questions covering the general principles already discussed in microeconomics seems appropriate. The reader is urged to write answers to most of these questions. Only by written practice will the student acquire the facility he needs with words and ideas. The questions are deliberately *not* placed in any particular order.

1. What is the difference between private capital and social capital? Give five examples of each.

2. Consider the effects of the introduction of mammoth tankers on (a) the price of petrol, (b) the South African economy, and (c) the Port of Glasgow.

3. What is a price index? What difficulties arise in constructing one? What use are price indices when constructed?

4. What is
(a) The Balance of Payments on Current Account
(b) The Balance of Payments on Capital Account?
What is the connection between the two? Do both balance?

5. The International Monetary Fund authorities must sanction a devaluation if it exceeds 10 per cent. Under what circumstances might a country apply to devalue its currency, and what does it hope to achieve?

6. What factors determine the location of an industry today?

7. Why are small firms common in agriculture, building, and retailing?

8. 'Every additional mouth arrives in the world with a pair of hands. As a result there is no need to fear overpopulation.' Discuss.

9. For the marginal firm in perfect competition, what is the relationship between average cost, marginal cost, and price?

10. What is a free-trade area? How may it benefit (a) a developed nation, (b) a developing nation?

11. Analyse the economic effects of Jumbo-jets, each carrying 500 passengers, on (*a*) traffic density at London Airport, (*b*) pilots, (*c*) the economy of Tunisia.

12. U.K. Population and Estimated Population (Thousands):

Total	Under 15	%	15–64	%	65 & over	%
1967: 55,202	12,999	23·6	35,394	64·1	6,809	12·3
1980: 61,223	17,972	29·3	35,042	57·3	8,209	13·4

Comment on the economic implications of these figures.

13. What part does the Stock Exchange play in the provision of capital for industry?

14. The following changes occurred between 1958 and 1968: the index of retail prices was 1962 = 100, 1958 = 91, 1968 = 125.

	1958 £ million	1968 £ million
Earnings from employment	13,470	25,267
Expenditure on food	4,028	5,673
Expenditure on motor cars	425	999
Expenditure on cinema entertainment	85	60

Comment on these figures.

15. Consider the economic problems arising from the balance-of-payments figures shown in Fig. 88.

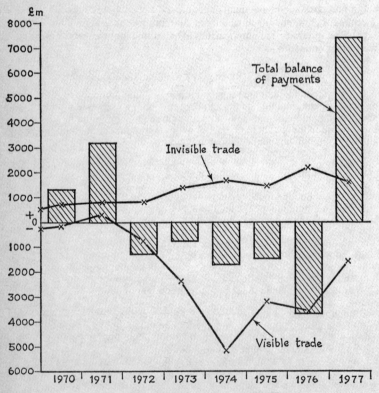

Fig. 88. Balance of payments, 1970–77

16. What is the function of the rate of interest in the economic system?

17. What is the meaning of 'optimum size' in business units? On what factors does the optimum size depend?

18. Why are film stars paid more than nurses?

19. 'High profits are essential for economic growth.' Discuss.

20. What gains arise from international trade? How are these gains shared between the countries concerned?

21. 'If we nationalize an industry it is because it will make that industry efficient.' Do you agree?

22. Why does the price of sugar fluctuate more than the price of transistor radios?

23. 'The use of container cranes will not benefit dockers.' 'The use of container cranes will enrich the nation.' Discuss these statements.

24. What is the likely effect on the price of rubber of the following?

(*a*) A war in Malaya.

(*b*) The development of a synthetic substitute for rubber.

(*c*) A 10 per cent rise in car sales.

(*d*) Legislation prohibiting the re-moulding of motor car tyres.

25. An increase in demand leads to a rise in price. An increase in price leads to a reduction in demand. Therefore prices can never change, except temporarily. Comment on this reasoning.

26. Economic forces play only a small part in wage determination these days. Do you agree?

27. What is economics? Use your definition to justify the study of economics in the further education of engineers.

28. 'It is unfair to expect a nation with a favourable balance of trade to adopt policies which will lead it into balance-of-payments difficulties.' What policies might it be asked to pursue, and why are they justified?

29. What is a non-insurable risk? What is its connection with profit?

30. Why do farm labourers earn less than doctors?

CHAPTER TWENTY-SIX

THE NATIONAL INCOME

(1) Definition

Alfred Marshall, the English economist already referred to on page 208, defined national income as *the aggregate net product of, and the sole source of payment for, all the agents of production*. It is an enduring definition, and the reader is strongly recommended to memorize it.

It needs, however, to be dissected carefully so that it is fully understood.

(*a*) *The agents of production*. These are the factors which create and then enjoy the National Income. We are back to Chapter One of this book with man's 'wants' leading to production, which is destroyed by consumption. The agents of production must ceaselessly be employed to create wealth, but their reward is to share in it.

(*b*) *The aggregate net product of*. What are the agents of production producing? They are producing a total (i.e. *aggregate*) collection of goods and services. However these goods and services cannot all be enjoyed as income, because in creating them depreciation has been suffered on the capital assets of the nation. Machines have been worn out, buildings have grown older, transport facilities have suffered wear and tear. If we do not replace this portion of the nation's capital then we shall in fact be living on our capital and consuming it. The true income created for current enjoyment is not the aggregate product of the agents of production, but the aggregate *net* product (net of depreciation on capital).

(*c*) *The sole source of payment for*. Who will enjoy this income? Who will consume the food, wear the clothing, find shelter in the homes, enjoy peace behind the defences, laugh at the entertainment, take pleasure in the beauty that these agents have created? The answer is: those very factors of production in their human forms. The landowner will enjoy a share paid for from his rents; the labourer will purchase a share with his wages; the investor will spend the interest and profits that accrue to him on purchasing a share. But will it be a fair share? That is a different matter, and it requires us to consider social policies, taxation to redistribute wealth etc. For the moment it is purely the income we are interested in: its distribution comes later (see page 354).

Let us now repeat and memorize Marshall's splendid definition of National Income:

The National Income is the aggregate net product of, and the sole source of payment for, all the agents of production.

(2) Why Measure the National Income?

In earlier times there was little interest in National Income statistics; income was regarded as essentially private, and if the nation had any interest at all it was in seeing that taxes (such as they were) were paid on the due date. In early Victorian times the total budget of the British Government was only about £30 million, and even by 1881 it was only about £69 million. In that year income tax raised a mere £21 million, while the tax on beer and spirits raised £31 million. This compares with the figure of about £58,000 million estimated to have been spent by various Government agencies in the 1977–8 financial year.

Clearly a great change has come over the economy since Gladstone s day. This change is chiefly an increase in welfare, using that word in the widest possible sense. We have gradually come to accept that certain standards of health, education, and housing are essential if society is to be kept peaceful; that income is a right to which a man and his family are entitled even if through illness, industrial reorganization, or old age he is temporarily or permanently unable to earn it. These principles seem to be generally accepted, although plenty of disputes are possible as to the level of services or income that should be made available.

The pressure towards equality is strong; and since resources are limited, planning becomes essential. It is quite unthinkable that we should ever return to the *laissez-faire* of the Victorian era. It follows that a close watch must be kept on the National Income, for that is the sole source of payment for all the welfare services that are to be provided. We must stimulate the aggregate net product of our people, so that they have a larger 'cake' to share out. This means we must devise optimum uses for our resources; we must train labour for a wide variety of new jobs, and we must retrain it when a change of technology results in the withering away of old industries.

The Government, then, is interested in the National Income. It must be measured, considered, and criticized. It must be stimulated and expanded if possible, and restrained if it changes in undesirable ways. As the chosen representative of the people, the Government has a mandate to pursue particular policies and exert particular influences on the nation's income.

(3) National Income Statistics

Every year the Central Statistical Office (C.S.O.) publishes a Government 'Blue Book' called *National Income and Expenditure*. It appears in the summer months and records the figures for income and expenditure up to the previous December. The 1976 issue therefore includes the figures up to December 1975. It also shows the figures for all the years since 1954, so that students of trends in business activity, Government expenditure etc. can compare the figures for over twenty years.

The compilation of these statistics is clearly a very laborious task. We have to add up the total income of the nation, and there are over 50 million of us. Moreover, in order to double-check and triple-check the answers, the C.S.O. works the figures out in three different ways, each way being based on a different aspect. The three aspects are:

(*a*) *The national output*—the creation of wealth by the nation's industries. This is valued at factor cost, so it must be the same as (*b*) below.

(*b*) *The national income*—the incomes of all the citizens.

(*c*) *The national expenditure*—because whatever we receive we spend, or lend to the banks who invest it, so that the addition of all the expenditure should come to the same as the other two figures.

Put in its simplest form we can express this as an equation:

National Output = National Income = National Expenditure

To understand the meaning of this relationship let us consider a packet of dehydrated mashed potato. What is the value of such a prepared food? The farmer rented his farm, paying rent to a landlord, and borrowed capital to buy machinery, paying interest on the loan. He employed a farmhand to help him, paying him wages, and he made a profit for himself. Suppose the price of the packet of mashed potato is 0·20. Possibly 0·02 represents the rent paid to the landlord, 0·02 represents the interest on the capital borrowed, 0·03 represents the wages of the labourer and 0·03 represents the farmer's profit. At this point the farmer sold the potatoes to a manufacturer who also pays rent, interest, and wages to his workers, and earns a profit for himself. Let us suppose that these payments are 0·01, 0·01, 0·02, and 0·02. This still leaves the wholesaler and retailer to perform their functions and there is only 0·04 left as their share. The production value of 0·20 is the same thing as the income paid to the various producers who have co-operated in the production of this commodity. Remember, to an economist a commodity is not fully produced until it reaches the final consumer, so that the income received by all these people is part of the production cost. Finally, as we all spend the income we receive, or lend it to the banks who loan it to others to spend, the total income is the same as the total expenditure.

(4) Using the National Output for calculating National Income

The National Output is the total of consumer goods and services, plus the total of the producer goods created by the various firms in the industries of the nation. The figures are collected on a 'value-added' basis to avoid double-counting. For example, suppose the forestry industry cuts timber and hauls it to a mill; the value of the timber when sold to the sawmill owner will be the value added by the primary producer, i.e. the forestry firm. When the sawmill has cut it to planks, weathered them for several months, and finally sells them to a furniture manufacturer, we cannot value the output of the sawmill at the total price paid by the furniture manufacturer. The price he pays includes the forestry price, so that only the 'value added' must be counted as the output of the millowner.

The total output of all the industries gives the **Gross National Product.** For several reasons this is not yet a correct answer for National Output. Since some of this output is for the benefit of owners abroad (i.e. foreign investors), it cannot be regarded as our output. Similarly we have the benefit of output achieved in foreign countries by our investments abroad. The result of these movements is a favourable balance to us, and appears in Table 39 as a net figure: net property income from abroad. Another modification in the figure is a deduction for stock appreciation. This adjustment is rather large because in 1975 stocks changed greatly in value due to inflation.

Another 'adjustment for financial services' was caused by high interest payments to foreigners. These reduce the output of banks, because foreigners get the benefit. The **residual error** is the result of errors in the collection of figures. It is only about one per cent of the total, and is unavoidable when so many figures are collected.

Finally, the total figure for the output has to be reduced by the amount of depreciation on capital assets. The 'net' national product, which citizens can enjoy, is thus determined.

Table 39. Calculating national income from national output

U.K. National Product by Industry, in £millions	1975	Enter current figures here
Agriculture, forestry and fishing	2,959	
Mining and quarrying	1,684	
Manufacturing	30,129	
Construction	6,539	
Gas, electricity and water	2,995	
Transport	5,772	
Communications	2,809	
Distributive trades	10,188	
Insurance, banking and finance	7,727	
Ownership of dwellings	5,535	
Public administration and defence	7,107	
Public health and education services	7,154	
Other services	10,454	
Total domestic output	101,052	
Deduct:		
Stock appreciation 5,203		
Adjustment for financial services 3,623	8826	
	92,226	
Add: Net property income from abroad 949		
Residual error 920	1,869	
	94,095	
Less:		
Estimated depreciation on capital assets	10,907	
Aggregate net national product	83,188	

(5) Using Factor Incomes for calculating National Income

What has the nation received as income? The answer is that every citizen has received his rewards as a factor of production, i.e. he has received rent, wages, interest, or profit. The 'Blue Book' lists these as shown in Table 40. It sometimes puzzles students to know why the figures for national output should agree with the figures for national income. The explanation is that when we value output, asking ourselves what it is worth, the answer is that it is worth what the producer received for it, and *that* must be the same as the factor income he paid. Since the sale price of his produce is the reward he pays to all his factors, with profit as the residue, then the national output and the national factor income must agree—for they are the same thing. Every commodity is merely a collection of services of those who proposed its production, made its raw materials available, worked on it in its progress to completion, transported, warehoused, marketed, and finally retailed it.

In Table 40 the following points are of interest:

(*a*) The contributions made by the employer to National Health Insurance and other funds are treated as part of the incomes of the employee. Clearly these funds are accumulated for the benefit of the employee who makes use of them when his circumstances (illness, unemployment, or old age) entitle him to do so. Similarly the cost of free clothing, food etc. to members of the Armed Forces are classed as income of the soldier, sailor etc.

(*b*) The surpluses of public corporations and public enterprises are part of the national income. Although not enjoyed by any individual they are part of the common fund administered by the Government.

(*c*) The total income received must be reduced by the amount of depreciation suffered on the nation's capital, whether privately or socially owned.

Table 40. Calculating national income from factor incomes

U.K. National Income Rewards to Factors in £millions		1975	Enter current figures here
Incomes from employment:			
Wages and salaries	59,292		
Pay in cash and kind of H.M. Forces	1,296		
Employers' contributions to National Health Insurance	4,043		
Employers' contributions to other funds	3,550		
		68,181	
Incomes from self-employment			
Professional persons	1,322		
Farmers	1,767		
Other sole traders and partnerships	5,616		
		8,705	
Other incomes			
Profits of companies		10,387	
Surpluses of public corporations		2,898	
Surpluses of other public enterprises		114	
Rent		7,144	
		97,429	
Less: Stock appreciation		5,203	
		92,226	
Add: Net property income from abroad	949		
Residual error	920	1,869	
		94,095	
Less: Estimated depreciation on capital assets		10,907	
Total factor incomes		£83,188	

(6) Using Total Expenditure for calculating National Income

The third method of calculating the National Income is by counting up the total expenditure of citizens and of firms, Government departments and local authorities. Some of this is expenditure on consumption goods, but some of it is investment in fixed assets, buildings, motor vehicles, plant and machinery, etc. This is listed as 'capital formation' in Table 41.

One difficulty in counting expenditure is that many items purchased have taxes added on to their sales price, while some are subsidized, i.e. sold cheaper than their cost price. Adjustments for taxes and subsidies are made in the Table.

Table 41. Calculating national income from total expenditure

U.K. National Expenditure in £ millions		1975	Enter current figures here
Expenditure of Consumers			
Food	12,092		
Alcoholic drink	4,902		
Tobacco	2,741		
Housing	9,201		
Fuel and Light	2,927		
Clothing	5,320		
Durable goods	4,858		
Other household goods	1,795		
Books, newspapers and magazines	973		
Chemists' goods	1,048		
Travel (including running cars)	5,929		
Other goods and services	11,587		
		63,373	
Public authority expenditure		22,907	
Capital formation		20,510	
Growth of stocks		-1,349	
Total domestic expenditure at market prices		105,441	
Deduct: Net result of exports and imports	2,155		
Indirect taxes on consumer goods	14,046		
		16,201	
Add:		89,240	
Subsidies	3,906		
Net property Income from abroad	949		
		4,855	
		94,095	
Less: Estimated depreciation on capital assets.		10,907	
		£ 83,188	

(7) Difficulties in Calculating National Income

When calculating the National Income there are very great difficulties to be overcome. The collection of data is never easy, but before it is even collected we must define clearly what information we require. The problems of definition, of double-counting, of collection (and compulsion if necessary), of analysis and interpretation, and finally of publication, are very great.

Definitions. A special volume of information (*National Accounts Statistics —Sources and Methods*) is published regularly by H.M. Stationery Office. It contains reference numbers for all the figures which appear in published tables of information. Wherever these figures are used the reference number is printed too, and the reader or student can turn up the exact definition for himself. Thus the definition of 'Consumers' Expenditure' in Table 41 is 'Expenditure on consumers' goods and services by persons and non-profit making bodies, *plus* the value of income in kind'.

It follows that if a limited company buys headed notepaper for use in the office it will not be included; but if the Automobile Association, a voluntary association of motorists, does the same thing it will be included as expenditure by consumers.

If the reader envisages the enormous variety of purchases made of the sort just described he will get some idea of the work involved in obtaining these statistics.

Double-counting. We have already seen that double-counting can occur when output is considered, so that each firm must only count the 'value added' to the product by its activities. A similar type of double-counting might occur where gifts take place. If a father earns an income of 2,500·00 and sends his son 100·00, this 100·00 must not be counted as income of both father and son. Similarly where a husband gives his wife housekeeping money the family income is not increased. Where taxation redistributes income from rich to poor we must be careful not to count both amounts: if it is counted as income to the rich we must leave out the welfare payments to the poor.

Inadequate Information caused by poor Collection Procedures

Some figures are derived from other figures collected for quite different purposes. Thus income tax payments are used to discover much information about incomes, but as many people pay no income tax there is a gap in the figures where these lower incomes are concerned. We can get some pretty broad ideas of how many there are of such persons because every employee pays National Health Contributions. The difference between the number of incomes that are taxed and the number of persons paying National Health contributions must be the lower-paid workers. How much do they earn, though? We shall have to employ sampling techniques to discover this, based on statistically selected samples from a range of industries and firms.

Analysis, Interpretation, and Publication

In the analysis and interpretation of these figures it is necessary to decide what will be the most useful information for the purposes of those eventually using the data. Often it is the trend that is interesting, for where public expenditure is involved the optimum use of resources requires us to avoid expenditure where possible. An education authority may force a few more children into classrooms for a few years to avoid building an extra school with a rather limited life use. The bulge in the birth-rate will soon pass, and an under-utilized building will then be left on the authority's hands.

If we wish to study trends the index-number approach may be the most useful. If we wish to know absolute figures is it desirable to publish also a table where these absolute figures have been adjusted to take account of price changes. For example, two of the tables in the *National Blue Book* are about Consumer Expenditure at Current Prices and at 'base year' prices. The following extracts from the 1976 Blue Book show the difference. The reader will notice what a contrast there is between the impressions conveyed about the consumption of these products by the two sets of figures.

Table 42. Consumers' expenditure at current prices and base-year prices

Consumers' expenditure in £ millions	1970 (Base year)	1975 At current prices	1975 (At 1970 prices)
Food	6,375	12,092	6,418
Alcoholic drink	2,299	4,902	3,091
Tobacco (etc. Tables 24 and 25)	1,720	2,741	1,746

In publication there is a further difficulty. Firms and industries using the published data will want them to be as useful as possible, but if definitions are repeatedly up-dated the figures of previous years become less useful for showing trends since the basis on which they were calculated has been changed. One has to accept a compromise between keeping a series of figures unbroken and keeping the series meaningful in a society that is changing. These are statistical problems too, and for a discussion of this topic the reader is referred to any appropriate text such as *Statistics Made Simple*.

(8) Uses and Limitations of National Income Statistics

There are many uses of National Income Statistics, but the economist must be careful in the conclusions he draws. Sweeping assertions made from statistical material have so often been proved wrong, that the popular view has become that there are 'lies, damned lies and statistics'. This is often unfair to the statisticians; it is the politician or economist who uses them carelessly and without remembering their limitations, who is responsible for the trouble.

The following uses are the most important:

(a) *As a Basis for Assessing and Comparing the Standards of Living*. When considering the standard of living of a people at any given time we must remember the difference between money incomes and real incomes, and must remember the distribution of income. A wealthy nation may have its wealth distributed evenly or unevenly. In comparing changes in the standard of living over the years the total population affects the average income, so that average income per head will be a more valuable indication of living standards than total National Income.

Comparisons between countries must take into account such matters as the climate of each country concerned. African incomes compare more favourably with British incomes if you leave out of the British income the portion necessarily expended on shelter, heating, and warm clothing. Economic welfare is not the same as social welfare, for the economist does not exclude antisocial production from production. Thus it may be argued that the creation of 'disservices' reduces national income rather than enhances it. Examples of disservices might be the creation of methods of destruction, gambling dens, and 'useless' advertising. A. C. Pigou, in his great work, *The Economics of Welfare*, saw any National Income as the source of the welfare of its people; but the figure of private net product must be reduced by the extent by which it embodies disservices, to give the Social Net Product. Thus the pollution of rivers by industries is a reduction in the social welfare that can be enjoyed by the people.

The division between consumption and investment is also important when comparing the National Incomes of different countries, or of the same country between one period and another. Thus if a country's wealth is being mainly used to create capital goods the standard of living will be reduced. Politicians in Britain were often accused in earlier times of promising 'Jam tomorrow, but never jam today'. This is currently true of many developing countries; the accumulation of capital is a bitter process.

(*b*) *As an Aid to Government in Planning the Economy*. The National Income figures are a useful base from which to start the control of the economy. By measuring what that income is we can see what is needed, and what is possible to achieve in the future. The Government becomes aware of the growth areas in the economy, and the areas where growth is less than average. This helps it to plan the location of industry before serious structural unemployment starts to occur, and to keep the whole nation making progress. It can correct tendencies which appear to be undesirable because they do not conform with the expressed national aspirations of the people, and it can see which industries need developing and which should be contracted.

(9) Summary of Chapter Twenty-six

1. Alfred Marshall defined National Income as 'the aggregate net product of, and the sole source of payment for, all the agents of production'.

2. We measure the National Income because we wish to control the economy to obtain the maximum economic welfare from it.

3. There are three methods of counting up the National Income. They are the aggregate-net-production method, the total-factor-incomes method, and the total-national-expenditure method.

4. In all these methods care is needed to avoid double-counting.

5. Clear definitions of the measurements to be made are essential, and must be borne in mind when using or interpreting the data.

(10) Suggested Further Reading

Beckerman, W.: *Introduction to National Income Analysis*. Weidenfeld & Nicolson: London, 1968.

Hicks, J. R.: *The Social Framework*. Oxford U.P.: London, 1960.

Stone, R., and Stone, G.: *National Income and Expenditure*. Bowes and Bowes: London, 1966.

Blue Book on National Income and Expenditure. H.M. Stationery Office: London (annually, about September).

Exercises Set 26

1. What is the National Income? How is it measured?

2. In what three ways can the National Income be measured? Why are the three methods sure to give the same answer apart from residual errors?

3. What are the main factors affecting the standard of living?

4. The National Income of Great Britain has changed as follows:

	£ million
1948	10,517
1958	20,408
1968	36,686
1972	48,116

Does this mean that the average Briton is better off? What other information would be helpful in giving a clear picture of the changes in the standard of living over these years.

5. Distinguish between 'real' National Income and 'money' National Income, using the following figures to illustrate your answer.

	1958	1963	1968	1973
National Income (£ million)	20,000	27,000	37,000	50,000
Index of final-output prices	90	100·0	120	160

6. Why is the standard of living lower in Zambia than in Great Britain?

7. Distinguish between National Income and National Capital. Under what circumstances could a nation be said to be living on its capital?

8. Why is it difficult to compare the National Income of one country with that of another?

9. Which of the following would you include in the National Income:

(*a*) Wages paid to farm labourers.

(*b*) Dividend paid to a member of a co-operative society.

(*c*) Family allowances.

(*d*) A win on the football pools.

(*e*) A husband's birthday gift to his wife of £5.

(*f*) The royalty earned by an author.

10. 'Wages' in National Incomes Statistics are defined as 'the cash earnings of wage-earners before deduction of personal tax and National Insurance contributions, plus income in kind less expenses of employment'. Why is such a definition necessary, and what are the implications behind each part of it?

CHAPTER TWENTY-SEVEN

FLUCTUATIONS IN ECONOMIC ACTIVITY

(1) History of the Trade Cycle

Throughout the nineteenth century, and until just before the start of the Second World War, economists recorded cycles of business activity without offering much that was helpful to cure them. These trade cycles were a serious problem for the mass of the population, who seemed destined to suffer endlessly the fear of unemployment. The inter-war period 1918–39 was particularly depressing, for it was one of unrelieved gloom in many industrial areas, reaching a peak in 1932 when there were twelve million unemployed in the United States and three million in Great Britain. The U.K. national average of unemployment was over 20 per cent, and in many areas it was over 30 per cent.

There were 15 cycles of business activity between 1792 and 1913, with an average of eight years to each cycle. Each cycle of activity consisted of an upward movement of business activity lasting about $3\frac{1}{2}$ years before reaching a peak from which it fell away rapidly into a depression, which endured rather more stubbornly, taking about $4\frac{1}{2}$ years on average to recover. The war activity of 1914–18 provided a particularly strong boom, followed by a very severe depression which was finally ended only by preparations for the Second World War.

It is hardly surprising that such a long experience of unemployment and under-employment bred very bitter feelings in the trade unions and political movements of those days. The prosperity enjoyed between 1945 and 1974, and even in the late 1970s, seems nothing short of a miracle (and just as transitory) to many who lived through the depression between the wars.

(2) Causes of Trade Cycles

No two cycles of business activity were alike, and all were to some extent related to their own peculiar economic level of development, or to some external event like war. For example, the boom years of 1791–4 were connected with a mania for building canals, and the boom years of 1825, 1836, and 1845 were all connected with surges of speculative activity connected with railway construction. The severity of the depressions following these booms were deepened by the loss of capital from private savings which had occurred during the speculations. Excessive saving is certainly connected with depressions.

Some of the chief causes of trade cycles are as follows:

(a) *Fluctuations caused by the durable nature of producer goods.* When a machine-tool industry is set up, it seems inescapable that fluctuations in business activity must occur. Suppose, for example, an industry is established to make a new type of machine for which there is a demand of 1,000. The life of these machines is ten years on average. At first the industry will be looking everywhere for engineers to make the first 1,000 machines, poaching labour from similar industries with offers of higher wages, and thus helping to create boom conditions. Once the first factories are equipped the boom will ease off, and eventually the industry will settle down to producing the annual requirement of, say, 100 machines. Engineers attracted to the industry in boom times will now be unemployed.

Not only this, but there is a multiplying effect in the economy of the boom enjoyed by the engineers, because they spent their wages instead of saving them. The boom wages of the engineers provided prosperity for grocers, publicans, landlords, bookmakers, and many other trades. The extent to which this multiplying effect ramifies through the economy depends on the propensity to consume of the original recipients of the income (this is explained more fully later on page 318). The point here is that there is also a multiplying effect when the depression comes along. The unemployed engineer buys less food, less clothing, less alcohol, and bets less frequently.

Pursuing the example further, this industry is now supplying 100 machines per year as a regular undertaking. Suppose there is a 10 per cent increase in demand for the product made by the machines. This requires 100 extra machines, because the industry consists of 1,000 machines. The 100 extra machines means that the size of the machine-tool industry is doubled. Once again a mad scramble starts for men to meet this increased demand; but when the order has been met there will again be a need for only 100 machines a year for nine years, when 200 will again be required.

The name 'accelerator' has been given to a movement of this sort which injects spending power into the economy and causes a surge of activity.

Clearly all sorts of variations are possible in such a cyclical activity. For instance the 10 per cent rise in demand might fall away in the following year leaving excess capacity in the industry. This would be corrected by not ordering any machines at all, thus leaving the industry in a very depressed state indeed.

(*b*) *Fluctuations caused by changing expectations.* Some primary industries are particularly susceptible to fluctuations because of climatic conditions. Thus sugar cane harvests can be decimated by hurricanes, wheat crops fail through diseases, frozen rivers interrupt supplies from particular regions. The initial effect is a sharp rise in prices which encourages producers in other areas to think that it will pay to turn factors over to that type of production. Once established such new regions form severe competition to the established suppliers, and in normal or good years the world price will fall to a very low level. Sometimes in such circumstances producers band together to control the price at which they will sell the product, but this only maintains the industries in existence and often encourages further suppliers to come in. Sooner or later someone cuts the price and 'the bottom falls out of the market'. Plantations are abandoned and the jungle creeps in. The whole cycle of activity starts again.

(*c*) *Fluctuations caused by monetary changes.* Some economists consider that changes in the quantity of money play a vital part in cyclical activity, and nearly all economists agree that monetary influences play some part in the development of booms and slumps. Monetary activities, as we shall see, are a chief method of influencing the economy today, and the post-war success in managing prosperity is certainly connected with these activities.

It also appears likely that the regularity of the trade cycles between 1792 and 1913 resulted from the monetary movements inseparable from the Gold-Standard mechanism. Of the fifteen cycles only three were longer than nine years and only one was less than seven years. By contrast, after the Gold Standard was abandoned in 1914, a very long depression set in. The return to the Gold Standard in 1925 did not cure this long depression because countries refused to honour the Gold-Standard rules, and this made the deflation in Great Britain more serious than ever. The beginnings of Keynesian economics, and the rearmament programme finally provided the increased demand needed to start recovery.

Monetary movements do not seem to start a trade cycle so much as keep it going once it has started. Bankers are cautious and have to look to the security of their investments. It follows that in the generally gloomy atmosphere of a prolonged slump they are the last persons to start up a bout of activity. In 1933 President F. D. Roosevelt begged and appealed to bankers to show a bit of optimism, but they were not to be roused. In the days of the Gold Standard there was a practical factor at work, the arrival of gold shipments to increase the reserves. Once something happens to promote confidence the bankers' more generous credit policies themselves generate the boom. Prospects of profitability get daily brighter, and the boom gathers momentum. In contrast to their inability to cure a slump, the banks can be very influential in curing a boom that is getting out of hand. All they need to do is to be a little more careful to whom they lend money. This will take the pressure out of a boom and start its down-hill movement into a slump.

(*d*) *Fluctuations caused by an excessive propensity to save.* One of the chief features of a depression is the tendency of those with some income to put it away for a rainy day, which seems all the closer because of the desperate unemployment all around. This keeps the monetary demand in the economy low, and reduces the prospects of profitability.

With reduced prospects of profitability, businessmen will not borrow at any price. In 1932 the rate of interest was only 2 per cent but businessmen would not borrow. It was Keynes who showed that spending was more important than saving if the economy was to recover. What was needed was more demand, so that the prospects of profitability would increase. This stood economics on its head. It turned established virtues into vices. Thrift was antisocial: the prodigal son was the man to admire. Keynesian economics kept the boom going for 30 years. But we are getting ahead of our argument. Before we consider the management of prosperity this is an appropriate moment to take a detailed look at unemployment. It will enable us then to move on to look at the present-day problems of inflation, stagflation and slumpflation.

(3) Types of Unemployment

There are many types of unemployment. We may classify them according to their persistence. In increasing order of persistence we have:

(*a*) *Normal, transitional unemployment.* This exists at nearly all times, and some economists argue that a normal rate of unemployment of 2–3 per cent does no harm to anyone. For many years British policy aimed at keeping unemployment at the 2 per cent level overall, but of course there were pockets where the level of unemployment was higher. Normal transitional unemployment is unemployment that lasts only a week or two as a man moves between jobs, or around the country to work. Where wages are high, and income-tax rebates occur at times of unemployment, a man is under less pressure to resume work at once. He may feel he is scoring off the Government by recouping his tax and taking a short 'holiday' between jobs. Clearly this sort of unemployment is not a serious matter.

(*b*) *Casual and seasonal unemployment.* Some occupations are adversely affected by weather conditions, and workers in these trades expect a certain amount of casual unemployment. The building trade is one such occupation, and stevedoring is another. Ships' hatches have to be kept covered in bad weather, and casual labour has been a chief complaint of dockers for many years. In Britain this casual employment has recently been changed, but it is still a feature of other countries' dock work. Seasonal unemployment affects hotels and restaurants, and is also a feature of agriculture. Generally speaking such unemployment is inevitable and tends to be overcome by casual labour. The housewife in a seaside resort helps in a cafe during the holiday season; students wash dishes at holiday camps and prepare vegetables in kitchens of holiday hotels.

(*c*) *Frictional unemployment.* As its name implies this type of unemployment only exists because of economic frictions in the labour market. For example, where engineers are required on Merseyside it would seem reasonable for an unemployed man in Newcastle to move there to new work. He may be unable to do so for domestic reasons, or may have some psychological objection. Sometimes such difficulties can be overcome if housing can be made available, or if the costs of moving are paid.

(*d*) *Structural or local unemployment.* Structural unemployment, which often affects particular localities, is caused by a change in the demand for the products of a given industry. The structure of the nation's industry as a whole is altered by the closing down of this particular industry; the factors are transferred to other uses. This often results in unemployment because labour may be highly specific, and therefore immobile between industries. A cotton-mill operative is unlikely to succeed in a shoe factory, and a rivetter cannot immediately transfer to electronics. These types of unemployment need special solutions. Retraining and resettlement are difficult, but must be undertaken. The pace of modern technology indicates that such problems are likely to increase, not decrease. It has been estimated that within twenty years one-fifth of all production will be with materials not yet invented. This type of unemployment is discussed more fully on page 358, where Government policies to cure it are discussed.

(*e*) *Cyclical unemployment.* As already mentioned, this type of unemployment presented extremely serious problems a quarter of a century ago. It has now been largely mastered by Government activity to control the development of cycles. It is discussed fully in Chapter Twenty-eight.

(*f*) *Unemployment in slumpflation.* In inflationary times cuts in expenditure are called for, particularly in the public sector, while in the private sector employers will seek to reduce labour forces, since wages represent a major cost item. Unemployment is therefore a feature of inflation today, and the term 'slumpflation' has been coined to describe it. The ability of strong trade unions to restrict entry to their industries prevents wage rates falling. This fuels both the unemployment and the inflation.

(4) Summary of Chapter Twenty-seven

1. An enduring feature of free-enterprise capitalism from the earliest times was the trade cycle, regularly recurring rhythms of business activity: boom–slump–boom–slump.

2. These trade cycles have been partly explained by real situations inevitable to production, like the durable character of capital equipment, natural events like climatic changes and human events like wars.

3. The monetary system seems to be very influential in cyclical changes, but it is less effective in curing a slump than in collapsing a boom. It may therefore be said to have a neutral rather than a positive effect on the trade cycle.

4. The excessive preoccupation of individuals with saving for hard times has a particularly unfortunate effect on the economy when times are indeed hard.

5. Unemployment may be temporary, seasonal, structural, or cyclical in nature. Each type of unemployment requires appropriate treatment, and the cure for one type of unemployment may cause harmful effects if applied wrongly in another situation. Slumpflation may also cause unemployment.

(5) Suggested Further Reading

Beveridge, Lord: *Full Employment in a Free Society*. Allen & Unwin: London, 1960.
Harvey, J., *Intermediate Economics*. 2nd. Edn. Macmillan: London, 1971.
Hobsbawn, E. J.: *Labouring Men*. Weidenfeld & Nicolson: London, 1968.

Exercises Set 27

1. What is meant by 'the trade cycle'? Describe a typical 'cycle' and the economic fluctuations that take place during it.

2. Before 1914 trade cycles were fairly regular, from 1914 to 1939 they were extended, from 1939 we have hardly noticed them. Explain.

3. Trade cycles can partly be explained by the durable nature of producer goods. Explain.

4. 'The banks are a great help in curing a depression, and are never involved in starting one.' Analyse this statement critically.

5. What is meant by (*a*) frictional unemployment, (*b*) structural unemployment?

6. 'The most difficult problem with declining industries is to transfer the men to new employments. Somehow you have to teach old dogs new tricks.' Discuss.

7. 'The industry has used us all our lives and now we are getting old it is failing us just as we need support.' 'You joined the industry to help yourselves, not to help the industry. On the contrary, we have provided 5,000·00 capital for every one of you. You must retrain for new employment. This industry is dying.'
Discuss these two attitudes to a declining industry's problems.

8. 'Structural unemployment will occur more and more frequently as the pace of technology increases. We envisage retraining a worker four times during his working life' (French education official). Explain this statement.

9. 'Manufacturers are welcome in Cornwall, especially if they will arrange their manufacturing to fit in with the peak tourist trade from June 30th to August 31st.' How might a manufacturer do this? What benefits might he achieve by leaving the London area to set up in Cornwall? What extra costs might he incur?

10. What is cyclical unemployment? What suggestions have been made regarding its causes?

CHAPTER TWENTY-EIGHT

MANAGING PROSPERITY

(1) Introduction

Since the great slump of the 1930s the management of prosperity has been the major preoccupation of governments. In the 1930s the problem was to cure the slump, and the solution was the adoption of 'Keynesian Economics'. This managed the economy by controlling the total demand in the economy, for the slump was caused by insufficient total monetary demand. This **aggregate monetary demand (A.M.D.** for short) was supplied as explained later in this chapter. The result was a quarter of a century of prosperity, with the general standard of living of the majority of the population in the United Kingdom rising all the time. Later this general prosperity produced side effects which caused demand to become greater than was desirable. The problem then became one of limiting aggregate monetary demand, and the control of **domestic credit expansion (D.C.E.** for short) became the essential policy. In this chapter we try to follow these two major developments.

(2) Persistent General Unemployment

If unemployment is so general throughout the economy that in every area there are unemployed, and in some areas there are very bad levels of unemployment, with men who have not worked for years, then we have a situation described by economists as 'persistent general unemployment'. It is no good trying to solve this problem by microeconomic methods, by looking at individual areas, or individual firms or individual industries. We have to use macroeconomic methods, looking at the whole economy.

What is usually wrong in these conditions of persistent general unemployment? It is not the shortage of capital, for often capital is freely available and very cheap indeed. During the slump of the 1930s all Governments pursued cheap-money policies. Bank rate was 2 per cent from 1932 until 1951. At these rates anyone who wanted to borrow money for entrepreneurial purposes should have been able to do so. Why did they not borrow? Because in order to proceed with business activity the entrepreneur must feel sure that he is going to receive back what he has invested with a reasonable profit. In times of general persistent unemployment he cannot feel that this will happen. In other words the **prospects of profitability** are poor. The entrepreneur lacks confidence in the chances of success. This was what led President Roosevelt, struggling to cure the massive slump in the United States in 1933, to cry 'All we want is confidence'.

(3) Aggregate Monetary Demand

We have said several times that there is a circular flow of money round the economy, from the firms to the individual members of the public and back again. We must now build up a detailed picture of this circular flow of income, and in particular look for fluctuations in it. We can best do so by considering a set of diagrams of which Fig. 89 (overleaf) is the first.

Fig. 89 shows how the earnings of the general public are used to demand goods and services. This total demand for goods and services is called

aggregate monetary demand (A.M.D. for short). We shall see that this is the most crucial factor to be considered when there is general persistent unemployment.

Fig. 89 is, however, rather unrealistic, because in fact people rarely spend all they earn. Some of their earnings are saved, but if we imagine that the savings are banked, and loaned by the banks to the entrepreneurs, then there is no real change from the situation in Fig. 89. Let us now consider the question of saving: what makes people save?

Savings

Out of the incomes individuals receive they spend in order to buy a reasonable 'basket' of the world's goods and services. The residue is savings. This

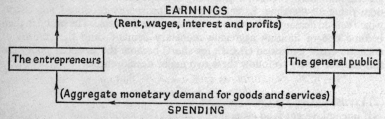

Fig. 89. Circular flow of income in a static economy (earnings = spending)

Notes:
1. The entrepreneurs running the firms are paying out in rent, wages, interest, and profit the entire proceeds of their activities. For the moment we can ignore corporation tax.
2. Imagine that the public spend all that they receive, so that the aggregate monetary demand for goods and services (which are of course supplied by the firms) is the same as the earnings. The entrepreneurs are therefore receiving back all they paid out.
3. The economy is in equilibrium, i.e. in the next period of activity the level of earnings paid will be the same as in the previous period, and all the earnings received will be returned to the entrepreneurs in the form of spending.
4. The economy is static, neither expanding nor contracting.

makes saving appear to be a rather passive activity, but in fact spending and saving are opposite sides of the same coin.

The general public at any given time have a certain propensity to consume and a certain propensity to save. The poor have a higher propensity to consume than the rich, and the rich have a higher propensity to save. We are, of course, talking relatively here, as already explained (see page 201).

Generally speaking people spend (*a*) to provide themselves with the basic necessities of life, and (*b*) when they are confident of future prosperity, so that they feel less need to provide for hard times. However they also tend to spend (*c*) when they feel that the value of money is falling so that savings will leave them worse off in the future.

Generally speaking people save when (*a*) their incomes are large, so that the bare necessities etc. are easily provided, and (*b*) they are unsure of future prosperity, fearing a decline in their future living standards due to a slump.

They also tend to save more when (c) they feel that money is stable in value, or even rising in value, so that they will not lose by saving.

Spending is further encouraged by:

(a) *A more equal division of the National Income*, because this gives poorer people a larger share in the income and they have a high propensity to consume. Thus taxation to redistribute income from rich to poor tends to increase spending. The rich would probably have saved the money if they had not been taxed. The pensioner, or the housewife who receives a family allowance, will almost certainly spend it.

(b) *Easy payment schemes*, like hire purchase, continuous credit, budget accounts, and bankers' credit cards. All these schemes enable a person to enjoy goods and services today and pay for them in instalments later. They therefore increase spending, and aggregate demand rises.

(c) *Persuasive advertising and new products*. Branded goods, artificially made 'differently new' encourage ostentation, and spending therefore increases.

Saving is further encouraged by:

(a) *The activities of institutions* such as banks, building societies, save-as-you-earn schemes, unit trusts, stock exchanges etc.

(b) *High rates of interest*. Although the influence of the rate of interest is probably less than was at one time supposed, the fact remains that private individuals are much concerned by it. Building-society deposits by small savers always rise when the interest rate is raised, and at the first sign of a shortage of funds for mortgage purposes the societies consider raising the rates.

Saving also takes place through the activities of business and the Government. Firms plough back profits into expansion, and also create reserve funds to meet future contingencies by buying portfolios of investments or insurance policies. In Britain today savings by firms are responsible for over £12,500 million per annum, while individuals save a further £12,500 million. Corporate saving is therefore as important as private saving.

Government saving is chiefly in the form of budget surpluses, but it may also result from surplus contributions to specific contributary schemes like national insurance funds, superannuation funds etc.

To return to the circular flow of income, if we include savings in our picture the result will be as shown overleaf in Fig. 90.

Even this picture is not quite advanced enough for real life, for we have left out the whole question of taxation and the part the Government plays in the economy. Before we move on to include these aspects, let us look for a moment at investment and what it means to the economy.

Investment

Investment is the employment of factors (land, labour, and capital) in the creation of capital goods (producer goods) and stocks of raw materials and finished goods.

Investment is not the same thing to an economist as it is to a stockbroker. The purchase of bonds or stocks or shares in a company is a financial investment; the economist is interested in investment as a 'real' activity creating plant and machinery, buildings, roads and railways, harbours and airports.

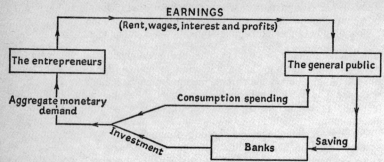

Fig. 90. Circular flow of income in an economy with dynamic potential (savings turned into investment)

Notes:

1. People are not consuming their entire incomes, saving is now taking place.
2. If the savings are *hoarded*, i.e. hidden away like a miser's gold, they will be lost to the circular flow of income.
3. Fortunately most people save through one of the institutional investors; the diagram shows 'banks' collecting the savings of the general public and passing them on to the entrepreneurs. Savings become investment.
4. As both 'spending' and 'investment' return to the entrepreneurs they form together the aggregate monetary demand. If the investment exactly equals the saving, the level of activity in the economy will be the same as before, i.e. the economy is static. *But* now we have a possible point where a static economy could become a dynamic, or changing, economy. The banks may 'create credit' if the entrepreneurs wish to invest more than the people have saved. This will increase the level of activity in the economy, and move it up into a boom. If the banks are nervous about prospects, or entrepreneurs are not optimistic, some of the savings will lie idle and the economy will turn down into a slump.

Some of these assets are created by public investment, others by private entrepreneurs, but both must use the savings that have been collected from the public. We shall first consider what motivates the entrepreneur to invest.

Private investment and the prospects of profitability. Entrepreneurs are in business to make profit; the chief factor governing the level of investment is the entrepreneur's view of the prospects of profitability. Many influences contribute to the view he holds, for he must continually weigh up the changes taking place around him. New developments in technology may require him to re-equip his factory if he is to keep ahead of rivals. Government policy may make the prospects brighter, or more gloomy. Changes of taste or fashion may lead him to expand in a particular direction, or introduce new lines.

The entrepreneur who is about to invest money in a project has to estimate the marginal-revenue productivity of the capital he is about to employ. It will be costing him the current rate of interest, but what return will it bring? Capital goods last a long time, and the revenue earned from them is therefore difficult to predict. Will demand continue strong? Will new techniques render this capital obsolete?

The entrepreneur does his best to estimate what the earnings in each of the future years will be. By discounting the yields back to a present value he can compare the cost of the project with the eventual proceeds from it. The arithmetic involved in such calculations is a little tricky, but it is possible to find a rate of interest which makes the present value of the project equal to the future yield from the project. *This rate of interest is called the marginal efficiency of the capital.* If this marginal efficiency is sufficiently above the rate of interest, the entrepreneur will proceed with the project.

Thus an entrepreneur who calculates that the purchase of a vehicle of a certain type will yield him on average a 24 per cent return on capital invested, whereas the rate of interest he must pay to borrow the money to purchase the vehicle is only 10 per cent, will feel confident in proceeding with the project. Certainly he would never proceed with a project where the marginal efficiency of capital is less than the current rate of interest.

Public Investment. Public investment is investment by the Government, by local-government bodies, and by nationalized corporations, to achieve socially desirable aims. Profit does not enter into the consideration except that waste should clearly be avoided wherever possible. The provision of necessary social services is the guideline, whether these are welfare services, education, defence, or more commercial activities like public transport and electricity and gas supply. The social investment required for these services is very great, and some measure of priority has to be decided for each.

In recent years a new technique for deciding these priorities has been developed. It is called **cost benefit analysis**, and has been used with particular success in transport problems such as the construction of motorways and the new Victoria Line of the London Underground.

The essence of cost benefit analysis is the detailed attempt for the first time to quantify (i.e. place a value on) not only the costs but the benefits of any capital project. For example, in deciding whether to construct a new Underground line we must not only calculate the costs of its construction, but the *social costs* involved, which we might describe as 'dis-benefits'. The proposed Underground line might make the lives of people living in houses over it miserable because their sleep is disturbed by the rumble of trains. Placing a monetary valuation on a sleepless night seems a little difficult, but it is surprising how soon standard charges for such dis-benefits can be calculated with reasonable accuracy after objective field research has been carried out. Now against these costs must be set monetary valuations of the benefits. There will of course be income from the fares charged, which will offset a good deal of the cost involved. There are easily calculable benefits like the saving of x minutes on every journey to destinations along the route. There are also less tangible benefits like the happiness of mothers whose children have not been run over because there are y per cent less cars on the roads, their owners having decided to travel by Underground instead. A comparison of the relative merits of various projects enables those concerned with making decisions to do so in full knowledge of the costs and benefits involved.

Investment Generates Savings

One of the major influences on savings is the level of income being received; for as we have seen, the well-to-do save more. It follows that investment must generate savings because every investment in producer goods is paid out as income to the factors constructing the goods produced. A high level of investment makes people more prosperous, and more likely to save.

Savings Equals Investment

One of Lord Keynes's assertions in his famous work, *The General Theory of Employment, Interest and Money*, caused great controversy. It was the proposition that savings and investment are always equal. His proof ran like this:

(i)					*National Income* = *Consumption* + *Saving*

What the public receive as income they either use (consumption) or save.

(ii)	$National\ Income = \dfrac{Production\ of}{consumer\ goods} + \dfrac{Production\ of}{producer\ goods}$
			= *Consumption* + *Investment*

It follows that

Consumption + *Saving* = *Consumption* + *Investment*

Therefore

Savings = *Investment*

In the early days of Capitalism when individual entrepreneurs postponed consumption to accumulate capital, their savings certainly equalled investment. Keynes's explanation of why savings and investment are always equal even in modern times is a little involved, and caused much controversy. Since it was chiefly concerned with a period of mass unemployment it is of less interest today than formerly. The idea seems to go against common sense, for the chief cause of slumps is that everyone is saving and no one is investing. The apparent contradiction here has been reconciled by taking into account the period involved.

We must now return to the circular flow of income around the economy and develop the idea to include the Government's position in the economy. The situation is illustrated in Fig. 91, and explained in the notes below it.

(4) Managing Prosperity—the Nature of the Problem

We must start our consideration of the control of the economy in the 1930s when the capitalist world was staggering through the worst slump it had ever experienced. The persistent general unemployment which had been such a feature of the troughs of the trade cycles over the previous century was more persistent and more general than ever before. A good deal of criticism of the capitalist system prevailed as a result, and since previous booms had been solved by the Boer War and the First World War, one of these criticisms was that capitalism was inseparable from wars. It even proved to be true that recovery from the slump of the 1930s was largely achieved by rearmament. But just before the Second World War, Keynes and others showed how to cure the depression: the solution was to inject purchasing power (i.e. increased aggregate monetary demand) into the economy. The reason why wars cured slumps was that they did just that; the demand for guns, ships, and uniforms raised aggregate monetary demand. It didn't have to be wartime demand, any sort of demand would do. The more massive the unemployment, the more massive the injections of extra monetary demand that would be necessary to cure it; but however much extra spending power was injected there would be

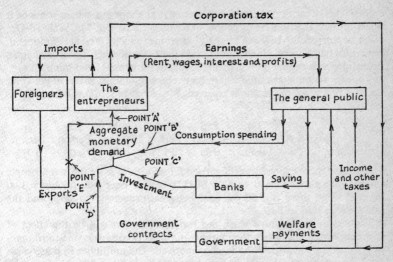

Fig. 91. Circular flow of income in an economy with four possible agents of change (the consumers, the banks, foreigners and the Government)

Notes:

1. Firms have to reduce the profits they distribute to their shareholders because corporation tax is payable to the Government.
2. The general public also pay taxes to the Government, but in return receive, where necessary, welfare payments.
3. There are now four agencies able to affect aggregate monetary demand: the consumers, the banks, foreigners, and the Government.
4. Thus the Government can 'manage' the prosperity of the nation. If a slump begins to develop (due to savings exceeding investment) the Government can compensate for it by increasing aggregate monetary demand. This it does with increased welfare payments, or increased Government contracts.
5. Points 'A', 'B', 'C' 'D', and 'E' are explained later (see page 324).

a multiplying effect, because the money injected would be spent several times, not once. Let us now consider the 'multiplier'.

The Multiplier

To begin, let us consider Mr. Average, who earns a low wage and has a high propensity to consume, while Mr. Well-To-Do earns a very high wage and has a low propensity to consume.

Suppose Mr. Average receives an increase in wages of 1·00 per week. He will promptly spend it, and aggregate monetary demand (A.M.D.) rises by 1·00. Suppose the person he gives it to is also rather poor, and promptly spends it. A.M.D. has now risen by 2·00. If the third person also spends it, A.M.D. will have risen by 3·00. If this went on fast enough and often enough, that single 1·00 would multiply around the economy an infinite number of times. This is rather unrealistic because Mr. Average does not spend his money with other poor people, but spends it at shops etc. where some of it filters off into the pockets of people like Mr. Well-To-Do. Mr. Well-To-Do, when he receives the 1·00 can't think of anything to spend it on at the moment, having all he requires. He therefore saves the 1·00; whether it gets used again or not depends on the entrepreneurs' demand for capital from the banks.

To take a simple example where on average the public saves 50 per cent, i.e. half of any extra income it received, Mr. Average's 1·00 will be spent as follows:

	Mr. A	1st Person	2nd Person	3rd Person	4th Person	5th Person	6th Person
Expenditure	1·00	0·50	0·25	0·12½	0·06	0·03	0·01½

The sum of these expenditures if carried far enough is 2·00; the seven people shown have already spent 1·98. A.M.D. therefore rises 2·00 for every 1·00 injected when there is a 50 per cent marginal propensity to save, and the multiplier is said to be 2.

The reader should now work out for himself what will be the effect of spending Mr. A's £1 when the marginal propensity to save is one-third, one-quarter, and one-tenth of the income received. The multiplier in these cases are 3, 4, and 10, respectively. In fact the multiplier is always the inverse of the fraction saved, i.e. the fraction turned upside down.

It follows that in managing prosperity we must inject sufficient spending power into the economy to raise A.M.D. and expand the economy towards the full-employment level. If we make the money available in the first place to the poorer section of the community the multiplying effect will be large. Unemployment will be cured more quickly, and we shall escape from the slump.

The **marginal propensity to save** is the inclination of the individual to save any *extra* income he happens to receive. The **multiplier** is found by the fraction

$$\frac{1}{marginal\ propensity\ to\ save}$$

Thus if the nation on average saves half of any increment in its income the multiplier is 2, if the nation saves one-third the multiplier is 3, if the nation saves one-tenth the multiplier is 10, and if the nation only saves one-twentieth of its extra income the multiplier is 20. The multiplier is that amount by which any injection of spending power into the economy will be multiplied round the economy by people passing the extra income on to others, who pass it on to third persons, etc.

(5) How does the extra A.M.D. cure a Slump?

A slump is a situation where there is a general persistent unemployment, not only of men but of land and capital too. Factors are lying idle and unproductive. The National Income is reduced, and therefore each individual's share of it is reduced; there is general dissatisfaction and possibly social unrest. Referring to Fig. 91, at point 'A' there is insufficient demand for goods and services. If the economy is to recover, the flow of resources into the firms has to be increased. Who can increase the flow through point 'A'? There are four possibilities: the general public, the banks, the Government, and the foreigners, because they control the flows through points 'B', 'C', 'D', and 'E', respectively. Let us consider each in turn.

(*a*) *The general public.* If the general public are to increase their consumption they must stop saving and start spending. It is all this thrift that is causing the trouble. The rainy day has arrived for which the public have been saving so long, the time has come to go out and spend, spend, spend. Unfortunately they can't do it. The ones who are poorest have spent up long ago; those who have remained in employment are nervous about the future, fearing to become unemployed themselves. The rich fear to spend any more for their present prosperous circumstances are already inviting social unrest: extra expenditure now might appear ostentatious. Charitable works might help, but charity is notoriously chilly, and therefore unfavourably received. Flowpoint 'B' is therefore difficult to open.

(*b*) *The banks.* If the banks are to increase the flow through point 'C' in Fig. 91 they will need the assistance of the entrepreneurs who are running the firms. The banks cannot lend money to, or create credit for, people who do not *want* to borrow. Unfortunately the entrepreneurs are feeling particularly gloomy because the prospects of profitability are so poor. It is a vicious circle really; the prospects cannot improve unless the firms invest in new capital goods, but the firms will not invest in new capital goods until the prospects improve. The following reasons are also important why the banks are of little help in curing slumps.

(i) If the multiplier is to be large the extra income ought to be given to the poor. As the banks never lend to the poor they are not likely to be much help. Any extra loans they make to the well-to-do will promptly be saved by the first recipient taking the income from the borrower of it.

(ii) Banks only lend against collateral, and the unemployed have no collateral. It is therefore of little use expecting banks to cure slumps, for bankers are by definition cautious, and we are looking for a spendthrift—to spend someone else's thrift.

(*c*) *The Government.* We are left with the Government as the only agent able to promote prosperity during slumps. Most readers would agree that there is no one like the Government for spending other people's savings, and this is exactly what is required. It also has two weapons at its command in defeating general persistent unemployment. It can increase A.M.D. in two ways: (i) by increasing welfare payments, (ii) by proceeding with Government contracts for socially desirable projects.

(i) *Welfare payments.* As the name implies, welfare payments are payments to members of the general public whose present welfare is for some reason unsatisfactory. This means the unemployed. If we make generous payments to them they will immediately spend the money, having an infinite capacity to consume after their recent deprivations. The multiplying effect will be great, and increased demand will reach the firms through point B. The firms will cheer up and take a more optimistic view of affairs, and before long they will be worrying the banks for loans. Recovery will be on the way.

(ii) *Government contracts.* Every Government has projects in reserve which it can put into operation. It may be a road, or a school, or a hospital extension, some slum clearance or an atomic-energy project. These will employ factors on socially useful work and the economy will receive the injection of income it requires. To replace the de-pigeonholed projects, a new set must be brought to the design stage. This will offer employment to draughtsmen, architects, etc., and will again raise the level of A.M.D. through Point D.

These major projects are the sort of schemes that would be used to cure a major slump, like the depression of the 1930s. They are not quite so useful for the short-term injections of extra demand needed today. More immediate improvements are achieved by changes in Minimum Lending Rate, hire-purchase controls, etc. Whichever methods are used, within a short while the slump will be cured and we shall be worrying about controlling a boom.

(*d*) *The Foreigners—Export and import effects on the circular flow of income.* One final point about the circular flow of income is that the volume of exports and imports does affect the amount of A.M.D. (aggregate monetary demand) in the system. If we import goods or services the incomes spent are not returned to the entrepreneurs for the following period, but are paid to foreign entrepreneurs instead. If we export goods and services the foreigners buying from us inject spending power into the economy. Therefore a favourable balance of payments increases aggregate monetary demand, and unfavourable balances result in reduced monetary demand through Point E.

Let us now look at the exact mechanism which extra monetary demand triggers off to fire the economy into a boom, using '*Keynesian*' *Economics*. Let us then look at what happens when the boom becomes inflation, and has to be controlled using '*Monetarist*' *Economics*.

(6) Achieving Equilibrium at the Correct Level

An economy is self-regulating in that it will always adjust automatically to a level where the incomes flowing to the public as a result of their ownership of factors (rent, wages, interest and profits) exactly match what they spend either in consumption or as investment by entrepreneurs. How this happens is explained in Fig. 92(*a*) and the notes below it. Before reading these notes and looking carefully at the diagram the reader is urged to watch for the concluding paragraph (5) of the notes. The economy has regulated itself to a steady level of activity, but there is no guarantee that the level is a 'full-employment' level. If it is not, and a large proportion of the factors are unemployed, the government must take steps to put it right. Now study Fig. 92(*a*) and Fig. 92(*b*) which follows from it.

(7) Curing a Slump—Keynesian Measures

Keynesian Economics showed how to cure slumps, a major preoccupation of pre-war governments. From 1946 to 1970 policies of managed prosperity were pursued in the United Kingdom. A common name for such policies is 'demand management policies' because they are concerned with controlling the amount of demand present in the economy.

Unemployment is so debilitating an experience that its prevention is essential if social unrest is to be avoided. The aim of demand management policies is to keep employment somewhere near the 98 per cent level, the other 2 per cent being normal transitional unemployment. When unemployment exceeded 2 per cent the Government used one of its measures for increasing A.M.D. The most useful of these are welfare measures, public-sector activities, monetary measures, fiscal measures, and direct controls.

(*a*) *Welfare measures.* The Government can always inject more spending power into the economy by welfare payments to the poorer section of the population. Although these measures were of great importance in curing the major slump of the 1930s they were of less importance in the years 1946–70, when the economy was managed so 'satisfactorily' that the problem became

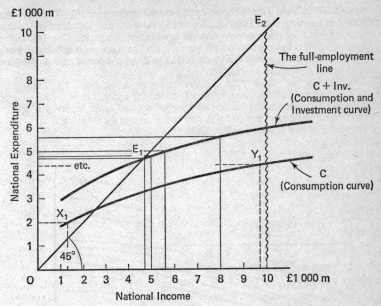

Fig. 92(*a*). The National Income Equilibrium Diagram (Part I)

Notes:

1. In this diagram the income of the nation has been plotted against the expenditure of the nation, on the same scale. The line OE_2 is at 45° to the axes and must represent the situation where income equals expenditure. In mathematical terms it is the locus of points where income equals expenditure.

2. Consider the Point X_1. At this point the citizens are being paid incomes of about £1,300 million but are spending almost twice as much, about £2,000 million. This means they must be dis-saving, or borrowing from their friendly bank manager. Expenditure is greater than income, and the economy is not in equilibrium.

3. Now consider the point Y_1. The citizens are being paid income of £9,700 million but expenditure is much lower, only £4,400 million. They must be saving a large part of their incomes. Income is greater than expenditure, and the economy is not in equilibrium.

4. When an economy is in either of these conditions it will tend to move towards equilibrium. In the first case it will expand to reach equilibrium at a higher level. In the second case the economy will contract to reach equilibrium at a lower level. The series of rectangles shows how this happens. The whole process depends upon the fact that this period's expenditure is next period's income. First let us note that the two curves on the diagram are the consumption curve and the consumption + investment curve. Some of the savings made by the citizens are loaned out to entrepreneurs or people seeking mortgages and do not lie idle. So the true level of activity in the economy is shown by the consumption + investment curve.

   Consider the largest rectangle. Incomes are £8,000 million, but expenditure is only about £5,600 million. This means the firms have £5,600 million to pay out in the next period as incomes to factors, and of course they have a great deal of unsold stock. No firm can keep going like this. They will cut output, lay off workers, close down plant and probably cut dividends (profits are lower). In the next period they pay out £5,600 million as incomes to factors, but expenditure is only £5,000 million. This is shown by the second largest rectangle. Therefore the firms can only pay out £5,000 million, and in the next period incomes fall to this figure. Eventually the economy reaches equilibrium, where the C + Inv. curve cuts the 45° line. Income now equals expenditure. The economy is in balance. Each period the firms receive back as much as they paid out last period, and they do not need to cut production any further.

5. There is only one snag—about half the factors are unemployed. Land is under-utilized; there is excess capacity in all major industries; mass unemployment prevails; the queues at the job centres have grown, and as the economy is now in equilibrium the queues are going to stay the same size for a long while.

6. *The reader should now turn to Fig. 92(b).*

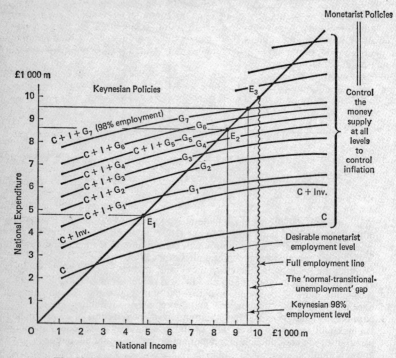

Fig. 92(*b*). The National Income Equilibrium Diagram (Part II)
(Controlling the economy with 'Keynesian' and 'Monetarist' policies)

Notes:

1. In Fig. 92(*b*) we have the same national income equilibrium diagram as in Fig. 92(*a*) but the influence of government policies is now shown, using both Keynesian and Monetarist policies.

2. The starting point is the equilibrium point E_1, where incomes and expenditure are at £4,800 million. The trouble is half the factors are out of work. Let us call this the 'great slump' situation.

Keynesian Policies

3. How did Keynesian policies cure this? They cured it by successive governmental injections of extra purchasing power. These pushed the consumption and invest-ment curve up to higher and higher levels, shown in the diagram as $C + I + G_1$,

$C + I + G_2$, $C + I + G_3$, etc. The purchasing power might be of many sorts. It could be payments to the unemployed, or government contracts for new roads, schools, aircraft, armaments, etc. As the curves rose, unemployed factors were taken on, business began to gain confidence, the slump began to recede.

4. It is important to note that inflation does not set in at this stage. The extra income is matched by extra production, because previously unemployed factors are being taken on. The new employees are so happy to be back in work they work hard. Prices need not rise because they are making extra goods.

5. The danger begins to creep in at about 95 per cent of full employment. Now we are beginning to offer jobs to the really hard cases. The halt and the blind can't help it, but the ignorant and the lazy are a different matter. Whatever the reason the output of these hard cases does not match their wages, and inflation begins to creep in. Governments did not try to go up to the full-employment level. They stopped at about 98 per cent of full employment. At that level, apart from a very small number of hard cases, no one was really out of work. The 2 per cent unemployed were just people changing jobs. This came to be called *normal transitional unemployment*.

6. Years pass by. Keynesian prosperity abounds. People come to expect that their standard of living should double every 25 years. They resent 'Stop–Go' policies; a little stop to check inflation, a little go to get back to 98 per cent of full employment. We are all more sophisticated; we know how the 'other half' of the world is living. Setbacks in the economy are necessary, but not if they affect me. Like a herd of Gadarene swine we burst through the full-employment income level (E_3 in the diagram) and over the inflationary cliff.

7. The trouble with full employment is that once you have it it is difficult to increase output any more. You cannot produce more goods, unless you use new technology. You cannot use new technology if trade unions demand the full fruits of its output, for there is nothing left for the inventor, or the tertiary services which are also trying to grow. Most of these services are run by the Government as non-profit-making services. If the public sector policies for which the Government was elected cannot be implemented because of over-full employment the Government must hold down the rest of the economy. Keynes is abandoned, for of course his policies are no longer necessary; we have too much aggregate demand. The problem now is to hold down the money supply to control inflation.

Monetarist Policies

8. National income has now gone up well above the full employment level (E_3 on the diagram). What has pushed it there? Clearly it is not deliberate injections of Government spending because Keynesian policies have now been abandoned. There is a strong mixture of forces at work to raise all the curves in the diagram. Briefly we may list:

(a) High incomes paid to strongly organized work forces;

(b) Easily available credit—not just hire purchase but sophisticated help-yourself schemes like Barclaycard and Access, and large-scale loans from fringe banks and finance companies;

(c) Sophisticated behaviour by the mass of the people—especially the tendency to increase the velocity of money, i.e. to spend money as soon as we get it;

(d) Low productivity, work-sharing, and other devices which make it necessary to employ three men to do one job;

(e) Wage drift under the influence of bogus productivity deals;

(f) Generous welfare arrangements, redundancy payments, golden handshakes and silver-lined retirement benefits;

(g) The rescue of lame duck industries of notional (rather than national) importance.

9. To control the money supply Government policies can act at every level. Since each layer in the diagram is built upon the layers lower down it will help to reduce incomes anywhere in the scale. Monetarist policies try to reduce incomes wherever possibly by putting a tight framework on wage-bargaining, credit, public expenditure, (including local government expenditure), taxation, bogus productivity deals, the rescue of lame ducklings (the ducks just have to be saved), welfare dodging, etc.

10. The aim of all these policies ultimately is to bring income down to about the 90 per cent level of full employment. This is because, with more generous welfare, etc., the band of 'normal transitional unemployment' is widened—people take a holiday between jobs, even if this lowers their consumption level. The actual measures taken, and the effect of monetarist policies on unemployment, are described in the main text (turn to page 359).

more a matter of decelerating. Most people achieved satisfactory levels of prosperity and all that was necessary was to keep really disadvantaged people up to a reasonable standard of welfare.

(*b*) *Public-sector activities*. These have already been referred to on pages 325–6. They consist of Government contracts for socially desirable capital projects without pushing the economy into inflation. In 1964, when the Conservatives were replaced after 13 years of power, the election was won on the grounds that socially desirable policies could not be pursued because private sector prosperity was too great. The expansion of university education and the switch to comprehensive education were two aspects of social policies that had been postponed repeatedly up to that time.

(*c*) *Monetary measures*. Monetary measures work through the monetary system and permit an increased level of activity where desired. Thus *the lowering of Minimum Lending Rate* will make all other interest rates fall, and this will mean that many individuals and firms will proceed with projects which they had been postponing because the cost of borrowing the money was too high. This increased demand for cars, other durable goods, extensions to premises, etc., will be multiplied throughout the economy and will lead to higher levels of employment.

Open-market operations will also assist the general level of monetary demand. Open-market operations are the activities of the Government broker on the Stock Exchange. If he buys back gilt-edged securities from investors and adds them to the Government store of securities, the money thus released to the investors will be banked. The increased liquidity of the banks will enable them to expand credit levels to their customers, who will consequently be able to proceed with projects held up for lack of finance.

The release of *Special Deposits*—that portion of the commercial banks' liquid assets which is frozen in the central bank—will similarly increase the ability of the banks to lend to their customers, and will thus increase aggregate monetary demand.

(*d*) *Fiscal measures* are taxation measures (the word 'fiscal' is derived from *fiscus*, a Roman emperor's privy purse). If we lower taxation, more money will be left in the pockets of the people. If we are careful to lower the taxation which affects poorer people, the multiplying effect will be large and the economy will receive an accelerating boost of extra demand.

(*e*) *Direct controls*. These are perhaps the most effective measures of all to stimulate the economy. The control of hire purchase is the most useful, since hire-purchase credit is chiefly used by the poorer section of the population. Thus a reduction of the H.P. deposit from, say, 25 per cent to 20 per cent would reduce the deposit payable on a £1,500 car from £375 to £300. It would mean that many people who had been saving up a deposit would suddenly find the car within their reach. Similarly, an extension of the period of repayment will enable many more families to afford the repayments. The £1,500 car, with a deposit of £375, leaves £1,125 plus interest to be paid. Over two years, at 10 per cent interest, this would mean £1,350 to be paid in 24 instalments, which is £56·25 per month. After the change of deposit rate and an extension of the repayment period to three years, the figures are £1,500 − £300 = £1,200. Add interest at 10 per cent for three years (£360) and we find that the total instalments due are £1,560. Divide into 36 payments this becomes £43·33 per month.

(8) Managing a Prosperous Economy

Once Keynesian measures have achieved an equilibrium state in the economy just below the full employment level the problem is to keep the economy at this desirable level in a changing world. Alternate touches of the brake and of the accelerator are necessary. Fine tuning of the economy by adept manipulation of the controls is not an easy art, and there are forces at work in the real world to upset delicate adjustments. Here let us divert for one moment to explain a word popularly used in the late sixties and early seventies—the **accelerator**.

The Accelerator

In Chapter Twenty-seven reference was made to the 'accelerator', a naturally occurring increase in aggregate monetary demand resulting from the durability of the machinery used in industry. Replacement at intervals of the capital equipment used in industry triggered off the trade cycles of the nineteenth century. Today there are other accelerators, for households also use relatively durable capital goods, particularly the motorcar, the television set, the washing machine, the refrigerator, and the vacuum cleaner. Each of these can lead to a sudden demand for new consumer goods, and produce the accelerating effect on investment.

The accelerator is any injection of extra spending power into the economy which has a more than proportional effect on the capital-goods industries, causing them to change in such a way as to inject extra monetary demand into the economy.

The word 'accelerator' is also used loosely by politicans when they feel it is time the Government injected extra spending power into the economy.

Forces at Work to Interfere with Fine-tuning of the Economy

In the notes to Fig. 92(*b*) a list of forces at work to interfere with fine-tuning of the economy is given in note 8. The most fundamental difficulty, perhaps an insoluble one, is the inherent difficulty of the mixed economy itself. Reference has already been made to the election of 1964, which was fought over the basic problem; how can we achieve more Socialism in a Capitalist society? In trying to achieve the best of both worlds, the mixed economy ends up by pleasing no one. Of course there are many citizens who are well content, and feel that the middle way really is the best solution in the end, but they are less vocal than those on either side. In such a situation it is for the Government to give a lead, and strike a balance. The reader may judge for himself whether an appropriate style of leadership has been available in the years since 1964. Without strong leadership it is all too easy for the economy to burst through the full-employment barrier into an inflationary boom.

Inflation. Inflation is a situation where too much money is chasing too few goods and services, so that they rise in price. Long before attempts were made to manage economies, businessmen and bankers had experienced inflationary times. For example, when Spain discovered the New World and gold flooded in from Mexico and Peru, increases of prices occurred all over Europe. There was more money about, but only the same quantity of real goods, so that money was worth less and goods were worth more. Similar inflations occurred during the 'Gold Rush' days in California and the Klondyke. Mark Twain tells an amusing story of the falling value of money as he journeyed by stage-coach from the Mississippi to Nevada. At the start of the journey he gave the porter a quarter of a dollar. The man expressed his sincere gratitude at such a generous tip. Further on the same coin at subsequent staging posts aroused less and less enthusiasm. When he finally reached Nevada the porter held it in the palm of his hand, squinted at it, said he had heard of one but had never seen one, and vowed he'd remember its 'generous' donor.

These experiences led economists to see a relationship between the quantity of money in circulation, the price of goods, and the quantity of goods. Later this was refined by Prof. Irving Fisher to take account of another feature which may cause changes at times when no sudden increase has occurred in the quantity of money in circulation. This is the velocity of circulation of money —in other words, the speed at which it is passed on. Velocity changes with the propensity to consume of the recipient, but even more with expectations of future events. The maddest inflations occur among well-to-do rather than poor populations, for the well-to-do have so much more wealth to get rid of when the value of money is falling. Readers who remember the gold crisis of 1968 when a concerted attempt was made to raise the price of gold above the world parity with the dollar, will recall the frenzy on the Paris Bourse, the South African exchanges, and even on the London exchanges.

Irving Fishers equation of exchange reads

$$MV = PT$$

where *M* is the quantity of money in circulation, *V* is its velocity, *P* is the price of goods, and *T* is the number of transactions that take place. This equation has been much criticized, chiefly on the grounds that it is so obvious that it is hardly worth saying. Clearly the quantity of money (*M*) multiplied by the number of times you spend it (*V*) must be the same thing as the number of goods you buy (*T*) multiplied by the price you pay (*P*). However, even the obvious is sometimes well worth saying, and the equation does give a useful clue in shorthand form to what happens in the economy. The following examples will illustrate the implications of Fisher's equations.

(*a*) Who controls *M*? Chiefly the monetary authorities, i.e. the Government. If they reduce the quantity of money in circulation it ought to stop prices rising—in other words, stop inflation. But while the Government proposes the people dispose. If the people change *V* by spending more rapidly, the

Government's activities may be undone. One of the major influences at work in 1967 to force devaluation on Britain was the refusal of the people to be 'squeezed' out of their prosperity. The more the Government squeezed the more the velocity of money increased. Entrepreneurs who could not get money from the banks borrowed from the finance houses and even the moneylenders to overcome their difficulties.

Similarly, in times of depression the Government's activities aimed at encouraging the economy by pumping in more money can be upset by the people, who have such a low V. If the spending power the Government pumps in is immediately removed as savings, the economy cannot advance. 'All we need is confidence': the confidence to spend, not save, and keep V going.

(*b*) On the other side of the equation, the significant point is that if prices are rising they can be checked by more T. More goods, more transactions, will keep the price of each transaction down. To produce more T the productivity of our fields and factories must be raised.

(9) Over-full Employment, Stagflation and Slumpflation

Inflation begins with over-full employment caused by too much A.M.D. in the economy. Attempts to control the inflation by credit squeezes and other Keynesian measures are resisted. Inflation then becomes 'stagflation' and finally 'slumpflation'. These paradoxical situations occur respectively when there are mixtures of stagnation and inflation (stagflation) and serious unemployment and inflation (slumpflation).

The danger is that stagflation may turn into **hyperinflation**, a madly spiralling series of wage and price increases. To prevent this governments establish tight controls wherever they can, particularly by control of the money supply. These tight controls on the money supply are called 'monetarist' policies. Their chief exponent is Prof. Milton Friedman, a critic of Keynesian economics. The monetarist policies of the mid-1970s are discussed more fully on pages 359–60.

(10) Summary of Chapter Twenty-eight

1. Persistent general unemployment, or a slump, is caused by insufficient demand in the economy.

2. Demand arises from the general public for consumption goods, from entrepreneurs for investment in capital goods, or from Government and local government bodies for investment in social capital assets.

3. Savings are a major source of investment capital, but may not be invested if entrepreneurs are unwilling to demand loans from the banks.

4. To 'manage' the economy the Government must inject purchasing power when required, or reduce purchasing power when inflation is developing.

5. The multiplier is a number which shows how many times a given njection of monetary demand will be multiplied round the economy.

6. To manage an economy it must be brought into stable equilibrium at a level of activity which is just below full-employment level.

7. Over-full employment produces inflation, where too much money is chasing too few goods. The only satisfactory solution is higher productivity. Where this is not forthcoming there is a grave risk of hyperinflation, which must be prevented by strict control of the money supply. This prevents expansion of domestic credit to reduce aggregate monetary demand.

CHAPTER TWENTY-NINE

PUBLIC FINANCE

(1) The Public Sector of the Economy

At one time the activities of a central Government were limited to the keeping of internal and external peace. In return for the security which it provided, a portion of the national output in the form of taxation was surrendered to the sovereign power. The extent of this tax contribution varied with the rapacity of the sovereign, and the ability of the lesser nobles, merchants, and ordinary people to resist or to control him.

Today the situation is very different; the powers of the sovereign have been curbed by a code of laws and conventions, and the duties of Governments extend far beyond the traditional powers of peace-keeping. Governments now control a large sector of the economy, providing not only security but welfare services of all sorts, and also providing through nationalized industries a range of goods and services which for some reason are produced more satisfactorily in this way. Thus in the United Kingdom a National Health Service provides a wide range of benefits from before birth until death. These services could be provided privately, but we have chosen to provide them socially. Similarly, but by a different process of development, electricity supply is controlled by a public authority, the Electricity Council.

A full picture of such activities can be gained by considering the 1974 figures for public expenditure given in Table 43.

The Public Sector and the Private Sector

Public debate rages over the level of resources which should be allocated to the public sector. During the early sixties management of the economy tended to act against the interests of the public sector and in favour of the private sector. The Keynesian idea was to expand the public sector whenever the private sector suffered a setback. When Governments became adept at keeping the economy booming by injecting an appropriate amount of A.M.D. into the economy, setbacks in the private sector did not occur, and the public sector was starved of resources. In the late sixties this imbalance was corrected, and socially desirable policies were pushed ahead, particularly in education and higher education, but also in the social services, and welfare fields.

These advances in social aspirations could only be achieved by a reduction in the private sector or by growth in the economy. In the late sixties and early seventies growth proved very difficult to achieve, so that controls over the private sector increased. Not only was taxation heavy, but the social aspirations included measures to promote such aims as security of employment, equality of opportunity, equality of the sexes, etc. These measures raised costs to the private sector. We are therefore now hearing claims that the private sector is being reduced more than is wise. Provisional figures for 1978–9 show that despite taxation of almost £54,000 million the Government still needed to borrow almost £8,500 million to carry out its social programme. The comparison with the 1974 figures is interesting.

Whatever decisions are made, the volume of public-sector activity is already large and is likely to increase in the future. The finance of such a huge

Table 43. United Kingdom public income and expenditure, 1974

Public expenditure in £ millions			Public receipts in £ millions		
Defence and external relations			**Taxation**		
Defence budget	4,235		On income	12,131	
Overseas aid	654		On expenditure	11,351	
		4,889	National insurance contributions	4,986	
Commerce and industry					28,468
Assistance to employment and industry	3,999		**Trading surpluses**		
Research councils	326		Central and local government	119	
Agriculture, etc.	1,049		Public corporations	2,426	
		5,374			2,545
Environmental services			Rents		1,948
Roads and lighting	1,195		**Interest and dividend**		830
Transport	1,894				33,791
Housing	3,942		**Capital items**		
Local environmental services	1,865		Receipts on capital account	1,174	
Law and order	1,245		Finance of deficit by borrowing	6,641	
Arts	222				7,815
		10,363			
Social services					
Education	4,864				
Health and Welfare	4,778				
Social security	6,845				
		16,487			
Other services					
Financial administration	496				
Common services	265				
		761			
Total current expenditure	37,874				
Debt interest	3,732				
	£m	41,606		£m	41,606

(Source: Blue Book of National Income and Expenditure, 1975)

range of activities is not easy, and involves a burden of taxation which consumes about 38 per cent of the national income. What principles govern such taxation?

(2) Adam Smith's Canons of Taxation

Adam Smith listed four principles of taxation policy which should, he said, be observed by Governments. These were:

(*a*) Taxation should be equal, by which he meant proportional to the tax-payers' incomes.

(*b*) Taxes should be certain, and not at the whim of the tax collector.

(*c*) Taxes should be arranged so that collection is convenient.

(*d*) Taxes should be economic, that is the yield should be greater than the cost of collection.

A modern Chancellor might add other principles, such as:

(*e*) Impartial treatment of all taxpayers.

(*f*) Absence of disincentive effects on hard work or enterprise.

(*g*) Consistency with Government policies.

(*h*) Adjustability if necessary.

(*i*) The cost of compliance should be kept as low as possible.

(*a*) *Taxation should be equal.* There are three ways of collecting tax from individuals so that it falls 'equally'. These are:

(i) The *per capita* tax, in which everyone pays the same contribution, say £50·00 per head.

(ii) The proportional tax, in which everyone pays the same proportion of their income in tax, say 10 per cent. This was Adam Smith's 'equal' tax.

(iii) The progressive tax, in which the amount of tax is adjusted to fall most heavily on the rich.

Table 44 shows the tax burden falling on three individuals under each of these three classes.

Table 44. 'Equal' taxation: the three methods

Type of tax	Income per annum					
	Mr. A £500·00		Mr. B £2,500·00		Mr. C £25,000·00	
	Tax	Balance to spend	Tax	Balance to spend	Tax	Balance to spend
Per capita (£50·00) (per head)	£50·00	£450·00	£ 50·00	£2,450·00	£ 50·00	£24,950·00
Proportional (10%)	£50·00	£450·00	£250·00	£2,250·00	£2,500·00	£22,500·00
Progressive	£ 5·00	£495·00	£125·00	£2,375·00	£10,000·00	£15,000·00

Which of these tax systems gives the fairest tax? We must judge them not from the weight of the burden in absolute terms, but relative to the utility to the taxpayer of the income surrendered. Clearly the *per capita* tax is most unfair; while even the proportional tax is unjust. The point here is that the utility of each pound given up is very much greater to Mr. A. earning £500 than the utility of that same pound to Mr. B. or Mr. C. Mr. B. is still left with 4½ times Mr. A.'s whole income, while Mr. C. is left with 43 times Mr. A.'s whole income. If the total tax needed is only £2,800 the fairest way would have been to let Mr. C. pay it all.

The progressive system is therefore the 'fairest' system for direct taxation, and this system has been adopted by most nations. However, it is not possible to take enough tax from the rich to finance all the nation's needs, and tax does fall upon all citizens in an indirect way.

(*b*) *Taxes should be certain.* A system of tax collection which is not certain will almost invariably cause discontent. For example, the system of tax-farming used in medieval times gave a local official the power to collect taxes from a given area. So long as the required sum was paid to the ruler no questions were asked as to how much profit the collector earned from his 'farm'. A rapacious and extortionate tax gatherer could therefore collect whatever taxes he wished, and could show favouritism or discrimination as it pleased him.

(*c*) *Taxes should be arranged so that collection is convenient.* Taxes are invariably a burden at the time of payment, even when the taxpayer agrees that they are just and equitable. To collect them at the most convenient point reduces losses by non-payment and simplifies the whole process. For example, income tax in Britain used to be a very nominal sum, twopence or threepence in the £1, and it was reasonable to collect it as a lump sum every six months. It now represents a very much larger fraction of earned income and payment every six months would require the ordinary citizens to save up several weeks' wages to pay taxes when required. A great many of them might default on such payments. The P.A.Y.E. (pay-as-you-earn) system relieves them of this necessity. The tax is extracted from the pay packet before it is even received and the employer pays it over to the Inland Revenue authorities. In 1972 a new system was suggested in a Green Paper called '*Proposals for a Tax Credit System*'. Under this system not only would tax be deducted from the wages of taxpayers, but the welfare payments to families with children, or those in need of rent allowances or family income supplements would be added to the wage packet. This would be done by a system of 'Tax Credits', to those needing extra income. A man whose tax credits exceeded his tax debits would find money added to the pay packet by his employer.

(*d*) *Taxes should be economic, i.e. productive of revenue.* Any tax which costs more to collect than it raises in revenue is clearly a waste of time. Of course taxation might be introduced for reasons other than raising revenue (for example to discourage an undesirable habit like gambling), but if it is a revenue-raising tax it ought to be abandoned if it is uneconomic. During the nineteenth century dozens of taxes which were barely economic were abandoned. They included taxes on windows, shops, horses, carriages, servants, coal, salt, wine, beer, leather, calico, candles, slates, earthenware, sweets, glass, brick, soap, and paper. By 1881 the entire revenue (admittedly only £69 million) came from five taxes: income tax £21 million, stamp duty £4 million, spirits £31 million, tobacco £9 million, and tea £4 million.

(*e*) *Taxes should be impartial.* Complete impartiality is achieved by direct taxation, if it is designed so as to be progressive in as 'fair' a way as possible. Two citizens in the same situation as regards income, dependents etc. are taxed the same. Impartiality is much more difficult when indirect taxes are imposed. A tax on hair-dressing will not affect some people, the non-smoker avoids tobacco duty and the teetotaller avoids the alcohol tax. In many cases of tax on goods the incidence of the tax is on someone other than the person who consumes the goods, and it is usually the supplier or the manufacturer who is forced to suffer the tax. This is explained more fully on page 345.

The impartiality achieved by progressive taxation is often called 'vertical equity'. 'Horizontal equity', by contrast, seeks to ensure that two persons with the same income and the same commitments pay the same tax. While this is fairly easy to achieve with direct taxation it cannot be achieved with indirect taxation unless all taxpayers have the same scale of preferences for goods.

(*f*) *Absence of disincentive effect on hard workers or enterprise.* It is very important to a nation that its people should work hard, should be industrious and busy. They will work best when personal incentives are great and personal prosperity is desired by all. Only a particularly dedicated man will keep working year after year for philanthropic or patriotic reasons. If taxation is so heavy that overtime becomes pointless, so progressive that responsibility is not worth accepting, then the tax is having a disincentive effect. People will 'vote with their feet' and leave the country; a 'brain-drain' or a 'capital-drain' develops as useful factors which cannot, in their estimation, earn a suitable reward, emigrate to other countries where their services are required.

(*g*) *The costs of compliance should be as low as possible.* It is expensive to comply with tax laws, and to employ accountants who will discover exactly what the laws say so that you need not pay more than a proper amount. If costs of compliance can be reduced, dissatisfaction will be avoided.

(3) Tax Structure of the United Kingdom

The first classification of taxes is into **direct taxes** and **indirect taxes**. Direct taxes are levied directly on the individual taxpayer; the burden is personal and inescapable. Indirect taxes are not levied directly on individuals, but on the activities of individuals. They can be avoided by refraining from the taxed activity, or they may be passed on to other people if the economic conditions are favourable. Thus we need to study the *incidence of taxation*, i.e. on whom does the tax fall, with indirect taxes.

Direct Taxes

Direct Taxes have in the past included income tax, surtax, corporation tax, capital gains tax and estate duty (death duty). A radical reform of personal direct taxation took place in 1973, so that income tax and surtax were replaced by a graduated personal tax. Corporation Tax was also re-shaped in 1973. These measures constitute one of the most far-reaching reviews of taxation for a century. The full impact of these changes is still being studied. The main features of the changes are described below.

Personal taxation. The income of individuals, instead of paying income tax, followed by surtax for those with very high incomes, now suffers a graduated personal tax. It includes (*a*) taxation at a basic rate on a broad band of income after certain personal allowances have been granted, (*b*) higher rates of tax on higher incomes, (*c*) a special rate of tax on investment incomes over a certain figure, but lower levels of investment income are treated like ordinary income to encourage saving.

Corporation Tax is a tax levied on companies. It has been revised to end the discrimination against distributed profits. At present it is a 52 per cent tax.

Capital taxes. It sometimes happens that where wealth has been accumulated to an excessive extent by particular classes of people, the Government will wish to redistribute it by taxing away the actual capital. An interesting Parliamentary Green Paper on a Wealth Tax appeared in 1974 (Cmnd 5704).

Capital-gains tax. A 'capital gain' is an increase in the value of an asset arising from some change in demand or market situation. There is an element of luck in some capital gains, which arise as a result of events rather than any special effort on the part of the asset's owner. For many years there was no tax payable on this kind of capital appreciation, for it was held that capital gains could not be taxed as income. This was an anomaly in tax law, because it gave immunity from tax to a class of relatively affluent persons who conducted regular activities on markets like the Stock Exchange, the New Issue Market, the property market, the markets for fine art etc. Where these transactions are occasional there might be some case for holding that only a capital appreciation is involved, but where they are repeated frequently as a series of short-term activities, they are clearly in the nature of business activities. The 1962 and 1965 Finance Acts therefore brought these short-term activities within the tax net.

If you buy certain assets and resell them, it is assumed that you are trading in them, and the profit is taxable. If you make a loss you can set this off against any profits which you have made on other things. Examples are investments, property (apart from private dwelling houses), and works of art. It follows, although the rules on any given transaction are complicated, that if your income is increased by capital gains you are caught in the tax net.

Development Gains Tax. This tax was first introduced in the United Kingdom in 1974. It is payable at a flat rate of 80 per cent when the development value of land is realized. Aimed at the profits of land speculators it may result in less land becoming available for development.

Capital Transfer (Gift) Tax. This tax replaced Estate Duty (Death Duty) in the April 1975 budget. It covers gifts made in the lifetime of the taxpayer as well as at death. It starts on assets over £25,000 (5% in life, 10% at death) and rises in steps to 75 per cent on gifts or estates of more than £2 million. The widespread evasion of death duty by giving gifts during the lifetime of the taxpayer has thus been controlled. The principle of death duties is that where a person makes a fortune in his lifetime, that fortune must be contributed by the mass of the citizens in the excellent profits he made by his trade or professional activities. It has been generally agreed that such rewards, however well deserved, ought to be returned to the mass of the people at his death (while still leaving reasonable provision for heirs or dependants).

Advantages of Direct Taxation

The chief advantages of direct taxes, like personal taxation, and corporation tax, are that they have a high yield relative to cost; they are reasonably certain in their application, and equitable because they fall most heavily on those who can afford to pay.

A personal tax of 0.05 in the £1 raises about £400 million in Great Britain, and gives a Chancellor considerable control of any uncertainty in the economy. (The use of the Budget as a regulator of the economy is discussed on page 343.) Direct taxation is thus a very effective method of regulating the economy. By removing money from, or restoring money to, the pockets of the nation's citizens, it enables very rapid alterations in spending policy to be achieved, to change the level of aggregate monetary demand.

The progressive nature of personal taxes and death duties redistributes national income and national capital to avoid gross inequalities of income and wealth. This promotes social harmony.

Disadvantages of Direct Taxation

The chief disadvantage of these taxes is that they constitute a disincentive to hard work. Cases are on record where authors who write a single volume which sells well are forced to emigrate because taxation removes such a large proportion of the income. The author's next book will earn income for another country, and his talents have been lost. Similarly a dramatist who could write several film scripts or plays per year may decide to write only a single script because any extra output would yield so little extra income. At more routine levels a high rate of tax on eventual earnings discourages individuals from working overtime, or taking extra responsibilities even if salary is raised. Leisure becomes more attractive than income.

High tax levels increase the advantages of evading taxation by discovering loopholes in the tax laws. Clever accountants can save their companies enormous sums, and a transference of good brains into socially unprofitable tax-avoidance activities wastes talent. High taxation repels foreign capital which would otherwise seek investment in a country, and encourages firms and individuals to invest abroad in tax havens. The development of 'flags of convenience' in the shipping field enables entrepreneurs to escape taxation.

Direct taxation on a company's profits reduces the capital available for ploughing back into the industry. This possibly lowers productivity since the latest equipment would usually mean faster working speeds and higher output. The overall effects of corporation tax are very difficult to assess.

Indirect Taxes

Indirect taxes include purchase taxes, sales taxes, taxes on tobacco, spirits and wines, petrol and fuel oil, motor taxes, betting and gaming taxes, stamp duties, and many more. In particular a recent controversial tax was the Selective Employment Tax. Value Added Tax began in April 1973.

Some of these taxes are specific taxes, i.e. a definite sum is charged per unit. For example petrol duty stands at £0·19½ per gallon at present, and tobacco tax is currently £0·25½ per pack of 20 normal-size cigarettes. Other taxes are *ad valorem*, i.e. at a percentage rate on the value of the item. Thus luxury goods have carried a 55 per cent purchase tax.

Indirect taxes called **customs duties** are levied at the port on imported goods. Others called **excise duties** are levied on home-produced goods or services. Tobacco tax and the tax on wines are examples of customs duties. The alcohol taxes on whisky and beer produced within the United Kingdom, and the licences charged for betting shops and gaming houses are examples of excise duties.

Motor taxes are payable on all vehicles, and form an additional cost to the motorist of £50 per annum. On commercial vehicles they are very heavy indeed, and may be as much as £1,000 per vehicle per annum.

A widespread change in indirect taxation took place during 1973, when Britain entered the E.E.C. It involves the abolition of purchase tax, an *ad valorem* tax imposed on wholesalers at the point where goods were passed on to retailers. The retailer then passed the tax on to the final consumers, who were therefore taxed upon the 'purchases' they made. Selective Employment

Tax was also abolished. This tax was imposed in 1966, by the Labour administration. Its purpose was to reduce employment in service industries. These taxes were replaced by Value Added Tax.

Value Added Tax. Value added tax is a tax imposed at every level of economic activity, over the very widest ranges of goods and services. The tax is applied at each stage where value is added. Imagine a gravel pit owner whose product is bought by a manufacturer of precast concrete bridge sections. These are purchased by a civil engineering contractor for use in a roadbuilding project. Value is added at three points: (*a*) where the natural product is removed from the pit for use; (*b*) when the raw material is manufactured into the semi-finished product; (*c*) when the pre-cast units are assembled into the civil engineering facility. At each stage value added tax is levied at—say—the 10% level. Let us imagine that £1,000 of gravel is turned into £3,000 of pre-cast units which are turned into a £10,000 bridge. Tax is added by the pit-owner at 10% (£100), by the manufacturer (£300), and by the civil engineering contractor (£1,000). The total tax payable by the consumer (say the local authority that ordered the bridge) is £1,000. This sum will be collected in the manner shown below, using a system of calculations involving Input Taxes and Output Taxes.

Input Tax is that part of his 'purchases' which the individual is paying extra as Value Added Tax.

Output Tax is that part of his 'sales' which the individual is receiving extra as Value Added Tax.

The difference between the two, Output Tax—Input Tax, is the net tax collected by the individual on behalf of H.M. Customs. This is accounted for to the Customs and Excise Department.

Tax Collection under the V.A.T. Scheme.

Tax Collector	Gravel Pit Owner £	Manufacturer £	Civil Engineer £
1. Cost price of output (without tax)	— (gift of nature)	1,000	3,000
2. Sale price of output (without tax)	1,000	3,000	10,000
3. Value Added	1,000	2,000	7,000
4. Sale Price (with tax at 10%)	1,100	3,300	11,000
5. Tax position	Input:Output 0:100	Input:Output 100:300	Input:Output 300:1,000
6. Tax collected: Output—Input (payable to H.M. Customs)	100	200	700
7. Tax paid personally	0	0	0
	(the entire tax falls upon the final consumer)		

The Advantages of Indirect Taxation

The chief advantages of indirect taxation are that the effects are spread more widely throughout the community, and the tax is often paid without the taxpayer being conscious of it, as it appears to him to be part of the purchase price of the commodity or service he requires.

Without indirect taxation the Government would find it difficult to raise the revenue it requires to finance its activities. Direct taxation would have to be raised to a level where the disincentive effects were very strong. Indirect taxation, by spreading the taxes over most citizens, promotes a sense of social responsibility. The demand for free goods is highly elastic, and without their present tax increments many goods would appear to be so cheap as to be almost 'free'. This would increase demand to points where the marginal utility of the goods was very small, so that the commodity was almost being wasted. When indirect taxes raise prices they cause citizens to take a desirable interest in the uses made of these revenues.

Indirect taxes do not have a disincentive effect on effort; they may even increase effort if they are placed on desirable goods and services. So long as the level of tax is kept reasonable, so that goods are not placed hopelessly out of reach of ordinary people, the incentive effect of indirect taxes may raise productivity and benefit the nation as a whole.

Indirect taxes may be used for a wide variety of Government purposes, to promote policies deemed desirable. For instance, an infant industry may be protected by tariffs from foreign competition. Improvements in social standards may be achieved by the removal or imposition of taxes: thus the abolition of the window tax in nineteenth-century Britain produced improvements in house design to give better light to the inhabitants. The imposition of betting taxes may reduce undesirable gambling, and the tobacco tax may reduce lung cancer. Links with overseas countries may be strengthened by reciprocal trading agreements involving tariff changes, and effects on the balance of payments may be achieved by encouraging exports and restricting imports.

Regressive Nature of Indirect Taxation

One criticism that is often made of indirect taxation is that it is regressive, in other words it falls more heavily on the poor than on the rich. For example, to tax household durables like vacuum cleaners, washing machines, or refrigerators with perhaps 20 per cent purchase tax is to tax regressively. Since no household really needs two of these articles the poor man and the rich man will pay the same tax. As the income surrendered in tax has greater utility to the poor man than it has to the rich man, the burden falls more heavily upon him. Similarly as motor tax is the same on a small saloon car as on a Rolls Royce it is a regressive tax. The adverse effects of regressive taxation are to some extent reduced if basic necessities are not taxed at all. Thus it is rare to tax bread or potatoes, meat, eggs, and vegetables. Indirect taxation, by contrast, is often quite heavy on tobacco, alcoholic beverages, and tea, which have been called the poor man's luxuries. The heavy tax on these items is partly connected with the inelastic nature of the demand for them which makes them particularly suitable for taxation purposes (*see page 107*).

Other criticisms of indirect taxes include their lack of impartiality, since they can be avoided by abstaining from the use of the article taxed. Thus the teetotal non-smoker who does not drive a car escapes enormous tax burdens in the United Kingdom.

Nearly all indirect taxes are inflationary. They lead to demands for higher wages to offset the higher taxes, and when these are granted the Chancellor is forced to raise taxation again. It is particularly difficult to avoid this sort of spiral in a free-enterprise society. For example, after the oil states raised their prices in 1973 heavy levels of both direct and indirect taxation were imposed with the deliberate intention of reducing the standard of living being enjoyed by the British public, which was out of step with their productivity at the time. The complex price rises that followed included three elements:

(*a*) an element caused by the increased raw-material prices due to depreciation of the currency as the pound floated downwards;

(*b*) increased indirect taxation deliberately imposed by the Government;

(*c*) an element of unfair price increases caused by the desire of corporations to keep ahead of inflation.

To avert massive pressure for increases in wages the Government formed a 'social contract' with the trade unions to limit wage increases to agreed levels. This, and high levels of unemployment, forced a reduction in real incomes.

(4) The Budget as an Instrument of Economic Management

In the United Kingdom the Chancellor of the Exchequer presents his tax proposals to Parliament every April. The Budget is not just designed to raise revenue to meet Government expenditure, but is an instrument for achieving control of the economy during the coming year. The true function of Governments in modern advanced societies is to preserve the general prosperity. This is done by keeping aggregate monetary demand strong enough to avoid recessions and slumps, but not so strong that inflation develops. The new budgetary measures are later set out in a Finance Bill which, upon receiving the Royal Assent, becomes legally enforceable. Powers to collect taxes have to be renewed annually as a protection to the common people, so that the Budget can never be delayed without the whole administrative machine being in grave danger of illegality.

The Chancellor's main task therefore is to assess the economic situation. Does the economy need stimulating severely, or moderately, or does it need to be restrained? He brings in a Budget which will have an accelerating effect, or a neutral effect or a restraining effect, according to the Government's estimates of what is required.

Budgeting for a Deficit

When the Chancellor 'budgets for a deficit', he plans to spend more in the year than he collects in tax. This can only mean that in his view the economy is in need of stimulation; the level of aggregate monetary demand needs to be raised. The signs will be obvious to all. Unemployment will be higher than the normal transitional-unemployment level. Entrepreneurs will have lost confidence a little and will be waiting to see whether the prospects of profitability are going to improve or worsen before proceeding with marginal projects. Order books will be looking rather thin in some of the major industries, and stocks will be accumulating in warehouses and retail outlets.

By budgeting for a deficit, i.e. reducing taxation, the Chancellor leaves the average citizen with more money to spend. If the average citizen does go ahead and spend, the economy will revive. If he does not do so, the Government will proceed to increase welfare benefits to needy persons and to press ahead with capital projects already in the pipeline. This will accelerate the economy, and recovery will start.

Budgeting for a Surplus

When the Chancellor's view is that there is inflationary pressure in the economy, he will take measures to raise taxation and reduce spending. This will leave him with a surplus. The resulting contraction of aggregate monetary demand will reduce the demands for goods and services. This will prevent prices rising and ease the inflationary pressure in the economy.

Whether the policy is successful or not depends on the reactions of the taxpayers. The extra taxation may lead to such a round of wage demands that it proves inflationary not deflationary. The people may give up extra work because the tax burden is too heavy, so that productivity falls. Again, this is inflationary. Fearful of heavier taxation in the future, they may increase the velocity of money and keep the inflation going by using their smaller incomes more rapidly.

A Neutral Budget

Where the economy is believed to be about right, with neither a stimulus nor restraint required, the Chancellor will bring in a 'neutral' budget. This means that any tax changes he makes will cancel one another out. They may still be important as far as individuals are concerned. For example, an increase in the tax on petrol and a reduction in higher rates of income tax would effectively transfer incomes from motorists to the well-to-do, but leave the aggregate monetary demand unchanged if the amounts concerned were the same (assuming the well-to-do do not save the extra income).

The Budget Accounts

There are two main accounts where records are kept of Government Income and Expenditure. The **Consolidated Fund** is an Account which records current transactions, expenditure against income. The National Loans Fund records the Governments' lending and borrowing. The Consolidated Fund records taxation moneys received and expenditure disbursed, most of it on 'supply services'. This name is given to the major expenditures of Government departments for civil and defence purposes, education, local-government activities etc. The surplus or deficit for which the Chancellor has budgeted will appear as a balance on this account at the end of the year. This surplus or deficit is transferred to the National Loans Fund and either reduces or increases the amount which the Government has to borrow to finance the loans which it makes. The government finances most of the capital expenditure of the nationalized industries and the local authorities, using the surplus, if one was achieved, or borrowed money. The borrowed money may be National Savings, or money from the sale of gilt-edged securities. The increase or decrease of the National Loans Fund during a year is thus the final measure of the Government's surplus or deficit.

(5) Is there a Taxable Limit?

Economists sometimes debate where there is a 'taxable limit' beyond which taxes cannot be raised because people will emigrate or revolt. While clearly there must be some point where this is so, it depends on the national circumstances as to how far taxation can go. People may be prepared to give their last penny and even their lives in the defence of their country. During the Second World War taxation rose to 50 per cent. The taxable limit in peacetime appears to be about 45 per cent.

Table 45 shows how countries compare for taxation. It appears that, contrary to common belief, Britain is not the most heavily taxed country. The Netherlands enjoys that doubtful privilege, with about 47 per cent of the gross national product being taxed away.

Table 45. Taxation in 1975: some international comparisons

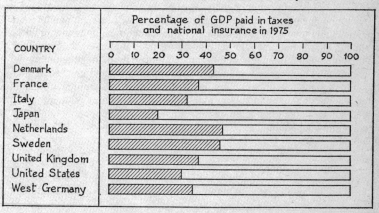

(Reproduced by permission of the Consumers' Association from *Which?*, June 1978)

Notes:

1. Taxation is calculated as a percentage of national income at factor cost. U.K. comes out at 37 per cent, while Sweden, the Netherlands and Denmark exceed this. Taxation in the U.S.A. is about 30 per cent, and in Japan about 20 per cent.
2. The figures include both central and local taxation, and a reasonable attempt has been made to ensure comparability between the nations, which are operating rather different tax systems on occasions.
3. Of the U.K. taxation shown, 46 per cent was taxation on personal incomes in the form of income tax, national insurance contributions paid by employees and the self employed, and capital gains tax.
4. A further 26 per cent of U.K. tax was taxes on spending, including value added tax, motor vehicle taxation, customs and excise duties (on alcohol, petrol, etc) and gambling taxes.
5. A further 23 per cent of the U.K. taxation was tax on business, chiefly Corporation Tax and Employer's National Insurance contributions, but also including rates on business premises.
6. The small remaining part (5 per cent of the 37 per cent of national income paid in taxation) consisted of capital transfer taxes and rates on domestic premises.

(6) The Incidence of Taxation

Taxation is an unpleasant experience for the person taxed, since it removes a portion of his income for the public use. It has been established in the courts of law that a person is entitled to do his best by all legal means to reduce his tax burden; it is for the tax authorities to make the tax net secure. The Chancellor proposes taxation on particular persons, goods, and services, but he is by no means sure that the burden will eventually fall where he intended it to fall. The 'incidence' of a tax is the place where it falls; it is of interest to the economist to be able to predict this so that the tax burden can be adjusted fairly.

Direct Taxation. The incidence of most direct taxation is clearly upon the individual taxed. The individual can rarely pass on his tax to any other person, though collectively a group may be able to achieve a compensating rise in wages. Heavy taxation may be inflationary if it leads to a round of wage demands, and the burden of such wage increases is shared among the entire population as an increase in the price of the goods or services produced. This means that those strongly organized workers whose goods are in inelastic demand, or who occupy 'bottleneck' positions in the economy, pass on their taxation to workers in less well organized industries or to pensioners.

Similarly, corporations may very easily pass on some of their increased taxation by raising prices to the public. Although this results in increased profits which bear tax in the normal way at 52 per cent, say, there is 48 per cent of each extra pound left to compensate the shareholders for the extra burden the Chancellor has imposed. Once again an inelastic demand for the product is essential if prices are to be raised without loss of trade.

Indirect taxation. Here the incidence of the tax can be demonstrated diagrammatically, and there are useful implications for a Chancellor attempting to devise a tax system which will raise the revenue required or implement the social policy proposed. Although a full discussion is too advanced for our present purpose, the main points are illustrated in Fig. 93.

A specific tax on consumer goods. This acts like an increased cost of production to the manufacturer, who will therefore bring in a smaller quantity at each price. In other words, the supply curve moves to the left, forming a new supply curve above the previous one and displaced from it by the amount of the tax. How this will affect the price of the goods, and on whom will the tax fall, depend on the elasticity of demand for the goods. Fig. 93 illustrates the position.

The implications here are important. If a Chancellor wishes to raise revenue he must tax goods which, because they have no close substitutes, are in inelastic demand. The consumer, being unable to change to other goods, will bear most of the tax burden, and the industry will be affected only to a small degree. Thus cigarettes, alcoholic drinks, petrol, and tea will support quite heavy taxation. Similarly, a tax on goods in elastic demand will raise little revenue, but will seriously affect the industry concerned. This may be an agreeable result of the taxation if the industry is antisocial in the Chancellor's view, or if it causes social costs which amount to disservices to the community. Thus a tax on betting may reduce gambling, while raising very little tax. A tax on vehicles emitting harmful exhausts would encourage a change to other forms of transport.

Taxation of Economic Rents

Where a factor is in inelastic supply and the factor owner is able to command economic rents, the imposition of tax will not cause any change in either supply or demand. The tax will have to be borne entirely by the supplier and will reduce the benefits he has been achieving hitherto from his fortunate position. Thus a monopolist earning economic rents cannot alter his position, which is already the most profitable one, and the tax will simply cream off these profits (see Fig. 94, page 348).

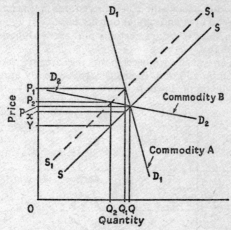

Fig. 93. Incidence of an indirect tax

Notes:

1. D_1D_1 and D_2D_2 are the demand curves of two goods. Commodity A is in inelastic demand; the demand for B is elastic. The supply curves are similar.
2. When the tax is imposed, suppliers lose the amount of the tax from whatever price they receive. As a result they are only willing to bring in a smaller supply at every price, and the supply curve moves to the left. The vertical distance between SS and S_1S_1 is the amount of the tax.
3. The effect on commodity A is that the price rises a good deal, and the quantity supplied falls off slightly to OQ_1. Of the total price OP_1, the entrepreneur is now receiving OX, compared with OP before tax was imposed. The industry has only contracted a small amount, and the bulk of the tax is being paid by the consumer.
4. With commodity B, which is in elastic demand, the consumers abandon their purchases to a much greater extent, turning to other substitutes. The result is that price only rises to P_2, the entrepreneurs only receive OY, and the incidence of the tax is largely upon them. Moreover the industry is seriously affected, with excess capacity forced upon it by the Chancellor's policy.
5. The reader should try now to draw a similar diagram with a more elastic supply curve. The result is to place a bigger share of the tax on the consumer, and a reduced burden on the supplier. The fact is that the incidence of the tax varies with both the elasticity of demand and the elasticity of supply. As the elasticity of demand is less affected by time than the elasticity of supply, the incidence of the tax will fall more lightly at first on the consumer; but as time goes on and suppliers adjust their outputs to take account of the less profitable situation the consumer's burden grows.

(7) Summary of Chapter Twenty-nine

1. The Government today provides a wide range of goods and services: security, education, welfare, basic economic services, and housing. These services have to be financed by taxation.

2. Taxation should be fair, easy to collect, of certain amount rather than at the whim of the tax collector, and impartial between different taxpayers. It should not discourage enterprise or hard work. It may be in the form of direct taxes levied on persons, or indirect taxes levied on goods and services.

3. In the United Kingdom the chief direct taxes are income tax, capital gains tax, corporation tax and capital transfer tax.

4. The chief indirect taxes are customs and excise duties, motor taxes, and Value Added Tax.

5. Direct taxes are usually arranged so that they are progressive, i.e. falling most heavily on the well-to-do. Indirect taxes are nearly always regressive, falling more heavily on the lower paid.

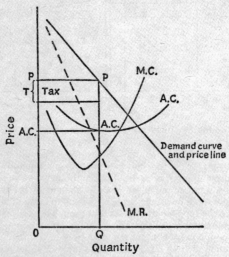

Fig. 94. Taxation of 'economic rents'

Notes:

1. The monopolist is making 'economic rents' equal to *A.C., A.C., P, P.*
2. The tax *T* will be paid by the monopolist, since at an output of *OQ* he is already producing at maximum profit.
3. Whatever proportion of this maximum is taxed away he will still be better off if he stays where he is than if he alters his position to a different level of output. 60 per cent of maximum profits it still better than 60 per cent of less-than-maximum profits.

6. The Budget is an instrument of economic management, used to control the economy.

7. A taxable limit appears to exist somewhere beyond the 40 per cent mark, at which point people will prefer to emigrate.

8. The incidence of taxation is the place where the tax falls. It is usually upon the individual in personal taxation, but with indirect taxation it depends on the price elasticities of demand and supply as to whether the tax can be passed on by suppliers to consumers.

9. Taxation of economic rents does not affect supply or demand, and falls on the rentier. (A rentier is someone who enjoys unearned income.)

(8) Suggested Further Reading

Dalton, H.: *Principles of Public Finance*. Routledge & Kegan Paul: London, 1967.

Hicks, U.: *Public Finance*. Cambridge University Press: London, 1951.

Pen, J.: *Modern Economics*. Penguin Books: London, 1965.

Prest, A. R.: *Public Finance in Theory and Practice*. 3rd. Edn. Weidenfeld & Nicolson: London, 1971.

Sandford, C. T.: *Economics of Public Finance*. Pergamon: 1969.

Exercises Set 29

1. Why should a good system of taxation include both direct and indirect taxes?

2. What were Adam Smith's canons of taxation? What other criteria might a modern Chancellor add to them?

3. Explain the difference between progressive and regressive taxation. On what grounds can each be justified?

4. Outline the tax structure of the United Kingdom. How are the revenues which have been raised eventually disbursed?

5. Direct taxation falls on the person taxed; indirect taxation falls more uncertainly. Explain.

6. In what ways may the Budget be described as an instrument for managing the economy? Who decides what management policies are to be followed, and what pressures are at work to influence these decisions in your own country?

7. Distinguish between 'budgeting for a surplus' and 'budgeting for a deficit'. In what circumstances is each appropriate?

8. What influence have the price elasticities of demand and supply on the incidence of an indirect tax? Illustrate your answer by the tax on tobacco, which is deemed to be a product in inelastic demand and fairly elastic supply.

9. 'If the demand for a particular commodity or service is elastic, the Chancellor can reduce its consumption by taxation. If it is in inelastic demand he can only make those consuming it pay heavily for the privilege.' Explain.

10. For each of the following give an example of an actual tax:

(*a*) A direct tax on a business enterprise.
(*b*) A tax convenient to the taxpayer.
(*c*) A tax which the taxpayer cannot possibly notice.
(*d*) A tax that is fair to different income groups.
(*e*) A tax that is highly regressive.

CHAPTER THIRTY

ASPECTS OF GOVERNMENT POLICY TODAY

(1) Introduction

We live in an age where instantaneous communication between places a world apart is an everyday experience. Over half the world's population watches the World Cup football series or the Olympic Games. In such circumstances, in free societies at least, everyone knows or gets to know everyone else's situation. Inequalities stand out more obviously. It follows that there is a strong drive towards achieving economic equality both among nations and within a nation. Such equality of standards of living requires a multitude of choices to be made. These choices are made by elected Governments. What major problems face such Governments? Today they include the problem of stabilizing prices in an inflationary world; the 'Balance of Payments' problem; maintenance of a high employment level and how to achieve growth in the economy so that the people's aspirations may be fulfilled.

(2) Rate of Growth of the Economy

If an economy 'grows', a higher standard of living can be enjoyed by the people of that country. Growth means an increase in the National Income in real terms, not money terms, so that there are more goods and services available. This growth can then be enjoyed by the people in one of the following ways:

(*a*) by enjoying more goods and services;
(*b*) by having more children, who then consume the extra product;
(*c*) by investing the extra output so that even more is available in the future.

As pressures towards equality raise the standards of living of the mass of the people by redistributing income through the tax system, growth becomes more difficult to achieve. First, even with a relatively sophisticated population like the United Kingdom, it is still true that the poorer section of the population tends to have more children per family. This tendency is much more pronounced in less developed countries, where whatever growth is achieved tends to be consumed by the extra mouths to feed. Secondly, the higher marginal propensity to consume of the mass of the population leads them to consume the growth in current production as goods and services for present enjoyment. Saving for future growth appeals less to people experiencing a better standard of living for the first time. The propensity to save of the nation as a whole declines, and this reduces growth. In the last few decades people have come to expect their standards of living to double every 25 years. In order to do this we must have growth at 2·5 per cent per annum, for at compound interest 2·5 per cent comes to 100 per cent in 25 years. For some years in the 1960s real growth in the United Kingdom was estimated to be as low as 1 per cent; in the U.S.A. it commonly reaches 5 per cent, Japan and Mexico have been achieving rates of growth of about 10–12 per cent. The reader must remember though, that 10–12 per cent of *what* is always an important point. A country may be top of the 'growth' list and yet in absolute terms may be falling farther and farther behind. The figures below illustrate this point. Gross National Product for the two countries shown reveals that while the growth rate in percentage terms of the Country B is very much better, she is starting from such a low base point that in real terms she is making nowhere near as big an increase.

Table 46. Growth in relative and actual terms

Country	Gross national product in £millions	Rate of growth, %	Actual increase in £ millions
A	30,000	$2\frac{1}{2}$	750
B	500	10	50

Among the chief factors influencing growth are the following:

(*a*) *Availability of factors, especially labour.* Where an economy has vast supplies of labour in under-utilized forms available, its rate of growth can be very rapid. These labour resources usually mean a peasantry, which can leave the land to come to the towns. In eighteenth-century Britain the Enclosure Acts which drove the peasantry off the land and forced them to become a landless proletariat generated the growth of the Industrial Revolution. The same sort of development has led to recent growth in the countries of Europe: the Dutch have been able to reinforce the labour of Rotterdam with workers from rural areas; the German, French, and Italian peasantries have become more industrialized, and surplus labour from Spain, Greece, Turkey, and Portugal has been imported to ease particular shortages. South Africa's growth is associated with the willingness of Africans to seek work in her industries despite the limited opportunities offered, and even by illegal entry. Mexico's growth is associated with an agricultural revolution which has raised productivity in agriculture, releasing peasants for industrial activities in the towns.

(*b*) *Changes in the hours of work per day and weeks of work per year.* Growth is vitally affected by the number of hours per week worked on average, and the vacation period per year. Where the hours of work are excessive, as they were in Victorian England, a reduction of hours of work may actually increase output. In more recent times the reduction of the working day to eight or seven hours, and the working week to five days, has definitely slowed growth.

If we all choose to have more leisure the country can produce more goods and services only if more intensive production takes place.

(*c*) *Changes in productivity per man-hour.* These are the most important changes from the point of view of growth in the economy. If extra output per man-hour can be achieved by new equipment and new methods of work, it may still be possible for both extra mouths to be fed and extra leisure to be enjoyed. A crucial element of growth is therefore the willingness of men to accept new equipment and machines, to be redeployed into new fields when they are no longer required in older industries, and to accept new systems of work.

Any sort of work-sharing (sharing reduced levels of work among the same-sized labour force to prevent unemployment in a particular trade) hinders national growth and is reprehensible from the point of view of the general community, even if it appears justified to the particular workers concerned. National growth can best be secured by adopting methods of work which are capital intensive; backing every worker with an array of power tools which perform the activities more rapidly and more effectively. This type of improvement comes about in two ways: first by increasing actual investment, secondly by technological change. This means that as the new investment takes place it replaces the existing asset by the latest type of machine, so that the output is raised.

Since this type of growth depends on investment it must also depend on savings. Today's standard of living must be reduced to achieve a fuller life tomorrow. In advanced and wealthy societies it becomes very easy to save. In less developed countries the sacrifices are real, and enduring.

Is growth desirable? There is much controversy today as to whether growth is desirable. It does appear that certain constraints on growth are being approached. They are (*a*) the finiteness of the earth's resources, (*b*) the pollutant effects of further growth—man is beginning to influence the biosphere (the natural framework within which life is possible) upsetting such fundamental matters as the carbon and nitrogen cycles, the ozone layer in the stratosphere etc.—(*c*) population expansion, which is accelerating in an overcrowded world. To these points advocates of growth retort that present growth still leaves many people below the poverty level; that conservation requires capital which can only be created by further growth and that man's ingenuity is great enough to solve these problems. The debate seems likely to continue.

Whether growth is desirable or not it has not been easy to achieve in the mid-seventies. The gross domestic product of the United Kingdom barely rose at all between 1974 and 1977 in real terms. There are signs that some growth may be occurring in 1978, assisted by improvements in the Balance of Payments as North Sea oil comes fully on stream.

(3) A Policy for Unemployment

The late seventies is a time of high world-wide unemployment. In 1977 the average number of unemployed was 1·5 million in the United Kingdom, a figure which compares with 559,000 in 1967 and 360,000 in 1965. Not surprisingly the large increase in unemployment has made the whole country more aware of the need for a policy for unemployment. Formerly there were certain areas where unemployment was particularly bad and in others 'normal transitional unemployment' was the rule (less than 2 per cent unemployed—and most of those only changing jobs). In 1977 no region had less than 4·4 per cent unemployed while in the North, Wales and Scotland unemployment exceeded 8·4 per cent. In Northern Ireland it was 11·2 per cent.

In the post-war years unemployment was associated with declining industries suffering from 'structural' unemployment. All countries must eventually suffer from structural unemployment, because it is in the nature of technology to advance. We have experienced in modern times a succession of materials, forms of power, and 'prime movers'. Since 1760 Britain has experienced an iron age, a steel age, an aluminium age, and a plastics age. We have had a steam era, an electrical era, and we are moving into an electronics era. Of prime movers (i.e. sources of motive power) we have used steam engines, electric motors, diesel engines, steam turbines, petrol and jet engines. Not all of these materials and processes die out completely, they go on being used but the demand declines to such an extent that factories, machines, and skilled tradesmen become redundant and have to be turned over to other uses. It has been estimated that at any given time 30 per cent of employment will be engaged in trades that have developed over the previous 25 years. The plastics industry today, with its wide variety of products and processes, gives a good example of the pace of technology.

In its worst form structural unemployment means that formerly prosperous areas which once had economic advantages become derelict and depressed. Capital has gone elsewhere; the active workers have moved to more prosperous regions or have gone overseas. The land has often been worked out and is covered with industrial waste, coal tips, and slag heaps. The service industries have declined; empty premises abound. Under-utilized social assets, many of them suited to former ages, exist all over the region. Thus there are large schools with old-fashioned coal-burning open fires, desks that have been used for 100 years or more, roofs that are worm-eaten and floors that are splintered. The problem was to put new heart into such areas, by a mixture of activities. For example, re-training programmes were needed to teach new skills to redundant employees. Financial assistance to improve the mobility of labour enabled people to leave areas of high unemployment to seek employment in more prosperous areas. To prevent the areas themselves becoming wastelands it was necessary to attract new industries into the area by granting 'regional development grants', 'regional employment premiums' and tax concessions. Areas of high unemployment were designated 'Development Areas' and regions where statistics showed that new investment was falling away although they were not yet facing serious unemployment were designated 'Intermediate Areas'.

A long succession of post-war legislation began with the Distribution of Industries Act, 1948. The latest legislation is the Industry Act 1972. The Government continues to develop measures to attack problems in the 'Regions' —to use the E.E.C. term for these areas of stubborn unemployment. Some of the measures in use are:

Regional Development Grants. Roughly 20 per cent of capital expenditure on new machinery, plant, buildings and mining work.

Government Factories. These are available for rent or sale. A rent-free period is possible for certain new undertakings.

Selective Assistance. This is available, on the merits of every case, in the form of loans, interest relief grants, removal grants and service industry removal grants.

Tax Allowances. Although available to the whole country at 100 per cent of cost for the first year, regional development grants given (as above) are not deducted from the value of the capital asset, and thus give a firm making profits in its first year an extra relief from tax.

Regional Employment Premium. This is payable to manufacturers at £3 per week for each adult male (and smaller sums for other labour).

Training Allowances. These are available for special courses.

Help for transferred workers. Free fares, lodging allowances and help with removal expenses are given to assist the mobility of labour.

Contract Preference Schemes. These divert Government contracts to Development Areas.

E.E.C. Regional Policy

The European Economic Community is developing a regional policy which provided a total of 950 million European Units of Account in 1975–7 for assistance to the Development Regions. A further 1850 million E.U.A.'s is proposed for the three years 1978–80. Criteria for assistance include: a lower gross domestic product than the Community average; heavy dependence on employment in declining industries (with at least one fifth of local jobs in such a category); a persistently high rate of unemployment (at least 20 per cent above the national average over a period of years) or a persistent rate of net emigration of at least 10 per 1,000 inhabitants over several years. Contributions from the fund can only be used to supplement an existing regional aid policy. Loans may be available on favourable terms from the European Investment Bank and the European Coal and Steel Community.

Of the 1975–7 expenditure the United Kingdom received the second largest allocation of 270 million E.U.A.'s spent on a total of 1,450 investment projects in the development regions.

Curing Unemployment in Slumpflation

One of the important developments in the mid-seventies was the increase in unemployment due to the recession sparked off by the increase in oil prices in 1973. The world financial crisis that developed as a result of this price increase presented unemployment problems which could not be solved by the 'Regional' policies described above. Instead of being regional in its effect, slumpflation brings with it general unemployment, and this can only be solved by a rise in A.M.D. (aggregate monetary demand). Unfortunately, an individual nation which pursued an expansionist policy on its own, without other nations pursuing similar policies, would only produce for itself a massive Balance of Payments problem. It is therefore essential that all nations move forward together in going for growth to overcome unemployment problems. In this respect it is clearly most desirable for the world in general that the countries with large surpluses on their Balance of Payments do more to expand their economies than those with deficits. During the mid-seventies the pressure has been on country's with Balance of Payments deficits, who apply to the I.M.F. for help, to take steps in their own countries (by deflating demand) to bring their payments back into surplus. This intensifies their own slumpflation.

In the United Kingdom the difficulties are intensified by the pressures (chiefly from strongly organized trade unions) to preserve traditional industries even though these industries make things the world no longer wants. Even the British do not want them, for every rise in real income tends to be spent on more imports. This can only mean that it is the foreigners who are making what the people of the United Kingdom need. If imports were shut out, and a protectionist policy was applied to United Kingdom industries, this would still mean that if people want their 'basket of goods' to include things previously imported then the United Kingdom must kill off the obsolete industries which the trade unions are doing their utmost to preserve. Job-saving in obsolete industries does not actually save jobs. It prevents new industries developing, in the interest of those in traditional industries who seek to preserve a level of income to which they have become accustomed but to which they are no longer entitled. Trade unionists have always decried 'vested interests' as a reprehensible element in the capitalist system. Yet with 80 per cent of all incomes going to the factor labour, when labour itself becomes a vested interest it must be four times as reprehensible as land and capital—the factors only taking 20 per cent of the total national income.

Even so, there is some reason to believe that a serious reassessment of the place of work in modern advanced societies needs to be made. When we do switch over to modern industries they will naturally be capital intensive industries. *They will not provide the employment necessary to cure the slump in slumpflation. What they will do is create the wealth that will enable the un-employed to be diverted into labour intensive occupations.* These labour intensive occupations are in the service industries, such as the National Health Service, education, entertainment, etc. If machines can create wealth for us then humans can turn their minds from production of goods to the production of services which enrich and enhance the quality of life. We now know how to distribute wealth fairly. The solution to the problems of slumpflation is to create wealth more abundantly by highly productive industries using the latest technologies, and then distribute it in such a way that employment in service industries expands. This means abandoning such traditional beliefs as the dogma that those who produce the wealth are entitled to the 'full fruit of production'. If they insist, they will not liberate the under-utilized resources which are unemployed at present, and consequently will have inadequate health and education services, and less leisure (for the full burden of leisure is being forced upon the unemployed).

(4) A Policy for Trade

Since the end of the Second World War the general climate in international affairs has been in favour of free trade. In the 1930s strongly protectionist policies led to an almost complete decline in international trade and consequent lack of growth around the world, but particularly in the less developed countries. The advantages of free trade are that it leads to increased special-ization and consequently higher world wealth. How that increased world wealth is shared up depends upon the terms of trade. For a quarter of a century, under the influence of the General Agreement on Tariffs and Trade, all nations achieved a steadily improving standard of living. In the 1970s a number of factors have led to calls for a more protectionist attitude on trade. Some of these factors are:

(*a*) A tendency of some advanced nations, notably the Japanese but also the West Germans and the Swiss, to run huge surpluses on their Balance of Payments by not sticking to the rules. The rules are that nations with large balances should allow their economies to expand by giving higher rewards to employees and other factors. This would raise their own costs and stimulate imports from countries around the world with deficits. It is difficult for politicians in deficit countries to agree to restrain demand in the interests of a Balance of Payments if this means more unemployment at home. Calls for protectionist policies to choke off the flood of imports will naturally be made.

(*b*) Workforces in less developed countries continue to expand, and in the seventies reached employment age. By contrast in the advanced nations populations are either static or even declining. It follows that a shift in world trade must take place for less developed countries must have a comparative advantage in labour-intensive industries. This must mean that they can undercut traditional industries in developed nations, which consequently call for protectionist measures.

(*c*) Other nations which do not stick to the rules in rather a different way are the controlled (Communist) economies which restrict the standard of living in their own economies by physical controls. They also operate veiled 'dumping' activities in order to earn foreign exchange; dumping which is not easily detected because these nations do not have a proper monetary system which is susceptible to analysis. They also compete in such fields as shipping services by direct subsidized fleets. This may be deliberately intended to undercut the economies of advanced nations, or may be a mere sideline effect of controlled economies; they tend to go on producing excess capacity in all sorts of directions because their industries are not subject to the laws of supply and demand and are consequently slow in taking corrective action with a cumbersome 'planning' programme. These nations really cheat because they engage in international trade without being a party to international agreements on trade.

In the face of these developments politicians are beginning to call for protectionist measures—**for 'organized trade' rather than 'free trade'**. This calls for world trade to be shared up in some agreed way, which would obviously be a way that redressed the present imbalances of payments. How desirable it is for this type of policy to be introduced is debatable, but probably it is unwise. The best solution to obsolete methods of working is to close them down, not protect them. Experience has shown that industries protected by tariffs remain ineffective high-cost industries and require further protective measures in the future.

(5) A Policy for Incomes

Incomes policy was originally based on the following propositions:

(*a*) Where full employment (or nearly full employment) is being maintained by policies of managed prosperity, any increase in incomes must mean rising prices unless it is accompanied by increased productivity.

(*b*) Such increases are most likely to be conceded by entrepreneurs in growth industries to workers able, because of boom conditions, to demand wage increases as the price of uninterrupted production of goods and services. Another group of entrepreneurs who may concede wage increases unjustifiably is those in nationalized industries who do not face competition and consequently may hope to pass the increased costs onto the general public without too much opposition.

(*c*) Any concessions granted will mean a redistribution of incomes from the exploitable section of the population (the unorganized, the unskilled, the pensioner, and the immigrant) to the prosperous section (the well-organized, the skilled, and the owners of land and capital).

(*d*) Such changes are socially unjust, and must be corrected by Government policies or they will lead to social unrest.

(*e*) In any case there is no need for one group to win advances at the expense of other groups, since equal or larger and perfectly honourable advances can be won by increased productivity—especially in countries like Britain where restrictive practices in industry are widespread.

(*f*) In these circumstances it is for the Government to 'hold the ring' for the benefit of the less privileged sections of the population. They must do so by ensuring that wage advances are only made when they are justified by higher output. This may be achieved by voluntary cooperation on the part of the trade unions, because they recognize the social injustice involved, or by control of incomes. Difficulty of course is experienced where it is impossible to measure productivity, particularly in the service industries where there is no end product except an increase in human satisfaction.

In recent years the criteria for having an incomes policy have changed somewhat. Some groups previously under-organized and under-represented have learned to be 'bloody-minded'; some skilled workers have been so co-operative that they have lost ground in the incomes battle and found them-selves earning less than the semi-skilled workers below them. It remains largely true that only the Government can hold the ring for the rest of the parties not directly involved in wage bargaining. The people whom they represent at any given time may change somewhat as the strengths of various groups wax and wane, but in the last analysis only the Government can govern. All those who have advocated the abandonment of incomes policies have been proved wrong—and the louder they have advocated a free-for-all the quicker that free-for-all has forced them to resume control of incomes. *There seems no prospect at all that incomes policy can cease to be a major feature of Government programmes for years to come.*

Difficulties of Incomes Policy

The implementation of an incomes policy is made difficult because of the following requirements:

(*a*) The need to maintain an adequate supply of factors into production requires that all factors are reasonably rewarded. In the absence of compulsory powers to direct factors where they are required the only way to encourage factors into particular areas is by varying the rewards to them. Thus North Sea divers earn larger incomes than waiters. We cannot totally freeze wages without producing severe shortages in certain fields.

(*b*) The pattern of wages has never been satisfactory (and probably never will be). Some manifestly low paid workers have to be raised more than proportionately if hardship is to be avoided. Thus a 10 per cent increase awarded to both the chairman of a nationalized industry earning £25,000 per year and to a waiter on £1,000 a year is 'unfair'. The chairman's rise is more than twice the other's whole income. Convincing arguments might be pre-sented to justify the chairman's rise but the waiter is unlikely to concede them.

(*c*) The tax system distorts the arrangements made. Because of fiscal drag—the tendency of progressive taxation to recoup in the tax net a large proportion of increases paid to higher income groups—it is difficult to achieve a fair system, and almost impossible to demonstrate that it is fair.

Lessons of Incomes Policy

Since 1945 there have been four complete wage freezes, in 1948–50, 1961, 1966 and 1972–3. There have been seven other periods when pay policies were still being implemented but the freeze was incomplete or voluntary. Generally speaking, we can say that really firm control of wages, if accompanied by price controls, can reduce inflation very considerably and have a favourable effect on the Balance of Payments. Profits tend to decline in such periods due to close supervision of prices. Firm control seems to be quite willingly accepted by the majority of workers; productivity rises marginally and time lost by industrial action declines considerably. Even the most headstrong advocates of wage explosions are held in check and lower their sights in the industrial battlefield.

A major difficulty in incomes policy arises when the attempt is made to return to free wage bargaining. A period of control increases tension among groups who for some reason have done badly during the wage restraint period. They inevitably look to the new opportunity for free negotiations to win back what they have lost during the earlier period and there is a grave danger of inflation rebounding under the influence of a cost-push from higher wages. Similarly, investors may look to higher profit margins as price controls come off. The educative effect of a period of restraint does seem to have some effect though in reducing unreasonable demands and in some cases increases in inflation have been caused by external influences such as increased raw material prices rather than excessive claims by factors for higher rewards.

Indexation

The argument for 'indexation' in wages holds that if inflation occurs factors should be rewarded with extra incomes linked to changes in the price index. This would reassure factors that real incomes would not decline; an increase in wages and other rewards to factors being automatic if prices rose. With incomes indexed in this way the pressure by unions to keep ahead of inflation which produces such a scramble in inflationary times would be reduced. Unions asking for an increase now have to justify their claim on the grounds either of productivity, or of the relative inadequacy of the share their workers receive out of the National Income. We are back to the National Income as 'the sole source of payment for all the factors of production'. Although indexation has become a way of life in some South American countries, it has not won wide acceptance in the United Kingdom except as far as pensions and social security payments are concerned. These now tend to be raised so that inflation does not reduce the real incomes of these (low-paid) groups. It has proved less than satisfactory in other cases—for example, 'blue chip' pensions indexed in this way have moved ahead of un-indexed incomes of those still at work in some cases. Clearly this is an anomaly.

Perhaps the great weakness about indexation is that it reduces the fear of inflation. In the short period when Mr. Heath's threshold agreements were in use, people began to hope inflation would increase by the necessary 1 per cent so that they would receive an automatic rise. This is not psychologically favourable to the control of inflation. A grudging concession by a niggardly Chancellor of the Exchequer of a final level of wage increase agreed after long debate, and a suitable airing of all the portents of disaster discoverable on the economic horizon, proved a much better way to reduce the rate of inflation in the subsequent period.

(6) A Policy to Control Inflation

In Chapter Twenty-eight reference was made to 'monetarist policies' and the way in which they may be used to check inflation.

Since about 1970 the 'demand–management' policies, which are generally known as 'Keynesian' after the great economist John Maynard Keynes, have been followed less enthusiastically. Some politicians hold that they have been abandoned, but the reader will observe Keynesian policies still being tried in many situations. The new policies are called 'monetarist policies', and seek to achieve control by influencing the money supply.

The Money Supply. The aim of monetary policy is to achieve a balance between the encouragement of expansion and the restraint of inflation. It is also hoped that the Government will be able to borrow the money it needs (the P.S.B.R.—public-sector borrowing requirement) and will be able to avoid pressure on the exchange rate (in other words it is hoped that a Balance of Payments will be achieved).

Why is money supply so important? The monetarists argue that inflation only occurs because the money is available to permit price increases. For example, if building societies get more funds, house prices will begin to rise. It is the availability of domestic credit that enables the prices to rise. *To contain inflation restrict domestic credit expansion.*

The question now arises, by how much shall we restrict domestic credit? Shall we set a target of a 'nil' increase in the money supply? If prices are rising anyway by, say, 10 per cent this will mean a severe cut in real standards of living in the year ahead. If we set a target of 5 per cent increase in the money supply and prices rise by 10 per cent the cut in living standards will be less severe. But what about growth in the economy. Suppose the Government hopes to achieve a $2\frac{1}{2}$ per cent expansion when prices are rising at 10 per cent anyway. This would require a $12\frac{1}{2}$ per cent growth in the money supply, if standards of living are to rise by $2\frac{1}{2}$ per cent. In fact, the targets are said to be **restrictive** if they are less than the combined rate of inflation and the proposed rate of expansion. They are said to be **accommodating** targets if they permit expansion of domestic credit (money supply) so as to accommodate both inflation and expansion. Obviously any nation that has problems with inflation and its Balance of Payments must set itself restrictive targets, but is entitled to take a long-term view as well. So a less restrictive target may be permissible if the horizon is beginning to be lit up at night by the flares of North Sea oil rigs, about to come on stream.

To set targets of money supply it is essential to know what the stock of money is at the moment.

Measures of Money Supply. There are almost as many measures of money supply in the world as there are nations to tinker with them. In the United Kingdom there are three definitions called M1, sterling M3 and M3. M2, another definition, was abandoned in 1971 when changes in the banking system made it rather misleading. However, in late 1976 the United Kingdom Government was forced to turn to the International Monetary Fund for assistance in controlling its Balance of Payments deficit, and the I.M.F. insisted, as part of a package of measures designed to improve the situation, that monetary targets should be based not on M1 or M3 but on the I.M.F.'s favourite measure **D.C.E. (Domestic Credit Expansion)**. This D.C.E. measure is the best measure to use to set money supply targets in a country which is having Balance of Payments difficulties, for it is not favourably affected by adverse balances on foreign trade. M1 and M3 are favourably affected for fairly complex reasons. It follows that if a nation sets its target for money supply on M1 or M3 and then has an adverse trade balance, the adverse trade balance will help it hit the target. Clearly, that is cheating. If the target is set on the D.C.E. basis it will be much harder to hit, because the target will have to be hit by careful management of domestic credit. The Chancellor also agreed with the I.M.F. that in future more attention would be paid to the sterling M3 figures than to M3 itself. This is because the M3 figures include large balances of foreign currencies held in London banks for purposes which are nothing to do with the United Kingdom's domestic economy. For example, insurance companies keep a good proportion of foreign premiums paid by foreigners to meet claims that are sure to arise in the near future, and which will have to be honoured in foreign currency. As these fluctuate a good deal they may make it appear that the United Kingdom has met its targets when in fact it has not met a domestic target at all. This would again be cheating.

The four measures of money supply, which enable targets for monetary expansion to be set are compared in Table 47. (See facing page.)

The Bank of England and the Money Supply. Clearly, it is no easy problem to manage the money supply, and the system of monetary targets is relatively new. The Bank of England is developing its techniques and fashioning new tools for influencing domestic credit expansion. It will certainly be helped by restrained behaviour by all citizens, for in the final analysis the money supply is the 'factor incomes' we pay ourselves for our efforts in the production process, plus the amounts we borrow from those 'friendly' local bank managers, plus the amounts we insist the Government overspends for countless 'necessary' purposes.

In the final analysis it seems that a mixture of Keynesian economics and monetarism is really required. The Keynesian economics will be an underlying theme, which in the absence of a major slump of 1930 proportions seeks to ensure that the economy expands each year in line with the growth of the national income. If the excessive optimism of politicians (for instance, in the late 1960s) can be curbed by a Treasury now grown wiser by a long succession of inaccurate forecasts, this Keynesian 'growth' will be set somewhere fairly low—say at about the 2 per cent level. The monetarist target, in line with this, should err on the side of a restrictive target, i.e. *somewhat less than the combined figure of* '*expected inflation rate*' *and* '*envisaged growth rate*'. At the first sign that this target is not going to be achieved a severe credit squeeze should be imposed to jam on the brakes with a salutary shock, reminding everyone that Stop–Go is still a fact of life which cannot be avoided. It is not an unacceptable facet of capitalism, but a highly desirable aspect of the mixed economy, which ensures the greatest good of the greatest number.

(7) A Policy for Population?

Population has given man concern since time immemorial. Primitive men practise infanticide so that only the strongest children are reared. The Eskimos used to practise polyandry (one wife with many husbands) because so many girls were killed off in infancy. Darwin found the inhabitants of Tierra del Fuego eating their grandparents when times were hard: it had a double effect on the food situation, reducing demand and increasing supply.

Mention has already been made of the Malthusian Doctrine (page 190), which held that population was likely to rise beyond the ability of agriculture

Table 47. Measures of Money Supply

Name of measure	M1	Sterling M3	M3	D.C.E.
Purpose of measure:	Measures the stock of money on a narrow definition	Measures stock of money on a broader definition which relates only to the U.K. domestic money supply	Measures stock of money on a very broad definition	Measures *changes* in domestic credit —the I.M.F.'s favourite
Items included:				
(a) Notes and coins in circulation	Yes	Yes	Yes	The change in this
(b) Bank current accounts of private sector (less an adjustment for items in transit)	Yes	Yes	Yes	No
(c) Bank deposit accounts, in sterling including certificates of deposit, both private sector and public sector	No	Yes	Yes	No
(d) Bank deposit accounts as in (c) but designated in foreign currencies	No	No	Yes	No
(e) Loans in sterling by U.K. banks to private, public and overseas sector during period	No	No	No	Yes
(f) Overseas lending to public sector and bank lending to public sector in foreign currencies during period.	No	No	No	Yes

Some seasonally adjusted figures for each measure:	Money supply at date shown			Change during year ending on date shown
	M1	Sterling M3	M3	D.C.E.
1975	£17,350 m	£37,270 m	£40,240 m	+£4,468 m
1976	£19,140 m	£40,580 m	£44,550 m	+£7,248 m
1977	£23,330 m	£44,660 m	£48,760 m	+£1,181 m

Advantages	Easy to understand as 'money'; it is cash and cheques	Is the best measure of purely domestic money supply	Includes all 'money'including some fairly illiquid items	The I. M .F. prefers it because a target can only be achieved if the domestic money supply is controlled
Disadvantages	Does not include deposits, and these are so easily moved into current accounts that they are virtually current account items		Not the best definition for a country with Balance of Payments problems	It is aimed at correcting Balance of Payments imbalancerather than at other targets

to supply food. Although the severity of the problem was much reduced by the opening up of new countries like the U.S.A., Australia, New Zealand, and Argentina, present-day calculations seem to indicate that Malthus may yet be proved right. Some population statistics bearing on this situation are given in Table 48.

Table 48. Estimated world population, 1650–2000

Year	Estimated world population (millions)
1650	450
1900	2,000
1960	3,000
1970	3,600
1980	4,000
2000	6,250

The phase 'Gigabirth Nightmare' has been coined to describe the serious trends in world population. Table 49 illustrates the same figures by comparing the speeds with which a gigabirth increase has taken place.

Table 49. World population trends

Population in thousand millions	Reached by A.D.	Number of years needed to produce an increase of one thousand million inhabitants
1	1830	From the dawn of life, say 100,000 years
2	1930	100
3	1960	30
4	1980	20
5	1990	10
6	2000	10

The staggering increase predicted for 1980–2000 (twice as large an increase in 20 years as was produced in the period from the dawn of history to 1830) gives some idea of the problems to be faced. Already in parts of Africa nomadic people, whose whole economy for hundreds of years has depended on their ability to graze large areas of land in times of drought, are finding barbed-wire fences across their ancient migration routes. More settled people need the land for intensive farming, and the disputes and battles that result are not pleasant. Thirsty cattle cannot wait.

These predictions, sometimes called **Neo-Malthusianism**, have revived interest in Malthus's arguments. The development of more intensive agricultural methods and some form of population control can probably postpone a crisis for some years in the advanced countries, but in the less developed nations population pressures are likely to become insurmountable. These countries to not have the capital to establish intensive agriculture, or to keep both population and the standard of living rising. The natural aspirations of such people cannot be realized in the slum shanty towns on the outskirts of great cities. The overwhelming advance of population requires national and international policies to be devised.

In 1949 a Royal Commission on Population reported in favour of stabilizing Britain's population, and appointing a body to review the problems of population and national policies affected by it. For years little was done, but the aim now seems to have been largely achieved through the improved methods of birth control available and the free availability of abortion. If this trend continues, the almost universal demand for increased living standards becomes much easier to manage, and the imbalance of population less severe. The imbalance in the population is centred on the changing proportion of working and non-working people. While successive bulges in the birth rate mean a high proportion of young people, each of whom tends on average to stay at school longer, the increasing longevity associated with medical developments results in a larger number of retired people. As both these groups have to be supported by the declining proportion of people actually at work, the burden on these becomes greater.

A full discussion of population is beyond the scope of this book. For the beginner in economics it is sufficient to note that population changes take a lifetime to work their way through the economy. A bulge in the birth-rate produces a wave of requirements that changes as the years go by. The high birth-rate in 1945–50 has produced successively a need for infant schools, junior schools, secondary schools, university places and by 1965–70 a new wave of babies as the larger number of young people marry and set up homes. The birth-rate of today is the housing problem of 20 years from now, the pensioner problem of 60 years ahead, and will produce intense pressure in the cemeteries a little later on.

(8) A Policy for Controlling Monopolies

Throughout the nineteenth century monopolies were regarded quite rightly with great suspicion, for the early capitalists did not hesitate to abuse their monopoly positions. A continuing battle was fought for Parliamentary control of the railway companies, for example. This control was finally achieved by the Railway and Canal Traffic Act of 1888. The climate of public opinion at that time was firmly against amalgamations, yet by 1911 the Russell Rea Report was saying that amalgamations were inevitable and even desirable. There is a conflict here between the achievement of economies of scale and the protection of the consumer from exploitation. As the Russell Rea Report said, the time to complain is when you get hurt, not before you have been hurt, or when beneficial effects may even be derived from an extension of monopoly.

A further illustration, this time of oligopoly, is the case of the British Cement Ring. Traditionally it has been assumed that this ring of cement manufacturers was against the public interest. An investigation in 1946 showed that in fact the Ring had been careful not to exploit its monopoly position; it had achieved a 10 per cent return on capital invested and this was about fair for this type of industrial enterprise.

By contrast, the restrictive practices to be found in many fields of industry and commerce have been held to be undesirable.

In 1948 a Monopolies and Restrictive Practices Commission was set up to inquire into the manufacturing conditions of a wide range of commodities. Later, the 1956 Restrictive Trade Practices Act split the control of restrictive practices away from the control of monopolies and set up a Restrictive Practices Court to investigate them. A Restrictive Practices Registrar was appointed to register such practices and bring before the Court any which seemed to be against the public interest. The reader should note that a restrictive practice is an arrangement made between suppliers not to compete with one another in some way. For example, where a dozen firms tender for a public contract and all submit the same tender it is clear there is collusion between them to keep up the price of projects at the expense of the public.

Of about 2,500 practices registered in the early years of the Registrar's activities over three-fifths were voluntarily abandoned by firms rather than face the expense of a court hearing.

Later still the Resale Prices Act, 1964, rendered illegal all resale-price-maintenance clauses designed to keep prices at prescribed levels, unless these were registered with the Registrar. The vast majority of such restrictions on competition have been either abandoned voluntarily or declared illegal by the Courts.

The Monopolies Commission itself has issued reports on many products. For example, a recent investigation into the detergent industry decided that the repetitive advertising of washing powders was wasteful and against the public interest. It recommended a reduction of 40 per cent in this advertising, and of 20 per cent in the price of products.

Under the Fair Trading Act, 1973, the Monopolies Commission was renamed the Monopolies and Mergers Commission. A Director General of Fair Trading was appointed to review the whole field of commercial activity and to take over the duties of the Registrar of Restrictive Trading Agreements. The official definition of a 'monopoly' situation was redefined as one where 'at least one quarter of all the goods or services of that description which are supplied in the United Kingdom are supplied by one person, or one group of bodies corporate'.

(9) The Future of Nationalization

Certain sections of economic activity ought clearly to be conducted by Governments, but there is a continuing debate as to whether major industries which are functioning satisfactorily ought to be nationalized or not. We have to set against the idealistic principle that all the essential instruments of production should be socially owned, the disturbance likely to be caused by the nationalization process. While experience has shown that nationalization is not as great a disturbance as at one time was feared, and indeed attempts to de-nationalize have been singularly unsuccessful, the fact remains that many major industries have still not been nationalized, for example the cement industry, the oil industry, petrochemicals, glass, and paint manufacture. There are many more.

The fact is that we have moved into nationalization 'by the back door' in many ways. There is little point in nationalization where the shares of a company are already widely owned, if not by the general public then at least by institutional investors acting on their behalf; or where the control of monopolies and restrictive practices is sufficiently good to prevent exploitation of the public; or where taxation restores many of the proceeds of industrial and commercial activity to the people. While in most respects the nationalized industries are excellently run, there are many who believe that diseconomies of large scale pass unnoticed and unchecked in these industries, especially on the distribution side. In one case the author has found as many as twenty-two documents being processed for the purchase of a single household appliance—surely an excessively complicated system.

The Petroleum and Submarine Pipelines Act, 1975, set up BNOC, the British National Oil Corporation. It came into existence on January 1, 1976, with Lord Kearton as Chairman and Chief Executive. On that day, for £90 million it took over the National Coal Board's North Sea activities, including interests in the Thistle, Dunlin, Hutton and Statfjord fields. It has negotiated to buy the Ninian field from Burmah Oil, and has a majority interest in Burmah's stake in Thistle—a field where Burmah is the operating company. BNOC has the right to $12\frac{1}{2}$ per cent of North Sea oil as a royalty, and if it starts to take this oil it will have an immense output to refine. In the future it is also empowered to take 51 per cent of all North Sea businesses into public ownership. This is reputed to mean a 51 per cent participation, not a cash purchase, and details remain to be worked out before 1980.

In 1977 the shipbuilding and aerospace industries were nationalized as British Shipbuilders and British Aerospace. The case for nationalization rested upon the need in both industries to achieve a basis of operations of the most viable size. Shipbuilding is a highly competitive world-wide industry and British yards have found it difficult to retain their share of the world market. In aerospace the major consideration perhaps was the large share of total output for which the government is the only customer. A bill to nationalize the ports was not proceeded with, despite the strong arguments for nationalization. Despite the success of some very small ports like Shoreham and Felixstowe, the case for making the best possible use of large ports is strong. New methods of transport have meant excess capacity in our ports and haphazard development could mean a waste of scarce capital.

(10) A Policy to Deal with a Surplus on the Balance of Payments

It seems likely that a major preoccupation for United Kingdom Governments since 1945—the problem of achieving a Balance of Payments—is about to disappear. The prospect of self-sufficiency in 1980 as far as oil supplies is concerned means that the Balance of Payments could be in surplus for a generation or so, provided wise policies are pursued. The changed circumstances can best be followed by considering Table 50. This clearly shows that since the huge rise in oil prices in 1973 the purchase of oil has had a major

Table 50. Balance of Payments figures (£ million)

Year	Deficit on Visible Trade	Deficit on Current Account	Amount spent on Foreign oil supplies
1974	5,195	3,515	4,211
1975	3,205	1,614	3,948
1976	3,510	1,107	5,243
1977	1,612	35	3,888

(*Source*: Bank of England Quarterly Bulletin)

influence on the adverse Balance of Payments. In each year shown the deficit on current account would have been cleared altogether if there had been no need to purchase oil from abroad. This is the happy prospect that opens up before the United Kingdom as 1980 approaches and self-sufficiency in oil is achieved. The prospect is that an over-all surplus on the Balance of Payments should be achieved by that date, even though a good deal of capital expenditure will be needed to keep the development of the North Sea fields going. We are therefore at a watershed as far as the Balance of Payments is concerned. Estimates of what will happen vary from optimistic forecasts of real growth in the national income to dire forebodings about a further decline in competitiveness in world markets and a return to imbalance in the mid-1980s. How can the pundits disagree so enormously? The answer lies in the interconnection between policies pursued at home, developments abroad, the movement of hot money, changes in the exchange rate of sterling and other factors. In a dynamic world who can guess correctly and even if someone does, will we recognize it?

In 1977 the Balance of Payments ceased to be a major problem for a number of reasons. First the traditional methods for solving an adverse Balance of Payments had been very successful under the tight control of the I.M.F.'s domestic credit expansion (D.C.E.) controls. Let us remind ourselves what the traditional methods of correcting a disequilibrium in the Balance of Payments are. They may be listed as follows:

(*a*) Pay up out of the reserves.

(*b*) Borrow enough money to bridge the gap until a favourable balance is achieved at some future date (in other words, official financing).

(*c*) Lower the price of exports and raise the price of imports.

(*d*) Deflate the home market.

(*e*) Import restrictions.

(*a*) *Pay up out of the reserves*. Where a nation has adequate reserves, a deficit can simply be financed by running down the reserves. Like an ordinary householder who, faced with heavy bills he must pay, moves funds out of his deposit account at the bank and into his current account, the nation's reserves are used to pay for the excess imports for the year.

(*b*) *Borrow from abroad to finance the deficit*. One way of overcoming an adverse balance until such time as a favourable balance returns is to borrow enough money to cover the deficit. Forecasts of what will be saved and earned by North Sea oil have been such that during 1977 foreign confidence in the United Kingdom increased enormously, aided by the aura of political stability the country appeared to display under very severe pressures. Foreign money therefore flooded in to the United Kingdom so that nearly £10,000 million was added to the official reserves. This confidence reflected the success of other measures described below, but as this type of borrowing is very responsive to the slightest change in the business and economic climate, it would not have occurred without them and therefore did not render them unnecessary.

(*c*) *Lower the price of exports and raise the price of imports*. This will make our exports more attractive to foreign customers and our imports less attractive to home consumers. One way of doing this is to allow the pound to depreciate (since all currencies are now floating, devaluation in a single sharp jump is not necessary). This has certainly been a major aspect of government policy in the years 1974–7. To be successful it requires that the elasticity of demand for British exports be high, and that the demand for imports is also elastic. It also requires that the supply of exports be elastic. If the elasticities are favourable it means that foreigners will increase their demand for our exports more than proportionately; we shall be able to meet this increase in demand because the supply of exports is elastic, and we shall give up demanding imports because we react very strongly against their increases in price.

In fact, the elasticities tend not to be all that favourable, especially as the developing world industrializes. The fall in the exchange rate cannot go beyond a certain point for any currency without creating a spiralling collapse of the currency concerned, and this can induce violent movements of capital out of the country by foreign investors which will completely offset any extra competitiveness.

There is also the point that too heavy a decline in the value of the pound must mean that import price increases will begin to affect the costs of industry and generate a cost-push inflation. This will force up the price of exports within a short while and reduce the advantages obtained by the original depreciation of the currency.

(*d*) *Deflate the home market*. The fourth way to improve the Balance of Payments position is to deflate the home market. This the Government has hesitated to do, though the idea that 1½ million unemployed can exist without a deflation of the home market might appear at first sight to be doubtful. The fact is that successive developments in the Welfare State have ensured that real hardship is not suffered by those experiencing even long-term unemployment. The chief benefits derived from a firm control of domestic credit have been in the voluntary surrender of current purchasing that has occurred as a result of employment uncertainty. The propensity to consume of those in employment has been reduced, and the loss of production by strikes and other types of industrial action has been reduced very considerably to the general benefit of production.

(*e*) *Import restrictions*. The one policy that has really not been tried is import restrictions, despite really strong pressure from trade unions in some industries. The difficulty is that to introduce controls on imports would require a fundamental reappraisal of much of our current policy and a recognition that we have failed to make the things that other people want, because neither depreciation of the currency nor deflation of the home market can cure the balance of payments. This means we shall have to cease making many sophisticated products which we have developed as part of the specialization in international trade, and turn to reviving more basic industries in a self-sufficient economy. This hardly seems sensible in the long run, even if it meets with the approval of unemployed people in certain industries. It would also have a serious impact on developing countries and on nations with whom we have agreed to trade freely. To renege on agreed policies rather than to set our house in order is both dishonourable and unfair. To this extent government policy is right in hesitating to introduce import controls.

The Post-1980 Situation

If the indications are correct the United Kingdom will be self-sufficient in oil by 1980. All that enormous expenditure on oil products shown in Table 50 will be saved, and it is possible that the country will become a net exporter of oil. If so, the adverse balances on visible trade, which have been a constant feature of United Kingdom trading since 1945, should disappear. However, this disappearance is not automatic: it depends upon what is done with the increased gross national product as to whether the Balance of Payments will cease to be a problem. What are the alternatives? They appear to be:

(a) Going for oil 'growth'.
(b) Avoiding 'growth' in favour of consolidation.

(a) Going for Oil Growth

With high unemployment (above 1½ million) the drive to improve the unemployment situation by stimulating the economy is a strong one. Many unemployed people will look to the Government to do this, and thus allow them to share in the oil bonus which the nation is enjoying. However, this is not as easy to achieve as it sounds, if only because the increased wealth is relatively small, between 3 and 5 per cent of present gross national product. In the early years—say to 1985—a portion of this must go back into North Sea investment if the oil is to continue to flow. The balance, if used to stimulate demand, may only result in a flood of imports which will not improve the employment situation very much. This raises again the major problem of British industry, that it is failing to change over to new industries which supply the things the world wants, including the British consumer. Feather-bedding dying industries does no good to the economy as a whole, offers no help to the unemployed, and saves jobs only at a high price which is greater than the rewards the unemployed receive. It is therefore unfair to the un-employed, who could justifiably claim that misery, like everything else, should be fairly shared.

What could make a successful contribution to the employment situation is much tighter control of incomes so that those still in employment do not have any share in the oil bonus, which should then be channelled into new, highly productive industries which would be import-saving because they competed both in price and quality with overseas goods. This would enable the unem-ployed to be taken on—partly in the new industries but even more in the labour-intensive service trades financed from the growth in national income created by the new highly productive industries. The Balance of Payments, instead of going 'into the red' with a flood of imports, would be kept in the black (a) because of import-saving now that British industry is making the right type of goods and (b) because of import-saving due to the enforcement on those already employed of a steady standard of living rather than a rising living standard at the expense of their unemployed fellow citizens.

(b) Avoiding Growth in Favour of Consolidation

If the Government opted to use the extra 'national product' to consolidate the national situation it could simply allow the 'oil bonus' to be applied to the reduction of the public-sector borrowing requirement, so that the current level of national expenditure could be maintained without further borrowing, and the very considerable mountain of medium-term borrowing could be reduced. Most of these debts are repayable in the 1980s, unless they are re-financed at that time. There is every chance that in the 1980s the United Kingdom would be in a satisfactory position and able to re-finance these loans without diffi-culty, but it would be better to repay them so that these funds become available for other countries whose need is greater at that time. The I.M.F. does not favour countries with a surplus on their Balance of Payments taking scarce loans. An important aspect of 'consolidation' is the need to regenerate United Kingdom business activity. The tendency to import more and more of the basic secondary manufactured goods is increasing, and is being masked by a favourable Balance of Payments position secured by North Sea oil production.

(11) A Policy for Energy

The United Kingdom is better supplied than most countries with sources of energy. It has coal reserves estimated at 100,000 million tons, of which it uses slightly over 100 million tons each year. Over 50 million tons (coal equivalent) of natural gas per year supplies 95 per cent of all home needs. North Sea oil should replace the 150 million tons (coal equivalent) of petroleum imported each year by 1980. Nuclear energy provides about 12 million tons of coal equivalent each year and hydroelectric power about 2 million tons of coal equivalent. Despite this comforting position, and until North Sea oil comes on stream fully, it is essential to have a sound energy policy, partly to assist the balance of payments and partly to conserve what are finite resources of hydrocarbon fuels. The reserves of natural gas and oil in the North Sea are not by any means fully assessed as yet. Estimates vary from about 30 years' to 45 years' supply, but this is a relatively short lifetime and it makes considerable sense to conserve these fuels so far as possible.

Among the measures instituted to conserve energy the following were significant:

(*a*) A phasing out of the subsidies given to the nationalized industries to help keep down the price of domestic fuels. These subsidies were introduced as part of the government's anti-inflation policy. The decision to allow fuel prices to rise reflects the official view that householders forced to carry the true cost of the energy they use will be more likely to save fuel by switching off where they can. This has in fact been the case and the saving that has resulted has exceeded £50 million per year.

(*b*) Investment allowances (a form of tax relief) have been extended to enable firms to institute programmes of insulation on industrial buildings, while a determined campaign of improvements in government offices was also started to cut fuel bills.

(*c*) Industry frequently fails to make use of energy that could be recycled. Heat escapes up chimneys, through ventilation systems, etc. Grants of up to £100,000 per project can now be obtained to assist in the installation of heat interchangers, automatic control devices and other energy-saving appliances.

(*d*) An energy Technology Unit based at Harwell has been set up to pursue studies in the field of energy conservation, and to examine schemes for the use of other energy sources, such as solar energy, geothermal energy, wind and tidal power, etc.

(*e*) Increases in the price of petrol have been designed to reduce public demand for petroleum products. These have certainly reduced demand for petrol for less-essential purposes.

(*f*) An Advisory Council on Energy Conservation was set up in 1974 to review the energy situation and advise the Minister on energy conservation generally.

(12) A Policy for Public Expenditure

Public expenditure has become a matter of public concern in recent years, as the growth of the public sector at the expense of the private sector has transferred more and more of total Gross National Product to the spending Departments. Almost 60 per cent of all wealth created is now at the disposal of Government and Local Government Departments. The review of public spending plans which is held each winter rolls the plans forward for a further year on a five-year programme, and the resulting proposals appear as a White Paper in January or February. The preparation of the White Paper gives an opportunity to review the trends in the economy, to predict the gross domestic product in the years ahead and to consider what proportion of that product should be applied to the alternative ends envisaged by the Government and the people. Out of a total G.N.P. of £93 billion in 1975 £49 billion was spent by Central Government Departments, of which about £27 billion went on goods and services and £17 billion on transfer payments such as grants, subsidies and social security (£8 billion). Almost £5 billion went on interest on public borrowing. This extremely high level of Government spending still does not complete the programmes the Government envisaged in its election manifesto, and the White Paper refers to the Government's need to reduce public expenditure programmes in the years ahead in order that industry and commerce may meet overseas and home demand. Future increases in public expenditure can only come out of growth in the G.N.P. To this end forecasts of public expenditure on all main programmes have been reduced for 1977–8 and 1978–9; only in three cases are they maintained at the 1976–7 level. These three cases are housebuilding, social security and overseas aid. A digest of figures is given in Table 47 opposite.

Clearly the expenditure of so large a proportion of total national output on public expenditure calls for a rigorous control policy to ensure that money is not idly wasted and that improper disbursements do not pass unnoticed in the huge sums being expended. To achieve this control a system of 'cash limits' was introduced in 1976, to supplement the ordinary control by Parliament through the Supply Estimates. During inflationary times the Supply Estimates have proved rather inaccurate as a control method, since it has proved difficult to predict the rate of inflation. Estimates often have to be revised and 'Supplementary Estimates' passed if necessary. The 'cash limits' system will provide a closer check on actual expenditure.

More than 120 blocks of cash expenditure have been specified for the year 1976–7, which is being regarded as an experimental year for this type of control. In each of these blocks cash limits have been set, and they will not normally be revised in the year. This means that Authorities and Departments cannot look automatically to Supplementary Estimates to get them out of difficulty if they overspend. As the year progresses the expenditure on each block will be monitored against a planned programme of expenditure, so that overspending is detected early, in time to take corrective action. Thus while salaries will be evenly distributed over the year in most departments a high level of activity in summer on building work might be built into the planned profile of expenditure in a particular block. The 'budgetary control' thus achieved should reduce the necessity for Supplementary Estimates, though in an experimental year it might still be necessary to review the cash limits if an unexpectedly adverse rate of inflation developed.

Table 51. Public Expenditure Programmes, 1974–75, 1976–77 and 1979–80

(£million at 1975 Survey prices)

	Expenditure on goods and services: investment and consumption			Transfer payments: grants, subsidies, loans, interest		
	1974–75	1976–77	1979–80	1974–75	1976–77	1979–80
1 Defence	4,318	4,571	4,527	13	15	14
2 Overseas aid and other overseas services	200	220	216	598	662	869
3 Agriculture, fisheries and forestry	138	145	143	1,330	842	469
4 Trade, industry and employment	472	518	519	2,393	1,754	1,595
5 Nationalised industries' capital expenditure	2,813	3,154	3,040	9	–104	–133
6 Roads and transport	1,555	1,573	1,348	626	620	504
7 Housing	2,171	2,000	1,804	2,258	2,097	2,286
8 Other environmental services	2,033	2,011	1,940	55	34	41
9 Law, order and protective services	1,325	1,450	1,417	14	20	21
10 Education and libraries, science and arts	5,010	5,069	4,827	1,094	1,165	1,168
11 Health and personal social services	5,020	5,292	5,522	36	25	26
12 Social security	373	424	393	8,209	9,578	9,570
13 Other public services	601	661	663	27	25	16
14 Common services	606	678	739			
15 Northern Ireland	602	723	676	598	613	582
Civil service staff costs	—	—	130	—	—	—
Total programmes	27,237	28,489	27,644	17,260	17,346	17,028
Debt interest	—	—	—	4,757	6,200	7,500
Total	27,237	28,489	27,644	22,017	23,546	24,528

Source: Economics Progress Report, March 1976.

Certain services are excluded from cash limits because it would be an inappropriate method. For example, where expenditure depends on numbers involved (as with unemployment benefit) it would be imappropriate to exclude some from benefit because the cash limit had been reached.

(13) A Strategy for Industry

United Kingdom prosperity is closely related to the prosperity of its manufacturing industry which is responsible for about four-fifths of all visible exports and three-tenths of G.N.P. A number of factors have led to a deterioration in industrial performance. These include a low rate of investment and a relatively poor use of such new investment as has taken place, so that the return on capital investment in the United Kingdom tends to be lower than our competitors achieve. Industrial activity is not as attractive to labour as employment in other fields; industry's recruits are generally speaking less well qualified and less dedicated than in other nations. The rewards they receive are not as high and their working conditions are less attractive than in many service trades and their status is too low in the community generally.

In order to transform the economy the Government has agreed with the unions and the representatives of management a new approach to the developmentment of a strategy for industry. The aim of the strategy is to achieve the best possible co-ordination of policies for the finance of industry, and provision of adequate manpower and the planning of industrial development. It has been clearly stated that industry must take precedence over consumption and social objectives, since it is fundamental to any sustained advance in standards of living. Our ability to create wealth is basic to any agreement on how wealth is to be distributed.

To develop the strategy, a series of working parties has been set up to review the situation in 30 major industries. These are listed below:

(1) Food
(2) Drink
(3) Mineral oil refining
(4) Organic chemicals
(5) Pharmaceuticals
(6) Synthetic resins and plastics
(7) Iron and steel (general) and steel tubes
(8) Ferrous foundries
(9) Non-ferrous foundries
(10) Metal-working machine tools
(11) Pumps, valves. compressors
(12) Industrial engines
(13) Mechanical machinery
(14) Construction and earthmoving equipment
(15) Mechanical handling equipment
(16) Industrial plant and steelwork
(17) Mechanical engineering and metal industries
(18) Scientific and industrial instruments and systems
(19) Electrical machinery
(20) Radio and electronic components
(21) Electronic computers
(22) Radio, radar and electronic capital goods
(23) Domestic electrical appliances
(24) Shipbuilding and marine engineering
(25) Motor vehicles
(26) Aerospace equipment
(27) Production of man-made fibres
(28) Woollen and worsted industries
(29) Hosiery and knitwear
(30) Rubber industries

The working parties will draw up a programme of action for achieving improvements in the industry.

(14) Summary of Chapter Thirty

1. Growth of the National Income is very important if citizens are to achieve higher standards of living from year to year. This depends on the supply of factors and their co-ordination to achieve high levels of productivity.

2. The problems of structural unemployment caused by the development of new technologies have called for a wide range of measures in recent years. These problems have recently been extended by unemployment associated with inflation. The whole position of 'work' in modern society needs re-thinking.

3. In recent years it has become more difficult to preserve the 'free trade' which seeks to promote world-wide prosperity. In times of world-wide unemployment nations turn to protectionist measures to safeguard their own national positions.

4. Incomes policy seeks to ensure the orderly advancement of the standard of living of all citizens, rather than only the advance of a few. The problem is to restrain those in growth areas or profitable situations from achieving an unfair share of the national income just because they happen to be producing it. The government has to act in the interests of the greatest good of the greatest number.

5. The control of inflation essentially depends upon high productivity. In the absence of this, severe controls on domestic credit expansion are necessary if increases in incomes are to be held down to that level which reflects the growth of national output. The control of the money supply is the chief weapon in this battle.

6. Population growth is becoming a major world problem. In the United Kingdom, however, recent trends in birth control appear to have stabilized the population with a consequent easing of pressure on certain types of welfare and education services.

7. Monopolies in Britain are not regarded as prima facie bad. The policy is to look out for any abuse of their monopoly powers, and to restrain them so that their activities do not turn against the public interest.

8. Nationalization of many key industries has been achieved in Britain. The shipbuilding and aerospace industries have recently been nationalized while the British Oil Corporation is taking control of a national stake in the North Sea oil and gas industries.

9. The prospects for the United Kindom Balance of Payments seem very favourable as North Sea oil comes on stream. The problem now is to decide what use should be made of this bonus. The desirable policy seems to be to use it for a permanent improvement in the industrial structure of the United Kingdom rather than for a temporary boost in the standard of living.

Exercises Set 30

1. Why is the rate of growth of an economy important? What factors influence growth and how can it be induced?

2. 'No one should have a wage increase unless his output rises to deserve it.' Criticize this statement.

3. What was the Industrial Reorganization Corporation? Is this sort of interference with private firms justified?

4. What is an 'incomes policy'? Discuss the advantages and disadvantages of such a policy.

5. What do you understand by 'wage drift'? Why has it developed in recent years?

6. 'Productivity has risen. The men work less, and earn more.' Give a detailed analysis of the implications of this remark.

7. U.K. Population and estimated population (thousands):

	Total	Under 15	15 to 64	65 and over
1967	55,202	12,999 (23·6%)	35,394 (64·1%)	6,809 (12·3%)
1980	61,223	17,972 (29·3%)	35,042 (57·3%)	8,209 (13·4%)

Comment on the economic implications of these figures.

8. 'The Malthusian Doctrine may yet be proved right.' What is the Malthusian Doctrine, and why is it still of interest in the second half of the twentieth century?

9. What is structural unemployment? How may it be cured?

10. We may have cured cyclical unemployment, but we shall always be faced with structural unemployment. Explain the differences between them. Why does the cure for cyclical unemployment not solve the problem of structural unemployment?

11. What do we mean by a monopoly? Are monopolies against the public interest? How are they controlled in Great Britain?

12. 'Monopolistic practices should be tolerated because they achieve valuable economies of scale.' Discuss this statement.

CHAPTER THIRTY-ONE

THE FUTURE OF ECONOMICS

(1) The Greeks had a Word for it

The modern word 'economics' has its origin in the Greek word *oikonomos* meaning a steward. The two parts of this word *oikos*, a house, and *nomos*, a manager, show what economics is all about. How do we manage our house, what account of our stewardship can we render to our families, to the nation, to our descendants?

From Socrates and Aristotle to J. M. Keynes, and Prof. J. K. Galbraith is a span of 2,250 years. It takes us from a slave society, where all but the few were poor, to an affluent democracy. Great changes of taste and fashion have occurred. Socrates rose in the morning, put on his cloak and went out into the public square to engage in conversation and discussion. His needs were few, and he was unencumbered by worldly possessions. Today we are obsessed with material wants, and struggle to the beach with a car loaded with deck chairs, aqua-lungs, and assorted paraphernalia, towing a yacht or a power boat behind us.

Economics is the study of mankind in the everyday business of providing this enormous variety of goods and services. This book has attempted to describe the major aspects of production, distribution, and exchange. It is clearly only a beginning to the vast study of specialized aspects of the economy. The author hopes the reader will continue into this more specialized field of applied economics. Before doing so, and to conclude this book, let us note two final points about elementary economics. First, economics is a valuable liberal study in its own right. Secondly, while economics can never cease to be important, the time is fast approaching when its relative importance should decline.

(2) A Liberal Study

The current fashion is to advocate liberal education, that is education over a wide field. Specialisms are condemned in education on the ground that specialists become divorced from everyday life, immersed in their own peculiar interests. The author does not subscribe to this view, for economics is about specialization as the key to a fuller life. Specialization increases wealth; as a general principle the ploughing of deep furrows is as advantageous in education as it is in agriculture. There are many liberal men who are also specialists.

Certainly economics is a liberal study. Everyone needs to know some economics, for it explains the framework of prosperity and a liberal life is only possible when prosperity exists. Follow historically the flowering of art, literature, and science around the world and you will find they flourished most where prosperity was to be found. Even today only where the economy is strong can men be spared from production to think sublime thoughts, create beautiful objects, paint immortal pictures, or compose imperishable melodies.

The humblest worker in such societies is ennobled by his labour, for it alone makes possible the culture of his times.

(3) No Longer the Dismal Science

Within the last 30 years Thomas Carlyle's characterization of economics as 'the Dismal Science' has been invalidated. The new economics can handle the cycles of depression which gave such distress in the early years of the capitalist system. There are still problems to be solved, but reasonable affluence appears to be within the reach of all men if the political and social framework can be adjusted to suit the new situation. No longer do the greatest economists of their age stand aghast at the enormity of the problems. Instead they look blithely and optimistically forward to a future where the stockpiling of consumer goods ceases to be the major preoccupation of men's minds. Even the recent (1973–6) setback to the advanced economies is little more than a temporary halt in the rapid progress of recent years. A particular group of nations—the oil producers—has demanded a larger share of the world's wealth. The adjustment can be speedily—if not easily—made. We have looked in *Economics Made Simple* at the writings of many great economists. The last to be mentioned is Prof. J. K. Galbraith, whose book *The Affluent Society* is another of those volumes that have won wide recognition as an important contribution to economics. The reader is urged to read for himself Prof. Galbraith's critical appraisal of modern society. His conclusion is that, while a poverty-stricken society must inevitably revere productivity, an affluent society should turn its attention in other directions. When private wealth is assured, social well-being becomes a possibility. We turn from investment in things to investment in man himself.

Part of that investment must include a re-appraisal of our attitude to material things. If we are to avoid the exhaustion of the earth's resources, to preserve natural beauty, to prevent the destruction of our traditional environment and protect what little innocence is left we must examine what economic growth implies for world society. Inevitably controls over economic activity seem bound to increase unless individuals can show restraint. The fullest development of man requires a return to Socratic contemplation of the state of 'The Republic'. Let us don our cloaks and go out into the market place to discuss it.

(4) Suggested Further Reading

Galbraith, J. K.: *The Affluent Society*. Penguin Books: London, 1962.
Galbraith, J. K.: *The New Industrial Estate*. Penguin Books: London, 1969.